PLANNING THE ETERNAL CITY

# PLANNING
# THE
# ETERNAL
# CITY

ROMAN POLITICS AND PLANNING

SINCE WORLD WAR II

BY ROBERT C. FRIED

NEW HAVEN AND LONDON

YALE UNIVERSITY PRESS, 1973

Library of Congress catalog card number: 72–91312
International standard book number: 0–300–01554–2

Designed by Sally Sullivan
and set in Times Roman type.
Printed in the United States of America by
The Murray Printing Co., Forge Village, Massachusetts.

Published in Great Britain, Europe, and Africa by
Yale University Press, Ltd., London.
Distributed in Canada by McGill-Queen's University Press, Montreal;
in Latin America by Kaiman & Polon, Inc., New York City;
in Australasia and Southeast Asia by John Wiley & Sons Australasia Pty. Ltd.,
Sydney; in India by UBS Publishers' Distributors Pvt., Ltd., Delhi;
in Japan by John Weatherhill, Inc., Tokyo.

TO TOM

AND

TO ROME

# CONTENTS

vii

# LIST OF FIGURES

# LIST OF TABLES

# ACKNOWLEDGMENTS

For the opportunity to visit, study, and live in Rome, I would like to thank the following institutions: the Fulbright Commission (1953–55), the Carnegie Corporation of New York (1957–59), the U.S. Department of Commerce (1966–67), and the Academic Senate of the University of California, Los Angeles.

Planning experts who were particularly helpful to me in writing this book include Ing. Armando Borgata, Dott. Antonio Cederna, Ing. Mario D'Erme, Arch. Italo Insolera, Arch. Carlo Melograni, Dott. Mario Pacelli, Arch. Luigi Piccinato, Avv. Alberto Predieri, Arch. Lisa Ronchi, Prof. Gabriele Scimemi, Arch. Michele Valori, Ing. Marcello Vittorini, and Prof. Giulio Tirincanti.

Special insights into the workings of Roman politics were provided by Dott. Paolo Cabras, Dott. Oscar Mammi, Dott. Aldo Natoli, Avv. Adriano Paglietti, and Dott. Luigi Pallottini.

My particular thanks go to the Ufficio Stampa of the City of Rome (Dott. Enzo Bellizzi) for permission to consult press office files on the master plan. The Ufficio Speciale Nuovo Piano Regolatore made available some of the documentation upon which the book is based. Officials in the Segretariato Generale provided useful information on the functioning of the city departments and the city council.

My understanding of Roman and Italian city planning was enhanced by talks with Arch. Augusto Baccin, Ing. Vincenzo Di Gioia, Arch. Luciano Pontuale, and Ing. Cesare Valle—all of the Ministry of Public Works.

Invaluable general assistance was provided by Dott. Giovanni Beccheloni, Prof. Elio Gizzi, Dott. Dolves Guidi, Prof. Joseph LaPalombara, Dott. Antonio Maccanico, Prof. Guglielmo Negri, and Prof. Alberto Spreafico.

In tracking down information, help from Dottoressa Gloria Ammassari, Miss Laura Cardiff, Mr. Rajmelic Odinec, and Miss Lorene Salkow is gratefully acknowledged.

The manuscript has been much improved by the insightful criticisms of Mrs. Ruth Kaufman and Prof. Aaron Wildavsky and much embellished by the maps and figures drawn by Mr. Noel Diaz.

As ever, my wife, Catherine, and my children, Maura and Thomas, have helped me to understand, tolerate, and delight in the quality of Roman life.

R.C.F.

# ABBREVIATIONS

ACEA Azienda Comunale Elettricità ed Acque (City Water and Power Company)

ACER Associazione Costruttori Edili di Roma (Association of Roman Builders)

ANAS Azienda Nazionale Autonomo Strade (State Highway Corporation)

ANCE Associazione Nazionale Costruttori Edili (National Association of Builders)

ATAC Azienda Tramvie ed Autobus (City Tram and Bus Company)

CET Comitato di Elaborazione Tecnica (Technical Drafting Committee)

CLN Comitato di Liberazione Nazionale (Committee of National Liberation)

CONI Comitato Olimpico Nazionale Italiano (Italian National Olympic Committee)

CSLP Consiglio Superiore dei Lavori Pubblici (Superior Council for Public Works, highest technical advisory organ in the Ministry of Public Works)

DC Democrazia Cristiana (Christian Democratic party)

ECA Ente Comunale di Assistenza (City Welfare Board)

ENEL Ente Nazionale Elettricità (National Electric Corporation)

ENI Ente Nazionale Idrocarburi (National Hydrocarbon Corporation)

ENPI Ente Nazionale Prevenzioni Infortuni (National Industrial Safety Agency)

EUR Ente Autonomo Esposizione Universale di Roma (Autonomous Corporation for the World's Fair of Rome)

GESCAL Gestione Case per Lavoratori (Agency for Worker Housing, formerly INA-Casa).

IACP Istituto Autonomo per le Case Popolari della Provincia di Roma (Autonomous Institute for Low-Cost Housing of Rome Province)

ILSES Istituto Lombardo per gli Studi Economici e Sociali (Lombard Institute for Economic and Social Studies)

IN/arch Istituto Nazionale di Architettura (National Institute of Architecture)

INCIS Istituto Nazionale Case per gli Impiegati dello Stato (National Housing Institute for State Employees)

INU Istituto Nazionale di Urbanistica (National Institute of Planners)

IRES     Istituto di Ricerche Economico-Sociali "Aldo Valente" (The Aldo Valente Institute for Economic and Social Research)

IRI     Istituto per la Ricostruzione Industriale (Institute for Industrial Recovery)

Istat     Istituto Centrale di Statistica (Central Statistical Institute)

MSI     Movimento Sociale Italiano (Italian Social Movement, the neofascist party)

ONMI     Opera Nazionale Maternità e Infanzia (National Maternal and Child Care Agency)

PCI     Partito Comunista Italiano (Italian Communist Party)

PLI     Partito Liberale Italiano (Italian Liberal [i.e. conservative] Party)

PRI     Partito Repubblicano Italiano (Italian Republican [i.e. progressive] Party)

PSDI     Partito Socialista Democratico Italiano (Italian Social Democratic Party)

PSI     Partito Socialista Italiano (Italian Socialist Party)

PSIUP     Partito Socialista Italiano di Unità Proletaria (Italian Socialist Party of Proletarian Unity)

SGI     Società Generale Immobiliare (General Real Estate Corporation)

STEFER     Società Tramvie e Ferrovie Elettriche (Tram and Electric Railway Company)

UCIT     Unione Cattolica Italiana Tecnici (Association of Italian Catholic Technicians)

UCR     Unione Costruttori Romani (Association of Roman Builders)

USNPR     Ufficio Speciale Nuovo Piano Regolatore (Special Office for the New Master Plan)

# 1

# JUDGING

# AND

# UNDERSTANDING

# PLANNING PERFORMANCE

There is much to be learned about planning and urban politics from the study of planning in Rome, for in several ways Rome resembles other cities. The attempt there has been to preserve through planning a very old city now overwhelmed by a very new city. The problem of preserving physical ties with the past—at least those ties that sustain a sense of civic identity and attachment—is common to a large and increasing number of cities all over the world. The problem of organizing decent patterns of settlement under conditions of very rapid demographic and economic growth is common to an even larger number of cities. Rome is an old city and a rapidly growing city; it is also a democratically governed city. The difficult task of adjusting old interests to new interests is being attempted through the fiercely competitive and chaotic processes of urban multiparty democracy. Roman planning experience is therefore also instructive about the capabilities of democratic urban political systems under conditions of intense ideological conflict and rapid social change.

But if interest in Roman planning politics derives in part from the fact that Rome resembles other cities, it derives also from the fact that Rome is unique. Rome is old, rapidly growing, and democratic in its own fashion. Roman planning is of intrinsic importance precisely because its overriding goal, its guiding principle, has been to save and enhance the unique legacy we all have inherited from the city's past.

## POSTWAR ROMAN PLANNING

On February 11, 1966, the *Gazzetta Ufficiale* of the Republic of Italy published a decree promulgating the new master plan of Rome. Promulgation of the plan, adopted by the Rome city council some three years before, marked a major step toward the goal of bringing the growth of the city under some form of rational or at least public control. The struggle to formulate and secure adoption of a new plan for the city began soon after World War II, and it was nearly twenty years later that an officially approved document appeared. During this time the city's population swelled from one and one-half to more than three million. The built-up area of the city, some fifty-eight square miles in 1940, spread out to cover more than twice that space by 1966. The number of occupied dwellings rose from 308,982 in 1951 to 653,095 in 1966; the number of occupied rooms, from 1.1 million to 2.3 million.[1] Thus the plan appeared after much of the growth it was designed to regulate had already taken place.

In the absence of a new plan, the city had grown in accordance with the provisions, modified by hundreds of formal and informal variances, of the Mussolini master plan of 1931, or in accordance with the convenience, interests, and opportunities of thousands of builders, operating outside any legal framework. Around the old historic center of the city there emerged a ring of new residential districts as densely packed with people, as poor in services, and as badly engineered for modern traffic as the slums of the historic center itself, built hundreds of years before. Illegal structures, some solid, some flimsy, appeared throughout the vast stretches of open countryside surrounding the city, just as they appeared—rather suddenly, and again illegally—on most of the rooftops of the historic center. Many large residential districts were built with the chrism of legality but even these were excessive in density, and, however luxurious, lacked adequate open and green space and services. By 1970, some fifty thousand people were still living in shacks, under the arches of ancient bridges and aqueducts, in caves and cellars, and in other places unfit for human habitation.[2]

1. Istituto Centrale di Statistica (henceforth "Istat"), *IX Censimento Generale della Popolazione, III Censimento Generale dell'Industria e del Commercio, Caratteristiche demografiche ed economiche dei grandi comuni,* vol. 1 (Rome, 1959), pp. 243–65; Istat, *X° Censimento Generale della Popolazione* (henceforth "10° Censimento"), vol. 1 (Rome, 1963), pp. 12–35; Comune di Roma, Ufficio Speciale Nuovo Piano Regolatore, *Raccolta di graffici* (Rome, 1958); Comune di Roma, Ufficio di Statistica e Censimento, *Roma: Popolazione e territorio dal 1860 al 1960* (henceforth "Popolazione e territorio") (Rome, 1960), p. 308; and Istat, *Indagine speciale sulle abitazioni al 20 gennaio 1066,* Note e relazioni No. 35, March 1968.
2. Estimates vary on the number of people living in *baracche.* The organ of the Union of Lazio Industrialists, *Industria di Roma,* on September. 15, 1969 (p. ix) estimated the number of people involved at over 300,000. An official city census of *"alloggi precari"* in 1967 counted 522 distinct settlements, with 8,980 dwellings, 9,417 families, and 38,248 people *(Notiziario Statistico Mensile del Comune di Roma,* October 1967). During the agitations of November 1969, when many of the *"senza tetto"* invaded and occupied long-vacant buildings in a well-to-do section of the city, the number of "roofless" was estimated at 70,000 (*Los Angeles Times,* November 20, 1969). See below, chap. 10, for other estimates. Uncertainties concerning the actual number of dwellings and people involved derive from the strong motivation of many of the "countees" *not* to be counted and the disinclination of the official "counters" to reveal the other side of *"la dolce vita."* On life in the baracche, see Pier Giorgio Liverani, "Un inferno chiamato baracca," *Capitolium,* January 1970, pp. 7–15.

Even with the approval of the new plan, the struggle to improve the quality of the city's growth has barely begun. The plan adopted by the city council in December 1962 and approved conditionally by the national government in 1966 has yet to be implemented. The implementation process does not promise to be any easier than the process of plan formulation and adoption. The plan calls upon builders to observe stringent new standards in the location and construction of new residences; more important, it calls upon them *not* to build in many of the as yet unbuilt parts of the city. The plan requests public agencies— important actors in any national capital—to observe the zoning provisions of the plan and in particular the plan's injunction to decentralize their offices to new office centers *("centri direzionali")* miles away from the existing center of the city. It calls upon the city and national governments to invest large sums of money in the construction of the new centers and of the new "eastern axis" freeway, which is eventually to become the "linear center" of the new Rome.[3]

To secure the cooperation of private and public investors has not been and will not be easy. Already hundreds, perhaps thousands, of new structures and entire subdivisions have been built—illegally—on sites designated as future parks, highways, streets, schools, and shops. The city government has been unable to police its territory in order to prevent the sabotage of its new plan. It has also been unable to raise funds for the capital improvements included in the plan. The agencies of the national government, for their part, have been none too sympathetic with the city's plight, nor generous in ministering to its needs, nor anxious to comply with its planning choices.

The planning experience that is the subject of this book is thus not exemplary, even if it may, indeed, be typical. In the absence of comparative studies of city planning politics, it is difficult to say whether what is being studied here is pathology or some form, albeit morbid, of normality.

EVALUATING PLANNING PERFORMANCE

Comparative study of planning, is made difficult by the lack of operational and consensual indicators of good planning. Most comparative studies of planning effectiveness have dealt with economic planning at the national level rather than physical planning at the local level. In the case of national economic planning, both policy and the presumed impact of policy are subject to quantification; there is a large measure of agreement on how to measure planning performance, including the use of such indicators as the growth of GNP. Some local policy outputs such as service levels in police, education, and welfare are much more measurable than planning outputs.[4] The effectiveness of municipal

3. For a recent description and analysis of the Rome master plan by an American city planner, see Corwin R. Mocine, "The New Plan for Rome," *Journal of the American Institute of Planners, 35* (November 1969), 376–82.
4. References to the mounting number of municipal output studies can be found in Philip B.

investment planning, where the outputs are quantifiable, can also be studied comparatively.[5] But in the case of local *physical* planning, inputs, outputs, and impacts are much less easily reduced to measurable units. This is especially true with regard to the more comprehensive forms of planning. General plans are rather difficult to reduce to common denominators for the purposes of comparative study; and their comparable elements may be the least significant thing about them.

We can, of course, measure some aspects of environmental quality, using statistics on housing and the distribution of services and facilities. But whether we are thereby measuring the impact of planning is problematical, just as it is open to question whether economic growth rates actually measure the effectiveness of planning; whether, that is, they reflect the impact of policy or of something else. Then, too, many of the goals of planning, the impacts sought, are more easily expressed in subjective and esthetic than in arithmetic terms. And as the goals of physical planning come increasingly to include social and psychological impacts, the evaluation of planning efforts will become even more difficult.[6]

In this study, given the lack of any single consensual, operational test of planning performance, I propose to use several criteria in the hope that, in combination, they may afford a fairer picture than any one of them would if applied singly. The criteria are the following: 1. planning technique or style; 2. planner power; 3. commitment to planning; 4. environmental amenity; 5. goal achievement; and 6. time costs.

*1. Planning style.* This criterion applies not to the results obtained but to the methods used. It is assumed that the use of appropriate methods and procedures and techniques will lead to or constitute effective planning.[7] If one is assessing comparative *master* planning, one looks at the kinds of information that have been collected about trends, preferences, intentions; the diversity of perspectives brought to play; the sophistication of research and analysis. Some yardsticks of comprehensiveness might be used, measuring the range and diversity of perspectives, disciplines, and sectorial preferences incorporated into the plan or planning process. Have the goals and interests of a wide variety of groups,

---

Coulter, "Comparative Community Politics and Public Policy," *Polity, 3* (Fall 1970), 22–43. Almost all such studies have dealt comparatively only with U.S. cities. References to some of the few comparative municipal studies of non-U.S. cities can be found in Robert Fried, "Communism, Urban Budgets, and the Two Italies," *Journal of Politics, 33* (November 1971), 1008–51, and Robert Fried and Francine Rabinovitz, *Comparative Urban Politics* (Englewood Cliffs, in press).

5. See W. H. Brown, Jr., and C. E. Gilbert, *Planning Municipal Investment: A Case Study of Philadelphia* (Philadelphia, 1961).

6. Efforts to broaden the social scope of planning are analyzed in Bernard J. Frieden and Robert Morris, eds., *Urban Planning and Social Policy* (New York, 1968).

7. This seems to be the approach also of Annmarie Hauck Walsh in her essay on comparative planning in *The Urban Challenge to Government* (New York, 1969), chap. 6.

institutions, and departments been consulted and incorporated into the plan? Has the plan sought to achieve some consistency of purpose among major public and private operators in all major sectors? Have local expectations been fitted into the calculations and choices made at higher levels? Of course, these tests do not measure the impact of the techniques, procedures, or research; they measure the style of planning rather than its effectiveness; they measure an input rather than an output.

*2. Planner power.* Another often used test of planning effectiveness focuses on the fate of planners, or rather of their proposals, in the policymaking process.[8] Effective planning here means the successful initiation and vetoing of policy proposals by planners; the adoption of their advice as government policy; perhaps even the obedience of private and public operators to planner decisions. But while effectiveness in the political arena is a prerequisite to successful planning, the two are not necessarily coterminous.

*3. Planning commitment.* Another indicator of performance may be found in government budgets: we might measure planning effectiveness by examining the amount of money spent on planning in a given jurisdiction, as Professors Eulau and Eyestone have recently done. Unfortunately, absolute and relative levels of spending on planning, or on any other public activity, are no certain indicators of performance quality.[9] Differences in efficiency might mean that equal expenditures had rather unequal results. Here again is a prerequisite condition for effective planning—a sufficient budget—in addition to the ones already discussed—proper technique and power. Budgetary allocations for planning may indeed correlate highly and positively with planning effectiveness, but without some independent measure of the latter we cannot tell.

*4. Environmental quality.* One can attempt also to measure the quality of the urban environment as a means of testing planning effectiveness. In recent article Professor John Burchard ranked the major cities of the world in accordance with a set of criteria for urban amenity.[10] In the resulting rank-order, Rome emerged second only to Paris as a "great city." (See Table 1.1.)

8. This is the test used by Francine F. Rabinovitz in *City Politics and Planning* (New York, 1969); David C. Ranney in *Planning and Politics in the Metropolis* (Columbus, 1969); and Alan Altschuler in *The City Planning Process: A Political Analysis* (Ithaca, 1965). I have myself analyzed Roman planning in terms of the political effectiveness of planners in "Professionalism and Politics in Roman Planning," *Journal of the American Institute of Planners, 35* (May 1969), 150–59.

9. Expenditures are the key output indicators used by Heinz Eulau and Robert Eyestone, "Policy Maps of City Councils and Policy Outcomes: A Developmental Analysis," *American Political Science Review, 62* (March 1968), 124–43. Caution in the use of expenditures as output indicators is suggested by Ira Sharkansky in "Government Expenditures and Public Services in the American States," *American Political Science Review, 41* (December 1967), 1066.

10. John Burchard, "The Culture of Urban America," in *Environment and Change: The Next Fifty Years,* ed. William R. Ewald, Jr. (Bloomington, 1968), p. 209.

Table 1.1. Urban Amenity Score Sheet

| | *Paris* | *Rome* | *London* | *New York* | *Stockholm* | *Chicago* | *Boston* | *Rio de Janeiro* | *San Francisco* | *Sydney* | *Venice* | *Washington* | *Istanbul* | *Pittsburgh* | *Los Angeles* | *Dallas/Ft. Worth* | *Totals* |
|---|---|---|---|---|---|---|---|---|---|---|---|---|---|---|---|---|---|
| Fine river, lake, etc. | 1 | 1 | 1 | 1 | 1 | 1 | 1 | 1 | 1 | 1 | 1 | ½ | 1 | 1 | 0 | 0 | 13½ |
| Great park(s) | 1 | 1 | 1 | 1 | 1 | 1 | ½ | 1 | 1 | 1 | 0 | 1 | 0 | 1 | ½ | 1 | 13 |
| Distinguished buildings | 1 | 1 | 1 | 1 | ½ | 1 | 1 | 1 | ½ | ½ | 1 | 1 | 1 | ½ | ½ | ½ | 13 |
| Distinguished museum(s) | 1 | 1 | 1 | 1 | ½ | 1 | 1 | ½ | 0 | 0 | 1 | 1 | 1 | 1 | 1 | ½ | 12½ |
| Readable plan | 1 | ½ | 1 | 1 | 1 | 1 | ½ | 1 | 1 | ½ | 1 | 1 | ½ | 1 | ½ | 0 | 12½ |
| Great university | 1 | ½ | 1 | 1 | 1 | 1 | 1 | 0 | 1 | 1 | 0 | 7 | 1 | 1 | 1 | ½ | 12½ |
| Diverse neighborhoods | 1 | 1 | 1 | 1 | ½ | ½ | ½ | 1 | 1 | ½ | 1 | ½ | ½ | ½ | ½ | ½ | 11 |
| Great eating | 1 | 1 | ½ | 1 | ½ | ½ | ½ | 1 | 1 | ½ | 1 | ½ | ½ | 0 | 1 | ½ | 11 |
| Fine music | ½ | 1 | 1 | 1 | ½ | 1 | 1 | ½ | 1 | ½ | 0 | ½ | 0 | 1 | 1 | ½ | 11 |
| General boscage | 1 | 1 | 1 | ½ | 1 | ½ | 1 | 1 | ½ | 1 | 0 | 1 | 0 | 0 | ½ | ½ | 10½ |
| Glamorous site | ½ | ½ | ½ | 1 | 1 | ½ | ½ | 1 | 1 | 1 | 1 | 0 | 1 | 1 | 0 | 0 | 10½ |
| Great sports | 1 | 1 | 1 | 1 | 0 | 1 | 1 | 1 | 1 | 1 | 0 | 0 | 0 | 0 | 1 | ½ | 10½ |
| Great avenue(s) | 1 | ½ | 1 | 1 | ½ | 1 | ½ | 1 | 0 | ½ | 1 | 1 | ½ | 0 | 0 | 0 | 9½ |
| Fine squares | 1 | 1 | 1 | ½ | 1 | 0 | ½ | 0 | ½ | ½ | 1 | 0 | ½ | ½ | 0 | 0 | 8 |
| Important visible past | 1 | 1 | 1 | 1 | ½ | 0 | 1 | 0 | 0 | 0 | 1 | ½ | 1 | 0 | 0 | 0 | 8 |
| Good air | 0 | 1 | 0 | 0 | 1 | 0 | 0 | 1 | 1 | 1 | 1 | 0 | 1 | 0 | 0 | ½ | 7½ |
| Fine libraries | 1 | 1 | 1 | 1 | 0 | 1 | 1 | 0 | 0 | 0 | 0 | 1 | 0 | 0 | 0 | 0 | ½ |
| Exciting shop windows | 1 | ½ | 1 | 1 | 0 | ½ | 0 | ½ | 0 | 0 | 0 | 0 | 0 | ½ | 0 | 1 | 6 |
| Generally pleasant climate | ½ | 1 | 0 | ½ | ½ | 0 | ½ | ½ | 1 | 1 | 0 | 0 | 0 | 0 | ½ | 0 | 6 |
| Fountains | 1 | 1 | 1 | 0 | 1 | 1 | 0 | 0 | 0 | 0 | 0 | 0 | 0 | 0 | 0 | 0 | 5 |
| Theater | 1 | 1 | 1 | 1 | ½ | 0 | 0 | 0 | 0 | 0 | 0 | 0 | 0 | 0 | 0 | ½ | 5 |
| Art in the streets | 1 | 1 | 0 | 0 | 1 | 0 | 0 | 0 | ½ | 0 | 1 | 0 | 0 | 0 | 0 | 0 | 4½ |
| Private galleries | 1 | ½ | 1 | 1 | 0 | ½ | ½ | 0 | 0 | 0 | 0 | 0 | 0 | 0 | 0 | 0 | 4½ |
| Many opportunities for participatory recreation | 0 | 0 | 0 | ½ | 1 | ½ | ½ | ½ | 0 | 1 | 0 | 0 | 0 | 0 | 0 | 0 | 4 |
| Totals | 20½ | 20 | 19 | 19 | 15½ | 14½ | 14 | 13½ | 13 | 12½ | 12 | 10 | 9½ | 9 | 8 | 6½ | |

*Source:* John Burchard, "The Culture of Urban America," in *Environment and Change: The Next Fifty Years* edited by William R. Ewald, Jr. (Bloomington: Indiana University Press, 1968), p. 209.

Ironically, it is just such impressionistic rankings that have made it difficult for planners to achieve their goals in Rome. To some people, Rome is a completed achievement of civilization: to view it as a social problem, requiring basic reform, seems sacrilegious. It is sometimes difficult to remember that the grand and elegant Rome described in art books and tourist guides is the same Rome described with lamentations and despair in the books of Italian city planners. The discrepancy arises, in part, from the structure of the city itself, which contains most of its grandeur within the confines of the Aurelian walls, leaving outside the far less picturesque districts inhabited by 90 percent of the Roman people. Quite properly, the tourist sees the great parks in and near the historic center, such as Villa Borghese, but has no reason to notice the virtual absence of parks in most neighborhoods of the city. Tourist Rome, the six square miles within the old walls, covers only about one percent of the city's six hundred square miles of land; it houses only one-tenth of the city's population. The historic center makes Rome a "great" city, but the amenities in that center are not very helpful in making the surrounding residential districts more livable and enjoyable.

If subjective estimates of environmental quality are used, it may be rather important whose estimates they are. There is accumulating evidence that environmental quality is perceived and assessed differently by different social groups. Perspectives and standards differ between social classes and between professional planners and laymen. Until recently, little has been known about how Rome is perceived by ordinary Romans. Planners and officials in Italy have hitherto not taken pains to inquire into the preferences and values of those for whom they presumably are planning. Recent surveys have begun to disclose that the city and its neighborhoods as seen by professional planners may not be the same city perceived by most of its inhabitants.[11]

Most measures of environmental quality are subjective, but even if consensual, valid, and reliable indicators of environmental quality could be found, they would not necessarily help to measure planning performance. Some of the most admired aspects of Rome are the result of government planning, as are some of its least admired aspects. Much of what different kinds of people like or dislike about the city has little to do with government planning, past or present. The quality of the Roman environment indicates less the quality of Roman planning than the impact of history, social and cultural values, and regional economics.

*5. Goal achievement.* We might attempt to measure the effectiveness of Roman planning by setting the achievements of the planners against their stated goals. The goals of planners tend to be descriptive and prescriptive: descriptive (predictive) for those allowed to make their own decisions and prescriptive for those subject to collective choice. The effectiveness of planning can be tested by the degree to which the prescriptions of the plan are obeyed and the descriptions (predicted behaviors) become reality. Effective planning exists (1) when public and private actors obey the ground rules laid down in the plan; (2) when they maintain the investment commitments contained in the plan; and (3) when, using their discretion, they act in accordance with the plan's predictions. The

11. Franco Crespi, "Aspetti del rapporto tra strutture urbanistiche e relazioni sociali in una borgata alla periferia di Roma," *Rivista di Socioloiga,* May-August 1967, pp. 5–50; F. Crespi and Franco Martinelli, "La dinamica delle relazioni sociali nel contesto urbano," *Rivista di Sociologia,* May 1968, pp. 5–62.

measure of planning effectiveness by the goal-achievement criterion is whether the rules are enforced and respected, investment commitments are kept, and predicted developments take place.

There are, to be sure, difficulties in applying this criterion. It is hard to apply when there is no plan with unequivocal rules, commitments, or predictions—no clearly stated goals by which to measure achievement. It is hard to apply in cities like Rome, where the plan has only recently been promulgated, where the implementation process has barely begun, and where it may accordingly be premature to make this kind of assessment.

Another difficulty with goal-achievement as a performance test is that the goals of planning include not only those manifested in the plan itself, but also the latent goals of many participants in the planning process—latent goals that may be unrelated or even antagonistic to the manifest goals of the plan. Planning effectiveness can also legitimately be assessed in terms of latent goal achievement because planning serves, or has served in Rome, a variety of ulterior purposes. Planning has been used to create and destroy private fortunes, help the poor, demonstrate fidelity to tradition, win personal or party credit, capture attention and prestige for planners, build and disrupt political alliances, affirm an ideology, win factional contests, apply professional doctrine, and engage in pseudo- or symbolic action. Latent planning goals may be more important to many actors than manifest goals, but if it is difficult to measure manifest goal achievement, it is next to impossible to measure latent goal achievement.

A further drawback in the use of the goal achievement standard, at least for the purposes of intercity planning comparisons, lies in the wide variations among cities—variations not only in the resources available for commitment to planning purposes but also in the pressure from the environment and the scope of the attempted response. City X achieves all of its goals, however defined, while City Y achieves few of them. City X is rich; the pressure on it from migrants is low; its plans are unambitious. City Y, on the other hand, is relatively poor; it suffers from a heavy influx of poor migrants; its plan is innovative, controversial, and comprehensive; its goals, in a word, are far more difficult to achieve. Which city, then, has the more effective planning? The one that deals successfully with an unchallenging environment or the one that deals poorly with an overwhelming environment? Goal achievement should be measured not only in some absolute sense but also relative to available resources and to the costs, complexity, and controversiality of the goals adopted.

6. *Time costs.* There is one other performance test to apply in assessing planning effectiveness in Rome, and that is simply the ability to produce and adopt a master plan within a reasonable period of time. Planning effectiveness involves in the first instance the ability to arrive at some kind of ongoing agreement, however provisional, however negative, as to what the future environment should be like and how and perhaps when it should become that way. Plans are

notoriously easier to design and adopt than to implement and, of course, only implementation (manifest and latent goal achievement) reveals the important payoffs of the planning process. Nonetheless, one can argue that it is already a planning achievement for a community to arrive at some kind of agreement as to its future state and to be able to adopt a general plan at all. It may take a long time to do so or only a few months. Other things being equal, planning is more effective when plans are swiftly made and implemented than when it takes long years to arrive at agreement. The longer the wait, presumably, the more unwanted developments are permitted to occur and the more desired improvements may be held up.

On the other hand, a long awaited plan may be a better plan and a swiftly adopted plan just as swiftly regretted. The more comprehensive the plan in the perspectives it seeks to incorporate, the interests it seeks to adjust and accommodate, and the aspects of reality it seeks to understand and predict, the longer its formulation will require, given environments of comparable complexity and diversity. How much such comprehensiveness is worth waiting for depends on the costs of delay. As the old saying goes, "the best may be the enemy of the good."

### EXPLAINING PLANNING PERFORMANCE

Evaluating performance is one thing, explaining performance is another. The task of evaluating planning performance in Rome is attempted in chapter 10, while the chapters preceding are devoted to explanation. The city planning process in postwar Rome is seen as being shaped by the following constraints:

1. the legacy of Roman history (Chapter 2)
2. the goals and ambitions of postwar planners (Chapter 3)
3. the roles of the city in the nation and in its region (Chapter 4)
4. the city's demography, social structure, and civic culture (Chapter 4)
5. the contrasting nature of the city's public and private economies (Chapter 5)
6. the machinery of city government (Chapter 6)
7. national politics and policy (Chapter 7)
8. Roman party politics (Chapter 8)
9. Roman interest group politics (Chapter 9)

In chapter 10, the suggested planning performance criteria are applied to Roman planning and Rome's performance is compared with that of the other large Italian cities. The findings of comparative studies of urban performance are brought in to suggest which of the constraints mentioned above may have been most crucial in shaping the outcomes of the Roman planning process. In the last chapter, the constraints on planning performance are again examined with a view to determining which of them is most subject to change and which therefore offers greatest hope for improving the effectiveness of Roman planning.

# 2

# PLANNING
# IN ROME'S
# PAST

PLANNING IN CLASSICAL ROME

Postwar efforts to plan development in Rome were by no means the first such efforts in the city's history. Planning schemes go back to classical times, when the difficulties seem to have been no less challenging than they are today. Classical Rome was not, in origin, a planned creation. It developed haphazardly from the unification of primitive communities on the hills above the Tiber about twelve miles inland from the Mediterranean Sea. The Tiber was both a boundary and a means of communication between the Etruscans in north-central Italy and the Latins to the south. As early as the eighth century B.C., the Latins created settlements on the steep Roman hills in sites that would provide them with control over the river traffic, protect them against malaria, floods, and tribal enemies, and give them a base for asserting and extending their hold over the lives and resources of neighboring peoples. The Forum emerged as the center of interaction among the hilltop villages, the site of public assemblies and of public buildings and temples. The first or Servian walls around the emerging city were built in the sixth century B.C. They did not suffice to prevent the devastating incursion of the Gauls in 390 B.C. After the Gauls had sacked and burned the city and left, it was decided to rebuild in the same place, within a second set of walls, but to allow complete freedom in the rebuilding of private dwellings. This freedom is blamed for the subsequent irregularity of the city's street scheme, but the unevenness of the terrain and the gradual nature of the city's growth must also have been important factors.[1]

1. Standard works on ancient Roman planning are Ferdinando Castagnoli, "Roma antica," in F. Castagnoli et al., *Topografia e urbanistica di Roma* (Bologna, 1958), pp. 1–186; and Léon Homo, *Rome Impériale et l'urbanisme dans l'antiquité* (Paris, 1951). Extensive bibliographies may be found in these and also in Istituto Nazionale di Urbanistica, *Roma: Città e piani*

By the fourth century B.C., Rome was the largest city in Italy, on its way to conquering the peninsula and to losing some of its primitive traditionalism. As the city's power expanded throughout the Mediterranean, its population grew as did its need for new forms of circulation and public intercourse. Conquest, which created these needs, also provided solutions to imitate (Hellenistic temples, porticos, and bridges), the means to finance those solutions (forced labor and imperial tributes), and new materials and techniques for utilizing them. The Romans themselves invented some forms, such as triumphal arches, basilicas, baths, and underground sewers, and used these and the borrowed forms in a great effort in the late republic to embellish the city so as to make it worthy of its growing political supremacy. Monumentality would serve to mitigate the contempt of the Hellenistic world; it would also advance the political ambitions of the city's rulers.[2]

By Caesar's time, Rome was a city of perhaps 400,000 people jammed into less than fifteen square miles of city territory. Most Romans lived in multistory wooden tenements without lighting, glass windows, or sanitation, and were constantly exposed to the perils of fire and building collapse. The city had grown largely without public direction or control. Elsewhere in their empire the Romans displayed great talent in the planning of roads and towns. But the features of Roman town planning—rectilinear house alignments and street axes, right angle street intersections, the *cardo* and *decumanus,* the checkerboard pattern—were thought to be appropriate to military outposts, not to the civilian capital. The Romans, moreover, opposed efforts to rationalize circulation within the city as destroying its "southern" comforts: the narrow, winding streets, lined with steep tenements, that kept out both wind and sun.[3]

Refusal to plan the building of the city after the Gallic invasion was characteristic of the Romans' private enterprise attitude toward urban development. Public authorities could alienate or lease public property, but they could obtain private land only on the open market. There was no right of eminent domain nor a concept of public law that made for effective public regulation of building.[4] The rulers of the city had, in any event, little incentive to attempt long-range or broad-scale civic planning, given the attitudes of the public toward civic improvement and private property. Authority over public works and improvements was scattered among several public officials, many of whom remained only one year in office and thus had neither ability nor reason to attempt long-

(Turin, n.d.), p. 327, and in Mario Morini, *Atlante di storia dell'urbanistica* (Milan, 1963). A most useful recent essay is that by Ludovico Quaroni, "Una città eterna: quattro lezioni da ventisette secoli," in *Roma: Città e piani,* pp. 5–72. For this paragraph, see Castagnoli, "Roma antica," pp. 3–19; Homo, *Rome Impériale,* pp. 48–49; and Quaroni, "Una città eterna," pp. 9–10.

2. Castagnoli, "Roma antica," pp. 21–22; Homo, *Rome Impériale,* pp. 49–57.
3. Italo Insolera, "Appunti per una storia urbanistica di Roma," in *Problemi urbanistici di Roma,* ed. Luigi Piccinato (Milan, 1960), p. 23.
4. Quaroni, "Una città eterna," p. 16.

term programs. Even when concentrated in the hands of consuls and emperors, such authority was more usefully employed for personal propaganda and immediate reward than for the gradual execution of a predetermined program that might redound to the credit of some future successor. Rome's governors typically preferred to enhance their power and prestige through bread and circuses, rather than through reform of the city's structure.

The result was a city composed of a series of spectacular monumental zones inserted in a cluttered mass of intricate, confused streets and neighborhoods; a city without public transportation and therefore without suburban development to relieve central congestion; a city without a rational circulation scheme, whose pattern remained whatever physical and historical accident had made it; a city in which many services were rudimentary, such as firefighting, or nonexistent, such as private water, street lighting, public education, private sanitation, and public cemeteries.[5]

Nonetheless, the planning heritage of ancient Rome is not entirely negative, for, compared to medieval and early modern cities, Rome as a city was rather advanced and represented a remarkable city-building achievement. It was a gigantic city for the times, sustaining without a very viable economy over a million people in what seems to have been for them reasonable comfort. The city possessed a vast network of streets and squares and a remarkable endowment of public facilities of all kinds—religious, governmental, economic, cultural, and recreational. The city did provide a large number of services: baths, vital statistics, records, street paving, police, firefighting, food supply, welfare, higher education, libraries, and drainage. The city enforced extensive bodies of regulations to enhance public safety and convenience in such fields as traffic, building, street cleaning and maintenance, health, and food. No less important a heritage were the attempts by city leaders to remedy some of the defects in the city's structure and functioning.[6]

The first major attempt at reform was Caesar's. In 45 B.C., Caesar promulgated the *Lex de Urbe Augenda* or the Law for the Extension of the City, which is considered the first modern planning law for the city, as well as a program for urban reorganization.[7] Caesar's plan aimed to improve communications between various parts of the city; to relieve the land shortage in the center; to expand the space available for public purposes; and, in general, to give the Roman state a suitable capital. Expansion of the city toward the west was blocked by the Tiber; toward the east, by the large estates of the powerful Roman upper classes; toward the south, by the port and its subproletarian population and connotations. Caesar accordingly chose to build new districts to the north, in the Campus Martius, even though this area, lying in the bend of the Tiber, was then outside the *pomerium,* or sacro-legal boundary of the city. The

5. Ibid., pp. 27–29; Insolera, "Appunti," p. 23; Homo, *Rome Impériale,* pp. 650–74.
6. Homo, *Rome Impériale,* pp. 650–51.
7. Quaroni, "Una città eterna," pp. 30–31.

Campus Martius was, however, flat, easily equipped with streets, and close to the Forum. (It was to become, in fact, the "modern" Rome of the period between the fall of the empire and 1870.)

Caesar's law also included a plan to divert the Tiber from its course to a new bed behind the Vatican and the Janiculum: this was to avoid the great expense of new bridges across the Tiber. Many joined Cicero in suspecting that this project was also designed to enhance the value of properties Caesar held on the right bank, in Trastevere. Given the customs of those days and our own, these suspicions seem not without foundation. It is reported in one history that in previous redevelopment projects Caesar had appropriated to himself the treasures found in the demolition of houses and temples.[8] To dispel such suspicions, perhaps, Caesar the following year bequeathed his gardens across the river to the Roman people.[9]

Execution of Caesar's plan was cut short by his assassination; it would, in any event, have encountered formidable opposition from a coalition of forces, led by Cicero, which opposed the plan because it would have forced many Romans to inhabit an area regarded hitherto as sacred and spirit-infested and because it called for change and sacrifice without presenting any prospect of immediate tangible personal gain.[10] Augustus, though Caesar's heir and executor, made no effort to carry out Caesar's program of urban reform. He sent Caesar's planner, Pomponius-Caecilius, back to Greece and, while completing the buildings and forum that Caesar had begun, abandoned the notions of diverting the Tiber and subdividing the Campus Martius for residential purposes. Instead he designated the Campus Martius as a monumental zone and secured residential expansion into the area by indirect rather than direct methods. He made the Campus Martius attractive for residential development not by direct subdivision but by the creation there of public works and monuments, such as his own tomb, and by administrative reorganization—neither apparently related to the purpose of major urban reform. His administrative reorganization scheme incorporated many of the suburbs, including the Campus Martius, into the city proper and divided the new greater Rome into fourteen regions. Through these methods Augustus opened up a vast new area for urban development, achieving by indirection what Caesar might not have been able to achieve in a frontal assault.[11] But if, under Augustus, some direction was given to the development process, most aspects, including the location and quality of housing, remained under the control of private interests.

Under Nero, greater public control over development was made possible by

8. Dion Cassius in his *History of Rome,* cited by Homo, *Rome Impériale,* p. 67.

9. Quaroni, "Una città eterna," PP. 30–31; Homo, *Rome Impériale,* pp. 59–66.

10. In the letter to Atticus in which he complains about Caesar's law, Cicero himself expressed regret that he had not bought land in the districts Caesar proposed to urbanize. See Quaroni, "Una città eterna," p. 31, and Homo, *Rome Impériale,* pp. 65–66.

11. Homo, *Rome Impériale,* pp. 68–90; on p. 100 there is a map of the regions. See also Quaroni, "Una citta eternà," pp. 31–37, and Castagnoli, "Roma antica," pp. 24–28.

the week-long fire in A.D. 64, which razed to the ground three of the fourteen regions of the city, destroyed most of the structures in seven, and left only four intact. While fire was destroying the nucleus of the old city, the emperor, according to popular rumor, recited poems on the burning of Troy.

Nero exploited the ruination caused by the fire to rebuild the central city along the more rational lines used by the Romans in their colonial cities. He provided a new street plan for the center, new building regulations, and state assistance in rebuilding. These measures resulted in a central Rome with broader, straighter streets, considerable open space, limited building heights, and protective porticos—all against the predilections of the populace, which considered the old center, with its tenements and its sunless, winding streets, to have been healthier. As in later redevelopment schemes, the poor were driven into the suburbs because of high rentals in the new planned districts of the center.[12]

Thus the major obstacle to the development of public control over development in ancient Rome seems to have been the public itself, which preferred a less rational, more traditional city to live in—almost anticipating Jane Jacobs in preferring the winding streets of overcrowded tenements to the rationalized, rectilinear roadways exposed to sun and wind. To the force of popular preferences opposed to centrally guided development must also be added the desire of the rulers themselves to produce benevolent surprises, to use public projects as a source of support for themselves rather than their successors, and to profit personally from the traffic in spectacular, if uncoordinated, public works. Greater public control over *private* activities would have been unpopular; greater coordination over *public* activities might have been unprofitable.

By the fourth century A.D., Rome began to live on, and to some extent in, its past: its eternal nature derived from its past glories rather than its present or future functions. By then the city was considered a most sacred place and efforts were made not to embellish it further but to preserve what had already been done. Effective planning now came to mean not control of future growth but prevention of future decay. But the rulers of the city were little more successful in preventing decline than they had been in guiding growth. Imperial edicts in the years 364, 376, and 390 banned new constructions that utilized building materials from the old monuments.[13] Even after it had ceased to be the capital of the empire in A.D. 331, Rome was still considered the most beautiful and sacred city in the world: all the greater, then, was the shock when, after eight centuries of immunity, the city was invaded, plundered, and burned for three days in 410 by the barbarians. This disaster was followed by earthquakes and further invasions which, together with the ravages of the weather and the use of the old monuments as quarries, left much of the city in ruins. Survival was assured only to those buildings and monuments that were converted to ecclesiastical purposes.[14]

12. Quaroni, "Una città eterna," pp. 37–39; Homo, *Rome Impériale,* pp. 303–8.
13. Castagnoli, "Roma antica," pp. 38–39.
14. Ibid., pp. 39–42.

Physically, little eventually remained of the Rome that had housed perhaps a million people or more. Surviving vandalism, foreign and domestic, were a small number of ruins, occupying relatively little area but possessing enormous powers of suggestion and attraction. The classical remains served to provide physical substance to the conception of Rome as sacred, universal, and eternal. The physical remains supported a monumental myth and a myth of monumentality. Already in the classical period the city as such had been an object of veneration as a symbol of moral and political grandeur. The cult of Rome was to survive the destruction of most of the classical city. The ruins of the ancient city have provided each regime that has governed the city with a set of challenges, issues, and problems. Each regime has developed a policy for the classical ruins; each has seen in them a different kind of problem and possible resource. The classical remains have supported a set of ideas and interests that continues to this day to play a major role in Italian culture and politics generally, and in Roman city planning in particular. The greatest issue of Roman city planning today is still the fate of the historic center, the core of which is formed by the legacy from ancient times.

### PLANNING IN PAPAL ROME

A Christian city was built upon the ruins of the pagan city just as the church was built upon the ruins of the pagan empire. Rome became the center of a world religion; its bishop, after A.D. 400, became the leader of world Christianity. The city became enhanced as the center of a universal religion, as the holy place in which St. Peter was martyred. Having declined to the provincial status of a dukedom, Rome was granted to the pope as a fief by Pepin, King of the Franks, in the middle of the eighth century A.D. As heir to the empire, and preserving many of its forms, customs, and organization, the church assumed the task of governing the city. But even the papacy proved as unable as its secular predecessors to arrest the process of urban decline. The city's population fell drastically after the cutting of the surface aqueducts by the Goths in 537. By the year 1000, the populated area of the city was reduced to one-fourth the area of the ancient city. (See Figure 2.1.) Surrounded by malarial swamps and sparsely inhabited plains, the city became completely dependent on the papal court—its Peter's pence and feudal rents—for a livelihood: again, Rome developed no productive life of its own but depended on its status as capital. When it lost even this, with the transfer of the papacy to Avignon, the population dropped still further, from about 35,000 in 1200 to about 17,000 in 1400.[15]

The city's dependency on the church, its lack of autonomous political develop-

15. For the medieval period, see Carlo Cecchelli, "Roma medioevale," in Castagnoli et al., *Topografia . . . di Roma,* pp. 187–341, and Mario Coppa, "Roma senza cuore," in Piccinato, *Problemi urbanistici di Roma,* pp. 63–107. On the city's decline, see Cecchelli, "Roma medioevale," pp. 189–210, and Coppa, "Roma senza cuore," pp. 70–77.

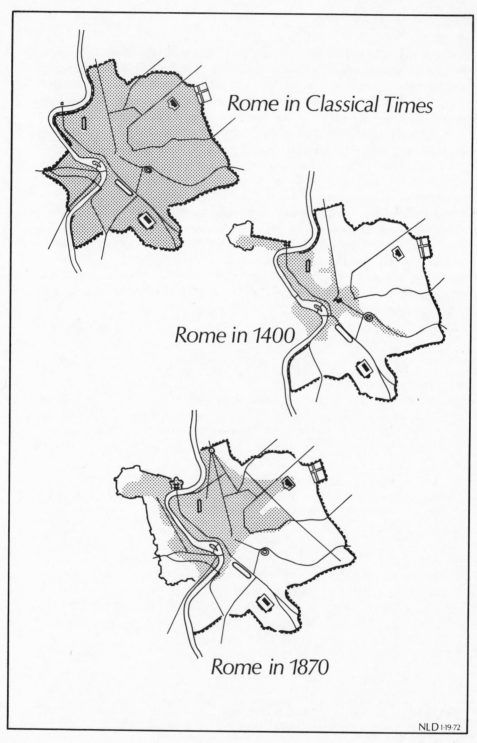

Figure 2.1

ment, became evident during the exile of the papacy in Avignon. The city, left to itself, failed to develop the flourishing civic and economic life that arose in the other cities of central and northern Italy at this time. Without the papacy the city declined into an arena for bloodletting among the feudal lords and factions that dominated the various districts of the city. The presence of classical monuments and the church inhibited rather than stimulated civic development and enterprise. Which civic authority could produce the monuments of the past? Which merely civic authority could approach the prestige of the Roman Empire or the medieval papacy?

Only with the return of the papacy to Rome in 1347 did the city again begin to grow. During the next three centuries the popes converted it into one of the most splendid cities in the world, the center of Italian and Western culture, the capital of triumphant Counter-Reformation Catholicism. The city was rebuilt, mostly between 1450 and 1650, by twenty popes and hundreds of architects, craftsmen, and administrators, working without any single master plan but achieving remarkable unity of style and effect. Each pope was expected to propose a building program and to hire architects and builders to carry the program out. Many grandiose plans were designed by artists anxious to apply Renaissance esthetic theories about geometry, "divine proportions," perspective, and the star-shaped city in order to link together the great Roman and Christian monuments in a single magnificent religious capital. Most of the grand plans were never implemented, owing to lack of time, funds, or real need. Instead the new Renaissance and Baroque city was built through a series of partial, incremental plans, seldom committed to paper. The greatest artists of the day—Bramante, Michelangelo, Raphael, Bernini, and Borromini—were enlisted in the task of city-building, and through their efforts Rome became the world's model for city planning.[16]

The program of creating the new Rome was begun by the first great humanist pope, Nicholas V (1447–55). Aided by Leon Battista Alberti, Pope Nicholas prepared grandiose plans to make Rome a great monumental and cultural center in preparation for the Jubilee of 1450. St. Peter's was to be restored; magnificent gardens and fountains to be built; city walls, bridges, and aqueducts to be repaired and constructed. Rome was to be restored to imperial splendor but recentered around the objects of Christian interest. As under later humanist popes, enthusiasm and admiration for the classical period did not prevent the systematic use of ancient monuments as quarries for the building of new papal Rome. Classicism did not protect individual monuments from this form of vandalism: indeed, the desire was to build in the ancient style in order to surpass ancient grandeur. There was no tenderness, either, toward the most venerable of ancient Christian monuments: in perhaps the major act of vandalism in the history of the city, the old St. Peter's—by then over one thousand years old—was

16. On this period, see Gustavo Giovannoni, "Roma del Rinascimento al 1870," in *Topografia . . . di Roma*, pp. 343–547, and Quaroni, "Una città eterna," pp. 41–68.

demolished and replaced by the present basilica. Classical monuments suffered much more during the period of Renaissance exaltation of the ancients than in all the previous centuries of abandonment. From this fact derived the wry schoolboy maxim: *"Quod non fecerunt barbari, fecerunt Barberini"* ("What the barbarians didn't do, the Barberini popes did.")[17]

Urban development was achieved at the expense of political development. Under the paternalistic and nepotistic rule of the popes, Romans became habituated to a life of servile dependency on the church. From the church came the city's moral, intellectual, and political leadership; from the church came the city's livelihood. Much of the population lived on the charity of innumerable religious institutions. Despite its artistic cosmopolitanism and its religious catholicism, Rome remained isolated from the currents of European thought and society that elsewhere were producing individualism, the scientific attitude, business enterprise, and community spirit. In an age of developing scientific and commercial agriculture, the land around Rome remained malaria-ridden and uncultivated—latifundia held by a small number of great aristocratic families allied to the church. The political tradition of the city consisted of absolute support for the one institution, the papacy, which gave the city its importance, its commerce, its economic and spiritual sustenance.

Table 2.1. Rome's Population under the Papacy

| | |
|---|---|
| 1513 | 40,000 |
| 1600 | 109,729 |
| 1656 | 120,596 |
| 1700 | 149,447 |
| 1702 | 138,568 |
| 1750 | 157.882 |
| 1760 | 155,124 |
| 1800 | 153,004 |
| 1805 | 134,973 |
| 1850 | 170,824 |
| 1870 | 226,022 |

*Source:* SVIMEZ, *Un secolo di statistiche italiane: Nord e Sud* (Rome, 1961), p. 1037.

After its Renaissance and Baroque splendor, the city began to vegetate and to fall behind the other European capitals in population growth and the development of public services and amenities. A brief exposure to progressive Napoleonic government (1807–14) was followed by a reversion to traditionalism: Rome became again a bastion against change, industrialism, liberalism, and nationalism. It stood virtually still while the other great cities of Europe and America forged ahead in size, productivity, and achievement. Only in its last days did the papacy attempt to regain lost time and to endow the city with some traits of

17. "Roma," in *Enciclopedia Italiana, 29* (Rome, 1936), 780–83; and Giovannoni, "Roma," pp. 372–73. Prof. Giovannoni conjectured (p. 373) that the popes might have been so little attached to Roman monuments because most of them were not native Romans.

modernity. In 1847, Pius IX granted the city for the first time in its history a limited form of self-government. From the city's professional and propertied classes, the pope appointed a city council of one hundred notables, thereafter to be recruited by a process of cooptation. An executive, called the Senate, was drawn from the council to govern the city under close papal supervision. Gas street lighting was installed in 1852. Following a long period of papal opposition, railways were built (1856–65), linking the city to Orte, Civitavecchia, and Frascati; a unified terminal was built for the lines at Termini, begun in 1867. The first modern building code for the city was promulgated in 1864—six months before the Syllabus of Errors.[18]

### PLANNING PERFORMANCE AFTER 1870

The city which rather abruptly became capital of united Italy one hundred years ago was strikingly different from other European capitals of the time. It was a small, backward, and provincial town, with little industry or commerce, surrounded by vast stretches of rural misery and malaria, visited by cultivated foreigners for its melancholy suggestions of past importance. The social structure of the city was still basically medieval, with, at the top, a stratum of high prelates and great noble families tied to the church; in the middle, the clergy, some clerks and professionals, and a number of artisans and merchants; and beneath these, the vast subproletariat that directly or indirectly depended on the church for a living.[19] The papal census of 1853 had classified the adult male population of the city as follows:

| | |
|---|---|
| Property-owners and nobles | 1,956 |
| Professionals | 4,911 |
| Employees | 3,540 |
| Merchants and artisans | 35,086 |
| Others | 57,614 |
| Total | 103,107[20] |

The city was backward culturally, as well, since the popes had deliberately isolated it from the currents of modern "enlightened" and "positive" thought, although nationalism and liberalism had made inroads during the previous decades among the middle classes. Segments of the city's middle classes, after all, had participated in the Revolution of 1848 and in the establishment in 1849 of the short-lived Roman Republic—one of the most advanced democratic

18. For nineteenth-century papal Rome, Silvio Negro, *Seconda Roma: 1850-1870* (Padua, 1966); Giovannoni, "Roma," 471–95; and Insolera, *Roma moderna,* chap. 1.
19. Alberto Caracciolo, *Roma capitale: dal risorgimento alla crisi dello stato liberale* (Rome, 1956), pp. 5–11.
20. Ibid., p. 8, n. 9.

regimes in Europe.[21] The Roman middle classes, however, had not played a major role in national unification, despite their growing opposition to papal autocracy and aristocratic privilege. The institutions for self-government created by Pius IX in 1847 had not been free enough from clerical control to create a tradition of self-government in the city.

But however backward, Rome was not unimportant. If inferior to other capitals in size and development, it was superior in the weight of its traditions, associations, and symbolic importance. Italians had exalted, if conflicting, images of the city. Rome had become the capital of Italy, despite its backwardness, because it had served the unification movement as a potent unifying symbol of the common Italian heritage, both Roman and Catholic. Rome alone had sufficient historical importance to overcome the rival municipal claims and pretensions of the other Italian cities. It was neutral from the point of view of geography, lying between North and South; it was neutral politically, having produced no considerable political class able to compete with northerners for national leadership; and it was neutral economically, given its weak and therefore unthreatening economy. Moreover, it was a city with magnificent buildings, villas, and monuments: if properly equipped, it would become an impressive capital of the new nation.[22]

One of the first actions of the new rulers of the city was to appoint, on September 30, 1870, a commission of architects and engineers to formulate a plan for the embellishment of the city and the regulation of its future development. Under the Italian Law No. 2359 of June 22, 1865, which now applied to Rome, local authorities were empowered to make master plans *(piani regolatori)* for the purposes of improving housing and circulation within existing districts and of ensuring the "health, safety, comfort, and decorum" of districts yet to be built. They were given powers of eminent domain to clear slums and cut new streets through old sections, They could force private builders to conform to the street alignments of official maps when building new housing. And they could condemn acreage on the city fringe, urbanize it, resell it to private interests for development, and in this way guide the development process, recoup some of the costs of urbanization, and regulate the price of land and housing. "Fair market value" had to be paid for properties taken, whatever the purpose. Plans regulating future development, designating the sites of public facilities, and marking property for expropriation required approval of the city council and of the national ministry of public works. Property owners were given a period in which to present "observations" against adopted plans—observations that the city or the ministry was free to accept or reject. Plans officially promulgated by the ministry of public works were valid for twenty-five years.[23]

21. Ibid., pp. 8–9.
22. Ibid., pp. 10–17.
23. On the 1865 act, see Camera dei Deputati, Segretariato Generale, *Ricerca sull'urbanistica, Parte prima* (Rome, 1965), pp. 19–33; bibliographical references can be found in the same

Thus planning authority existed by which to create the ground rules for the future growth and reorganization of the city. The task of planning was facilitated by the fact that very little of the city's enormous legal territory was actually built up. The city or, more properly, the commune of Rome was incorporated into Italy with 800 square miles of land. At its greatest length the communal territory ran fifty miles; parts of the territory were thirty-five miles from the center.[24] Most of this vast area was uninhabited. Almost all residents lived within the 3500 acres of land enclosed by the walls built by the Emperor Aurelian in A.D. 275. The area within the walls was divided into districts called *rioni,* the direct descendants of the *regiones* into which Rome had been divided in ancient times. Even within the old walls, only about half the land was built up; the rest was covered by luxurious private estates (villas), Roman ruins, and vineyards. Surrounding the *rioni* and the old walls was a rural district, the *Suburbio,* with some 22,500 acres, and surrounding this were the 507,000 acres of the *Agro Romano.* Of the city's 213,633 legal residents in 1871, 205,103 lived in the *rioni,* most of them packed into the square mile of land in the bend of the Tiber known since ancient times as the Campus Martius.[25] With so little of the city's territory built up and such a vast territory subject to city jurisdiction, there was considerable freedom of choice in directing the expansion of the new capital.

On some city development issues there was consensus. It was generally felt that the city should remain an administrative, religious, and cultural center and that industrialization should be discouraged in order to avoid the formation in the national capital of a restless and radical industrial proletariat. It was agreed that the Tiber should be banked in order to prevent the periodic inundations of the central portions of the city, such as occurred in 1870. It was also agreed that the existing city required extensive demolitions for the purposes of building new streets and clearing the worst slums such as the old ghetto. On other matters the city's new rulers disagreed. Some favored the formulation of a general plan under the 1865 act before approval of any new residential expansion or the construction of any new public facilities; in the interests of rapid private development, others wanted to postpone formulation of a plan and to consider each proposed new private development on its merits. Some favored the creation of a new administrative capital to the east of the existing city near Termini station, to serve as administrative and cultural center of the new nation. Others favored the less expensive and ambitious policy of locating new ministries in the convents and palaces of the existing city and modernizing the existing city to perform new roles. Some people favored expansion of the city toward the east, around and beyond Termini station, on high land not subject to the malaria and flooding

volume, pp. 159–81. On the early post-1870 planning, see Italo Insolera, "I primi anni di Roma capitale," in *Roma: Città e piani,* pp. 74–94.
  24. "Popolazione e territorio," map facing p. 54.
  25. Ibid., p. 62.

endemic to the parts of the city near the Tiber. Eastern development would also be a gesture of protest (or spite) against the Vatican, which had fought Italian unification so bitterly and which now refused to recognize the new national government. Other interests pressed for development in the Prati, to the west, just north of the Vatican, for speculative as well as symbolic reasons. Some people favored extensive use of the condemnation powers of the 1865 act in order to buy up development land for urbanization and resale to private developers; this would keep the initiative in shaping future development in public hands. Others favored residential expansion through ad hoc conventions between private developers and the city, primary reliance on private initiative and enterprise, and basically private control of the development process.

After three years of study and debate, the city council that had been elected in November 1870, the first elected city council in Roman history, decided not to adopt a legally binding general plan and opted for a general policy of giving private investors maximal freedom and encouragement.[26] It approved, for advisory purposes only, a general plan calling for the eventual clearance of the ghetto slums near the Tiber and the slums near St. Peter's. The advisory plan also provided for the cutting of major new arteries through and across the older parts of the city, showing little awe for the physical legacy of the past in order to modernize the old city to serve new purposes. The city council decided to allow residential development in both the west (Prati) and east, thus pleasing both sets of contending developer interests and symbolic-ideological factions. Westward development in the Prati district, in effect, meant that the old city was gradually to be ringed on all sides by new residential and business districts and would thus become the center of a modern city, but without the capacity to bear modern traffic. The policy of city purchase, urbanization, and resale of land was dropped in favor of a policy of private subdivision and urbanization. Only the ministries of war and finance decided to locate in the new eastern section near Termini station; the other ministries were lodged in former convents, papal buildings, and embassies, in which many of them remain to this day.

In the laissez-faire spirit of the times, the city government rejected the idea of a legally binding regulatory plan and of an active municipal role in land development. To most members of the city council (and Parliament), municipal regulation of development seemed an illegitimate interference with private property rights. Municipal authority over development should, they felt, be used to legalize and ratify the initiatives proposed by private investors, who were to be encouraged. There seemed to be no constituency for public planning, while pressures to approve private planning decisions were specific and intense. Planning involved choices among competing development proposals and

26. On the failure of the first master planning operation, see Insolera, "I primi anni," and his *Roma moderna,* chaps. 2–3; Caracciolo, *Roma capitale,* pp. 60–81; and Mario Zocca, "Roma capitale d'Italia," in Castagnoli et al., *Topografia . . . di Roma,* pp. 551–77. The council was elected by 3,170 of the city's 7,897 eligible voters (3.4% of the total population); see Enrico Zampetti, "Le elezioni comunali a Roma dal 1870 ad oggi," *Concretezza,* June 1, 1966, p. 28.

public leadership in development: neither role was particularly gratifying to the economic conservatives who dominated the council or to the chief planner himself, the city engineer, a strict adherent to the principles of laissez faire. Planning meant holding up approval of private subdivision applications, and the city fathers were too anxious for the city to grow and prosper under the new Liberal regime to accept any such delay.[27]

Thus development of Rome in the decade after 1870 took place through ad hoc conventions between the city and private developers and through ad hoc measures of public improvement, without benefit of, or hindrance from, an overall design. A large street-building program was carried out in the heart of the rioni. Boulevards à la Haussmann were cut through old neighborhoods, usually with little respect for the monuments and sites of the past. New residential districts were built, resembling those of Paris and Turin, with broad avenues, checkerboard street plans, and portico-lined squares. After considerable agitation by Giuseppe Garibaldi, the most illustrious member of the Rome city council, work was also begun on the embankment of the Tiber. Many more works would have been built and many more demolitions carried out had there been the necessary funds: poverty was to keep the city poor in public facilities and rich in historic reminders for many years to come.

The city was given its first *piano regolatore,* or master plan, only at the instigation of the national government, anxious that Rome, as the new capital of united Italy, should become a physical symbol of the superiority of the new liberal-national constitutional regime over previous clerical-reactionary regimes. In 1881 the national government agreed to finance the construction of a number of public works in the capital, on condition that the city locate them in a duly approved plan. The city engineer drafted a plan which located the new facilities—barracks, hospitals, prisons, university faculties, and ministries—and, with respect to residential development, ratified the proposals and accomplishments of private owners and syndicates. The plan was presented to the council on April 27, 1882, and unanimously approved on June 20, 1882. On the recommendation of the Ministry of Public Works, the plan was promulgated as law by a royal decree of March 8, 1883.

The master plan of 1883 assumed that rapid growth of the city, resulting from the influx of immigrants attracted by the employment and investment opportunities of the capital, would continue. Under the 1883 plan the old city was to be surrounded by new residential districts and crisscrossed by large avenues. Parts of the old city, including the Ghetto, whose walls, erected in 1555, had been taken down in 1848, were marked for clearance and redevelopment. The entire area within the Aurelian walls was eventually to be built up, plus some districts outside, such as Prati.[28]

Parts of the 1883 plan were actually carried out. Many of the proposed streets

27. Caracciolo, *Roma capitale,* pp. 74–81.
28. On the 1883 master plan, see Italo Insolera, "I piani regolatori dal 1880 alla seconda guerra mondiale," in *Roma: Città e piani,* pp. 114–15 and Caracciolo, *Roma capitale,* pp. 148–64.

were cut; the new public facilities were built; and the ghetto, picturesque but unhygienic, was rebuilt. The infusion of funds under the law of 1881 set off a boom in Roman real estate and construction that became famous in the annals of Roman planning. The 1880s became known as the years of the *"febbre edilizia"* or "building fever." Roman real estate became one of the most profitable investments in Italy, indeed in Europe, and northern and foreign syndicates rushed in to buy and trade lots, materials, and buildings. The boom of the 1880s far surpassed the smaller boom of the seventies, when demand for new housing and office space in the new capital had promoted feverish speculation and construction. Religious orders had sold off their properties as fast as they could before they were secularized and expropriated under Italian law. Some members of the nobility sold their estates to foreign and Italian syndicates. Ownership of land and buildings passed in many cases from religious orders and aristocratic families to capitalistic real estate corporations, which became powerful actors in the process of shaping the new city, sharing with the national and city governments the decisions as to where new neighborhoods would be built, with what kind of housing and street plans. In many of the new corporations the church and the church-related nobility acquired considerable interests.[29]

Most of the building fever of the eighties occurred outside of the Aurelian walls, that is, outside the perimeter of the 1883 master plan. Outside the walls, the excise tax on building materials did not have to be paid and builders could benefit from legislation designed to promote the development and reclamation of the Agro Romano, including a ten-year exemption from the tax on buildings. Most residential building during the boom was thus located behind the reach of the master plan. Construction inside the walls suffered, while the new districts outside were hastily built up, often without city authorization or supervision, in the certain knowledge that the city government would be forced by reasons of public health to recognize the faits accomplis and to incorporate the new districts in the city map.[30]

In the process, one of the great tragedies in Roman planning history took place: the gardens of the magnificent patrician villas, forming a band of green around the city much admired by foreign visitors since the eighteenth century, were destroyed to make space for subdivisions.[31] One after another of the great estates was broken up; Villa Boncompagni-Ludovisi, for example, was subdivided to become the Via Veneto district. Worst hit were the estates in the northeast, along Via Salaria and Via Nomentana, and those in the east, behind the railway station and the Colosseum. The destruction of the villas was perhaps inevitable, given the insatiable demand for land and the city's lack of legal or

29. Caracciolo, *Roma capitale*, pp. 125–33, 173–85.

30 Insolera, *Roma moderna*, pp. 54–77.

31. Henry Hope Reed, "Rome: The Third Sack," *The Architectural Review*, February 1950, pp. 91–110.

financial means of preserving the villas through zoning restrictions or purchase. Had the master plan's provisions for the development of public parks been carried out, the loss of the villas would have more than compensated for, but, as usual, the city and the national government lacked the required funds. The lack of funds, of course, was also serving to protect the old city from some of the demolition projects contained in that same plan. It is said in extenuation that the villas had been private and inaccessible to the public, and that the Roman people did not like large parks, preferring the pleasures of such built-up sites as the Spanish steps and the tree-lined boulevards.[32]

The boom of the eighties, involving for the most part a few big operators and large tracts of land, came to an abrupt end in 1887, when the stock of Roman land and building companies dropped suddenly and sharply on foreign, then Italian, stock exchanges. The boom had been based on *cambiali* or promissory notes, discounted abroad; when these *cambiali* began to be turned back from abroad, the house of cards collapsed. The boom had ignored and undermined the master plan of 1883. Building had followed expectations of maximum short-term profit rather than plan indications or market possibilities. More rooms were built than were needed to house the entire population, yet the index of crowding rose to its historically highest level, given the fact that the "wrong" type of housing was being built. Areas marked in the plan for development remained unbuilt, while the city was forced to pay for urbanizing the areas outside the plan where speculators had built entire neighborhoods without services. The crash of 1887 left half-finished houses all over the city. Twenty-nine thousand building workers were required by the police to leave the city and return to their native towns. The city lay prostrate in an economic depression that was to last for more than a decade.[33]

The crisis gave a boost to the nascent socialist movement in the city, just as the boom had tended to bring together the previously alienated legitimist Catholics and upper class Liberals in common speculative ventures. By 1900, the population of the city had risen to more than 400,000, almost doubling in the thirty years since Rome had become the capital. Although growth had taken place without the aid of industry, which remained small in scale and importance, an industrial proletariat of sorts had been formed in the shops of the public utilities—among the railway, trolley, water company, and sanitation workers. These, plus the building workers, gave added force to the native radical, anarchist, anticlerical, and republican traditions among the poor and the artisan classes.[34]

Since 1870 the city had been governed, except for brief intervals, by a conser-

32. For a map of the destroyed estates, see *Roma: Città e piani*, p. 117.
33. Caracciolo, *Roma capitale*, pp. 173–85.
34. Paolo Basevi, "Il movimento operaio romano dal 1870 alla Liberazione," in Aldo Natoli et al., *Introduzione a Roma contemporanea: note e saggi per lo studio di Rome dal 1870 ad oggi* (Rome, 1954), pp. 9–22.

vative Catholic coalition, based on the Catholic election organization, the *Unione Romana.* While Catholics were forbidden by papal order from participating in national politics, they were allowed to be active in local politics. The continued power of the church in Roman politics was based not only on the leadership of the great Catholic families, the so-called "black aristocracy," but on the mass of faithful Catholics in all classes, especially women, who still followed the leadership of the parish clergy and, somewhat like Irish peasants, saw in the clergy and the church a native institution opposed to the invading anticlerical "foreigners" from the north. Thousands of Romans had suffered when the temporal power was ended; the church and its religious orders could no longer provide charity or employment as before. Romans lost the many forms of ecclesiastical patronage, while they acquired new burdens in the form of higher taxes, higher rents, and military conscription. Low income Catholics provided the clerical coalition with fanatical and aggressive elements that frequently engaged in violent clashes with the secularists at public ceremonies, as during the unveiling of the statue to Giordano Bruno in 1889. The anticlerical Liberals, who dominated the national government and the bureaucracy, drew their support from the secularist upper and middle classes, who were united on the question of church vs. state, but increasingly divided on the question of labor vs. capital. Two rival issues struggled for supremacy: the clerical issue and the social issue. The social issue united Liberal and Catholic members of the upper classes, while the clerical issue united Liberal and leftist members of the middle and lower classes. The clerical issue tended to prevail and the balance of power shifted back and forth between the clerical and the anticlerical coalition.[35]

In a wave of progressivism that affected both national and city politics, a coalition of the anticlerical Left came into power after 1900, based on an alliance between the secular and progressive middle classes and the secular, progressive, and socialist lower middle and lower classes. Nationally, the coalition was led by Liberal Prime Minister Giovanni Giolitti; in Rome, by Republican Ernesto Nathan, Grand Master of Italian Freemasons, who was elected mayor in 1907 and remained in office until 1913.[36]

The Nathan administration is regarded by the left today as one of the few progressive administrations in the city's history. It was strongly anticlerical in tone and ended religious instruction in the city school system. It made major efforts to improve the public education system by building sixteen new schools.[37]

35. Alberto Caracciolo et al., "Il movimento cattolico e la Chiesa," in Natoli, *Introduzione,* pp. 23–30.
36. Mayor Nathan was born in London into a family of wealthy Jewish Italophiles, who entertained Giuseppe Mazzini as a houseguest during his London exile. Nathan emigrated to Italy, became a citizen in 1888, and was elected Grand Master of the Italian Freemasons. As such he was asked to head the anticlerical coalition in the Rome city elections of 1907. See "Nathan antipapa laico," *L'Espresso,* May 19, 1957.
37. Caracciolo, *Roma capitale,* pp. 240–58.

It attempted to weaken the conservative front by municipalizing the bus and trolley system in 1911 and part of the water and power system in 1912, thus eliminating the private utility companies, which had been major elements in that front. It widened popular participation in government by holding the only referendum in the city's history: the 1909 referendum on municipalization of the trolleys, in which 21,460 of the 44,595 eligible voters participated—a large majority of them favorable to municipalization.[38] Even as late as 1909, it should be noted, literacy requirements restricted voting rights to a small portion (8 percent) of the population.

The 1883 master plan, which had not been effective at all in regulating development, was due to expire in 1906. The national government again intervened provide financial and planning assistance to the city. The expiration of the 1883 plan was postponed in order to allow for the preparation of a new plan. Parliamentary approval was secured for two laws—the so-called Giolitti laws— designed to provide the city with funds for new public works and for the creation of a public land domain in zones to be marked for development. An Act of 1904 instituted, for the city of Rome only, a tax on building lots *(aree fabbricabili)*, defined as "parcels of land included in a network of streets capable of bearing traffic or adjacent to same, that are not in a stable way dedicated to agricultural or industrial use, and that are not accessory to existing edifices, such as villas or gardens." Law 502 of July 11, 1907, raised the tax rate from 1 to 3 percent ad valorem and established an ingenious method of self-assessment. Property value for purposes of taxation was to be declared by the owner, or by the city if the owner failed to make any declaration. At the same time, the city was authorized to take land for public purposes at precisely the value declared by its owners. It was hoped that this tax on unimproved land would reduce the cost of building, make real estate speculation less attractive, and stimulate investment in industry. Half the revenues collected were to be assigned to the newly created public agency for low-cost housing, the *Istituto Autonomo per le Case Popolari di Roma*. The city was required to issue a new building code for housing to be built both inside and outside the perimeter of the new master plan. It was authorized to borrow fifteen million lire for the purchase of building lots; in this way, the threat of city purchase was to be made credible. The city, it was hoped, would be able to prevent scattered and leapfrog development in remote suburbs and thus avoid heavy expenditures for sewers, streets, and street lighting. The 1907 act also allowed the city to take land for public works, using, as the basis for compensation, values previous to the publication of the new master plan. The act implied that not all land in the city was "building land," but only such land as was designated for development under the master plan. A new plan and building code were to specify the order in which districts were to be built up; this would prevent both scatteration and political favoritism.

38. Insolera, *Roma moderna*, pp. 88–90.

With the strong backing of the national government, Mayor Nathan brought in a leading member of the national Corps of Engineers to draft a new plan. Some two years later, in October 1908, the plan was presented to the council, and adopted on February 10, 1909. After approval by the Ministry of Public Works it was promulgated by royal decree of August 29, 1909.

The 1909 master plan had powerful backing from both the national and city governments. It was a major element in a joint national-local attempt to alleviate the city's chronic financial difficulties, to crush the land speculation "trust," and to ease the housing shortage for low income groups. The 1909 plan was the first Rome plan to zone the areas of proposed new residential development in terms of permissible building types. There were no land-use zones in the plan, however. Many of the new residential districts were marked for low density housing, composed of *villini,* that is, apartment houses with a maximum of three stories. Facilities were to be built in proportion to permitted densities. The new districts were to be located, as before, all around the older center, which was again marked for extensive streetbuilding and demolition. The protests of the Society of Engineers and Architects, the Artists' Circle, and the Artistic Association of Architectural Amateurs to Mayor Nathan brought elimination from the plan of some proposed *"sventramenti"* (literally: "disembowelings") or demolition projects.[39]

The 1909 plan was no more successful than its predecessor in regulating development. It was undermined, first of all, by violent, organized resistance to the tax on building land. An Association of Building-Land Owners was formed, which successfully urged landowners to refuse to make self-assessments and to contest assessments then made by the city. By 1914, the city was involved in litigating 2,500 appeals; the first collections were made only in 1919. Four years later, in one of its first acts, the Fascist regime abolished the tax altogether.[40] The plan was undermined, secondly, by the fall from power in 1914 of its major sponsors, the Nathan administration in the city government and the Giolitti cabinet in the national government. The result of introducing nearly universal male suffrage in 1914 was to remove the progressives from office in the city, replacing them with a coalition of Catholics, Nationalists, and conservatives. This coalition was unenthusiastic about the land tax. Thirdly, the tax, as administered, was unable to offset the effects of World War I on Roman land prices, which rose steeply, making it practically impossible the for city to enforce the low-density zoning provisions of the 1909 plan. Thousands of variances were approved, permitting the construction of so-called *"palazzine"* in zones marked for *"villini." "Palazzine,"* created expressly as a building type appropriate for higher-priced land, could be built as high as nineteen meters (61 feet), with four stories and an attic, surrounded on all sides except the street front by

39. The 1909 master plan is described in ibid., pp. 91–103 and in Zocca, "Roma capitale," pp. 613–30.
    40. Caracciolo, *Roma capitale,* pp. 258–68.

six meters of "garden." The national government in royal decree No. 1937 of December 12, 1920, allowed the building of palazzine in all zones marked for villini.

Many of the apartment houses built in Rome after 1920 were of the palazzina type, which became the housing preferred by the Roman middle class. Single-family dwellings have remained a rarity in the city in striking contrast to the American pattern.[41] The lower income groups in Rome have been housed in so-called *intensivi*—ten or twelve-story tenements, holding between thirty and forty families. Middle and upper income groups consider themselves fortunate to live in twelve-family, four-story houses, separated from each other by 37 feet of setback and facing, across the street, buildings only sixty feet high. Unfortunately, the post-World War I changeover from villini to palazzine was not accompanied by revision of the master plan to increase the provision of space for streets and facilities, so that middle-class districts were only relatively better off than high-density districts.

Rising land prices caused much postwar development to take place *outside* the 1909 plan perimeter. Some of this development consisted of illegal settlements *(borgate)* build by poor migrants out in the countryside. Some was built, legally, by the two major low-cost housing agencies, the *Istituto Autonomo per le Case Popolari* (IACP) and the *Istituto Nazionale Case per gli Impiegati dello Stato* (INCIS), created specifically for state (that is, national) employees. After World War I, both agencies began to build low-density projects on the model of English garden cities on cheap land far outside the 1909 plan perimeter. Once the city brought services out to these projects, the land between them and the central city became desirable for building, although most of it lay outside the plan perimeter and accordingly was not designated for building. The goals and provisions of the plan notwithstanding, the area between the garden cities and the city became filled in, mostly with intensivi, as in the so-called "African" quarters, whose street names were taken from Italian colonies in Africa. In time, the green in the garden cities disappeared and the villini built there were replaced by palazzine.[42]

PLANNING PERFORMANCE UNDER FASCISM

In October 1925, on the third anniversary of the Fascist accession to power, the dictatorship abolished democratic self-government for Rome and placed the city under a governor directly appointed by and responsible to the national

41. Most single family houses at that time were probably farmhouses and illegally built squatter dwellings; since then some luxury single-family houses have been built, but not on a large scale. For a description of the predominant Roman building types, based on the codes of 1912 and 1935, see Italo Insolera, "L'istituto del Regolamento Edilizio nell'ultimo secolo di urbanistica romana," in *Roma: Città e piani,* pp. 305–16.

42. Insolera, *Roma moderna,* pp. 104–16.

government. The governor, a national functionary, was given the ordinance-making powers of the former city council, as well as the executive powers lodged in the *giunta* and mayor elected by the council. The policymaking process for the city was simplified by the abolition of all autonomous political and labor organizations and the abolition of a free press. The absence of a free press and legitimate opposition did create serious problems of corruption in the city government: the first governor of the city, an industrialist, was forced to resign in November 1926 subsequent to a scandal of such proportions that the national Italian press was ordered not to report it.[43]

After this, with one exception, only members of the "black aristocracy" of princely rank were appointed to the governorship. The one exception, party boss Giuseppe Bottai, governor between 1935 and 1937, left a few months after his appointment to serve in the Italian campaign in Ethiopia and as governor of Addis Ababa, though still governor of Rome.

It was under fascism that *urbanistica* or city planning received official recognition as a discipline and a profession. In 1921, just before the Fascists came into power, the first separate architecture and urban planning facilities were created in some Italian universities, including the University of Rome. Until that time, architecture and planning had been taught in the academies of fine arts; planning was considered to be a matter of esthetics, on the one hand, and law and engineering on the other. The Italian city planning movement of the 1920s and 1930s, or at least its vanguard, attempted to balance esthetic, technical, and legal concerns and to add to the mixture some attention to social and economic problems. The movement also attempted to strike some balance between concern for the preservation and enhancement of old monuments and entire historic districts and concern for the housing, traffic, business and recreational problems of the modern city. The 1929 congress of the International Federation of Housing and Town Planning was held in Rome, and the following year the *Istituto Nazionale di Urbanistica* (INU) or National Institute of Planners was established. INU was given legal recognition by the government as the official source of professional advice in the planning field and its members were called upon to design new towns, such as Sabaudia and Aprilia in the newly reclaimed Pontine marshes, and to formulate master plans for the renovation and expansion of existing centers. After a long campaign the planning movement secured the passage of the *Legge Urbanistica* or Urban Planning Act of 1942, which marked the acceptance—albeit only in form—by the Fascist regime of many of the doctrines advocated by the planning profession.[44]

In practice, however, apart from the new towns in the Pontine marshes and the African colonies, professional planners had relatively less impact on Italian

43. Alberto Aquarone, *L'organizzazione dello Stato totalitario* (Turin, 1965), pp. 83–84.

44. Some aspects of the evolution of the Italian city planning movement under Fascism are described by Manfredo Tafuri in *Ludovico Quaroni e lo sviluppo dell'architettura moderna in Italia* (Milan, 1964).

urban development than did city engineers and bureaucrats, private owners and developers, and Fascist party officials, their friends, "clients," and relations.

Official planning remained primarily esthetic, technical, and legalistic, rather than social and economic. The professional planners had relatively little impact, partly because they were so strongly divided among themselves in the policies they recommended. This became quite apparent during the 1929 congress of the Housing and Town Planning Federation, when two radically different proposals were presented for a new master plan of Rome.[45]

One plan was presented by an older group of well-established architects, headed by Professor Gustavo Giovannoni, the leading planning consultant for the city since before the World War. Professor Giovannoni had begun to develop a theory of planning that rejected "Haussmanization," or the attempt to modernize old cities through massive rebuilding, in favor of conservation, restoration, and rehabilitation. His group now proposed to apply these conservationist principles to the so-called *quartiere del Rinascimento* or Renaissance quarter—the district lying in the bend of the Tiber, between the river and Via del Corso. But in the neighboring Baroque districts, the Giovannoni plan mercilessly proposed massive demolitions and the building of a *cardo* and a *decumanus*—the two great intersecting roads of the classical Roman military town. At the intersection, located a few blocks from Piazza di Spagna, there was to be a vast open square decorated in Assyro-Babylonian style with monuments to Mussolini. The principles of classical Roman city planning, which the ancient Romans had never dared to apply to Rome itself, were finally to receive application two thousand years after the fact. Such a proposal was possible only given the then current contempt for the Baroque and Mussolini's declared passion for demolishing all traces of the "centuries of [Italian] decadence."[46]

Planning Rome had become a central instrument of Fascist policy, for Fascism turned back to ancient Rome—imperial, not republican Rome—for its symbolism, manners, and pedigree. The city of Rome was once again to become an imperial capital. Romans and Italians were to draw from the monuments of ancient Rome a sense of pride, power, and discipline. Mussolini set the tone in December 1925 when he declared:

> My ideas are clear. My orders are precise. Within five years, Rome must appear marvellous to all the peoples of the world—vast, orderly, powerful, as in the time of the empire of Augustus.
>
> You [addressing the first governor of Rome] shall continue to free the trunk of the great oak from everything that darkens it: you shall create vast spaces around the Theater of Marcellus, the Capitoline Hill, and the Pantheon. All that has grown up around them in the centuries of decadence must disappear.

45. See Luigi Lenzi, "The New Rome," *The Town Planning Review,* May 1931, pp. 145–62.
46. The Giovannoni plan is described in Insolera, *Roma moderna,* pp. 127–29. For maps, see *Roma: Città e piani,* facing p. 138, and Zocca, "Roma capitale," figs. 158–159.

Within five years, the mass of the Pantheon must be visible through a vast opening from Piazza Colonna.

You shall also free the majestic temples of Christian Rome from parasitic and profane constructions.

The millenary monuments of our history must loom gigantic in the necessary solitude.

Thus the Third Rome will spread itself onto other hills, along the banks of the sacred river, to reach the shores of the Tyrrhenian sea. A straight line—the broadest in the world—shall carry the fury of *mare nostrum* from arisen Ostia to the heart of the city where the Unknown Soldier stands guard.[47]

Il Duce himself began to implement this policy of emphasizing classical Rome by moving the offices of the prime minister from Palazzo Chigi, next to Parliament, to Piazza Venezia, next to the Tomb of the Unknown Soldier and the Roman forums. Piazza Venezia became the political center of Italy. The square, with its balcony, became the world-famous stage setting for Fascist "oceanic" rallies and ceremonies. Guides to the city, which formerly began their description of the city with the Campidoglio or the Vatican, now began with Piazza Venezia. From this derived the need to enlarge the square and to open up monumental access routes to it from the various parts of the city, so as to make it the focal point of city traffic, activity, and attention.[48]

The objective of emphasizing both classical Rome and the centrality of Piazza Venezia was actually self-contradictory. A huge effort went into the excavation of the various forums, which were then covered over to permit the building of the colossal Via dell'Impero (today Via dei Fori Imperiali) between Piazza Venezia and the Colosseum, which has served since then for the annual display of Italian military might. Exaltation of the classical monuments and sites was accompanied by indifference or hostility to those of later periods. Classical monuments were isolated at the expense of the medieval and Renaissance accretions and environments that had grown up around them. Medieval and Renaissance districts were perceived as so much "picturesque filth" *("sudicio pittoresco")* in Mussolini's phrase, to be redeveloped and crisscrossed with modern traffic arteries, although the press was able to save some monuments and sites from casual demolition.[49]

It took some courage therefore and the protection of architect Marcello Piacentini, the leading architect in Rome and Italy under Fascism, for a group of young Roman architects—among the first products of the new architecture faculty and adherents of the modern architecture movement—to challenge the

47. Edoardo and Duilio Susmel, *Opera omnia di Benito Mussolini* (Florence 1956–64), *22,* 47–48. (Translation, of this and subsequent passages, by the author unless otherwise noted.)
48. Zocca, "Roma capitale," pp. 650–52.
49. Paving Via dell'Impero meant covering up 97 percent of Trajan's Forum; 85 percent of Nerva's Forum, etc. Seventy-six thousand square meters of the eighty thousand square meters of the imperial forums had been excavated; 84 percent of this uncovered area was now covered over to build the road! (Insolera, *Roma moderna,* p. 136.)

ideas of the Giovannoni group, ideas that so closely echoed Mussolini's planning dicta for Rome. The Piacentini group proposed to shift the center of the city and the railway station at Termini[50] to the east so as to drain traffic from the historic center and permit its conservation. Their proposals were based on studies of existing traffic patterns rather than the principles of ancient Roman town building. They advocated shifting the city's center of gravity toward the east, while Mussolini had called for its growth southward "along the banks of the sacred river to reach the shores of the Tyrrhenian sea."[51]

Following the 1929 Congress of the Town Planning Federation, Governor Boncompagni of Rome, its chairman, secured consent from Mussolini to formulate a new master plan for the city. Mussolini himself installed an ad hoc drafting committee, composed of architects, engineers, and city officials, on April 30, 1930, and charged the committee to present him with a plan six months later, by October 28, eighth anniversary of Il Duce's assumption of power. In typical Fascist style, marked by "unshakeable decisions, precise programs, and absolute deadlines," a new plan was presented to Mussolini on the appointed date. Architect Piacentini drafted the report accompanying the plan. The plan was approved with amendments by the Ministry of Education (Superior Council for Fine Arts and Antiquities) and the Ministry of Public Works (Superior Council of Public Works), then promulgated by royal decree No. 981 of July 6, 1931.[52]

The plan, as adopted by the city, had the following set of manifest goals and means to achieve them:

| GOAL | MEANS |
|---|---|
| 1. Create a splendid, monumental capital. | Proposed new boulevards. |
| | Isolation of Roman monuments. |
| | Retention of the historic city as the center of the modern city. |
| 2. Modernize, yet preserve the historic center. | Massive street-cutting in the old city. |
| | Zoning and building code restrictions on alterations. |
| 3. Improve communications within the city. | Subway system. |
| | Street-cutting in the old city. |
| | Relocation of the major railway station to the east. |

50. Note that Termini is a place name, rather than the word for terminal, though Stazione Termini is, in fact, a terminal station.

51. On the Piacentini group proposal, see Luigi Piccinato, "Il momento urbanistico alla prima Mostra Nazionale dei Piani Regolatori," *Architettura e Arti Decorative,* January 1930, pp. 199–235.

52. The 1931 master plan is described in Zocca, "Roma capitale," pp. 664–66; in Ludovico Quaroni, "I problemi del Piano Regolatore di Roma," *Urbanistica,* Nos. 15–16 (1955), pp. 96–99; and in Leonardo Benevolo, "Osservazioni sui lavori per il piano regolatore di Roma," *Casabella,* May 1958, pp. 4–15. The map and legal norms can be found in *Roma: Città e piani,* pp. 141–43.

4. Permit the city to guide and finance new expansion, and regulate development outside the plan perimeter.

Condemnation of properties in expansion zones for urbanization and resale.

District-by-district expansion through detailed implementation plans.

Zoning and building code restrictions on development rights, even outside the plan perimeter.

5. Permit landowners to develop their properties.

Generous allocation of development rights in all directions, rather than selective expansion.

6. Provide for a variety of housing needs, including low-cost housing

Depression of land prices through condemnation at preplan prices.

Ample zoning for intensivi (tenements).

Zoning also for palazzine, villini, and row-houses.

Authority to permit building outside of plan perimeter.

7. Place some restrictions on permitted densities in the new districts.

Zoning and building code restrictions.

8. Ensure adequate provision of facilities in the new districts.

Reservation of space for facilities through zoning, indicating location of public buildings, parks, recreation facilities, and streets.

9. Improve the quantity and quality of parks and recreation facilities.

Unified scheme of public and private parks.

Restrictions on subdivision of private estates.

Designation of properties for condemnation as public parks.

Development restrictions in zones of scenic or archeological importance

10. Interrelate and guide policymakers in various sectors of the city and national government.

Master plan itself.

Interrelations between parks, railway, subway schemes.

Designation of sites for public building.

Rome thus had its third officially adopted master plan, backed by the will and might of a regime that had coined the word "totalitarian" to define its power. Under the provisions of the decree approving the new master plan, the national government even agreed to help defray some of the costs of implementing it. One would expect, then, that this plan, unlike its predecessors, might find prompt, strict, and faithful execution. But such was not the case: like its predecessors, the plan of 1931 was respected neither by its official sponsors nor the many actors whose activities the plan was designed to regulate. Most of the goals of the plan were never achieved, even though it remained in force, legally speaking, until 1959.

Some of the projects designed to make the city more grandiose and monumental, such as the Via dell'Impero between Piazza Venezia and the Colosseum, were carried out because of their immediate political significance. But the priority schedule for the remodeling of the historic center was generally ignored and the proposed demolition projects, fortunately, were only sporadically executed. Cost, not culture or nostalgia, was the great limiting factor in the planned modernization of the historic center. Since expansion was allowed generally on all sides of the historic center, and residences there were gradually replaced by offices, the historic center remained the center, albeit increasingly overwhelmed, of modern Rome. Public poverty kept most of the historic district intact, while private poverty meant that most of its residences remained airless, unhygienic slum dwellings. The subway system was not built, nor was the railway station relocated.[53] City powers to condemn land for urbanization and resale in expansion districts were never used, either to guide development or recoup some of the costs of urbanization. The detailed plan mechanism was not used to guide city growth; as will be seen, detailed plans were issued haphazardly, mostly in response to pressure from private developers and seldom in relation to the master plan they were designed to implement.

The new integrated system of private and public parks was never created and, in fact, between 1931 and 1943 no public park of any importance was created, despite the rise in the city's population from 940,000 in 1931 to 1.5 million in 1943. Instead, variances were approved that rezoned for intensive development areas originally designated as parks. Zones under scenic-archeological restrictions were used to create ultraluxurious homes for movie stars—legally through variances as well as illegally through the creation of faits accomplis. From 2.8 square meters per capita of green in 1925, the city fell to 2.2 square meters in 1940, 1.7 in 1957, and 1.5 in 1964—as compared to 80 square meters in Stockholm and 16 square meters in Amsterdam (1964).[54]

Private developers everywhere were given the maximum leeway to develop what they wished, where they wished. The 1931 plan was interpreted and implemented so as to reflect the policies of private operators and of the many

53. The State Railways intervened at the last moment to remove this from the plan, when it was too late for the planners to oppose them or to develop a substitute scheme. See Quaroni, "I problemi," p. 97.

54. Antonio Cederna, "Il verde a Roma: cronaca di una rovina," Casabella, April 1964, pp. 29–36, reprinted in Mirabilia Urbis, pp. 469–502. The figures come from pp. 482, 497 of the latter.

public agencies that acted in the same way as private operators. As it was, the plan allowed in many places the continued building of intensivi and actually raised their maximum height to 35 meters: by 1957, 61 percent of Roman residential buildings were intensivi; 33 percent were palazzine; 3 percent villini; and 3 percent other unspecified types.[55] Middle-class districts came to be almost as crowded and lacking in facilities as working-class districts, because of the way the master plan was implemented through detailed plans and altered through variances.

The master plan had been drafted by an ad hoc committee of ten experts and bureaucrats, who had worked feverishly for six months and then retired from the scene. They had been sufficiently isolated from administrative burdens and private pressures during this time to take a detached and broad view of the city's problems. There was no way to ensure that detailed plans of implementation respected the spirit and letter of the master plan: pressures operated on the city planning offices to make sure they did not. The planning department was, unlike the committee that drafted the master plan, a permanent organization, enmeshed in administrative detail and the tangle of public and private particularism. In designing detailed plans it made decisions affecting individual fortunes and specific pieces of property; it dealt with determinate persons and organizations. It could not and did not have the detachment or overview of the drafters of the master plan. The policies of the 1931 plan, calling for private sacrifices in the public interest, lay beyond the enforcement capabilities of the implementing agency.[56]

When detailed plans emerged, the broad boulevards and scenic squares of the master plan reappeared as building lots. The result was a neomedieval street pattern in many of the residential districts built in Rome after 1931, including some of the most luxurious (for example Via Archimede). The planning department systematically distorted the intentions of the plan in order to allow owners and builders maximum exploitation of their properties. The building code was interpreted with a generosity that allowed intensivi to be built in zones marked for palazzine, and palazzine to be built in zones marked for villini. In the reservation of space for public facilities other than streets, however, the department generally remained faithful to the master plan. Thus, relatively crowded new districts were built with the facilities allocated for the much less densely built districts intended by the master planners. Resemblance of the detailed plans to the master plan was further reduced by the large number of amendments ("varianti") to detailed plans proposed by the city and accepted by the Ministry of Public Works—174 of them in the period 1931–57.[57]

55. *Relazione al piano regolatore generale, appendice parte seconda,* presented in 1957 by the Ufficio Speciale Nuovo Piano Regolatore and the Comitato di Elaborazione Tecnica, p. 3.

56. On the nonimplementation of the 1931 master plan, see Quaroni, "I problemi,"; Zocca, "Roma capitale," 666–88, 704–07; Insolera, *Roma moderna,* pp. 152–55; and Benevolo, "Osservazioni," pp. 4–5.

57. Insolera, *Roma moderna,* p. 153, n. 1. One can compare the maps of the 1931 master plan with the composite of the detailed plans of execution in *Roma: Città e piani,* pp. 143, 199.

The planning department "betrayed" the city's master plan in its zeal to accommodate private builders and landowners. The master plan itself, being necessarily general in its prescriptions, conferred considerable discretion on city officials as to how it should be interpreted and enforced. City officials, especially at the political level, provided no support and made little demand for effective regulation of development in the public interest—at least as defined in the master plan. The progressive Fascist elements, a minority, were usually kept contented with general policy enunciations in the form of master plans and statutes. Conservative Fascists, on the other hand, were plied with gratifications in the form of concrete administrative decisions—decisions that often involved the non-implementation of general policies.[58]

The master plan of 1931 applied, at least in the fashion described, to about 80 of the city's 600 square miles, that is, to about 13 percent of city territory. Like its predecessors, it was designed to regulate land use in the existing built-up portions of the city and in as much of the city's territory as necessary to house predicted population increases. But much of the city's development after 1931 took place in the vast areas outside of the plan perimeter but within the legal boundaries of the city of Rome.

Concentrated ownership, the slowness of the city in urbanizing new land, and the demand created by heavy immigration made land within the plan perimeter expensive, so that thousands of families were able to settle only on much cheaper land outside. The master plan sought to contain and shape all new development by restricting development outside the perimeter to officially approved subdivisions, whose developers agreed to pay for the basic costs of urbanization. But the drive of the poor to build and own their own homes could not be contained, especially since the city did not avail itself of its condemnation powers to make cheap land available *within* the plan perimeter. Single houses and entire villages sprang up all around the perimeter, the work of individual masons working at night to elude the few policemen assigned to patrol the hundreds of square miles outside the perimeter. Often these rural villages or *borgate* were started by big operators, who bought up large tracts, subdivided them without city permission, and promised lot buyers that city approval was imminent: almost always the city eventually agreed to accept the fait accompli and provide some services at the general taxpayer's expense.[59]

Two hundred thousand people thus came to live outside the plan perimeter,

---

58. The courts (i.e. the Council of State) were fairly tolerant of the way local authorities translated master plans into detailed plans, admitting the need to maintain some flexibility in the planning process. They were less tolerant, however, of those few detailed plans that actually reduced development rights. On this point, see Virgilio Testa, *Disciplina urbanistica* (Milan, 1961), p. 106, who covers the general legal relations between master plans and detailed plans on pp. 57–124. See also Insolera, *Roma moderna*, p. 1, n. 1. The Ministry of Public Works is also responsible for the way the plan was implemented, in that it had to approve all detailed plans before they came into effect.

59. On the borgate, see Quaroni, "I problemi," p. 98; Insolera, *Roma moderna*, pp. 139–45; and "I piani regolatori," pp. 153–63.

eluding the plan's intentions and standards.[60] Some of them lived in scattered houses; others in illegal settlements or shantytowns; still others in borgate built under official auspices by the Fascist regime to house those evicted in the course of demolitions in the historic center. Twelve such official borgate were built between 1924 and 1940, none based on the master plan, including five that lay *inside* the plan perimeter. Even these officially built houses in the early borgate were shoddily built, seldom maintained, and lacked private water and electricity. Some of the punitive spirit in which they were built is revealed in the following excerpt from a report to the governor of Rome from the City Welfare Department in 1930:

> All this mass of homeless and badly housed people, plus the farm workers and unemployed must be relocated [in the borgate]. The farmworkers, unskilled laborers and unemployed, on the one hand, and the families with irregular composition and poor moral precedents, on the other, might well be transferred to the city properties located in the open countryside, not visible from the highways, where they would be allowed to build houses with the materials from the demolished buildings. Through such a measure it would be possible to build real rural borgate, with between a thousand and fifteen hundred people, each under the vigilance of a station of the Royal Carabinieri and the Militia.[61]

The borgate built later under public auspices were of higher quality.

Public authorities felt as little bound by the master plan as private builders. They were happy to revise the plan, formally or informally, in order to suit the needs of interested parties. They willingly ignored the plan's set of priorities in the programing of public facilities, failing to build many called for by the plan and building others that were not called for in the master plan. The governor of Rome revealed the official attitude toward the plan in a decree of 1936 (November 9, No. 5792), which established the city's first standing planning commission, consisting of city bureaucrats and experts appointed by the governor, and a planning office in the Public Works Department. The master plan, declared the governor, "though studied by eminent technicians and realized on the basis of norms representing the most advanced planning legislation, is not sufficient to ensure a rational succession of initiatives on the part of the Administration or on the part of private citizens in the development and modification of the urban agglomeration." Planning policy would accordingly be made by the new planning commission, presumably free to define the rules as it went along, and executed by the planning office.[62]

By the late thirties, even the plan's authors were describing it as "bourgeois,"

60. Insolera, *Roma moderna*, p. 159.
61. Ibid., p. 109.
62. Insolera, "L'istituto del Regolamento Edilizio," pp. 312–13.

"agnostic," "outdated," "subverted by reality."[63] In the climate of euphoria following the conquest of Ethiopia, Mussolini decided to hold a world's fair in Rome in 1942, on the twentieth anniversary of the founding of the Fascist regime. *Esposizione Universale 1942* or *E42,* later rechristened EUR, was to be the most splendid world's fair ever held and was to become afterward a permanent new residential, commercial, and civic center. Control over this major new city-building enterprise in the southwest was given not to the city government but to an autonomous public corporation, Ente Autonomo Esposizione Universale di Roma (EUR), which became one of the richest, most powerful, and most independent actors in the Roman planning process. The site of E42 was located several miles south of the city, toward the sea, outside of the master plan perimeter; it eventually became an independent enclave, much like the sovereign state of Vatican City. The creation and siting of E42, the single most important decision regarding the future growth of the city taken during the thirties, was made with absolutely no reference to the master plan.[64]

Thus the 1931 plan, the so-called Mussolini Plan, fared little better than its predecessors despite the ample legal powers given to the implementing agency, the regular and generous appropriations from the national budget for this purpose, and the plan's association with the name of Il Duce himself. Despite the totalitarian powers of the regime, the planning of the city during the Fascist period suffered from the same pluralistic lack of coordination, the same discontinuity and improvisation, and the same susceptibility to private pressure characteristic of less pretentious, less fortified regimes. The totalitarian nature of the regime in fact enabled it to disregard and violate its own plan and to change course at will in the certainty that every change would be met with a chorus of ecstatic approval. There were repeated demands in the contemporary Roman press for a "unified command" in Roman planning, to bring about in practice the unity and coordination that totalitarianism claimed in theory.[65] But it was arduous, unrewarding, and perhaps dangerous for the dictator to establish any such "unified commands" below the very top. And thus planning under Fascism continued to be plagued by bureaucratic particularism; by conflicts of interest and value; by frequent changes in goals and priorities; by the resistance of interests, large and small, to regulation in the public interest, at least as defined by official plans; and by the regime's tendency to proclaim one set of policies and administer another.

Except for some on the extreme Right, few planners, administrators, politicians or general observers in Rome today see much to admire in the Roman plan-

63. Antonio Cederna, *I vandali in casa* (Bari, 1956), p. 399.

64. Zocca, "Roma capitale," pp. 683–86; Virgilio Testa, "L'E.U.R.: centro direzionale e quartiere moderno alla periferia di Roma," *Studi Romani,* January-March 1970, pp. 39–50.

65. See the citations from the Roman press in *Urbanistica,* January-February 1941, pp. 69–70, and March-April 1941, p. 72, and the observations of Mario Zocca, "Roma capitale," pp. 680–83.

ning tradition or care to defend that tradition. In the light of current values, past planning seems autocratic and socially insensible; ineffective and distorted by prejudice and rhetoric; corrupt and afflicted by what Professor Bruno Zevi has called "a sadistic pleasure in destroying green" and a "mania for demolition."[66] Indeed, many would say that the antiplanning tradition is much stronger, more deeply rooted in historic memories and current reflexes, and is in keeping with more of the realities of social power and with the dominant cultural norms. Unlike the cities of northern and northwestern Europe, Rome cannot build upon historical habits of civic pride, discipline, and enterprise. Neither in her classical past nor in the recent regime that modeled itself on that past can the city find precedents of successful collective guidance of the pattern of city development.

Knowing this, one can better understand the commentary of a neofascist city councilman, Luigi Turchi, following the adoption over neofascist opposition of the new master plan of 1962:

> Nothing could be done. The machine of the parties ripped to shreds any attempt to restore good sense, coherence, spirit of *"romanità"* and thoughtful moderation against the new wave in planning of the Christian Democratic council group. Rome has been planned. But will Rome allow itself to be planned? Rome is an anti-plan city because it is a city that refuses to be made flat, anonymous, regimented. Rome will not let itself be planned, certainly not in the name of an Eastern Axis. It will remain faithful to its "furrow," its traditions, its past and its hopes, its eternal becoming.[67]

Those who seek to plan Rome's future work against a mighty current indeed.

66. *L'Espresso,* February 3, 1963.
67. *Il Secolo,* December 19, 1962.

# 3

# PLANNING ROME'S FUTURE:
# THE DIMENSIONS OF
# POSTWAR PLANNING

PREWAR FAILURES AND POSTWAR ASPIRATIONS

Many facets of Roman planning performance—the long time it has taken to secure an approved plan, the difficulties of implementation, the vicissitudes of the planning movement—derive from the ambitions of postwar planners to surpass the performance of the master planners of 1931 by means of a bold plan involving heavy public expenditures, stringent restrictions on private development rights, the coordination of numerous public investment programs, and the design and execution of large-scale, complex, and controversial projects. Only such a plan, they felt, would be capable of making a clean break with the planning failures of the past—failures due primarily, they thought, to continued reliance on the historic center as the center of modern Rome. All previous plans had taken for granted that a modern city could be superimposed upon an ancient city, that the old center could be adapted to serve new purposes, and that new districts could be grafted on to the existing core so as to remain as close to the old center as possible. But as the population of the city grew and, with it, motor vehicular traffic, it became all too clear that the old center could no longer survive or perform effectively as the compulsory point of intersection for communications within the city. Even in the late forties and early fifties, with only about 50,000 automobiles on the streets (or one per thirty people), traffic congestion was considered at the breaking point.[1] Today there are some 800,000 vehicles using the same street system.

The alternatives were, in fact, equally radical, controversial, and costly: the old center could be modernized, that is, leveled, or a new center or centers could be created. These alternatives had been recognized as early as 1870, when

1. See the anguished complaints about traffic "saturation" in the early postwar articles indexed in "Ceccarius" (Giuseppe Ceccarelli), *Bibliografia Romana*, from 1950 onward.

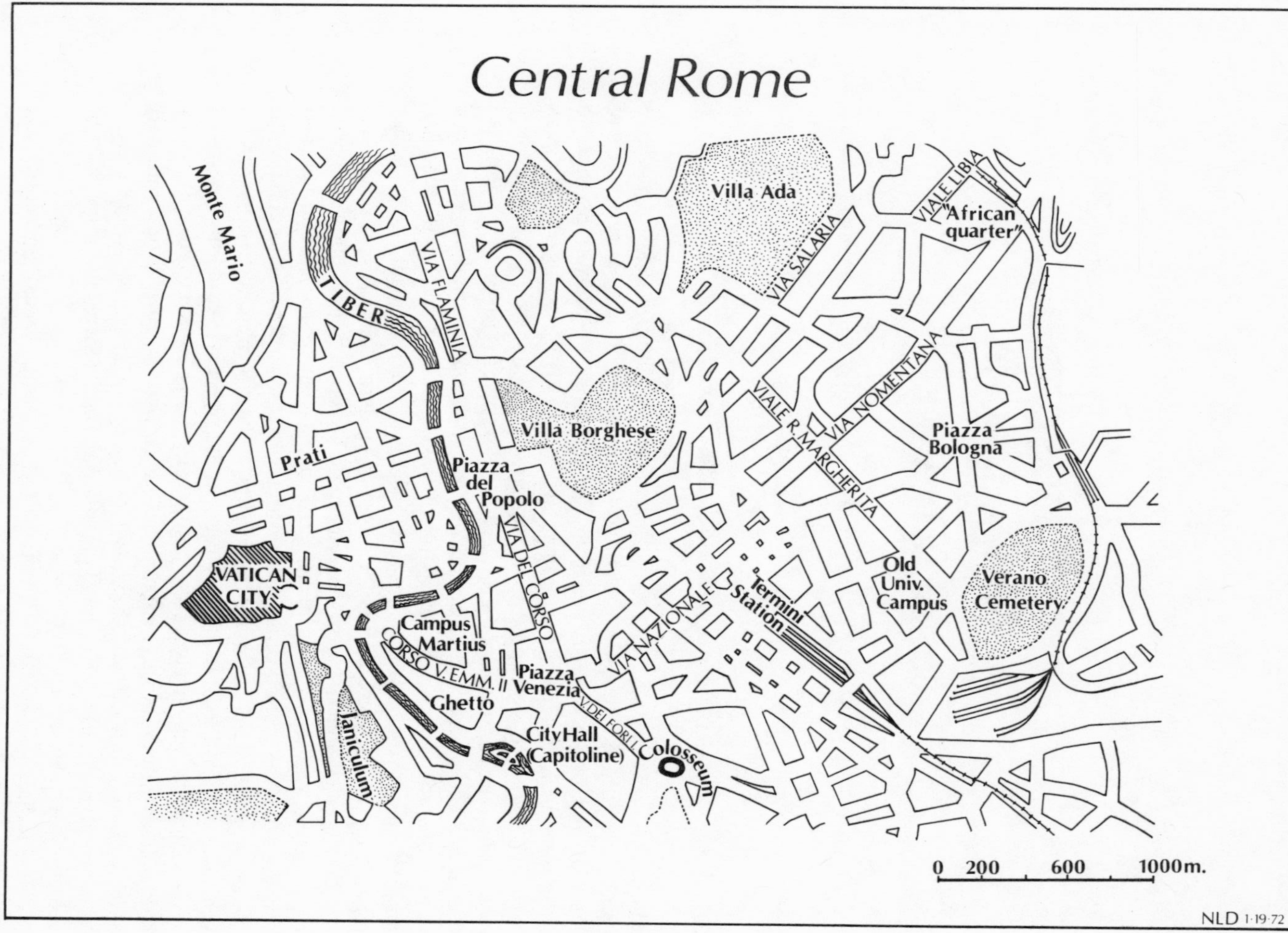

# Central Rome

Figure 3.1

African quarter
VIALE LIBIA
VIA SALARIA
Villa Ada
Monte Mario
VIA FLAMINIA
TIBER
Prati
Piazza del Popolo
Villa Borghese
VIA DEL CORSO
VIA NOMENTANA
Piazza Bologna
VIALE R.MARGHERITA
Old Univ. Campus
Termini Station
VIA NAZIONALE
VATICAN CITY
Campus Martius
CORSO V.EMM. II
Ghetto
Piazza Venezia
Janiculum
City Hall
Capitoline
VIA DEI FORI I
Colosseum
Verano Cemetery

0   200   600   1000 m.

NLD 1:19:72

Quintino Sella, the Italian Minister of Finance, proposed the building of a new capital to the east of the old city.[2] The question of centralized growth vs. decentralization was again posed in the rival plans for Rome presented to the 1929 World Congress of the International Federation of Housing and Town Planning. The master plan of 1931 attempted a compromise between the alternatives by, on the one hand, sanctioning expansion on all sides as in previous plans and, on the other hand, proposing to replace Termini station with three underground stations; the area formerly occupied by the station and railway yards was to become a major artery and civic center in the east. On the very eve of plan approval, too late for any response from the planners or for a substitute proposal, the Italian State Railways withdrew their support from the master plan, claiming that the new scheme was technically impossible. Thus the "oil-stain" pattern—expansion in ever-wider concentric wider around the historic center—remained unchecked by any eastern thrust. The decree approving the master plan simply removed the provisions concerning the railways.[3]

The same alternatives emerged after the war when, in 1951, the city council adopted a detailed plan derived from the 1931 master plan providing for a new road and tunnel to be built along Via Vittoria, between Piazza di Spagna and Piazza del Popolo, tying Via del Corso to Villa Borghese and to Via Veneto. (See Figure 3.2.) The new road was designed to speed up traffic in the historic district, and its construction involved extensive demolition, rebuilding, and alteration. The proposal was denounced in the press by leading writers and journalists, who made a successful appeal to the Ministry of Public Works to veto the proposed road. Arguments that the old center could never be adapted to modern traffic, no matter how many new streets were driven through it, seem to have persuaded many members of the cultural and political elite that some solution had to be found to the problem of congestion that did not involve destruction of the city's historical legacy. A general consensus emerged in the early fifties that, whatever happened, the historic part of the city must be preserved as an entire district, rather than modernized and destroyed.[4]

Preservation of the historic center became the basic axiom of the new plan. Unfortunately, it was not an axiom that led to one and only one set of conclusions. There were several ways of defining "preservation" and "historic center" and several more ways of identifying appropriate means of preservation. The city council, for example, in October 1951, approved in one and the same report both the principle of conserving the historic center and the demolition project involving the new street through the historic center.[5] The council agreed

2. On Sella's scheme, see Mario Zocca, "Roma capitale d'Italia," in *Topografia. . . di Roma,* ed. F. Castagnoli, pp. 567–69.
3. Quaroni, "I problemi del Piano Regolatore di Roma," pp. 96–97.
4. Cederna, *I vandali in casa,* pp. 35–42; INU, *Roma: Città e piani,* pp. 210–15; and Insolera, *Roma moderna,* pp. 203–04.
5. *Roma: Città e piani,* pp. 206–10.

# The Proposed Via Vittoria Redevelopment Project, 1950

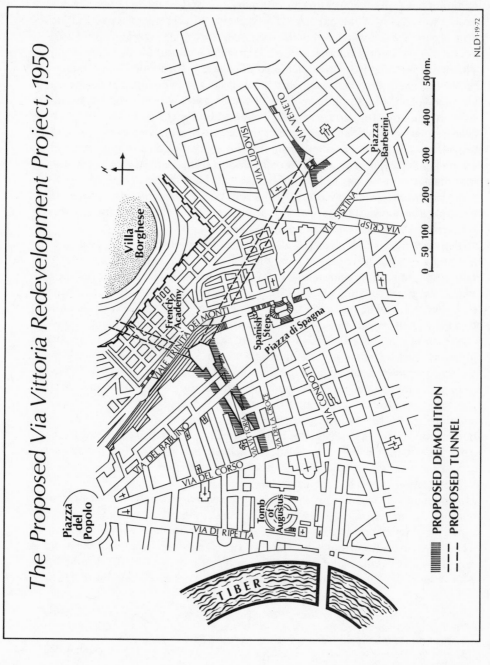

PROPOSED DEMOLITION
PROPOSED TUNNEL

0  50  100   200   300   400   500m.

NLD 1-19-72

in 1951 and again in 1954 that the historic center of the city must be preserved, but at the same time it agree that it must not be "sterilized," or deprived of its vitality. The council agreed that all *"sventramenti"*—modernizing demolition projects—in the old district must cease. After the 1951 incident involving the proposed new road and tunnel through the historic district, the council became aware of its inconsistency and no longer proposed, in the same breath, conservation and modernization. Councilmen of all parties came to agree that expansion of the city in all directions around old Rome must be stopped if the old center was not to be crushed under the increasing load of traffic. New residential districts, therefore, would have to be built only in predetermined sectors, selected so as to draw the epicenter of civic activity away from the existing central business district. Within the same asymmetrical development pattern, existing and new office and commercial building—generators of traffic—would be relocated in centers built specifically to cope with the demands of modern traffic and business. Decentralization of residences and businesses was considered not only necessary and desirable but, given modern means of transportation and communication, feasible as well.

But despite council agreement on what was necessary and desirable, as stated in the unanimous resolution of May 21, 1954, in favor of preserving the old center and creating new centers, formulation of a master plan embodying these principles took almost four years. More than a year was spent in deciding *which* directions for expansion were to be officially permitted and favored.

Most professional planners and the Left strongly preferred eastern expansion; political conservatives and a few conservative planners opposed any eastern expansion, preferring expansion to the west or north or, particularly, the southwest. The vast open spaces around the city made many choices possible: if there had been greater geographical constraint in the form of mountains or bodies of water, there would have been less to fight about. There was no way the progressives could prove that eastern expansion was preferable to expansion toward the sea. They attempted to show that eastern expansion was the most "natural" direction and were given support by the director of the city statistical office. But they could not show that, because the city had been growing in an easterly direction for some time, it followed that people preferred eastern expansion. The eastern sections of the city were occupied by factories, Verano cemetery, railway yards, shanty towns, and massive public housing tenements. Conservatives might reasonably argue that people came to the eastern sections to live because they could not afford to live elsewhere. Conservatives could see no reason why middle class groups should be forced to build and live "across the tracks" in the eastern sections as the planners wanted them to do. In November 1955, a compromise resolution was adopted which sacrificed selectivity to consensus. Instead of choosing the east, as the Left wanted, or the southwest, as most conservatives wanted, the new plan would sanction expansion both to the east and the southwest. Eventually the compromise resolution was translated into a percentage formula: 40 percent southwest, 30 percent east, 15 percent north, and 15 percent west. Even this formula was not completely satisfactory because the contending forces wanted some reassurance that the formula would be respected each year in the issuance of building permits. Leftists were afraid, for example, that the formula could be undermined or disregarded by biased administrators, anxious to favor or accommodate pressures for southwestern or noneastern development.[6]

Akin to the problem of choosing the direction of further residential expansion was that of selecting the number and location of the new office and commercial centers. The Left and most professional planners preferred immediate and maximum development of two new centers in the east—at Pietralata and at Centocelle—and minimal development of the existing new center at EUR. EUR, under dynamic and autonomous leadership, had grown from a deserted collection of grotesque, half-completed buildings and monuments, inhabited by refugees and goatherds, into a model community, linked by subway (as of 1955) to the Termini railway station. Ministries and city offices, including the planning offices, had acquired and built on EUR sites, and private developers were building there one of the most attractive new residential neighborhoods in the city.[7]

Ironically, to the professional planners, the good design and the very attractiveness of EUR posed a threat to the orderly development of the city, to the principle of asymmetrical expansion. For various reasons the planners preferred expansion to the east. Development at EUR, however, stimulated growth in the opposite direction, toward the Mediterranean. If the city expanded both east and west, the historic center would again be encircled and crushed under the weight of cross-city traffic and the rise in speculative values. EUR also had strong ideological associations; both EUR and the idea of expansion toward the sea were brainchildren of the former dictator. The portals of the EUR corporation building, after all, bore and still bear the Mussolinian inscription: "The Third Rome will spread onto other hills, along the banks of the sacred river, to reach the shores of the Tyrrhenian sea." EUR and development toward *mare nostrum* could not fail to be anathema in the eyes of the antifascist planners of INU—the Istituto Nazionale di Urbanistica (National Institute of Planners).

Some on the political right, in contrast, saw in EUR the symbol of a not inglorious past as well as a going entity under conservative and sound public management. They opposed creation of new city centers in the east, which would require heavy public investment and would be located in the midst of a broad, depressing band of slums and public housing. If successful, the new centers would compete with and threaten not only EUR but also the existing central business district in and near the historic center.

6. Ufficio Speciale Nuovo Piano Regolatore, Commissione Generale, *Resoconti stenografici delle sedute* (Rome, 1954–58), 3 vols. (henceforth, "Commissione Generale"), minutes for the meetings of February 3, 10; March 3, 17, 31; July 21; November 17, 1955.

7. *Roma: Città e piani,* pp. 164–68; Virgilio Testa, "L'E.U.R."; Corwin R. Mocine, "New Business Centers for Italian Cities," *Journal of the American Institute of Planners, 31,* (August 1965), 210–21.

The city council in June 1954 appointed a Grand Commission to draft a plan and resolve such differences of opinion. The Commission was to be provided with technical advice by a Comitato di Elaborazione Tecnica (Technical Drafting Committee, or CET), composed of professional city planners. It was months and years before agreement could be reached on how many new centers there would be, where they would be located, and how important each one would be. In May 1957 a compromise formula was achieved, whereby EUR was to be the principal focus of decentralization, containing 50 percent of new office space in the city. Two lesser centers were also to be created, at Pietralata and Centocelle in the eastern suburbs, to house and service the other half of new civic business.[8]

The new Rome, according to the proposals of the CET planners, was going to be organized along an imposing new communications axis, the *Asse Attrezzato* (literally: "equipped axis") or eastern axis, an expressway that would tie together the new civic centers at EUR, Pietralata, and Centocelle, and form the Roman segment of the national *Autostrada del Sole* linking northern Italy with Naples and Sicily.[9] The eastern axis would become the "linear center" of the new Rome. Conservative opponents felt that the axis would be extremely costly to build and they wanted to have some means of rapid communications in the western sectors, serving the growing districts in the northwest and southwest behind the Vatican. The planners were gravely disturbed by the prospect of such major highways in the west because they saw in them a further stimulus to western development. A western expressway, just like the development of EUR in the southwest, was seen as undermining the whole attempt to break the historic "oil-stain" pattern in the city's growth. After three years of negotiation (1954–57) on the Grand Commission, a compromise provided for both the axis in the east and a "rapid highway" of unspecified importance in the west.

The principle of selective rather than continued indiscriminate expansion—considered the only means of saving the historic center—meant that planners would have to engage in a painful and explosive process of choosing those districts where development rights were going to be restricted or even excluded. Under existing legislation, moreover, there was no provision for compensating those whose properties were thus excluded from development. Planners felt nonetheless that if property owners all around the city were allowed to build in accordance with market conditions, rather than in accordance with predetermined zoning plans, the city would continue to grow in oil-stain fashion.

This had several negative consequences. First, it forced cross-city traffic to flow through the old center, which was bad not only for the old center but for the flow of traffic. Secondly, oil-stain development usually meant not only symmetrical, concentric development but also growth by accretion leading to an undifferentiated, compact urban mass. Planners hoped to create a different form of city

8. "Commissione Generale," 2, June 15, 1957.
9. See pp. 62–65 for further details on the eastern axis.

neighborhood—distinct new residential districts, adequately serviced, separated from each other by large amounts of open space. Thus selective expansion was designed to prevent concentricity and compactness in city growth. Strict control of new development through zoning was also going to be used to combat the equally prevalent and undesirable pattern of leapfrog or scattered growth, which created communities that were isolated, to be sure, but lacking in many essential services. Planners hoped to produce a new type of residential-employment district that combined separateness with low densities and adequate services. Outside of these new districts, building rights were to be sharply curtailed.

Many of the still unbuilt or only partially built suburbs that where zoned for development and even intensive development under the master plan of 1931 were, under the new zoning scheme, to be left as little developed as possible. If the building rights conferred by the 1931 master plan were allowed to be fully implemented, market conditions might channel all new growth into the densely packed, undifferentiated quarters provided for under the old plan rather than into the low-density, differentiated quarters provided for by the new master plan scheme. Instead, under the master plan of 1962, the uncompleted residential districts under the 1931 master plan were to remain "unsaturated"; this would allow the city to install more adequate services in these districts and ensure that new city growth took place instead in the brand-new residential districts designated in the new master plan.

Conservatives considered these proposals to be an illegitimate construction of and interference with property rights and legitimate vested interests. Conservatives felt that property owners should be allowed greater freedom to build what they wanted where they wanted, whether it be in the historic center, the unfinished quarters of the 1931 master plan, or out in the countryside; they felt that high subdivision and building standards would further increase the price of land and housing; and they felt that the community facility standards were not based on a realistic assessment of what the city could afford to provide, but rather on arbitrary definitions of community "needs." During the proceedings of the Grand Commission and its subcommittees, much time had to be spent working out compromise formulae on these standards as well as on the direction and intensity of expansion and decentralization.

The plan presented to the Grand Commission in November 1957 by the the professional planners on the CET represented an effort by the planners to find an overall compromise between their preference for eastern expansion, high standards, and low densities and the preference of the overwhelming majority of commission members for expansion in other quadrants, lower facility standards, and higher densities. The planners' attempt at compromise was not successful: the conservative majority on the Grand Commission considered the CET plan not a compromise at all but an attempt by the CET to impose a unilateral solution. After three years of debate the deadlocked commission simply turned responsibility for the plan back to the city council (April 30, 1958). The city council, now firmly under the control of right-wing forces sympathetic to the landowners and builders, in turn refused to accept the CET plan and in June 1958, passed *its* responsibility over to the *Giunta* or city executive committee. It was another year before the Giunta worked out and the council adopted a plan that satisfied both the requirements of the 1942 Planning Act and the requirements of the conservative planning coalition.

The plan adopted by the city council in June 1959—the so-called Plan of the Giunta—was a much more palatable plan than the one offered by the now defunct CET; it proposed to ratify existing inertial tendencies toward monocentric, compact development. The 1959 plan was a much more "realistic," feasible plan, economically, politically, and technically, because it called for little change in the structure of the city and in the operating procedures of private developers and builders. It called for little stringent public regulation and little public investment in projects or facilities. It attempted to minimize any public interference with the private planning of real estate investors and developers. It was perhaps more "democratic" than the CET plan in the sense that it attempted to please all active private interests or offend none of them. The CET plan was more "democratic," of course, in attempting to improve conditions for tenants and home buyers; but the tenants and home buyers were relatively uninterested, inactive, and unaware of their stake in the planning process, as compared to the landowner-contractor interests.[10]

Instead of reducing and eliminating development in large parts of the city, the 1959 plan provided for expansion all along the fringe and for new arteries in both east and west. In the unbuilt areas within the perimeter of the 1931 master plan, the 1959 plan allowed for much greater saturation than did the CET plan. In the Agro Romano, the vast open countryside around the built-up portion of the city, the CET plan had banned any structures except farmhouses, on minimum lots of five acres. The 1959 plan, in contrast, permitted private residences as well as farmhouses, on minimum lots of one acre (5000 sq. meters), scarcely a "rural" density. Volumetric building standards would permit as many as forty people per hectare.[11] Public spending under the 1959 plan was to be modest: there was to be only one new "directive" or office center, at EUR, a few miles south of the historic center; EUR was already urbanized and linked to the city by rapid transit. The CET plan's proposals for two new centers in the east— at Pietralata, about two miles northeast of Termini station, and at Centocelle, about three miles southeast of the station—and the elaborate new eastern axis were all dropped from the 1959 master plan.

10. For analysis of the defeat of the CET plan and comparisons between that plan and the 1959 giunta plan, see Insolera, *Roma moderna,* chap. 17; articles by Michele Valori, Leonardo Benevolo, and Luigi Piccinato in *Roma: Città e piani,* pp. 199–302; R. Fried, "Professionalism and Planning in Postwar Rome"; and Antonio Cederna, *Mirabilia Urbis: Cronache romane 1957–1965* (Turin, 1965), Part 1.

11. Comune di Roma, *Controdeduzioni alle osservazioni sul Nuovo Piano Regolatore Generale: Deliberazione della Giunta Municipale n. 187 del 20 gennaio 1960* (Rome, 1960) (henceforth, "Controdeduzioni, 1959"), p. 27.

Under the plan adopted in 1959, standards for public facilities in the new expansion districts were modest and rather vague, leaving scope for maximal private development and minimal public investment. Builders were given a five-year "transition period" after plan approval in which to build at the densities permitted under the 1934 building code.

There is no doubt that the 1959 type of plan could be both more easily adopted and more easily implemented. It proposed very little regulation and little public investment—in effect, minimal public intervention. It was basically a throwback to, or extension of, the 1931 master plan and as such would be carried through by the momentum of existing tendencies. Such a plan suited the existing capabilities of the city government, both its administrative frailties and its financial anemia. But the 1959 plan, if easily adopted and administered, would scarcely have achieved its stated major purpose: saving the historic center. While imposing stringent restrictions on alterations in the historic center, the 1959 plan, by allowing further oil-stain expansion and providing for a concentric circulation scheme, increased rather than diminished speculative and traffic pressures on the center—pressures that would eventually undermine restrictions on alteration. The old center would continue to lie at the intersection of cross-city traffic, and pressure to modernize its buildings and streets would become irresistible. Nor would the plan have achieved its other stated purpose: improving the quality of new residential districts. Standards for the new districts—densities, facilities, and so forth—were only slightly more stringent than those of the 1931 master plan. If the 1959 plan standards were observed, improvement in the quality of the new districts would not be noticeable.

The Ministry of Public Works in its November 1961 ruling on the 1959 master plan agreed with many of the INU criticisms; at the same time, the ruling stated that the plan was "worthy of approval as a whole"; and, in fact, the ruling was sufficiently sibylline to allow both defenders and critics of the giunta plan to find confirmation of their views.[12] Functionaries of the Ministry of Public Works found it just as difficult as local city officials to endorse proposals for radical reform of urban structure. The two years it took for the ministry to formulate its ruling, and the ambiguity of that ruling, reflected the strength of the cross-pressures to which the ministry was subject: pressures from the planning movement for innovative, expensive, and stringent plans; and pressures from private interests for plans embodying the principles of laissez-faire or for no plans at all. Until the formation in 1962 of the national Christian Democrat-Socialist alliance, the ministry lacked sufficient political support to take sides with the professional planners against local real estate interests and their political allies. Only in 1962 did the ministry begin a nationwide attempt (as of 1970 still not a

12. A summary of the Superior Council's ruling can be found in Ministero dei Lavori Pubblici, Ufficio Stampa, "Riassunto del parere espresso dal Consiglio Superiore dei Lavori Pubblici nella adunanza in assemblea generale in data 23 novembre 1961, in merito al progetto di piano regolatore generale di Roma adottato il 24 giugno 1959." The full text was published in *Informazioni Urbanistiche,* September-December 1961, pp. 3–68.

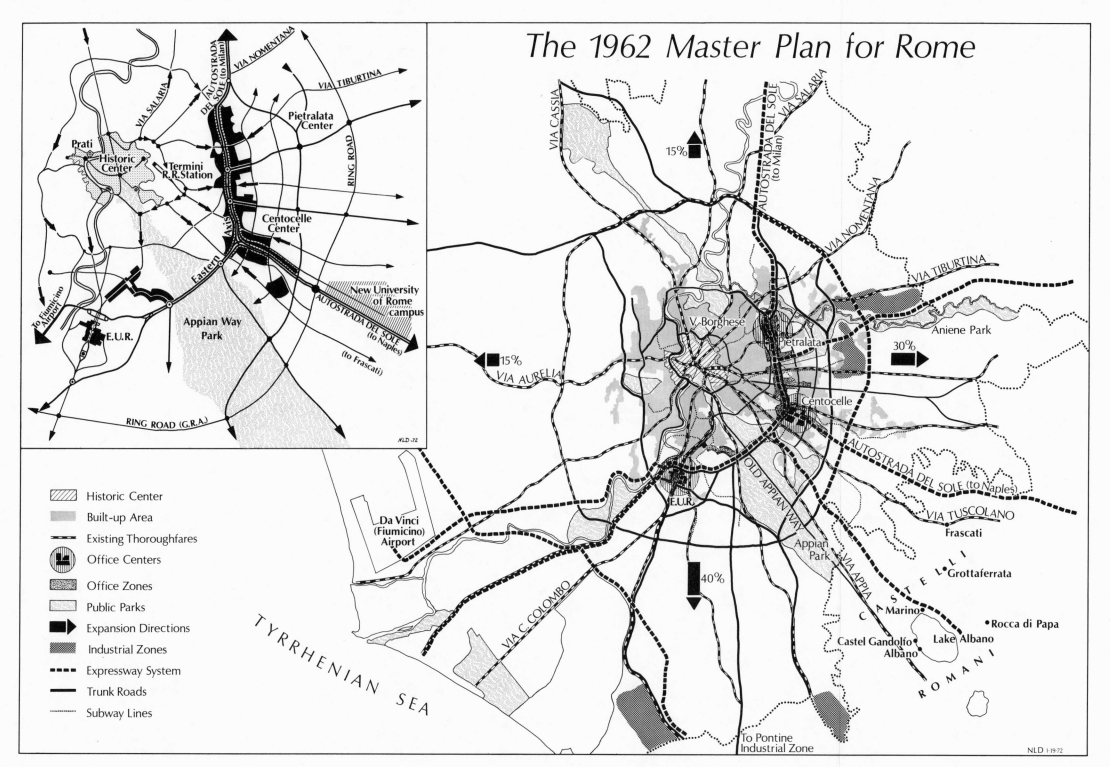

# The 1962 Master Plan for Rome

**Inset labels:**
VIA NOMENTANA · VIA TIBURTINA · AUTOSTRADA DEL SOLE (to Milan) · VIA SALARIA · Pietralata Center · RING ROAD · Prati · Historic Center · Termini R.R. Station · Centocelle Center · Eastern AXIS · New University of Rome campus · To Fiumicino Airport · E.U.R. · Appian Way Park · AUTOSTRADA DEL SOLE (to Naples) · (to Frascati) · RING ROAD (G.R.A.) · NLD-72

**Main map labels:**
VIA CASSIA · AUTOSTRADA DEL SOLE (to Milan) · VIA SALARIA · 15% · VIA NOMENTANA · VIA TIBURTINA · V. Borghese · Pietralata · Aniene Park · 30% · 15% · VIA AURELIA · Centocelle · OLD APPIAN WAY · AUTOSTRADA DEL SOLE (to Naples) · Da Vinci (Fiumicino) Airport · E.U.R. · Appian Park · VIA TUSCOLANO · Frascati · VIA APPIA · Grottaferrata · CASTELLI · 40% · Marino · Rocca di Papa · Castel Gandolfo · Albano · Lake Albano · ROMANI · VIA C. COLOMBO · To Pontine Industrial Zone · TYRRHENIAN SEA · NLD 1-19-72

**Legend:**
- Historic Center
- Built-up Area
- Existing Thoroughfares
- Office Centers
- Office Zones
- Public Parks
- Expansion Directions
- Industrial Zones
- Expressway System
- Trunk Roads
- Subway Lines

Figure 3.3

very successful one) to support local planners in their battles with private interests. The ministry's intervention in Roman planning in 1962 marked the first episode in this valiant campaign.[13]

The 1962 master plan of Rome, formulated and adopted under the ministry's aegis, was basically a reversion to the CET plan of 1957, just as the giunta's plan of 1959 had been a reversion to the master plan of 1931. It was not a reversion to pure progressive principles, however, but, like the CET plan, a compromise between progressive and conservative demands. The progressives won on several points; they secured sizable expansion to the east (30 percent); commitment to the two eastern directive centers and the eastern axis; the raising of minimum lot sizes in the Agro Romano from one acre to two acres, and a 50 per cent reduction in the permissible bulk of new building in the Agro. Expansion zones in the north and west were sharply reduced, as were permitted densities in the incompleted sections of the city within the 1931 master plan. The amount of land zoned for public parks was increased.

The progressives also won a commitment from the city to reform and reorganize the city planning offices and to create a new Permanent Planning Institute as a source of planning research. The specific and rather high standards for buildings and facilities in new expansion districts were a victory for them. And they won, for the first time in Roman and possibly in Italian city planning, the introduction of use controls. Previous zoning in the city had regulated building types rather than use; now building use was controlled as a means of protecting the historic center and decentralizing major traffic-generating uses to the new directive centers. The inclusion of dozens of borgate or illegal subdivisions as Zone F districts—"redevelopment"—was also a victory for progressives, anxious to have these settlements, with perhaps half a million people living in them, rationalized and converted into respectable residential communities with paved streets, sewers, and other basics.

In return, the progressives had to make important concessions. They had to agree, first of all, to allow 40 percent of future expansion to take place in the southwest in, around, and beyond EUR, where private developers had long been pressing for approval of their subdivision contracts. They had to accept EUR as the principal new directive center. In exchange for lower densities in the Agro, they had to consent to creation there of hundreds of G4 zones—private one-family houses on one-acre lots—with a possible future population of 100,000-250,000 people. More important, they had to agree to a zoning scheme based on an anticipated massive growth in the city's population: the new plan provided theoretical space for a population of some 2.5 million new residents by 1985 and 4.5 million in 2000. The resulting large number of new expansion districts thus provided in the plan might be used by conservative forces to steer expansion exclusively into the southwest.[14]

13. Giovanni Astengo, "Le nostre tigri di carta," *Il Ponte,* December 1968, pp. 1493–1510.
14. The trading involved in the formulation of the 1957 and 1962 master plans can be observ-

But however many concessions the progressives had to make, they still managed to secure a plan that met many of their demands, a plan that, under propitious circumstances, may bring about a major change in the structure and performance of the city as a place to live and work. The potential for change in the 1962 plan is great. Delay in adopting and implementing such a plan becomes understandable once it is realized how ambitious, controversial, and innovative the new master plan is. Unlike the 1959 plan, the new master plan involves heavy public expenditures, stringent restrictions on private development, the coordination of numerous public investment programs, and the design and execution of large-scale, complex, and controversial projects. It takes a good deal of time to adopt and a good deal more time to implement a plan that proposes fundamental reform.

There were some other gains deriving from the long delay in adopting the plan. Each successive version of the plan, while embodying different policy emphases, also became a more refined instrument of regulation and a more specific program of action. The CET plan of 1957 was relatively crude and general in its provisions, both graphic and regulatory, as compared to the 1959 plan. The 1962 plan was more specific and articulated than its predecessor, at least partly because its drafters could be guided by the detailed criticisms of the Ministry of Public Works ruling on the 1959 master plan. Further refinements have been introduced in the master plan since its adoption by the city council in 1962. Only time will tell, however, whether in this case the better is the enemy of the good, whether, that is, the search for a better or perfect plan has been worth the time involved, whether or not an early and immediate enforcement of a few crude but simple ground rules for development might have been better than the painful, time-consuming formulation of an elaborate document that seeks to resolve all outstanding issues at one blow.

There are many reasons why it took so long and was so difficult to produce and implement a new plan: the potentially heavy impact of the plan on property rights and values; the large number of agencies, institutions, and operators whose individual plans had to be coordinated; the national and even international prestige and influence of some of the actors; the radical scope of the changes proposed in the pattern of the city's development; and the large number of issues to be resolved. Some of the outstanding substantive issues are summarized in Table 3.1, but there were many others.

Much time was spent debating such questions as:

- Which aspect of the plan should be worked out first—the circulation scheme, the zoning of new residential districts, or the zoning of employment sites?

ed in "Commissione Generale" (cited above, n. 6); Comune di Roma, *Piano Regolatore Generale della Città di Roma: Estratto dal Verbale delle deliberazioni del Consiglio Comunale* (Rome, 1959) (henceforth, "Council Debates, 1959"); and Comune di Roma, *Piano Regolatore Generale della Città di Roma: Estratto dal verbale delle deliberazioni del Consiglio Comunale* (Roma, 1963) (henceforth, "Council Debates, 1962").

Table 3.1. Basic Planning Choices: 1957, 1959, 1962 Versions of the Master Plan

| | CET Plan (1957) | Giunta Plan (1959) | Master Plan (1962) |
|---|---|---|---|
| Expansion pattern | Asymmetrical Selective Specific | Concentric Indiscriminate Indeterminate | Asymmetrical Selective Specific |
| Number of new office centers ("centri direzionali") | Historic center EUR Pietralata (East) Centocelle (East) | Historic center EUR | Historic center EUR Pietralata (East) Centocelle (East) |
| Expansion directions | East Southwest (left bank of Tiber) | North South East West | East Southwest (left bank of Tiber) |
| Status of eastern axis | "Linear center of the new Rome" | "Urban segment of the Autostrada del Sole" (Milan-Naples) | "Linear center of the new Rome" |
| Circulation scheme | Heavy in east, light in west | Balanced, east and west | Eastern emphasis |
| Subway scheme | Tangential to historic center | Intersecting the historic center | Tangential to historic center |
| Development of countryside (Agro Romano) | Farm houses only | Farmhouses and one-acre residential lot development | Farmhouses (H2) on 4-acre lots; residences in Hl zones on 2-acre lots and 4-acre lots; no residences in Hl zones except farmhouses. |
| Development of unbuilt zones within 1931 master plan | Minimal | Saturation | Moderate |

– Should the city wait for national, regional, and metropolitan planning studies and decisions before attempting to make its own master plan? Would any local master plan made in the absence of national, regional, and metropolitan plans be viable?

– What kind of growth rate should be assumed for the city? Should existing tendencies be extrapolated? Should planners prepare for alternative growth rates? Should they take growth rates as "given," or assume that growth rates were subject to manipulation by public policy?

– Should the plan be based on the city's actual and prospective financial capabilities, or should it be based on the assumption that financing could be arranged after a proper plan was formulated and financial *needs* were determined?

– Should the plan be rigid, specific, airtight, difficult to misuse, misinterpret, and sabotage? Or should the plan be open, flexible, adaptable, and discretionary?

– How much study and research should be conducted before decisions were made? What kind of research was relevant and valid?

– How should standards for public facilities be determined? Were there objective standards on "needs" and "requirements" for various kinds of services and facilities?

– How restrictive could new zoning and building norms be without increasing the amount of black-market subdivisions and building, raising the price of land and housing, or reducing employment in the building industry?

– What was the proper basis for selecting areas for expansion as opposed to areas where public facilities would be built or minimal development would be allowed? How should choices be made among contending property interests as to who would be allowed intensive development rights and who would be forced to sell land at below market value?

– Given the city's financial straits, how much reliance should be placed on wholesale compulsory purchase of development land as a means of permitting the city to guide and pay for the process of urbanization?

– How much should the plan acknowledge vested interests and rights acquired under previous plans and building codes? Should the new plan provide a period of transition between old norms and new norms?

– How far could the city go in granting legal recognition and services to illegally built subdivisions without encouraging the establishment of new ones?

Many of these issues had never come up in the previous planning of the city and had to be explored for their financial, political, social, and ideological implications. To be sure, for some of the actors, the time spent debating these issues was worth it, not because issues were being explored but because adoption of a new plan was being postponed. Many of the participants in the deliberative process had an interest in seeing that no final decisions were made. Frequently, areas thought to have been decided came unstuck, possibly also because initial acceptance had not been sincere. But the very scope of the plan generated a large number of very difficult issues, even for those sincerely desirous of arriving at a workable set of arrangements within a reasonable amount of time.

SAVING THE HISTORIC CENTER

Saving the historic center has been one of the few goals that most groups in Rome have been able to agree on.[15] It is this goal that has been used to justify

15. A general treatment of the planning problems involved in the historic center can be found in Comune di Roma, *Urbanistica Romana*, No. 3 (1966) (also in *Capitolium*, April 1966) and No. 4 (also in *Capitolium*, September-October 1966). See also Salvatore Rebecchini, "Passato e avvenire del centro storico di Roma," *Studi Romani*, April-June 1965, pp. 200–19.

a plan of radical reform, that has permitted a measure of consensual planning, and that has given Roman planning national and a measure of international significance. Rome is the first important Italian city to attempt to save its historic form and identity. It is the first large-scale testing ground for the theories of urban conservation adumbrated by postwar Italian planners, who have come to believe that historic centers can be preserved only as wholes and not as collections of individual landmarks. They must be treated as specialized elements in a total urban context, including both old and new sections. Rejecting the notion that historic centers can or should be adapted to perform all modern functions, planners hope to identify those functions appropriate to these centers, which will give them a viable existence within the total urban system. Planners hope to transfer functions inappropriate to old centers, such as bearing heavy vehicular traffic, to other urban structures. Within the old districts they would allow only "conservative rehabilitation" *(risanamento conservativo)*—public and private programs to restore, maintain, and conserve the historic urban fabric, while eliminating hazards to health and safety. They would permit only such alterations as would remove from historic buildings and blocks the superfetations from later periods that have filled in courtyards and gardens. Conservationists hope to maintain not only single landmarks of particular importance but the traditional appearance of entire neighborhoods. Rehabilitation is to be based not only on the careful inventory and classification of physical structures but also on research into the sociology of the people who live and work in historic districts and who own them. Renovation by individual owners would be discouraged in favor of collective rehabilitation of entire blocks and neighborhoods. Collective renovation, it is felt, is more likely to respect conservationist standards than the renovation efforts of thousands of individual owners.

The historic center in Rome is usually defined as the part of the city that existed in 1870—the territory of the original fourteen *rioni,* covering about 3500 acres or about half the land within the old Aurelian walls. The major threats to the preservation of the buildings, monuments, and neighborhoods within this area come from decrepitude, traffic, and "wildcat" development. In 1870, the rioni had nearly 100 percent of the city's population; today they house only 10 percent. The demographic decline of the rioni has been not only relative but absolute; since World War, I they have gradually lost population to other districts. Steady population loss in the districts of the historic center will bring the population of those districts by 1980 back to what it was one hundred years before. Built centuries ago, many buildings in old Rome are no longer considered comfortable places to live.[16] Rising incomes and standards of living

16. On the evolving concepts concerning the preservation of historic centers, see Piero Maria Lugli, *Storia e cultura della città italiana* (Bari, 1967), particularly pp. 243–302; Cederna, *Mirabilia Urbis,* pp. 151–235; L. Benevolo, *L'architettura della città nell'Italia contemporanea* (Bari, 1968), pp. 139–48; the bulletin of the *Italia Nostra* society; Umberto deMartino, "Cento

have permitted and caused many families to move from the unfit habitations of the center to the newer apartment houses in the suburbs.[17]

The decay of the old buildings in the center has been partly the result of rent control, applied to all apartments built before 1947. Decades of rent control have made maintenance and renovation uneconomical for most landlords. In some cases, landlords have deliberately allowed their properties to fall to pieces so as to force out older tenants and permit the conversion of humble abodes into luxury flats for wealthy Italian and foreign tenants. Because of landlord pressure, parking difficulties, and general inconvenience, storekeepers and artisans have been deserting the old center; their departure has impoverished the street life that was an integral part of the historic aspect of the center.

While much of the center decays, other parts have been renovated or altered, often with little respect for the law or for conservationist values. Since the war, the center has witnessed illegal remodeling on a scale fully matching illegal building in the countryside. Illegal stories have appeared in all sections, on all streets, on practically all buildings. In many cases, owners have added a story *("sopraelevazione")* merely in order to restore the panoramic view obstructed by their neighbor's *sopraelevazione*. Illegal rooftop additions sometimes are massive structures, requiring weeks of effort and large amounts of materials. Others are shacks and huts especially treated to look old so as to acquire the protected status of an historically valuable or at least long-existing structure. Hundreds of small builders and contractors have become respected specialists in illegal rooftop additions. They usually arm themselves with building permits authorizing minor repairs that can be shown to neighbors and the city police. Thus the paraphernalia of the regulatory process is used to defeat the purposes of regulation.[18]

Protection of the historic fabric beneath the burgeoning rooftops has not been much more effective. Buildings have disappeared behind straw matting and scaffolding to reappear unrecognizably altered on the inside and sometimes, also, on the outside. The historic villas or estates occupied by foreign embassies and religious orders have been particularly vulnerable to illegal alteration. Such owners have frequently violated zoning codes to fill their private parks and gardens with housing, despite city efforts to stop them. The Soviet embassy, for example, sold to private speculators a portion of the estate on the Janiculum donated to it by the Italian government after the war; on the remaining land it began to build housing for embassy employees. The Communists joined the rest of the Rome city council in urging the Italian Ministry of Foreign Affairs to

anni di dibattiti sul problema dei centri storici," *Rassegna dell'Istituto di Architettura e Urbanistica* (Facoltà di Ingegneria, University of Rome), April 1966, pp. 75–116. The December 1960 issue of *Urbanistica* is entirely dedicated to the subject.

17. Migration from the historic center is described in *Il Messaggero*, September 10, 1969, and also in *The New York Times*, September 17, 1969. Statistics on postwar intracity migration can be found in the *Notiziario Statistico Mensile*, March and April 1969.

18. *Corriere della Sera*, November 19, 1966.

use its good offices with the embassy, to prevent the destruction of this traditional Roman villa, but to no avail. The master plan of 1962 zoned the embassy estate, Villa Abamelek, as a *"parco privato vincolato"* ("restricted private park"); that is, as a private estate in which new construction was forbidden. But the Soviet embassy, claiming the privileges of extraterritoriality, went ahead to build housing for its employees.[19]

Similarly, most other embassies have disregarded the building and planning policies of the Rome city council. Confronting two sets of embassies, one accredited to the Italian state and the other to the Vatican, many of them occupying sites of artistic, historic, and scenic importance, urban conservationists in Rome have an unusually difficult problem. Religious orders and national ministries have had as little respect for and as much immunity from city regulation as foreign embassies.

Traditionally, the city's historic form and structure have been saved by poverty, both public and private. Ambitious modernization schemes, from those of Pope Sixtus V and Napoleonic Prefect Camille de Tournon to those of Il Duce, have been curbed by budgetary realities. Relative poverty meant also that private renovations, which have made the historic district a compendium of architectural styles, were carried out at a slow, incrementalist pace. Today, poverty continues to be a constraint for the public authorities, but not for private entrepreneurs. Formerly, the city was protected by the gradual increase in population: it took some 250 years for Rome's population to grow from 100,000 in 1600 to 250,000 in 1850. Today the population of Rome increases by 150,000 every two to three years.[20]

The problem of conservation worsens with the continued growth of population and traffic. The basic circulation pattern of the city derives from ancient days, when all roads left from Rome. The major highways into the city today are still those built by the Roman consuls—the so-called "consular highways." The spread of the city outward converted these highways of another age into the chief interior arteries of a modern city, a function that most are badly equipped to serve. Just as all roads led to Rome, all major arterial roads now lead into the historic center, overloading with modern traffic a street system built to accommodate the pedestrians and coaches of the eighteenth century. The Rome traffic survey of 1964 founded that one-fifth of all pedestrian and vehicular movements within the city pass through the historic center—even though that center has only about one-tenth the urbanized area of the city.[21]

Prewar methods of conservation, involving mostly zoning and building ordinances, have not held up under the strain of rapid change, as owners have

19. Cederna, *Mirabilia Urbis,* pp. 317–18; *La Stampa,* January 31, 1965; *Paese Sera,* October 30, 1965; *Avvenire d'Italia* (Rome), July 28, 1965.
20. Comune di Roma, "Un programma quinquennale per Roma," attached to *Capitolium,* May-June 1967 (henceforth, "Five Year Plan"), pp. 19–20, 23–26.
21. *Il Traffico a Roma: La situazione attuale e le previsioni fino al 1985* (Rome, 1966).

sought to increase the value of their properties through more or less illegal additions and alterations. Landlords in the historic center have either ignored permit conditions and requirements altogether, or violated them, or secured official permission to violate them. Many of what conservationists consider the worst attacks on the historic center have been duly authorized by the major regulatory agency, the superintendent of monuments (a regional field official of the Ministry of Public Instruction), as well as by the city government. Unless spurred into action by the Roman press and by the *Italia Nostra* conservation society, those responsible for enforcing the conservation norms of the master plan and of the 1939 laws on historic, scenic, and artistic landmarks have tended to accommodate rather than to oppose entrepreneurial initiatives within the historic center, and to tolerate rather than remedy the inertia of landlords who refuse to carry out needed repairs and improvements.[22]

Postwar master planners have proposed not to do away with the ineffective regulatory apparatus for conservation but to strengthen it by providing an environment in which serious regulation is feasible. They have also introduced new forms of regulation, such as the previously noted control of building use as well as building type. Previous plans (1909, 1931) zoned the city in terms of building types and restrictions; apart from the provisions of the health code, there were no restrictions on building use except those imposed and implied by building type norms. The 1962 plan utilizes use controls *("destinazioni d'uso")* as one of the chief means of protecting the historic center and promoting decentralization. Thus within Zone A, the historic center, no new public offices, new private offices employing more than one hundred people, large department stores, or large hotels (with over 200-guest capacity) may be built or installed. Permitted uses in the center include offices for top corporate management, professional offices, newspaper editorial offices (but not printing plants), retail stores and artisan workshops, theaters and movie houses, restaurants, tourist and travel agencies, museums and cultural institutions, and the like. The ban on public offices employing or dealing with large numbers of people (excluding local field offices) extends to all other parts of the city except for the three new directive centers.[23]

In its ruling on the master plan, the national government (actually, the Council of State in this case) insisted that the use restrictions of the Rome master plan could not be made retroactive without expropriation.[24] Use controls can be applied, therefore, only to new structures, unless the city is willing and able to use its powers of eminent domain. Existing traffic generators in the

22. On the weakness of the superintendent of monuments, see Alfredo Barbacci, *Il guasto della città* (Florence, 1962); Cederna, *Mirabilia Urbis,* passim; and the series in *L'Espresso,* February-March 1970.

23. See the "Technical Implementation Norms" of the Rome Master Plan, as amended, *Urbanistica Romana,* No. 2 (1967); supplement to *Capitolium,* January 1968.

24. The opinion of the Consiglio di Stato on the Rome master plan is contained in *Urbanistica,* May 1966, pp. 131–34.

historic center—the "nonconforming uses"—will accordingly have to be induced to move out from their buildings in the old center into offices to be built
in the new directive centers. The palaces of the president of the republic, the
Chamber of Deputies, the prime minister, the mayor, and ecclesiastical digni-
taries will remain in their existing locations, while the ministries and public
institutions that have not already left will be encouraged to do so.

The introduction of use controls is based on a concept of the historic center
that sees it as continuing to play an important role in the city as the focus of
national leadership and prestige, culture, and tourism—all compatible with and
particularly suited to its unique nature. The center is also seen as performing a
less elegant but equally vital role as a traditional Roman place for living and for
handicrafts production. Planners are concerned to preserve not only old buildings and streets but also something of the social structure that still gives those
buildings and streets vitality.[25]

Police powers will also be used to regulate development and redevelopment
within specific subzones of Zone A to be defined in detailed plans of execution.
In Zone A1, containing buildings of the highest historical or artistic importance,
renovation will be allowed strictly for purposes of health and safety; identical
form, façade, color, volume and even internal structure have to be retained.
Buildings in A2 zones, in themselves less important than those in A1 but forming a characteristic *"ambiente,"* may be renovated, providing that their external
color and appearance are not changed or their total floor space increased. In
A3 districts, buildings may be renovated on a speculative basis, on condition
that the characteristic architecture of the district is preserved, adequate parking
space is provided, and no more than one-third additional floor space is added.
In no building within Zone A can any alterations or additions be made without
authorization of the superintendent of monuments.

One of the major goals of the planners is to encourage the collective rather
than individual renovation of the center. Collective renovation is felt to be more
susceptible to public supervision; in many cases it is also a financial necessity.
Many property owners in the center have little or no incentive to renovate;
unless the costs and benefits of renovation can be shared among a number of
owners, renovation will not be feasible. The planners hope to formulate a general
"frame plan" *(piano quadro)* for the historic district—on a scale between that
of the master plan (1:10,000) and that of detailed plans of execution (1:200,
1:500).[26] The *piano quadro* will identify the subzones within the district, following a careful survey and inventory of the district, and will provide the overall
framework for the definition of homogeneous renovation districts *(comprensori)*
for each of which a detailed plan will be designed. The detailed plan will show

25. Sergio Bonamico et al., "Studio metodologico propedeutico ad un restauro conservativo
nel Centro Storico," *Capitolium,* September-October 1966, pp. 5–38.
26. See *Urbanistica romana,* No. 3 (1966), for the initial attempts at a framework plan for the
historic center.

exactly what is to be preserved, what is to be removed as a superfetation, and exactly what changes are to be made. Within each renovation district, a consortium of property owners will be constituted and required to carry out the rehabilitation specified in the detailed plan. Failure to carry out the project will make their properties subject to the city's power of eminent domain. It is hoped that the public housing agencies can be induced to join rehabilitation consortia so as to provide subsidized housing for low income groups and also experienced and responsible project management.

In 1967, the city appointed a special subcommittee of the Building Commission, the Advisory Committee for the Old Rioni, to examine and advise city officials on permit applications, detailed plans, and general studies of the historic center. The advisory committee includes representatives of city and national agencies, the university, private planning groups, and the press, but in characteristic corporatist fashion it includes no representatives of the people who live, work, or own property in the old rioni.

Measures to relieve traffic congestion in the historic center are also planned and have, in part, been carried out.[27] Major relief for congestion will come only when the new directive centers and communication axis are built in the east and the subway system is functioning. Until then measures taken can only be stop-gap palliatives, with marginal effect. Against almost universal resistance, the city has banned parking in sections of the old center during certain periods of the day. It has begun, again despite resistance, to create "pedestrian islands" in some of the most famous piazzas, which have thus been reconverted from parking lots to oases of safety and quiet. Eventually a system of pedestrian paths will be created, permitting one to cross the historic district on foot with only minimal threat to life and limb from Roman motorists.

The major techniques, then, for saving and enhancing the quality of old Rome include decentralization, a new subway system, more effective regulation, and "conservative rehabilitation." None of these techniques promises to be easy to use or necessarily effective in securing the desired goal. Critics of the plan might even argue that there is a contradiction among techniques. For example, decentralization of activities from the historic center may damage its vitality, just as strict regulation of building may discourage rather than stimulate much needed renovation. It will certainly be difficult for the city, given the administrative apparatus at its disposal, to see that regulatory controls prevent only unwanted development and do not stifle desired improvements.

The task of adjusting regulatory policies and decisions to specific situations will not be easy. The little research that has been done on the historic center suggests the existence there of an enormous variety of situations, problems, and actors.[28] A pilot study of one block near the Pantheon, involving some fourteen

27. "Il Traffico a Roma"; Antonio Pala, "I problemi del traffico di una grande città," *L'Impresa Pubblica,* May 1967, pp. 24–32.
28. Bonamico, "Studio metodologico."

buildings, found structural elements ranging from portions of Nero's Baths to a 1937 bank building with, in between, elements from the thirteenth to the nineteenth centuries. Some of the buildings were in excellent shape, others required structural repairs. Some were primarily residential, others commercial. Some were owned by individuals, some by co-owners, some by public institutions, and some by private corporations. Some owners had incomes below $1,600 per annum, while others were well-off families or institutions. Among the various owners, investigators found widely divergent perspectives on the desirability of renovation. A voluntary consortium of owners for renovation seemed out of the question.

Major success with renovation—at least as a public program, rather than a series of disconnected, individual, sometimes unfortunate episodes—cannot really be expected under current legislative and financial conditions. As will be seen, much of the ineffectiveness of Roman planning derives from the lack of new national legislation in the field.[29] This is particularly true for conservation. A series of new urban planning bills has been proposed since 1960, but no general reform has been passed.[30] These bills have all contained provisions on the conservation of historic centers that would have been extremely helpful to the planners in Rome. The new laws would have given the city authority to form compulsory renovation consortia, with the consent of owners representing 60 percent of total property values. Renovation consortia so formed would expropriate all the properties within the renovation district for purposes of land reassembly. Each former owner would retain an option to purchase back a proportionate share of the renovated property.

New legislation would also have created programs to make renovation financially possible and attractive to private investors. In Italy today there are no programs of grants, loans, or tax credits to assist and encourage renovation, whether public or private. One of the reasons that such a program does not exist (except in the case of special laws for Venice and for the Southern Development Fund area) is that the problem of financing the conservation of Italian historic centers seems simply too overwhelming to tackle. But without some kind of program creating private incentives and public means for renovation, the conservationist goals are bound to be poorly achieved.

Even with national financing, however, renovation projects will be extremely difficult to do well. The pilot renovation project in Rome at Tor di Nona, along the Tiber, which was begun in 1954, has been an outstanding but perhaps instructive failure.[31] The city government is only slowly developing the ad-

29. See chap. 7.
30. Domenico Rodella, "La legge ponte urbanistica e la conservazione ambientale," *Città e Società,* October-December 1967, pp. 14–21. See more generally: Fiorentino Sullo, *Lo scandalo urbanistico: storia di un progetto di legge* (Florence, 1964); Francesco Forte, *La strategia delle riforme* (Milan, 1968), chap. 10; Giuseppe Campos Venuti, *Amministrare l'urbanistica* (Turin, 1967); and Astengo, "Le nostre tigri di carta."
31. Cederna, *Mirabilia Urbis,* pp. 136–60, 232–35.

ministrative capabilities that will enable it to use wisely the legal and financial
resources it already possesses and those it may eventually be given by the national government.

BUILDING A NEW ROME IN THE EAST

The crux of the plan to save the old center and improve the quality of urban
growth is the proposal to build and organize a new polycentric city to the east
and south of the existing city. This is to be accomplished by the building of an
impressive communication belt, the *Asse Attrezzato* or eastern axis, running
in a north-south direction about two and a half miles east of Termini railway
station, and the building of a series of new city and regional business centers
located along the axis.[32] The axis will serve several functions: it will allow national and interregional traffic to pass through the city without having to cross
the old center. It will tie together the two ends of the *Autostrada del Sole,* the
major nationwide expressway built in 1964 between Milan and Naples. It will
also link a number of the consular roads coming into the city from the various
parts of the surrounding region. It will be the major highway for traffic within
the city, joining together the southern and northeastern sections where 70 percent of future city growth is expected to take place. It will form the spine
supporting and connecting the new regional and urban administrative-commercial centers and will run some six miles between the existing center at EUR
to the still unbuilt centers at Centocelle and Pietralata. Separate roadways will
be established for each of these purposes, in descending order of anticipated
speed: roadways for high-speed national traffic; roadways for rapid intracity
traffic; and a system of local arteries to serve the directive centers and new
residential districts. Altogether the axis will be about thirteen one-half miles
long from where it meets the Autostrada del Sole, north of Pietralata, to the
point south of EUR where it meets Via Cristoforo Colombo. En route it will
pass through a tunnel beneath the Old Appian Way.

The system of directive centers is to include some 2,750 acres of land, including the 250 acres already built at EUR, with over 46 million cubic meters of
space. It will have some 540,000 rooms, about the number to be found in cities
like Florence, Bologna, or Athens.[33] Two-thirds of the space will be used for
offices, the rest for residences housing a population of 225,000 people. The new
system of centers is designed to perform five key functions:

  1. lighten the commercial and administrative pressure on the historic center

32. *Roma Oggi,* December 1968, p. 3; *Urbanistica Romana,* Nos. 2, 3, 4 (1968) *(Capitolium,*
September-October 1968); *Il Messaggero,* October 14, 25, December 18, 1966; January 1, 1967.
See also Carlo Aymonimo et all., *La città territorio: un esperimento didattico sul Centro direzionale di Centocelle in Roma* (Bari, 1964).
33. Edoardo Salzano, "Sull'asse attrezatto e i centri direzionali di Roma," *Città e Società,*
July-August 1969, pp. 102–08. See also Paolo Luzzi and Camilla Nucci, "Il sistema a Roma:
un dibattito ancora aperto," in ibid., March-April 1969, pp. 74–92.

2. provide attractive and functional new quarters for public offices, corporations, banks, department stores, hotels, major public facilities
3. raise the tone and amenity of the eastern sections of the city
4. encourage and organize new residential expansion of the city toward the
east and the south
5. promote the development of more polynucleated development within the
Lazio region in contrast to the monocentric tendencies of the past

Use restrictions will force institutions that wish to expand and those wishing
to locate in Rome to establish themselves in the new centers. Such relocation
will be positively stimulated by the attractiveness and convenience of the new
districts as compared to the congestion and inconvenience of sites now available. The new districts will have excellent parking facilities, transportation
connections (the axis and the new subway system), and attractive residential
possibilities.

Creation of the axis and the eastern centers has become the dominant issue in
Roman politics. Since 1962, every new mayor and every new Center-Left giunta
taking office has made creation of these projects a top-priority item, but without
concrete results. Frustration over lack of achievement has become an acute
source of tension within the ruling coalition. Left-wing Christian Democrats,
Republicans, and Socialists brought down the Center-Left coalition in March
1969 on the axis issue and almost did so again in November. Frustration over
the inability to make progress in this area led the Socialist vice-mayor of the
city, in August and again in December 1969, to propose enlargement of the
coalition to include the Communists. Conflict, tension, and delay are not surprising, given the scope of the proposed projects.

The key issues concern financing and control. The cost of the projects has been
estimated at over 1.6 billion dollars.[34] This would include the cost of land for the
axis and centers; the cost of building the axis; and the cost of providing basic
utilities and community facilities (schools, markets, city field offices, and parks)
for the new centers. A private corporation offered to spend two hundred million
dollars on the axis alone in return for the right to charge tolls, but its offer was
rejected because it is generally agreed that the axis and the centers from a single
project to be planned and built in unitary fashion. It is also generally agreed
that the project must be self-financing. The plan is for $800 million to come
from ministries and public agencies buying office space in the centers, with the
remaining cost to be financed by the sale of land and/or building rights to
private corporations and developers. The Socialists and Communists want the
city to sell not the land but only building rights within the centers, so as to prevent speculation, while the non-Marxist parties have expressed doubts as
to whether private interests would be willing to invest in the centers without
the traditional complete rights in land and buildings. The Republicans (a left-

34. Giulio Tirincanti, *Il Messaggero*, November 30, 1969.

of-center party), for example, wondered how the project could be self-financing
if the city did not sell the land it had taken by compulsory purchase. In the
summer of 1969 they withdrew from the governing coalition, disagreeing with
the compromise solution arrived at by the other parties concerning building
rights in the directive centers.[35]

Problems of financing spill over into problems of control. Because of the
immense cost of the project, there has been some support for turning the entire
matter over to a national public corporation to be controlled by the Istituto per
la Ricostruzione Industriale (IRI), the national industrial holding company. In
June 1968 the Interministerial Committee for Economic Planning, the cabinet
committee with responsibility for formulating national economic policy,
invited the city to turn to IRI for help in planning, financing, and executing the
project. Political forces in the city, especially those left of center, have reacted
very negatively to the prospect of losing control over the most important
planning operation in the city's history to an autonomous public corporation
responsible only to the national government. Leftists in particular see this
proposal as part of a general conservative strategy of using the admitted inefficiency of traditional ministries and local governments as pretext for turning vital
national programs, involving such sectors as the railways, ports, and highways,
over to autonomous IRI corporations controlled by conservative technocrats.
While there is general interparty agreement that some parts of the operation
must be turned over to semiautonomous authorities, there is considerable
disagreement over how much control should remain in city hands. The Communists would allow an IRI corporation to handle all the lower-level construction
operations, reserving to the city council or to an agency directly responsible to
the council, the right to formulate the project design, manage land transactions,
and exercise general supervisory authority. The national government, which
has agreed to help finance and support the project, is not, however, likely to
agree to delegate exclusive control over the project to the city. The issue will be
decided not by the city but by Parliament, which, in granting financial and
statutory backing for the operation, will undoubtedly insist on a 51 percent
controlling interest for the national government. By proposing such a major
restructuring of the city, the planners made virtually inevitable the surrender to
the national government of control over the city's destiny, insofar as such a
planning operation can affect that destiny.[36]

While the issues are weighty and deserving of long and careful deliberation,
delay is making the project ever more difficult to carry out. National agencies
and private corporations, in the absence of the new centers, have been locating
in semicentral areas all around the historic center. The area available for the
axis and the centers is being eroded by a series of minor transactions in which
particular parcels are given for much needed projects involving hospitals,

35. *Il Messaggero*, January 10, 1970
36. Salzano, "Sull'asse attrezzato."

schools, and housing. The land for the axis and centers is located in the midst
of some of the most densely built-up quarters of the city—quarters badly lacking
in basic facilities. Pressure to use still vacant land for such facilities, rather
than for the unitary design of the new axis and centers, is very strong. One
hundred ninety-two acres, or about 9 percent of the total area of the directive
centers at Pietralata and Centocelle, are already covered by illegally built
structures.[37] Most of the land at the proposed center at Centocelle comes from
the former military airport there, now controlled by the *Demanio dello Stato* in
the Ministry of Finance. That agency has parceled out ninety-four hectares to
the National Research Council, the Engineering School of the University of
Rome, the Air Force Ministry, and the Ministry of Transport. Meanwhile
neither the prime minister's office nor the Ministry of Public Works has been
able to help the city in discovering the future building plans and requirements
of the national ministries and agencies. Since 1870 there has been no coordination among the ministries with respect to their real estate activities and it is
difficult one hundred years later for anyone, especially a local-level authority,
to break down their longstanding habits of individual entrepreneurship. Successful implementation of the decentralization scheme requires, however, that
the city accomplish this minor revolution in the standard operating procedures
of national agencies.

### ESTABLISHING CONTROL

No less challenging to the modest capabilities of the city than conservation
of the historic center and creation of the eastern linear center is the goal of
establishing a measure of public control over the development process. One of
the prime purposes of the master planning operation has been to lay down
guidelines for all actors in the development and redevelopment process. The
professional planning movement has sought to establish not only public control,
but detailed, stringent, and precise public control— in sharp contrast to the
virtual lack of actual control obtaining during the postwar period.

Precise controls over development are considered essential for at least three
reasons. First of all, they are needed to implement the policy of selective expansion, which in turn is a vital aspect of the program to save the historic center by
building the eastern linear center. Breaking the existing combination of scattered
and oil-stain development in favor of clustered decentralization and a development thrust toward the south and the east requires that the city be able to
determine what can and cannot be built in every part of the city territory. The
compromise "40-30-15-15" percentage formula for expansion in specified
areas will work only if the city can, in fact, enforce it. The planners want this
formula enforced on a year-to-year basis, irrespective of market or other condi-

37. Piero Samperi, "Per un avvio degli studi sul sistema direzionale all'est di Roma," *Urbanistica Romana,* Nos. 2, 3, 4 (1968), p. 10.

tions. The city is expected to observe the terms of this formula when, from time to time, it approves private subdivision permits and low-cost housing projects.

Precise controls over development are also sought in order to improve the quality of new residential districts, most of which have hitherto lacked adequate or even essential services and facilities. Tight controls are designed to make sure that developments are not built and occupied before they are properly provided with sewers, utilities, schools, markets, and access to employment. New residential districts in Rome are to have carefully limited densities and a proportionate, ensured level of facilities; they are to be separated from existing and other new districts by parks and open space. Higher facility standards will be more feasible in the new districts since the city will be able to allocate its limited funds for capital investment in accordance with predetermined expansion programs. Close control over development is essential in order to reduce the costs of urbanization and thus permit the city to provide the needed facilities. Controls will be used to encourage large-scale development operations in preference to less easily regulated, more expensive to service, lot-by-lot development. Hopefully, requiring development on a larger scale will encourage industrialization of the building industry and thus reduce housing costs.

Finally, precise controls are necessary in order to save the archeological treasures and traditional scenic appearance of the Roman countryside.

Implementation of these controls would be an ambitious task in any city; it is especially ambitious in Rome, where the controls run so contrary to public mores and private interests. Given these mores and interests, the stronger the intended controls and the higher the standards prescribed, the greater become the incentive and necessity to evade. Stronger regulation of the legal market in land and housing seems merely to drive a larger share of land and building transactions into the extremely flourishing black market. Even in countries with stronger civic spirit and more respected, competent, and disciplined administrative services, such heavy reliance on the use of police powers to achieve land use goals would probably not be considered wise or even equitable. Even in such countries, it would probably be thought both prudent and fair to compensate those who stood to lose by the outcome of the planning process. In Rome, whose inhabitants admittedly lack much spirit of sacrifice for the public weal and who have, with some reason, little respect for the impartiality, fairness, and wisdom of public policy decisions, such heavy reliance on police powers seems, on the basis of historical precedent, to be doomed to failure.

Planners have relied so heavily on police powers at least partly because the legal and financial means of reducing resistance to their choices have simply not been available to them. Italian planning law does not permit cities to compensate those damaged by municipal zoning ordinances. Even if it did, Italian cities would lack the financial ability, had they the will, to make the results of their zoning choices more legitimate and palatable through compensation. As the chronology in the Appendix shows, however, Italian courts in recent years have become extremely disturbed by the apparently confiscatory nature of planning laws, regulations, and decisions. The courts have begun a general campaign against the use for planning purposes of police powers in ways that infringe upon constitutional guarantees of private property rights and constitutional requirements of just compensation.[38] Thus the police powers have become less available for use by planners, while at the same time, the national government has not acted to make it financially possible for city governments to secure planning goals by paying for them. City planners in Italy have thus found themselves without the stick of police powers or the carrot of compensation.

Elements in the Italian planning movement have also tended to rely heavily on police powers because of a generally hostile attitude toward private property and private enterprise in land and housing. Moral outrage at the results of speculative land and building practices has made the imposition of detailed and strict controls, without compensation, something of a punitive action against private entrepreneurs. The latter, in turn, have responded by denouncing the legitimacy of the planning process and by attempting to sabotage it. There has been little common ground between the planning movement and the real estate interests. Ironically, the leftist city planners of INU, in their hostility to private interests, have tended to propose planning instruments, such as the master plan of 1962, that rely heavily on administrative regulations for success. Yet, at the same time, leftist planners have little or no respect for the integrity, competence, or independence of existing city planning departments. This has been a general dilemma of the Italian Left: that its programs, involving massive intervention by public authorities, must depend for their execution on existing bureaucratic agencies in which the Left has little confidence and over which it has had little control.

In order to channel city growth into a decentralized network of carefully designed, well-serviced new residential centers, the planners proposed to ban development in over half the city's territory, zoning some three hundred square miles around the city as farmland. As farmland, the properties involved were worth in 1966 less than $640 an acre, while neighboring properties, zoned for residential development, were worth between $140,000 and $200,000 an acre. Marks on the master plan can ensure the fortune of some property owners and the despair of their neighbors.[39] The resistance of the Union of Roman Farmowners, the Rome Small Farmers Federation, and the Provincial Agrarian Inspector (Ministry of Agriculture) to low-density zoning is understandable.

38. Campos-Venuti, *Amministrare l'urbanistica*, pp. 209–71.
39. Enrico Sermonti, "Contributo della conoscenza dell'agricoltura nella scelta della localizzazione delle aree a bosco e a parco in Agro romano, "*Urbanistica*, May 1966, p. 117. Both major farm groups, the small-holders in the *Coltivatori Diretti* and the large landowners in the Provincial Agrarian Union, aided by the Ministry of Agriculture's provincial agrarian inspector, fought the restrictions on rural development proposed by the CET plan, the 1959 giunta plan, and the 1962 plan. The *Coltivatori Diretti*, who regularly elected their leader to the DC delegation on the council, where he in turn was regularly elected a member of the giunta, were a

There has also been resistance to the principle of selective expansion from other quarters: from property owners in unbuilt or partially built districts within the 1931 master plan perimeter, who would not be permitted to develop their properties; public housing agencies, which are reluctant to surrender the right to choose the location of their projects; city departments, such as public works, traffic, water and power, and the bus companies, equally reluctant to subordinate their sectorial planning to the dictates of master planners; small private building contractors, who rightly fear bankruptcy if the city insists on large-scale development and discourages lot-by-lot development; and private contractors generally, fearful of the impact on production costs of stricter city building standards and subdivision requirements.

In the end, the planners have secured acceptance of the principle of selective expansion by making the proposed expansion less selective. A large number of special, luxury-housing districts (G4 districts) have been zoned across the Roman countryside in order to increase the development rights available to the owners of rural acreage. A high rate of future population growth has been assumed as the basis for the plan; this permits a large number of regular residential districts to be planned and thus more properties to be developed. The exclusive emphasis on eastern development desired by the INU planners has been sharply modified to permit great emphasis on southwestern expansion and some degree of northern and western expansion; thus properties in districts all around the city will be valuable. Those property owners disappointed by the general zoning choices made in the master plan have been given some hope of better luck in the future when the detailed plans to execute the master plan are drafted and decisions regarding specific properties are made.

Acceptance of the idea of selective expansion and low density zoning for much of the city has been made possible also by the near certainty that the city government will be unable and/or unwilling to enforce its zoning decisions very strictly. Presumably, it is easier to accept the adverse decisions of the master plan if one knows that the city will, in practice, be neither willing nor able to stop illegal development. Before, during, and since the adoption of the master plan, subdividers and builders have had little difficulty in evading provisions of building and zoning ordinances that restrict their freedom of action. It is quite probable that the master plan, with its Draconian choices, may remain, in practice, a paper tiger.

---

powerful force in city politics, both because of their electoral weight and their financial importance to the DC party. Nonetheless, they were unable to block restrictive norms in the new master plan eventually adopted and promulgated. But since the city has no capability for enforcing the restrictions contained in the new plan, the farmers have, in effect, lost the battle only to win the war. On this, see *Il Messaggero,* February 1, 1960; *Il Popolo,* February 3, 1964; *Il Giornale d'Italia,* March 20, 1958.

# 4

# ROMAN

# SOCIETY

# AND CULTURE

One of the curious legacies of history is Rome's unique status among cities in Italy and in the world. It is at once uniquely important and uniquely unimportant—uniquely important as the capital of Roman Catholicism, a symbol of the origins of Western civilization, and the capital of a major nation state; and uniquely unimportant as a "primate city" within Italy. Rome was lowest in a recent ranking of the largest cities of 104 countries according to their demographic primacy. Defining primacy as the percentage of the population of the four largest cities in a country that is contained by the largest one, Rome has less primacy than any other city in the world. The Rome metropolitan area in 1955 had only 32 percent of the combined populations of the Rome, Milan, Turin, and Naples metropolitan areas. Paris has 74.7 percent; London has 60.3 percent; and Copenhagen, 76.2 percent.[1]

In 1870, when it became the national capital, Rome had only 0.8 percent of the national population; it reached one percent in 1885; 2 percent in 1927; 3 percent in 1940; and 4 percent in 1961.[2] In 1870 Rome was the third largest Italian city, after Naples and Milan. It became the largest city in Italy only in 1936. As a metropolitan area Rome is still second to Milan, which is also the leading commercial and industrial city of the peninsula. Milan province, with 6.6 percent of national population, produces 16 percent of the national industrial product, 14.5 percent of the national commercial product, and 11.5 percent of total gross national product. The province of Turin, with 3.8 percent of the population, produces 9.5 percent of the national industrial product. Rome province, with 6 percent of the national population, produces only 4.6 percent of

---

1. Norton Ginsburg, *Atlas of Economic Development* (Chicago, 1964), p. 36.
2. "Popolazione e territorio," pp. 21–22.

the national industrial product, following Turin.[3] Rome is the second most important Italian commercial center, accounting for 8 percent of gross national commercial income, but it has a much smaller percentage of its working force in industry (32 percent) than any other large Italian city: Turin leads with 61 percent; it is followed by Milan with 50 percent; Genoa, with 43 percent; Bologna, with 45 percent; Florence, with 40 percent; Naples, with 39 percent; Bari, with 42 percent; and Palermo, with 36 percent. This is due not so much to the absolute lack of industry as to the unusually large public administration sector (22 percent) in the city.[4]

If Rome is not the leading industrial or commercial city in Italy, neither is it the wealthiest, as measured by per capita income. Its relative position is shown in Table 4.1.

Table 4.1. Per Capita Provincial Income, 1965

| Milan | 925,670 lire |
|---|---|
| Turin | 834,784 |
| Genoa | 789,964 |
| Rome | 633,983 |
| Naples | 447,979 |
| Palermo | 401,077 |

Source: G. Tagliacarne, "I conti provinciale," Moneta e Credito (1966), p. 303.

Rome province ranks second to Milan province in total income produced, but on a per capita basis it ranks only 20th out of 92 provinces. In a study identifying 260 Italian "economic areas," Rome city was ranked in 150th position in terms of per capita income from the private sector of the economy but 23rd in overall economic development.[5] Rome has thus had to confront the consequences of rapid growth with a fragile economic base. This is reflected in the fact that in 1961 Rome led all Italian cities in the number of people (72,203) living in caves, shacks, cellars, and other improper dwellings, and was surpassed only by Reggio Calabria, Messina, Cagliari, and Foggia in the percentage of city population living in such housing.[6]

Rome has never dominated Italian culture. Its university has only recently come to rival that of Milan.[7] Milan still has the leading publishing houses, the editorial staffs of the leading weeklies, and the leading Italian national newspaper (Corriere della Sera). Roman newspapers, while important in central Italy, have never had the national importance of Milan's Corriere della Sera or Turin's La Stampa. The headquarters of Italian state broadcasting were brought to Rome only after World War II. Rome shares with Milan the most important libraries, laboratories, and other research facilities. Only in the field of film-

3. Tagliacarne, "I conti provinciali," pp. 277, 302, 319–21.
4. "Five Year Plan," pp. 37–38.
5. Guglielmo Tagliacarne, ed., 260 aree economiche in Italia (Milan, 1966), p. 116.
6. Calculated from Istat, 10° Censimento generale della popolazione 15 ottobre 1961, vol. 3, Dati sommari per comune, Fascicolo 58, Provincia di Roma, pp. 1–58.
7. Francesco Compagna, La politica della città (Bari,1967), p. 186.

making, an important field to be sure, has Rome established unquestioned primacy in Italy.[8]

In the length and weight of its historical tradition, Rome surpasses other Italian cities by far, but municipal pride and tradition are strong in many other cities, and mixed with recognition of Rome's historical primacy is considerable resentment and hostility toward the city and disesteem for its current institutions and inhabitants. Propaganda on behalf of Rome—so central to Fascist iconology—was in the end counterproductive: forcing all Italian cities, some with pedigrees as old as Rome's, to celebrate the "birthday" of Rome on April 21 was a repeated blow to Italian *municipalismo*. It reinforced an anti-Roman sentiment that continues to plague the city today in its quest for national sympathy, understanding, and financial aid.[9]

"Turin produces, Milan sells, and Rome consumes" is a slogan summing up attitudes toward the capital in most of the peninsula, especially in the North. Latter-day Italian Luthers see Rome as the great bureaucratic parasite, living off the incomes produced in more earnest and industrious centers. To many Italians, Rome is identified with hated institutions: Fascism, the Catholic church, and the state bureaucracy. Such attitudes severely undermine the pretensions of the city to moral primacy over, or even equality with, the other cities of the country.

But if Rome does not enjoy the primacy of a capital city such as Paris, it is still a city of importance. It is the largest Italian city. It is the capital of Italy and the capital of Roman Catholicism. It is the headquarters of the national political parties. It is visited by millions of tourists each year, including a million from foreign countries. Its airport is of major international importance. It has the fastest growing economy of any major Italian city. Between 1951 and 1965, its absolute income rose by 308 percent as compared to 257 percent in Turin, 232 percent in Milan, 214 percent in Genoa, and 235 percent in Italy as a whole.[10] It is a rich consumption market second only to Milan. While private corporations remain predominantly located in the North, Rome is the headquarters of the powerful public corporate enterprises—IRI (Istituto per la Ricostruzione Industriale), ENI (Ente Nazionale Idrocarburi), and ENEL (Ente Nazionale Elettricità). Rome is thus acquiring a measure of control over the Italian econo-

8. Ibid., pp. 171–89.

9. One of the continuing features of the annual *Bibliografia romana* is a section devoted to "Anti-Roma," with references to and extracts from the large number of anti-Rome articles appearing annually in the Italian press. Defense of Rome against outside criticism has united all the parties, from one extreme to the other. Even the Communists have taken up the cudgels on the city's behalf. See, for example, A. Caracciolo, *L'Unità,* April 1, 1954; Comune di Roma, *Decisioni del Consiglio Comunale in ordine all'urbanistica cittadina e al nuovo piano regolatore* (Rome, 1955) (henceforth, "Council Debates, 1953–54"), pp. 214–46 (unanimous approval of a resolution "of protest against the denigrators of the city and against the stupid insinuations about its status as an 'over-luxurious capital', maintained at the expense of an overly poor country"); and *Il Paese,* March 9, 1954.

10. Tagliacarne, "I conti provinciali," p. 305.

my, although Milan is likely to remain the principal center of management and operations for a long time to come. Symptomatically, trading on the Rome stock exchange reaches only one-sixth the volume of trading in the Milanese exchange.[11] Even so, Rome's importance in all spheres of Italian life has been increasing rather than decreasing, and it is likely to continue growing—even following execution of the scheme to decentralize Italian government to the regions.

Rome lies astride the major north-south transportation routes and has siphoned off much of the huge postwar migration of peasants from the under-developed regions of the South to the industrialized regions of the North. As Table 4.2 shows, a large and growing proportion of net migration to Rome in the sixties has come from the South and the islands, as well as the depressed rural areas of south-central Italy, which resemble the South in their under-development.

Table 4.2. Net Migration to Rome from Various Parts of Italy, 1961–1967
(Percentages)

|  | 1961 | 1964 | 1967 | Total |
|---|---|---|---|---|
| Lazio | 25.5 | 19.9 | 13.8 | 21.2 |
| North[a] | 12.3 | 9.7 | 9.8 | 9.0 |
| Center[b] | 16.6 | 15.9 | 15.5 | 15.6 |
| South and Islands[c] | 38.3 | 45.7 | 49.7 | 44.6 |
| Total net migration | 100.0 | 100.0 | 100.0 | 100.0 |

Source: Comune di Roma, Notiziario Statistico Mensile (May 1968), p.11.
a. 8 regions
b. 3 regions, excluding Lazio
c. 8 regions

Great efforts have been made to improve economic conditions in the South. Southern per capita income rose from 59.5 percent of the national average in 1951 to 64 percent of the national average in 1966; it increased at the same rate (4.6 percent per year) in the South as in Italy as a whole. But the South, with 36 percent of the population, still received in 1966 only 23 percent of total national personal income. Through government action the position of the South is improving, but not fast enough to slow down northward migration.[12] Rome has been a way-station for southern migrants who, even if initially attracted by northern employment opportunities, remain in Rome and bring in their families, relations, and neighbors. Rome has become the center for the collection of the excess population of the vast surrounding areas of depression.[13]

What are the consequences of this mixed picture for Roman planning? The national and international importance of the city has meant that efforts to

11. Compagna, La politica della città, p. 183.
12. Alberto Campolongo, "Sul divario del Mezzogiorno," Studi economici, January-April 1968, pp. 1–6.
13. Nicola Signorello, "La migrazione a Roma," Studi Romani, July-September 1965, pp. 328–45.

regulate and shape existing and new land uses in the city have enlisted the aid of highly competent professional planners, of whom there are a large number in the city. The city's planning problems have attracted the attention of some of the most qualified planners in Italy. The importance of the city has helped to strengthen the movement to save the historic center as an economic and cultural asset.

On the other hand, the importance of the capital, its relative visibility, the attention paid to its affairs by the mass media, both Italian and foreign, and the constant flow of travelers from other parts of Italy and the world have had negative consequences for planning. The stakes have been higher because the results of failure are too visible to too many people. The prominence of the city and its importance to the national government and to the church make city officials rather hesitant to take strong innovative steps, especially when no one is sure exactly what is at stake. Then, too, anti-Roman sentiment has made it difficult for city officials to secure special legislative, administrative, or financial consideration from national government officials. Other parts of the country have only grudgingly accepted the idea that, as national capital, Rome requires special treatment and consideration. The city government, upon which has fallen the major burden of planning, has been at a great disadvantage in attempting to deal with and regulate the prestigious and autonomous institutions of the church, the national government, and foreign governments. The prestige of the city government itself has not been enhanced by its financial distress and its inability to meet the service expectations of national and international observers. Also, with so many elites attentive to its affairs, city leaders may have had a rather more difficult time working out the deals and compromises inherent in the planning process.

### ROME AND ITS REGION

Rome is the capital of Lazio region, a set of five provinces lying physically and economically between the poor regions of the Italian South and the richer regions of the North. (See Figure 4.1.) Much of Lazio resembles the under-developed South, just as many of Rome's social and economic patterns are those of southern rather than northern cities. Lazio is the legal jurisdiction for the regional government, which was first elected in 1970. It is about 150 miles long and 35 miles wide, lying between the Mediterranean coast and the central Apennines. Though only one of the 371 communes in Lazio region, Rome city in 1966 had 58 percent of the entire regional population. Table 4.3 gives some idea of the domination of the region by its capital city.

While Rome province's per capita income in 1965 was 633,983 lire, the average in Italy as a whole was 533,756. The average for all north-central provinces was 633,044 lire, while the average for all southern provinces was 359,173 lire. The table makes clear that the provinces of Lazio outside Rome lay at

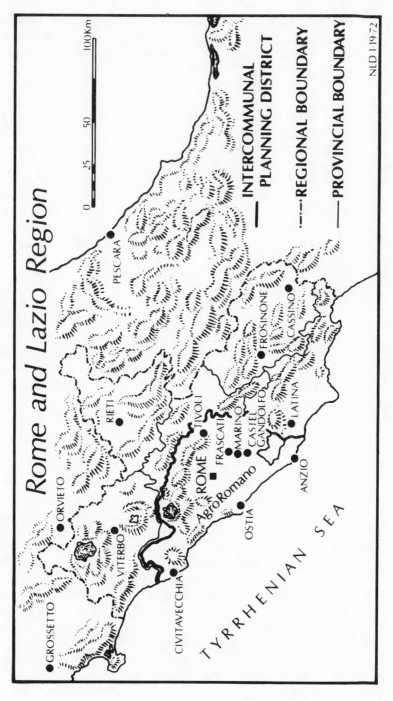

Figure 4.1

Table 4.3. Rome in Lazio Region, 1961

| Province | Provincial capital population | Total provincial population | Area in square kms. | Number of communes | Per capita income, 1965 |
|---|---|---|---|---|---|
| Frosinone | 31,155 | 438,254 | 3,240 | 91 | 316,823 lire |
| Latina | 49,331 | 319,056 | 2,250 | 33 | 440,865 |
| Rieti | 35,441 | 162,405 | 2,749 | 73 | 375,939 |
| Rome | 2,188,160 | 2,775,380 | 5,352 | 114 | 633,983 |
| Viterbo | 50,047 | 263,862 | 3,612 | 60 | 404,577 |
| Lazio | — | Regional total: 3,958,957 | Regional total: 17,203 | Regional total: 371 | Regional average: 563,352 |

*Source: Annuario Statistico Italiano 1967,* p. 11; G. Tagliacarne, "I conti provinciali," *Moneta e Credito* (September 1966), p. 289.

southern levels of development, while Rome province was at the northern level of economic development.[14] Apart from Rome, Lazio region actually lost population during the period 1951–65, with a negative net migration of 113,000 people. During this period Rome gained a net migration of 552,600 people.[15] The poverty of much of the Lazio region has been officially recognized: two provinces, Latina and Frosinone, and part of two others, Rome and Rieti, have been placed within the jurisdiction of the *Cassa per il Mezzogiorno* or Southern Development Fund. Sections of northern Lazio have been placed under the provisions of the 1966 Act for the Depressed Areas of Central and Northern Italy. Outside of Rome the only developed areas lie along the coast, around the port of Civitavecchia, in the Ente Maremma land reclamation zones, the beach communities, and the burgeoning industrial towns, such as Latina and Pomezia, to the south of Rome on the site of the reclaimed Pontine marshes. With these exceptions, the region around the city consists of depressed mountain and hill towns and stretches of abandoned farms.

Rome has been caught in the vise of four mass migrations: from the mountains to the plains; from the rural areas to the cities; from the South to the North; and from agriculture to industry and commerce.

As Tables 4.4 and 4.5 bring out, there was a massive exodus from the mountain and hill zones of Lazio after 1951 and most people seem to have gone to Rome. The area around Rome has never been heavily populated; it is tending to become even less so. Lazio has always been a poor market for Rome's goods and services and at the same time the major source of the city's demographic pressure. In recent years, however, the regions of the South have begun to displace Lazio as the principal sources of migrants to Rome.

Rome has an even more dominant position within Rome province. It is only one of 114 communes within the province, but in 1961 it had 70 percent of the province's population and 26 percent of its territory. The next largest commune

14. "Five Year Plan," p. 21.
15. Comitato Regionale per la Programmazione Economica del Lazio, *Schema generale del piano di studi e ricerche* (Rome, 1966), p. 13.

Table 4.4. Population Redistribution in Lazio by Altitude Zones,1951–1965
(Percentages)

|           | 1951  | 1965  |
|-----------|-------|-------|
| Plains    | 54.6  | 63.6  |
| Hills     | 34.8  | 29.3  |
| Mountains | 10.6  | 7.1   |
|           | 100.0 | 100.0 |

Source: "Un programma quinquennale per Roma," Capitolium, May-June 1967, p. 20.

Table 4.5. Population Redistribution within Lazio, 1951–1965
(Percentages)

|                           | 1951  | 1965  |
|---------------------------|-------|-------|
| Rome                      | 49.4  | 57.7  |
| Other provincial capitals | 4.1   | 4.2   |
| Other communes            | 46.5  | 38.1  |
|                           | 100.0 | 100.0 |

Source: "Un programma quinquennale," p. 20.

in Rome province is the port of Civitavecchia, thirty miles to the north, with some 40,000 people. Unlike Milan, which is itself almost completely built up and which merges into a densely developed network of cities and towns, constituting a genuine conurbation, Rome has hundreds of square miles of undeveloped city territory and is surrounded by sparsely populated communities. Rome does not have an important metropolitan area, consisting of heavily populated, economically integrated communities separated by legal boundaries.[16] The lack of a metropolitan hinterland has resulted, in part, from the vastness of the city's territory—602 square miles. Rome did not achieve this size, which makes it one of the largest cities in the world, through annexation. Indeed, when it was incorporated into the Italian state in 1870 it was even larger, with some 850 square miles, running fifty miles along the coast. It lost 250 square miles of territory when separate communes were carved out for Civitavecchia and for the towns in the reclaimed Pontine marshes.[17]

Despite rapid postwar growth the city still occupies little more than one-tenth of its legal territory. Unlike Milan and Turin, where rapid growth and attendant problems were forced into surrounding communes, Rome absorbed most of the problems and the growth within its own boundaries. The movement to suburbia that occurred in Rome took place within city boundaries, rather than spilling into neighboring communes. Within the city boundaries lies a large part of the Campagna Romana, a vast undulating plain limited by the Sabatine mountains in the northwest, about fifteen miles from the city; the Tiburtine and Prenestine mountains in the east, also about fifteen miles from the city center; the Lazio hills and Alban mountains to the southeast, about

16. Alberto Aquarone, Grandi città e aree metropolitane in Italia: Problemi amministrativi e prospettive di riforma (Bologna, 1961), chap. 8; Stefano Garano, "I problemi della ristrutturazione della periferia di Roma," Città e Società, May-June 1970, pp. 89–100.
17. "Popolazione e territorio," facing p. 54.

ten miles from the center; and by the Tyrrhenian Sea on the west, about thirteen miles from city hall.[18] Until recent decades, malaria kept most of the Campagna Romana as a kind of broad, desolate green belt around the city. Even today, 84 percent of the city's population lives concentrated in only 12 percent of the city's territory—some seventy square miles in and around the old city.[19] Sheep from the surrounding Campagna still pasture in and near the fringe streets of the built-up city.

The communes with closest relations with Rome are Tivoli toward the east, and, toward the south, Frascati, Marino, Castelgandolfo, and the other fifteen communes of the so-called *Castelli Romani*. Many residents of these towns are commuters who work and study in Rome. Residents of Rome in turn use surrounding towns, especially those of the Castelli Romani, for recreation and summer homes. Commuting traffic is particularly heavy when the Roman building industry is flourishing and can provide jobs for the unskilled workers who prefer to live outside the city. There is a strong tendency for the built-up area of Rome to merge with that of the Castelli Romani to the southeast. Neighboring communes have absorbed part of the migratory pressure on the city, though not as much as have the communes around Milan and Turin; this can be seen in Table 4.6.

This pattern of partial metropolitanization has had important consequences for Roman planning. The fact that there is so much empty space around the city is at once an advantage and a disadvantage. It is an advantage in that the city is free to choose the type, intensity, and direction of expansion, free from the constraints of natural obstacles, sunk costs in existing residences and infrastructures, and rival governing jurisdictions. Open space creates the kind of freedom of maneuver for planners that they do not possess in such cramped cities as Milan, Turin, or Genoa. Also, the vastness of the city makes it a little more difficult for builders to escape the city's planning jurisdiction by locating in suburban communes with less stringent building standards. In contrast, Milan,

Table 4.6. Population Increase, 1951–1961
(Percentages)

| Province | Capital city | Inner-belt communes | Outer-belt communes | Other communes | Provincial average |
|---|---|---|---|---|---|
| Turin | 42.6 | 49.5 | 26.6 | 2.7 | 27.3 |
| Milan | 24.2 | 78.0 | 46.5 | 14.5 | 26.0 |
| Genoa | 13.9 | 2.7 | 2.6 | 2.7 | 11.0 |
| Rome | 32.5 | 36.9 | 10.4 | 6.5 | 29.0 |
| Naples | 17.0 | 24.2 | 18.4 | 40.8 | 16.3 |
| Palermo | 19.8 | 7.3 | 1.7 | –4.1 | 8.8 |

*Source:* Franco Archibugi, "The Growth of Cities in Italy, *"Review of the Economic Conditions in Italy* (January 1965), adapted from p. 56.

18. *Enciclopedia Italiana,* "Roma," *29* (Rome, 1936), 589–93; Roberto Almagià, *Lazio* (Turin, 1966), chap. 12.

19. *Notiziario Statistico Mensile,* July 1968, p. 2.

its small territory almost solidly built-up, has to contend with strong neighbors who compete for industry and building by providing relief from the stringencies of the Milanese master plan. Rome's territory is vast and its neighboring communes, while extremely compliant to builders, are too far away to offer the same convenient escape from its master plan.[20] But, of course, in Rome evasion of building and land use regulation has been quite feasible *within* the city and there has been relatively little need to escape across the city line into friendlier territory.

If open space has been something of an advantage, it has also had some drawbacks. Part of the planning problem in Rome derives precisely from the range of available options. There are no major constraints on expansion in the form of rivers, mountains, canals, or factories; the city can expand in all directions. Nature did not stand in the way of oil-stain development. Since planners so adamantly insisted that the oil-stain pattern be broken once and for all, and be replaced by a pattern of selective expansion, the unlimited range of alternatives became a major hindrance to any political settlement. There was no compelling way of deciding which pattern of selective expansion was most suitable. The pattern of expansion became the single most controversial issue in postwar planning, involving as it did huge financial stakes for those whose land was zoned for development and those whose land was zoned for farming. The principle of selective expansion required an adjustment of competing interests made particularly painful by the size of the stakes and the large number of potential winners and losers.

Partial metropolitanization means that the city can solve some of its problems by itself, without consulting its neighbors. But the city is not really able to ignore its neighbors as completely as that. Long-range prospects of solving the city's problems depend on cooperation, not isolationism. Only more balanced regional and metropolitan development will begin to relieve migratory pressure on the city. Only regional and metropolitan planning and zoning will protect the city's own plan against cutthroat competition from its neighbors and protect the city's interests in preserving the scenic and recreational values available in neighboring localities. Some of the existing and emerging interdependencies between Rome and its neighbors were given official recognition in 1958 when the Ministry of Public Works sponsored the formation of an intercommunal (land use) plan for Rome and forty surrounding communes.[21] An intercommunal plan was formulated in 1960, but it has never been adopted by

20. Marco Romano, "L'esperienza del piano intercomunale milanese," *Urbanistica,* October 1967, p. 24.
21. The text of intercommunal plan discussion and reports is contained in the unpublished volumes entitled, Comune di Roma, Ufficio Speciale Nuovo Piano Regolatore, *Piano Regolatore Intercomunale,* 7 vols. The curiously noncontroversial intercommunal planning process in Rome is analyzed in Giuseppe Campos-Venuti, "Il Piano Intercomunale del comprensorio romano," *Urbanistica,* July 1960, pp. 92–93; in Aquarone, *Grandi città,* and chap. 8; and in Mario Coppa, "La lunga strada per il Piano di Roma," *Urbanistica,* March 1964, pp. 13–15.

any of the forty communes involved, who have preferred to go their own separate ways in regulating and not regulating land use. The Ministry of Public Works has not pressed the issue.

The city's attention has been drawn more recently to the south, to the communes of the Pontine area—Aprilia and Pomezia—where the Southern Development Fund has been successful in stimulating industrialization. In 1962 the Italian Council of Ministers designated a large area to the south of the city, but including about 5,000 acres in the city itself, as an industrial development area under the *Cassa per il Mezzogiorno* jurisdiction. The city has joined twenty-one other communes in forming the Consortium for the Rome-Latina Industrial Area, which is charged with formulating a master plan for industrial development of the entire Pontine plain—some five hundred square miles, with 180,000 people. The 200 factories in the area as of 1961 have become 320, now employing more than 25,000 workers. It is hoped that the Rome-Latina Industrial area will become one of the major economic development poles for the Italian South. Lying between Rome and Naples, it may help not only to provide employment for Romans but to divert migration from the city. Unfortunately, it may also discourage efforts to promote industrialization within the city itself.[22]

A similar effort to promote a more balanced development in Lazio has been made at the regional level by the Union of Lazio Provinces and by the Ministry of the Budget's Regional Economic Planning Committee. Most of the regional development plans proposed, including the regional plan adopted by the Regional Economic Planning Committee for Lazio in July 1969, attempt to check migratory pressures on Rome by stimulating development in northern and eastern Lazio. Here again, Rome is caught between the desire to reduce immigration by promoting industrialization in other centers of the region and the desire to cope with ongoing immigration and natural population increase by promoting industrialization within its own territories.

## ROMAN DEMOGRAPHY

Rome is unusual among Italian cities in having a high rate of growth both from natural increase and from immigration. Southern cities like Naples and Palermo have high rates of natural increase but low rates of migratory increase. The rich cities of the North, on the other hand, have experienced just the opposite pattern of growth. Only Rome, as Table 4.7 shows, has enjoyed (or suffered) both a high natural increase rate and a high migratory increase rate—reflecting once again its hybrid character as both a southern (high natural increase) and a northern (high migratory increase) city.

Migration has been a major cause of the city's growth since 1870, when Rome became the capital of united Italy. Without migration, someone has estimated,

22. *Roma oggi,* April 1967, pp. 1–2.

Table 4.7. Growth Rate by City and Cause, 1951–1961
(Percentage of average annual increase per thousand, 1951–1961)

| Group I | Natural | Migration |
|---|---|---|
| Naples | 15.0 | 0.9 |
| Palermo | 17.1 | 1.6 |
| Catania | 19.2 | 0.5 |
| Bari | 18.7 | –4.1 |
| Messina | 12.1 | 2.5 |
| Group II | | |
| Milan | 4.6 | 18.0 |
| Turin | 3.4 | 33.6 |
| Genoa | –0.4 | 13.5 |
| Florence | 1.2 | 14.4 |
| Bologna | 1.4 | 26.0 |
| Group III | | |
| Rome | 11.0 | 19.2 |
| Venice | 6.1 | 3.3 |
| Trieste | –1.9 | 1.9 |

Source: Adapted from Franco Archibugi, "The Growth of Cities in Italy," p. 47. The table is a corrected version of an apparent misprint in the original, which reversed the columns.

the city's population would today be half a million rather than three million.[23] Migration began with Italian occupation of the city and became heavy during the building boom of the 1880s. After the crash in the building industry in the late 1880s migration tapered off. After World War I, overseas migration outlets were cut off and Italian migrants turned instead toward the large Italian cities. Migration to Rome rose rapidly under the Fascist regime, reaching a peak in 1936 when Rome became the largest Italian city. The flow of people into the cities alarmed the Fascist regime which attempted to check it through anti-urbanization laws.[24] Migration to the cities was henceforth legally possible only by official permit. The anti-urbanization laws, however, were only indifferently enforced, especially in the case of Rome, as the Fascists wanted an appropriately large city to serve as the capital of the new Italian empire. Rome also grew, in spite of the Fascist anti-urbanization laws, because it was relatively difficult to enforce the laws in the larger cities. The anti-urbanization laws remained on the books long after the new constitution guaranteed freedom of movement; they were declared invalid by the Constitutional Court only in 1961. Reduced to very low levels during and after World War II, migration to Rome began to reach the level of the 1930s even before the anti-urbanization laws were abrogated. The legal population of the city, consisting of those duly registered with the city Vital Statistics Office, rose from 1.1 million in 1936 to 1.7 million in 1951 and to 2.2 million in 1961. (See Tables 4.8 and 4.9.)

23. Franco Martinelli, "Contributo allo studio della morfologia sociale della città di Roma," Rivista di Sociologia, January-April 1968, p. 199.
24. Robert Fried, "Urbanization and Italian Politics," Journal of Politics, 30 (August 1967), 505–34.

Table 4.8. Population Growth of Rome, 1871–1961

| Census year | Registered population | Percentage of increase over previous census |
|---|---|---|
| 1871 | 213,633 | — |
| 1881 | 275,637 | 29.9 |
| 1901 | 424,943 | 54.1 |
| 1911 | 522,123 | 22.9 |
| 1921 | 663,848 | 27.1 |
| 1931 | 937,177 | 41.2 |
| 1936 | 1,155,722 | 23.3 |
| 1951 | 1,651,754 | 42.9 |
| 1961 | 2,188,160 | 32.5 |

Source: Comune di Roma, *Bollettino Statistico,* June 1966, p. 7.

Table 4.9. Postwar Population Growth of Rome

| Year | Excess of births over deaths | Excess of registrations over cancellations | Total increase |
|---|---|---|---|
| 1945 | 7,263 | –9,069 | –1,806 |
| 1946 | 15,609 | 39,339 | 54,948 |
| 1947 | 15,089 | 25,259 | 40,348 |
| 1948 | 13,393 | 22,079 | 35,472 |
| 1949 | 12,602 | 10,447 | 23,049 |
| 1950 | 13,531 | 15,449 | 28,980 |
| 1951 | 12,136 | 21,931 | 34,067 |
| 1952 | 13,298 | 15,610 | 28,908 |
| 1953 | 13,555 | 9,357 | 22,912 |
| 1954 | 16,696 | 8,689 | 25,385 |
| 1955 | 17,897 | 20,484 | 38,381 |
| 1956 | 15,762 | 25,650 | 41,412 |
| 1957 | 16,271 | 28,792 | 45,063 |
| 1958 | 18,206 | 27,135 | 45,341 |
| 1959 | 20,268 | 43,208 | 63,476 |
| 1960 | 21,180 | 44,381 | 65,561 |
| 1961* | 25,659 | 104,002 | 129,661 |
| 1962 | 27,070 | 50,339 | 77,409 |
| 1963 | 30,025 | 70,071 | 100,096 |
| 1964 | 34,121 | 42,203 | 76,324 |
| 1965 | 32,305 | 26,564 | 58,869 |
| 1966 | 32,088 | 27,292 | 59,380 |
| 1967 | 29,237 | 27,747 | 56,984 |
| 1968 | 28,488 | 22,650 | 51,138 |

Source: Comune di Roma, *Bollettino Statistico,* April 1966, p. 7; *Notiziario Statistico Mensile,* June 1969, p. 3.
*Increased registrations for the year 1961 are due in part to the abrogation that year of the Fascist laws banning internal migration.

Even after the anti-urbanization laws were abrogated, many of the hundreds of thousands of "illegal," that is, non-registered, inhabitants failed to register, even though this meant they could not vote or be listed at the unemployment exchanges in the city. About hundred thousand people who live in Rome still retain legal residence in other communes. For a long time the city fought abrogation of the anti-urbanization laws, which served as a means of discouraging migration and of refusing assistance to those who came anyway. The city also feared that legalizing the status of hundreds of thousands of *"romani abusivi"* or "illegal Romans" would create a large new mass of Communist voters. Fortunately for the anticommunists, many of the *abusivi* refused to surrender their privacy as nonresidents; thus, despite the registration of 108,000 new voters, the Communist share of the vote actually dropped from 23.1 percent in 1960 to 22.8 percent in 1962.[25]

Migration to Rome occurs primarily because of the sharp differences in economic opportunities and living standards between the South and the North; between the mountains and the plains; between rural towns and cities; and between farming and other occupations.[26] Rome is an oasis of development surrounded by a vast region of underdevelopment and poverty. As in ancient times, Rome is still the major transit point between northern and southern Italy.

But it also has the fascination and glamor of a world-famous city, and thus not all migrants to the city are poor nor do they come always for economic reasons. Many of them are former peasants, tired of farming, who have sold their land and with the proceeds have come to Rome to buy a small store or obtain a post as *portiere* in an apartment house. Migrants account for the plethoric number of and frequent bankruptices among small businessmen in the city. Other migrants to the city are professionals, attracted by the prestige of the city and its ministries, offices, and cultural institutions. It is still common practice for professors in southern Italian universities to live in Rome and commute once a week to their classes in the provinces. A post in Rome is a widely sought goal for most Italian bureaucrats, especially since most of them are central and southern Italians—people who, unlike northerners, tend to find living in Rome attractive.

Most migrants to the city, however, are poor, unskilled, young laborers from the farms and mountain villages of central and southern Italy. Internal migration in Italy tends to be broadly intraregional: most northerners, when they migrate, remain in the North, and most central Italians remain the in Center. Relatively few southerners, however, remain in the South. Migration to Rome has thus consisted largely of people from central and southern Italy.[27] (See above, Table 4.2.)

One of the consequences of heavy migration has been to submerge among newcomers the original Roman population. In the papal census of 1853, 73 percent of the city residents were found to be natives; 17 percent had been born in other provinces; and 9 percent were foreigners. In 1921, the native-born population had dropped to 47 percent; in 1931, to 43 percent; in the 1960s to

25. *L'Unità*, June 6, 1962. Voter registration in Italy, as in most West European countries, is tied to a general system of citizen registration: Italians are required to register with the vital statistics office (*ufficio dello stato civile*) in the commune in which they reside. Perhaps 200,000 Italians, however, reside in Rome while maintaining their legal residence in other communes. There is thus a sizable gap between the city's legal population and its actual population.

26. "Five Year Plan," pp. 40–43.

27. Signorello, "La migrazione a Roma," p. 330.

20 percent.[28] Thus, demographically speaking, Rome is a relatively new city. Heavy migration has created and sustained an intense demand for jobs, business opportunities, land, housing, welfare, and infrastructure. Migration has raised the demand for city services while not providing the city with proportionately larger taxable resources. Most migrants do not earn enough to qualify for payment of the city income tax *(imposta di famiglia)*: the minimum taxable family income was raised in 1963 from $750 to $900. They do have to pay city consumption taxes *(imposte di consumo)*, many of which fall on items of necessity such as food, clothing, and utilities. On the whole, however, migration is one of the factors responsible for the relatively poor performance of the city in providing decent environmental conditions for all of its inhabitants.

Migrants have tended to depress wage levels in the city and to make the building industry extremely crucial for the city's political economy. They have created a huge demand for unskilled jobs—a demand that only the building industry has been able to meet. City officials have been reluctant to regulate building partly because disturbances to that industry might create or aggravate unemployment and social tension within the city. Migrant building workers have been a very unstable social and political force in the city; they have been very difficult to unionize and, especially before 1961, when their status was illegal, very easy to exploit.[29]

Migrants have also posed a major problem in social integration, particularly because of the city's large size, its lack of homogeneous traditions and values, and the scatteration of its settlements. Immigrants account for a disproportionate amount of the city's various forms of social disorganization. On the other hand, the city has done relatively little to facilitate their adjustment—much less than the cities in the North. Most assistance to immigrants has come from the church and the Communist party, rather than the city or the state. Unlike migrants in the United States, migrants to Rome do not create huge welfare burdens for local government mainly because Italian local governments do not provide many welfare services. A 1961 survey by the *Ente Comunale di Assistenza* (ECA) of migrants in Rome found that 54 percent of migrant families had state medical insurance and that most migrant families made heavy use of medical services in the city. Relatively few migrants took advantage of available welfare services, partly from pride, partly from lack of information.[30]

28. Martinelli, "Contributo morfologia," . . . p. 97.
29. "Domenico Sforza" (Marco Cesarini Sforza), *Il Mondo,* April 10, 1962.
30. Carlo Savini, "Fenomenologia delle migrazioni e indagini sociologiche in un inchiesta dell'E.C.A. di Roma," *Rassegna del Lazio,* July-September 1963, pp. 85–90. E.C.A. in Rome, as in other Italian cities, is financed almost entirely by the national government. The Rome E.C.A., however, spends 60 percent of its two million dollar budget on administrative overhead and 10 percent on interest payments; this leaves 30 percent to spend on food, clothing, and shelter for the poor (*Il Messaggero,* November 16, 1966). Most welfare is administered in Rome by private, church-related agencies, of which there are a very large number. Counting the 238 parishes, which play a role in welfare, there are some 588 independently operating welfare agencies in the city, with over one thousand distribution centers. On the ineffectiveness of the

Migrants are commonly blamed for the existence of the *baracche* or shanties that line the major roads into the city. The 1961 survey by the ECA found, however, that only 8 percent of migrant dwellings were *baracche*. Eighty-six percent of migrant families lived in "proper" dwellings. Shantytowns, the survey found, were inhabited mostly by older residents of the city rather than by newcomers. Most immigrants have been able to find housing either in the tenements of the semicentral working class districts or in solid, two-story houses that they themselves have built in illegal subdivisions. Most of these immigrant-built houses have electricity and running water; in most cases they are better than the houses the migrants have left behind in the mountains.

There are significant and not altogether expected differences between migrants' districts near the center and those located in the illegal subdivisions on the urban fringe. Migrants living in the peripheral borgate tend to be much younger, to have smaller families and legitimate family relations; their children are more apt to go to school and receive vocational training. Migrants in the peripheral borgate tend to be more socially integrated than those who face the greater social diversity and conflict of the semicentral proletarian districts. There is greater community cohesion in the peripheral areas because of the relatively greater social and sometimes "ethnic" homogeneity. But psychic support is purchased at the expense of access to city opportunities. Adjustment seems to be more difficult and dissatisfaction greater among migrant families living in the more central districts and among those families living beyond the periphery, far out in the countryside, without any community facilities whatsoever.

Most migrants, according to the same 1961 survey, felt that they had made an improvement in their living standards by coming to Rome. But most were highly suspicious of public authorities and disturbed by the lack of proper facilities in their communities. For their part, city officials generally blame migration for the weakness of civic spirit and identification of the populace with the city. Some planners find migration responsible for the low quality of postwar urban development. Vittoria Calzolari Ghio wrote in 1966 for example:

> It must be remembered that of the two and half million people residing in Rome today, three-fifths have come during the last thirty years and another fifth immigrated after World War I. People born in Rome, who remember it with its villas, its promenades, its boulevards, its countryside, its silence are now a rarity, as the are genuine Redskins of America. For the new immigrants, having come from the country or the small village, the eight-story apartment house with an elevator facing other eight-story apartment houses with elevators was from the start the symbol of urban living; they had no possibility of conceiving of another way of living in the city because in the

Roman welfare "system," see Gianni Cagianelli, "L'Assistenza," *Capitolium,* April-May 1969, pp. 85–86.

lack of green, space, and freedom, all the new quarters were perfectly the same.[31]

Unfortunately, there is no real evidence to support assertions that civic spirit and planning standards are any higher among native Romans than they are among the newer residents.

Migration may not have weakened civic spirit and lowered community service standards, but it most certainly has been a major factor in raising land and housing prices, creating a black market in building lots, and stimulating enormous but inadequate city investment in infrastructure. The cost to the city of each new migrant was estimated in 1961 to be more than $1,500.[32] Net migration for the period 1951–66 was 564,375 people—61 percent of the total increase. Natural increase accounted for the addition of 356,013 people to the city's population—39 percent of the total fifteen-year increase.[33]

Delay in approving and enforcing a new master plan was costly largely because of heavy migration: had there been less growth, speculative profits in land and apartments might have been lower. It might have been easier to formulate and adopt a plan under such conditions. Growth made planning more necessary but more difficult, precisely because it made the lack of planning so profitable, except to the city government.

If rapid growth made planning—regulating current growth—more difficult, it also made planning for the future more problematical. One of the basic issues in the formation of the new plan was the size of the future population to be planned for. Should the new master plan assume that existing growth trends would continue? Should it, on the contrary, assume that current trends were not likely to last? Should it, finally, assume that demographic trends were subject to some manipulation by public policy at national, regional, or local levels? There was a major argument between the Communists, on the one hand, and the Center-Left administration, on the other, over precisely this issue.

The Communists have attacked the plan, claiming that the master plan is predicated upon the failure of national policy designed to improve conditions in the South and in the depressed areas of central Italy. The master plan, they argue, assumes that current migration rates will continue, eventually producing an enormously "overdeveloped" metropolis surrounded by a miserable hinterland. They also argue that the basic principle of the master plan, selective expansion, will be undermined by the provision of all the expansion zones needed to accommodate an eventual population of four million people: nothing guaran-

31. Vittoria Calzolari Ghio, "Roma, luglio 1966: nuovo piano regolatore, nuova amministrazione, nuovo verde?" *Italia Nostra,* May-June 1966, pp. 35–36.

32. This is the estimate of Prof. Francesco Forte, *Saggi sull'economia urbanistica* (Naples, 1964), pp. 186–87, using data from the Milan metropolitan area. A Christian Democratic senator (Murgia) estimated in 1967 that each of the 900,000 immigrants to Rome in the previous fifteen years had cost the city a million lire ($1600) in urbanization costs. *Il Messaggero* (December 1, 1967), commenting on the estimate, considered it too high by half.

33. "Five Year Plan," p. 33.

tees that the actual choice of expansion zones will follow the agreed-upon "40–30–15–15" formula.[34]

Defenders of the new master plan reply that the plan's success is not tied to any particular rate of population growth. Rome, they say, may reach the four million figure at any time between 1985 and 2000.[35] It is assumed that the city will continue to grow, if only because Rome has an unusually small percentage of the national population for a European capital city. The plan has been left "open" in terms of its implementation and completion; it has been designed to work even if the city's growth rate does slow down.[36] However, some future growth is actually needed for the decentralization scheme to work: the plan assumes that the population of the existing built-up part of the city will remain constant; thus further growth will be needed to populate the new Rome to be built in the southeast and southwest, along the eastern axis.[37] Future population growth, unlike past growth, may thus become a help rather than a hindrance to the achievement of planning goals for the city.

### SOCIAL CHANGE AND STABILITY

Despite rapid economic and demographic growth, many elements in the city's social composition and structure have remained unaltered. The city is still socially rather homogeneous, with few of the cleavages that characterize American cities. There are no important racial, ethnic, or religious minority groups in the city. The city has few nonwhites. A sizable foreign colony of 20,000–30,000 people gives the city a cosmopolitan tone without creating ethnic, social, or political conflict. Foreigners working for the embassies, the church, international organizations, and the movie industry generally live at the margins of the city's public life. Even ethnic conflict based on regional differences among Italians has been latent rather than actual, especially as compared with Milan, Turin, or the Italian Riviera. This is partly because the city contains relatively few northerners. The assimilation of southerners and of mountain villagers from central Italy has not been terribly difficult, given the city's easygoing, "southern" traits, the large numbers of southerners already living there, and the city's large size, its openness, and its relatively fluid social values and patterns of behavior. The capital's relatively congenial atmosphere has obviously been a major reason why southerners on their way north decide instead to stay in Rome. Thus migration, whatever its other nefarious consequences, has not been a major source of social or political conflict. A number of distinct "ethnic" colonies and settlements have always existed in the city but they have seldom

34. Piero Della Seta, Carlo Melograni, and Aldo Natoli, *Il piano regolatore di Roma* (Rome, 1963), pp. 81–83.

35. See the reply to Communist criticisms of the plan by Planning Assessor Amerigo Petrucci in "Council Debates, 1962," pp. 246–58 (December 7, 1962).

36. See *Urbanistica Romana,* No. 2 (1967) (*Capitolium,* January 1968), p. 1.

37. Alberto Gatti, in *Urbanistica Romana,* No. 1 (1967), pp. 9–13.

become important elements in city politics. Roman mores and the Roman people are a regional blend, with only a small contribution from the sterner regions of the North.[38]

If ethnic cleavages lack great political significance, it is perhaps because those cleavages are intersected by more significant but equally traditional, cleavages along class and ideological lines. Thus, while southerners constitute a large segment of the poor migrant class, they also dominate the bureaucratic bourgeoisie. There have always been pronounced social and economic inequalities within the city, as well as violent strife among ideological subcultures.

There is no neat congruence, however, between social class and ideology, just as there is none between regional background, class, and ideology. The oldest ideological battle within the city, that between the clericals and anti-clericals, cuts across class lines. There are church sympathizers in every social class. This is one reason why the Communists and Socialists, seeking to organize people along class lines, have never been as anticlerical as the Radicals, who have drawn support almost exclusively from the middle class. This is also why the church party, the Christian Democrats, wins at least 30 percent of the vote in every district of the city, irrespective of class composition.[39] But if the Communists are constrained on the religious issue and the Christian Democrats are constrained on class issues, other parties have been free to exploit those issues to the hilt. Thus, class, "religious," and other ideological tensions have historically been quite severe.

Social inequalities continue to be marked within the city, especially when one contrasts the living conditions of the hundred thousand people living in shanty-towns with those of the people living "la dolce vita" in the wealthy districts, private villas, and the newer residential compounds. These inequalities are reflected in income, education, and housing statistics.

In 1969, two-thirds of the families in Rome were too poor to qualify for the family income tax, because family income was less than $900 a year. Thirty-one percent of the families in the city earned between $900 and $5,000 per year. Eighteen thousand families—2 percent of Roman families—earned over $5,000 a year; together they accounted for 70 percent of the total family tax receipts. The highest assessed income in the city in 1969 was that of Sophia Loren, who earned an estimated $580,000 and was required to pay $80,000 in city income tax. The next largest assessment was for film producer Carlo Ponti, Miss Loren's husband, who was required to pay $70,000 on an estimated income of $475,000.[40]

In 1961 only 4 percent of the population six years of age or older had a university degree and only 10 percent had a high school diploma. As Table 4.10

38. Signorello, "La migrazione a Roma," pp. 239–31; *Notiziario Statistico Mensile del Comune di Roma*, April 1968, pp. 11–12 (for the years 1961–67).
39. See Table 8.2, p. 201.
40. *L'Unità*, December 31, 1969.

Table 4.10. Educational Achievement Level in Rome, 1961

|  | Total |  | Males only |  |
|---|---|---|---|---|
| University degree *(laurea)* | 81,871 |  | 62,634 |  |
| Secondary diploma | 202,584 |  | 109,467 |  |
| Classical-scientific |  | 67,281 |  | 45,302 |
| Normal school |  | 57,810 |  | 8,348 |
| Technical, professional, artistic |  | 67,726 |  | 52,816 |
| Other |  | 9,767 |  | 3,001 |
| Junior high school diploma | 381,313 |  | 197,358 |  |
| Elementary diploma | 1,008,703 |  | 453,288 |  |
| Literates without diploma | 242,927 |  | 102,684 |  |
| Illiterates | 56,868 |  | 16,162 |  |
| 6-14 years old |  | 4,740 |  | 2,369 |
| 14-65 years |  | 33,719 |  | 9,496 |
| over 65 years |  | 18,409 |  | 4,297 |
| Total | 1,974,266 |  | 941,593 |  |

Source: Istat, *10° Censimento,* Vol. 3, Fasc. 58, pp. 38–39.

Table 4.11. Educational Achievement Level Changes, 1951–1961

Percentage of the Roman population (six years and older) with
varying levels of academic training

|  | 1951 | 1961 |
|---|---|---|
| Illiterates | 4 | 3 |
| Semiliterates | 14 | 12 |
| Elementary diploma | 54 | 51 |
| Junior high diploma | 14 | 19 |
| High school diploma | 9 | 10 |
| University degree | 4 | 4 |

Sources: *Roma: Popolazione e Territorio,* pp. 148–49) *10° Censimento,* Vol. 3, Fasc. 58,
pp. 38–39.

shows, there were almost as many illiterates in the city (56,868), as there were college graduates; a more accurate census would probably have shown an even higher rate of illiteracy. There was a minor improvement between 1951 and 1961, as shown in Table 4.11.

Considering the influx of poorly educated migrants during this period, the performance of the educational system is not as bad as these indicators might make it appear. Nonetheless, the percentage of the Roman population with secondary and higher education remains very small, despite the large number of high-level administrative personnel in the city. Higher education remains an elite privilege. Seventy-two percent of the population had five years of grade school or less. Junior high school for ages 11 to 14 became complusory only in 1965. The city's Five Year Plan, adopted in 1967, assumes that only 25 percent of junior high school students will go on to high school.[41]

Classification of family heads in Rome (see Tables 4.12 and 4.13) suggests a somewhat broader upper and middle class, if we include in that class supervisory personnel, white-collar employees, the self-employed, as well as the entrepre-

41. "Five Year Plan," p. 60.

Table 4.12. Occupational Status of the Family Head in Rome, 1961

|  | Families | Family members |
|---|---|---|
| Entrepreneurs, executives, professionals | 17,347 | 65,126 |
| Supervisory personnel and employees | 147,653 | 529,551 |
| Self-employed | 56,584 | 218,476 |
| Workers | 230,276 | 891,359 |
| Helpers | 1,647 | 6,367 |
| TOTAL | 453,507 | 1,710,879 |

Source: 10° Censimento, Vol. 3, Fasc. 58, pp. 54–57

Table 4.13. Economic Sector of Family-Head Occupation, 1961

|  | Families | Family members |
|---|---|---|
| Agriculture, forestry, hunting | 14,138 | 60,537 |
| Mining and manufacturing | 78,961 | 294,515 |
| Construction | 63,822 | 262,013 |
| Electricity, water, and gas | 5,776 | 22,811 |
| Commerce | 63,288 | 235,850 |
| Transportation and communication | 48.526 | 186,439 |
| Credit and insurance | 16,583 | 60,380 |
| Services | 52,911 | 183,504 |
| Public administration | 109,502 | 404,830 |
| Total | 453,507 | 1,710,879 |
| Unemployed Heads of Family | | |
| Housewives | 41,985 | 109,137 |
| Pensioners | 82,259 | 253,482 |
| Others (including those looking for first employment) | 14,099 | 48,189 |
| Total | 138,343 | 410,808 |
| TOTAL | 591,850 | 2,121,687 |

Source: 10° Censimento, Vol. 3, Fasc. 58, pp. 54–57.

neurs, executives, and professionals. By this criterion, about half the families in the city are working class and half belong to the lower middle class or above. One can stress the inequalities between haves and have-nots in the city, but the presence of a large intermediary sector should also be noted, as suggested by the large number of people in the white-collar occupational category and in public administrative and tertiary occupations generally.

The tendency in Rome has been toward a less obviously stratified society and this is clearly reflected in the growing social diversity within most of the city's residential districts.[42] The diffusion of wealth, increased geographic mobility of the population, and continued expansion of the tertiary sector have all been making for a more ambiguous social structure. The city still lacks a sizable industrial proletariat; the relatively few industrial workers in the city are employed by a large number of small and medium-sized firms scattered about the city. Almost half the city's industrial workers work in the building industry, itself highly atomized.[43] In 1951, only 89 out of 13,533 Roman manufacturing firms employed more than one hundred employees; they provided much less than half of total manufacturing empolyment. Only 191 of the 1,550 Roman construction

42. "Perchè tanti voti fascisti a Roma?" *Rinascita,* June 2, 1962, pp. 3–7.
43. Martinelli, "Contributo morfologia," . . . p. 115.

firms employed more than one hundred workers; these firms accounted for just over half of total employment in the industry.[44]

Despite rapid economic and social growth, the city remains basically an administrative-commercial center, dominated in tone by the middle and lower middle classes. Many traditional social patterns persist, such as the importance of the family, though no longer of the extended family.[45] Other Roman mores persist that have an impact on planning, such as the normal workday schedule, which runs from 8 A.M. to 1 P.M. and 5 P.M. to 8 P.M., six days a week. The split workday means that the streets and public transportation systems must cope with four, rather than two, rush hours six days out of seven.[46] It also means a general lack of leisure time and the resulting crushing Sunday pressure on recreational facilities. The workday pattern is also partly responsible for the low level of participation in associational life and sports.[47]

One social tradition that does *not* exist in Rome is that of the Mafia. Where the Mafia is active as in Palermo, it is even more difficult to carry out planning in the public interest. It is reported that master planning and plan administration in Palermo have been based on close cooperation between the city offices and "the Honored Society," as the Mafia is called. In Palermo the Mafia has apparently controlled the land market and building supplies, just as it has controlled gardening, water supply, markets, and funerals. Land speculators of the Mafia type use machine guns and explosives. In Rome, speculators achieve thier goals in less dramatic but sometimes equally effective ways.[48]

## ROMAN SOCIAL GEOGRAPHY

The city is divided, strictly for statistical purposes, into four kinds of districts: *rioni, quartieri, suburbi,* and the *Agro Romano.* The *rioni* descend, etymologically and physically, from the *regiones* created in fourth century Rome, when, according to one scholar's estimate, the city contained 2,319,530 inhabitants.[49] The entire population of the classical city, one or two million people, was jammed

44. "Popolazione e territorio," p. 394.
45. Crespi and Martinelli, "La dinamica delle relazioni sociali," p. 43.
46. Mario Ugazzi, "Una chimera, per i romani, l'orario continuato?" *Capitolium,* January 1967, pp. 5–9.
47. Armando Ravaglioli, "A Roma s'invecchia," *Capitolium,* January 1967, pp. 2–3.
48. Recently, however, Mafia activities appear to have been transplanted to the Roman suburbs. The Lazio regional government in 1971 appointed a committee to investigate ties between Mafia figures and leading officials of the regional government and of the province of Rome. The Mafia leader in the Rome area is alleged to be Frank ("Three Fingers") Coppola, who was deported from the United States in 1948 and who since that time has been a farm-owner and real estate entrepreneur in Pomezia, a town about ten miles south of Rome. The Rome city government and Roman real estate politics seem, so far, to have escaped Mafia influence. (*Il Messaggero,* September 14, October 24, 1971.) For the contrasting situation in Palermo, see Michele Pantaleone, *Antimafia: occasione mancata* (Turin, 1969), pp. 17–46, and Gian Luigi Capurso, "Cronache amministrative: Palermo," *Nord e Sud,* July 1964, pp. 52–56.
49. "Popolazione e territorio," p. 16.

Figure 4.2

into six square miles of territory, surrounded by walls built by the Emperor Aurelian in A.D. 275. The Aurelian walls, with the addition of walled territory around the Vatican on the right bank, contained the 225,000 people of the city when Rome became capital of Italy in 1870. At that time only the inner six rioni were fully urbanized; the rest of the territory within the Aurelian walls— mostly around the Colosseum, in Trastevere, and near present-day Via Veneto— was covered by pastures and vineyards. After 1870 the city grew by filling out the area within the old walls and then by expanding in concentric circles around the walls. The rioni, with all of the city's urbanized area in 1870 and nearly all of its population, gradually came to hold only one-tenth of the urbanized area and one-tenth of the population. After World War II the population of the rioni began to drop, as people moved into newer residential districts—the *quartieri*—and offices replaced their former residences.[50]

Around the rioni was a band of territory, the practically uninhabited *suburbio,* itself surrounded by the open vastness of the Agro Romano. In 1911, part of the suburbio was carved up into quartieri; later, when more quartieri were carved out, the suburbio was displaced outward into the Agro. The rioni today form a rough circle about two miles in radius around the bend of the Tiber. (See Figure 4.2.) The thirty-two *quartieri urbani,* holding three-quarters of the Roman population, form another circle about three miles in radius. The six suburbi lie further out in a band approximately four to six miles from the Capitoline Hill. Surrounding the rioni, quartieri, and suburbi is the Agro Romano, with 83 percent of the city's territory, but only 11 percent of its population. Part of the Agro itself, along the coast, has been carved into three *quartieri marini* (East Ostia, West Ostia, and Castel Fusano); these beach communities contain relatively few permanent residents.

Table 4.14 shows the shifts in the relative demographic importance of the various kinds of districts between 1871 and 1966, as well as the shift that is predicted by the planners for the year 2000. Table 4.15 shows the current importance of the various types of district in terms of area and population.

The master plan of 1931 covered only the rioni, quartieri, and suburbi, leaving the Agro Romano, with 83 percent of the city's territory, without effective building regulation. In the course of time, hundreds of settlements emerged in the suburbi and the Agro, in a few cases on the basis of an official subdivision contract with the city but in most cases through "spontaneous" subdivision. By 1951, before the postwar building boom began, the rioni had been completely urbanized, but only about one-third of the quartieri had been built up and serviced.[51]

The historic center—consisting of the twenty-two rioni, which as late as World War I had two-thirds of the city's population—began to lose population very rapidly after 1951. By 1980 it will probably have returned to its population of

50. Ibid., pp. 54–57.
51. Ibid., pp. 410–11.

Table 4.14. Population Distribution within the City, 1871–1966
(Percentages)

| Statistical district | 1871 | 1921 | 1936 | 1951 | 1961 | 1966 | 2000[b] |
|---|---|---|---|---|---|---|---|
| Rioni | 97 | 69 | 39 | 25 | 13 | 10 | 6 |
| Quartieri | — | 23 | 51 | 59 | 73 | 74 | 39 |
| Suburbi | 2 | 4 | 5 | 9 | 4 | 4 | } 55 |
| Agro | 1 | 4 | 5 | 7 | 10[a] | 12[a] | |
| | 100 | 100 | 100 | 100 | 100 | 100 | 100 |

Source: Calculated from Urbanistica romana, No. 1 (1967), p. 5; "Roma: Popolazione e territorio," pp. 56–57.
Note: The areas of the rioni, quartieri, suburbi, and Agro are not the same over time.
a. Includes 1% in the quartieri marini (established 1961).
b. Master plan prediction.

Table 4.15. Distribution of City Area and Population among the Various Types
of Statistical District, 1966

| Statistical district sector (no. of units) | Total area (sq. miles) | % of total area | (1966) % of city population | (1964) Density (persons per hectare) |
|---|---|---|---|---|
| Rioni (22) | 6.4 | 1 | 10 | 170 |
| Quartieri urbani (32) | 64.4 | 11 | 74 | 103 |
| Suburbi (6) | 21.6 | 4 | 4 | ⎰ |
| Quartieri marini (3) | 6.0 | 1 | 1 | ⎰ 2–3 |
| Agro Romano | 504.4 | 83 | 11 | ⎱ |
| Total City | 602.8 | 100 | 100 | 1.6 |

Source: Calculated from Urbanistica romana, No. 1 (1967), p. 7, and Bollettino Statistico June 1966, pp. 4–9.

1870.[52] Population declined rapidly as housing was reconverted into office space; as new housing became available in the quartieri; and as the ancient houses of the district fell further into decrepitude. Many apartments in the district were covered by rent controls and very poorly maintained. Parking for residents became nearly impossible. Where rent controls were lifted, higher rents drove poor residents out to the suburbs in search of cheaper housing. Better-off residents also left as much better housing became available in the newer sections.

All districts of the city have become more rather than less socially diversified, especially since World War II. Social segregation in Rome has never been absolute, although some districts have been more mixed socially than others. Class composition in most of the rioni is mixed, ranging from the poorest pensioners to wealthy Roman aristocrats and foreigners. Some rioni, however, are predominantly districts of the poor, such as Trastevere, Ponte, Parione, Testaccio, and Sant' Angelo. Some rioni are predominantly middle and upper class, such as Ludovisi (the Via Veneto area), Sallustiano, Esquilino, Castro Pretorio, Ripa, Prati, and Santa Saba.

52. Il Messaggero, September 10, 1969.

The same mixed picture is true for the quartieri, none of which is completely homogeneous in its class composition. Almost all quartieri contain middle-class and lower-class neighborhoods. In some of the wealthiest new sections luxury penthouses coexist with shanties. Intracity social differences are not easily defined precisely because statistical districts like the quartieri are mixtures of different kinds of neighborhoods. Some quartieri, mostly north of the historic center, however, are predominantly upper class: Flaminio, Parioli, Pianciano, Salario, Nomentano, Trieste, and Della Vittoria. Some quartieri, mostly in the south and east, are predominantly lower class: Tiburtino, Prenestino-Labicano, Tuscolano, Appio-Latino, Ostiense, and Portuense.

In contrast to American suburbs, the Roman suburbi are almost completely inhabited by poorly housed, poorly educated low income groups. In 1951, the suburbi had an average of over two persons per room, and between 0 and 2 percent college graduates.[53]

How did the social geography of the city affect the master planning process? Clearly there were some important social stakes involved although they usually were inseparable from political and ideological issues. Conservatives saw or claimed to see in the proposals of the Left an attempt to use the planning process for purposes of subverting existing social arrangements. The proposal to decentralize the city structure to new centers was seen as an attempt to create a new, modern, and secular Rome in the east which would rival and eventually overshadow the existing center of the city, associated with the city's past, particularly its Catholic past. Proposals to restrict expansion only toward the east were seen as attempts to proletarianize the Roman middle classes, to force them to live with the lower classes and to adopt lower class perspectives. At one point the CET planners were denounced as being dupes of Communists,[54]

> conceiving of the future Rome as "massified" in the East, around a giant industrial zone. . . . Historical Rome, cut off by the Eastern Axis, would become archeological Rome—something dead when compared to vital new Rome created in the East.
>
> The Communist game, their long-term strategy, is to concretize their ideas, pointing to "modern" Rome, industrialized and productive, in the East, as a contrast to the Hilton Hotel, the Rome of the billionaires, in the West, with, in between, the archeological Rome of the historic center.[54]

Planners' preferences for eastern expansion came up against the fact that the eastern suburbs had lower-class associations, while the northern and western suburbs, where the planners opposed any further development, had much

---

53. "Popolazione e territorio," pp. 267–69, 326–27; see also Dennis C. McElrath, "The Social Areas of Rome: A Comparative Analysis," *American Sociological Review, 27* (June 1962), 376–91.

54. Mario D'Erme, "L'elaborazione del piano regolatore di Roma," *Battaglie Politiche,* December 1, 1957, pp. 6–8.

higher social standing. Politically, then, the principle of selective expansion could be accepted only if some of the zones selected for development appealed to the middle and upper classes. The final formula, allocating 40 percent of future development to the southwest reflects this necessity to adjust zoning to social preferences, considerations of social status, and fears of political-ideological upheaval.

Social anxieties, connected again to politics and ideology, have affected not only zoning but site planning and building norms. For example when Spinaceto, one of the new residential districts under Law 167, was designed, both moderate and extreme conservatives criticized the proposed housing types, claiming that the large number of apartment houses would increase collectivistic thinking and behavior. The Socialists and Communists, who planned the new quarter, hoped to show that excellent housing could be built in a predesigned quarter and endowed with adequate services at relatively low cost. They pointed to the proposed quarter's 31 square meters of parks and gardens per person, as compared to the citywide average of 1.85; its 4 square meters of school playground per pupil, as compared to the citywide average of 0.04 square meters; its 2.7 square meters of sports fields, as compared to the citywide average of 0.4 square meters; and its total of 37 square meters of recreational green, as compared to the citywide average of 2.29. They also defended the proposed linear apartment houses as producing "positional parity," with every apartment facing both the main road, on one side, and the open countryside of the campagna romana on the other. As a result of criticism from the right-wing parties, business, and the church, the city council, in its vote approving the project on June 4, 1965, split the proposed linear apartment houses into segments so as to preclude the generating of "collectivistic mass psychology.[55] For some reason the conservatives have not expressed any similar fears with regard to the giant apartment houses built by speculative builders; apparently the laws of physical determinism of mass psychology apply only to housing built under public auspices.

It is doubtful whether any of these social anxieties, based mostly on class, match in intensity the social anxieties affecting American planning, based on race.

ROMAN SOCIAL VALUES AND PLANNING

One of the most revealing facts about social values in Rome is that we know so little about them. It is a characteristic result of Roman and Italian culture that we know far more about ancient and Renaissance Rome than we do about modern and contemporary Rome. Relatively little emphasis has been placed within the cultural elite, not to mention the political elite, on the development of "social intelligence" about the city. There are hundreds of works concerning the ancient city but no more than a handful describing the city since it became

55. *L'Avvenire d'Italia* (Rome ed.), April 11, 1965.

capital of Italy. Relatively little is known about modern Rome because until recently very few scholars or intellectuals have considered the subject worthy of attention. Most work on modern Rome has been done by Marxists who alone seem to have been able to escape the fascination of the classical and religious heritage in order to perceive the social organism that envelops and carries that heritage. Community social patterns and values have not, until recently, been considered suitable objects of academic study, at least by non-Marxist intellectuals. The fact that the Marxists paid attention to such matters has only served to reinforce the feeling among non-Marxist scholars and city officials that such study is disreputable and possibly dangerous. Thus, for example, when the city established a special office for the master plan in 1953, the director of the office forbade any member of the staff to engage in social research. Research on employment and income in the various districts of the city was considered controversial and unnecessary.[56]

Thus postwar planning has taken place in something of a vacuum as far as knowledge about the community is concerned. No economists, sociologists, or other social scientists participated in the formation of the successive versions of the master plan. The first major social research relevant to planning was begun *after* the master plan was adopted.[57] This was partly because of the attitude of officials and scholars toward the social sciences; partly because of the controversial and possibly threatening nature of research findings; but partly, also, because of elite attitudes toward the public.

Little is known about the values and preferences of ordinary Romans because the Italian educated elite has traditionally not considered mass preferences or values as intrinsically significant or decisive. Italian planners do not see planning as a means of identifying what groups in the community want and presenting alternative plans for community choice, but rather as identifying through professional doctrine what the community must have and presenting a plan designed accordingly. In all the disputes over the master plan, practically no reference was made to what various groups in the population would prefer. American government and planning are populistic; deference to public opinion and preferences makes planners uncertain of the legitimacy of proposals until they have been ratified by popular consent. Italian government and planning, under all regimes, assume, with Dr. Johnson, that the public is a "great beast"— ungovernable, unprincipled, litigious, and selfish, with no particular right to dominate public policymaking. The style of Italian public administration until recently has been predicated upon contempt for public convenience and preferences: the ordinary member of the public dealing with a city or national office

56. Manieri-Elia, "L'attività dell'Ufficio Speciale," in *Roma: Città e piani*, pp. 272–73. This is contrary to the usual notion that research is a relatively harmless activity and a useful distraction for restless minds.

57. See, for example, the work of sociologists Franco Crespi and Franco Martinelli, cited above, n. 45.

has been treated, as a matter of course, as a morally inferior petitioner.

The location of the city hall high on the Capitoline Hill symbolizes the historic remoteness of city government from the Romans—the detachment of the *Senatus* from the *Populus Romanus*. The presence of the papacy in the city long discouraged an active interest in city affairs, turning minds outward and upward to matters cosmopolitan and transcendental. Unlike many Italian cities, especially in the Center and North, Rome never developed a strong communal spirit. Roman citizenship has always been too Catholic and too universal to focus on a particular set of urban problems. The presence of the church and the national government has diverted attention and prestige from locally oriented leadership. Rome, moreover, as the national capital, lacked the capital-hating animus behind civic spirit in other Italian cities and towns.

Then, too, civic spirit was not encouraged by the oligarchical nature of papal government in the city. Only in 1847 was the city given its own governing organs, including a representative council appointed by the clergy. The first elected city council in the city's history took office only in 1870; those with education or wealth enough to be allowed to vote constituted 3.41 percent of the total population.[58] City elections under universal manhood suffrage were held only once (in 1920) before the Fascist regime abolished them. Universal suffrage is a relatively recent phenomenon in city politics, dating back only to 1946 when Roman men and women were allowed to elect the first post-Fascist city council.

With all its exaltation of Rome, Fascism did not strengthen civic pride in any way useful to the solution of the city's problems. The "Rome" that was glorified was only partly an existing community; the existing community that was glorified was only a small part of the city of Rome. Fascism increased pride in the city, but as an existing achievement, something universal and eternal, something to be embellished rather than reformed.

The sprawling form of the city, especially after the heavy migration of the thirties and fifties, weakened whatever sense of cohesion may have existed in the sleepy city of the nineteenth century. Rome came to be dominated by people neither born nor raised there, with little knowledge about its problems or concern for their solution. The educational system paid no attention whatsoever to civic matters and stressed authoritarian rather than participatory values.

Nor did the native social elites identify very much with the city and its problems. On the face of it, Rome might seem to have had a governing aristocracy. Of the fourteen mayors between 1871 and 1922, seven had titles. Four of the six governors appointed by Mussolini to govern the city were noblemen. Even the first post-Liberation mayor of the city, who was appointed by the Allies to head the Resistance giunta, was a prince, Prince Doria Pamphili, who had dared to defy Mussolini. But the appearance of an Aristotelian aristocracy is deceptive: aristocrats have been prominent in Roman affairs as prestigious individuals

58. Enrico Zampetti, "Le elezioni comunali a Roma dal 1870 ad oggi," *Concretezza*, June 1, 1966, p. 28.

rather than as representatives of a governing class. Even before 1870, government of the city rested in the hands of the clergy rather than in the hands of the black aristocracy. It has been to clergymen, rather than aristocrats, that traditionalist Romans have turned for leadership. The presence of the church discouraged the development of a responsible aristocracy, just as it discouraged the development of a responsible citizenry and an autonomous communal tradition.

After 1870 the papal aristocracy was swamped by an influx of rival aristocrats from other parts of Italy. For some time Catholic aristocrats remained aloof, within the separate subculture created by the church, which until 1929 refused to recognize the legitimacy of the new secular regime. A rival elite, loyal to the House of Savoy, with liberal-national values, emerged to form a secularized middle class based on political, professional, bureaucratic, cultural, and economic achievement. After 1900, other elites began to mobilize the support of the large sectors of the lower classes who were by no means deferential toward the Catholic aristocracy, and who were in stages acquiring the right to vote. The election in 1907 as mayor of Rome of Ernesto Nathan—foreign-born, Jewish, a Freemason and fervent Mazzinian, hostile to both clericalism and aristocracy —demonstrated how little the lower and lower middle classes in the city recognized the right of Catholic legitimists to rule. Catholic aristocrats, mirroring the stance of the church in Italian national politics, became a defensive minority in the city of the pope.[59]

The Fascist regime returned the Catholic nobility to leading positions and repressed the Radical-Socialist anticlerical movement.[60] But it did not make Roman aristocrats into the "natural" leaders of the community—into a cohesive elite that might threaten the power of the Fascist party iteslf. Real power resided in the hands of the Fascist party and the city bureaucracy. The Catholic aristocracy remained an influential and favored social elite whose prestige could be tapped by others.

It was perhaps fortunate that the aristocracy was not a governing class because it had and has little tradition of noblesse oblige. It has tended to a be self-regarding stratum of privilege, rather than a nobility of service and philanthropy.[61] Far from being a class with anticapitalist attitudes, the Roman nobili-

59. The Catholic conservative coalition regained control of the city government in the elections of 1914, with 52.3 percent of the vote as against 47.7 percent for the Nathan bloc and the Socialists (ibid., p. 31).

60. "Radical-Socialist" in Roman terms meant left-of-center progressive, rather than "radical" or "socialist."

61. Compare the role in planning of the Roman aristocracy with that of the aristocracy in London or Stockholm. In the northern European cities the leading families have often been major supporters and sponsors of the progressive city planning movement, while in Rome (and Italy), they have been close allies of the real estate interests opposed to progressive planning. On the role of the British aristocracy, see Alan Altschuler, *The City Planning Process*, pp. 438–51; on the role of the Swedish aristocracy, see the study by Bertil Lennart Hanson, "Stockholm Municipal Politics," mimeographed (Cambridge: Joint Center for Urban Studies of the Massachusetts Institute of Technology and Harvard University, 1960). The Roman aristocracy in their attitudes towards planning have apparently attempted to emulate the former

ty, which owns much of the land around the city, has pursued personal profit as ruthlessly as any nouveau riche, trading and speculating in Roman real estate with little regard for its historic, scenic, or archeological value. The core of this aristocracy—a small group of landowners—systematically used its economic power, social standing, and connections with the church to secure favors and immunities from the city government. The attitude of the Roman landowning nobility has been exploitative; rather than providing an example of "public regardingness," it has led the way in the the destruction of the monuments, buildings, and villas of the old Rome and the creation of the ignoble districts of the new.

Rome has also lacked a substantial civic-minded bourgeoisie. Its composite middle classes, consisting of professionals, bureaucrats, merchants, farm owners, rentiers, contractors, movie stars and producers, ecclesiastics, and politicians, have not compensated for the lack of a nobility based on service. Some observers have blamed the lack of a community achievement ethos in the city on the absence of industrialization and of an industrial bourgeoisie. Many of the less admired traits or reputed traits of the city's population—sloth, skepticism, sloppiness, rhetoric, chaos, disorder, corruption—have also been blamed on the fact that there is almost no industry, no production-minded bourgeoisie, no disciplined, "serious" working class. Evidence from northern Italy suggests, however, that industrialization does not convert Italian managers and workers into North European managers and workers. Existing industrialists in Rome have not seemed any more "enlightened" and public-regarding than other "economic operators" in the city.[62] It may indeed be the case that delayed industrialization has actually saved the historic city; the slow pace of industrialization has allowed a conservationist coalition to be formed and consolidated before the advent of factories and industrial wealth added to existing commercial pressures on the old city.

The planning values of the Roman middle classes may be inferred from the kinds of neighborhoods they have built and lived in. These neighborhoods, despite their individually attractive buildings, tend to be just as densely packed, traffic-jammed, and underserviced as the districts of the poor. Luxury districts have been built with almost as little amenity as lower class districts. Rare though impressive exceptions are the residential developments built at EUR and the private compounds built by the Società Generale Immobiliare (SGI), which provide

---

ruling family of Italy, the Savoys, who fought the city's attempt to convert their estate, Villa Savoia, now Villa Ada, into a public park. The Savoys pressed in the early fifties for rights to subdivide the 375-acre estate, located in a densely populated section of the city practically devoid of any parks. The master plan of 1962, however, zoned the entire estate for condemnation as a public park. See Giuseppe Lionello et al., "Il sistema dei parchi di Villa Ada e di Villa Glori e dell'Acqua Acetosa," Urbanistica, May 1966, pp. 53–56.

62. The leading case involves the FIAT company which, despite protests, located a major repair facility in the northern suburbs, exactly where the planners sought to discourage development.

amenity within the compound even though the street outside may be unpaved.[63] Middle-class Romans often regard the streets as a no-man's land, into which one casually throws lighted cigarettes and garbage; sidewalks in the finest districts are generally obstructed by private cars parked at the casual convenience of their owners. The Roman middle classes tend to show the same lack of social discipline and restraint as residents that they display when driving. There is relatively little sense of neighborhood pride, possibly because the predominant form of middle-class housing is the multifamily, cooperative apartment house. There might be more concern for neighborhood cleanliness, order, and amenity if the middle classes lived in single-family dwellings.

All members of the upper classes in Rome do not display the same level of incivility: the tone is set by a minority whose *prepotenze* (or acts of imposition) the rest of the population has long ago learned to suffer. Indeed, the progressive planning coalition was completely middle class in origins and for a time, also, in its backing. The Radicals, who "created" planning as a political-cultural issue in postwar Rome, were very much a party of bourgeois professionals and intellectuals. It was the Radical middle-class group that developed the themes and campaign later taken over by the proletarian parties of the Left. Radical attitudes, however, were not typical of the attitudes of the Roman middle and upper classes generally. Radicals were unusual in their concern for the community. On the other hand, they were like other members of the Roman social elite in their contempt for mass preferences and tastes.

The values of the lower income groups in the city were not generally much more conducive to effective planning than those of the middle classes. The lower classes did not become a powerful constituency for progressive planning, although the leftist parties did attempt to act as if they were. For one thing, low income groups were often *too* satisfied with the conditions around them because, however poor their housing and facilities were in Rome, they had usually been much worse back in the village. Many in the lower income proups had rural perspectives; their expectations and standards were remote from those of professional city planners. Surveys suggest that low-income families, in choosing where to live, are less concerned with neighborhood amenity than with neighborhood social composition.[64] Both middle-class and lower-class families are averse to living in the outer suburbs, but for different reasons: the middle class sees the outer districts as lacking in facilities, while the lower income groups see them as undesirable because they are inhabited by "uncivil" types of people *("gente poco civile")*.[65] Unlike the middle class, low income groups, who use public

63. SGI, formerly owned by the Vatican and the largest real estate company in Italy, has also been active abroad. Its most notable achievement in the U.S. is the Watergate complex in Washington, D.C., but it has built similarly impressive apartments in Montreal, Mexico City, and many Italian cities. See below, chap. 9, n. 56.

64. Crespi and Martinelli, "La dinamica," pp. 27–28.

65. Ibid., p. 33.

transportation, do not see Roman traffic as a particularly important problem.[66] Nor are they particularly sympathetic to city efforts to stop illegal subdivisions; they see attempts to prevent and demolish illegal building as acts of persecution rather than actions designed to protect the public interest.

Low-income groups were not demonstrably averse to land speculation on moral or other grounds. The literature of the progressive planning coalition has tended to understate or omit the role played by small lot-buyers in creating the antiplanning climate in postwar Rome. Speculation was not only, as the Left implied, an elite phenomenon but also a mass phenomenon. Trading in lots and apartments became a mass passion as well as an elite "conspiracy." Thousands upon thousands of Romans went into real estate ventures as the campaign *against* speculation gradually made clear to everyone the attractiveness of real estate investment.

Gianfranco Piazzesi, a perceptive observer of the Roman scene, has written:

It is not only in Rome that people complain about real estate speculation; but only here does it exist in a pure state. In the capital, the square meter is the unit of measure for wealth; it is the real currency. It supports the luxury of the *nouveaux riches* and sometimes leads the middle classes to live beyond their possibilities. The square meter has created many millionaires and above all has diffused a euphoria, which in the long run might be dangerous, among the army of apartment owners. Today [1964] all the Romans, from the shanty dwellers to the patricians, from the movie stars to the priests, betray a real estate mentality [*una mentalità immobiliare*].[67]

Small investors and potential investors swelled into a powerful antiplanning army, as former Minister of Public Works Fiorentino Sullo, a Christian Democrat, has testified from personal knowledge:

The climate of the "economic miracle" created expectations in all potential owners of land, including outlying and suburban land, especially among the very smallest [who often buy lots as dowries]. . . . [Among the most violent opponents of new planning legislation] in addition to the small landowners, were the new owners who had acquired their property in precent years. Some land they acquired with the intention of building their own homes. Other land was acquired with purely speculative intentions, as an investment with extremely high yields requiring no management. Some land was acquired through the help of intermediaries and politicians. . . . Not rarely the speculation was successfully brought off by charitable institutions which believe they have moral motivations for their actions and will not accept reproaches or interference.[68]

66. Ibid., p. 24.
67. *Corriere della Sera*, May 14, 1965.
68. Sullo, *Lo scandalo urbanistico*, pp. 21–22.

Roman speculators, large and small, became the most powerful opponents of the new planning legislation sponsored by Minister Sullo that would have made Italian urbanization somewhat more orderly.[69]

The ethos of the city is not favorable to planning. The general attitude toward achievement and effort is negative. The common Roman response to effort, especially altruistic effort, is to ask, *"Ma chi te lo fa fare?"* ("Who is making you do that?"). The general spirit of the city is considered by most observers to be conducive to laziness, sloppiness, disorder, and corruption rather than to the kind of orderly achievement admired by northern industrialists and Roman planners. It is difficult to tell just how far the stereotypes concerning Rome and the Romans are accurate. Evidence suggests that planning in the more "serious" northern cities is not as different as the stereotypes would imply. But that Rome has a nonachievement ethos is admitted by practically everyone, including the city's defenders; it is usually blamed on the lack of industry, the traditions of papal paternalism, and close ties to the feudal South.[70] The presence in the city of so many Italian bureaucrats, who are not noted, at least below the top echelons, for an aggressive achievement orientation, helps to reinforce the general tone of "la dolce vita." The admitted antifanaticism of the city that makes effective planning so difficult may, on occasion, be an important virtue. "Rome softens everything," one of its defenders, Leone Cattani, has noted; Fascism without Rome would have been Nazism.[71]

Attitudes toward government regulation are no more favorable than attitudes toward achievement. Regulations are not seen as designed to protect the public interest but as permitting officials to vex and victimize the public. Social types who demonstrate unusual ability to evade, flout, and escape regulation, who display *furberia* or cleverness in the sly pursuit of self interest, are widely admired. Law and regulations are seen by many Romans as instruments for personal gain, to be manipulated or resisted, depending on the immediate situation. The Roman public is highly litigious and is apt to challenge any and all administrative rulings as a matter of course. Thus enforcement of planning regulations is costly and unpopular. Laws and regulations are viewed positively only as the means for legitimizing, regularizing, and legalizing private behavior, however irregular.[72]

Cynicism and suspiciousness are important elements in the Roman political ethos. Studies of Italian political culture rightly stress that Italians know and understand relatively little about politics, do not see politics as relevant to their lives, have little pride in their form of government, and feel little sense of ob-

69. Sullo interview, *L'Espresso,* December 15, 1966.

70. Filippo Sacchi, "Perchè gli italiani non amano Roma," *La Stampa,* June 10, 1956; Alberto Caracciolo, *L'Unità,* April 1, 1954; Amerigo Petrucci, "Problemi della Roma d'oggi," *Studi Romani,* January-March 1965, pp. 44–73, esp. 44–48.

71. *L'Espresso,* June 9, 1957.

72. Virgilio Lilli, "Caos sui tetti di Roma," *Corriere della Sera,* November 19, 1966.

ligation to participate in community affairs.[73] The picture is probably over-drawn, for combined with a low sense of civic obligation is an unusually high tendency to participate in political life. Thus, while electoral turnouts of 30 to 50 percent are normal in British and U.S. local government, turnout in Rome city elections is usually at or near the 90 percent level, reaching even 95 percent in national elections.[74] (See Table 4.16.) There is some evidence, moreover, that Italians are better informed about local politics than about national politics and less dissatisfied with local government performance than with national government performance. In a nationwide public opinion survey in 1960, for example, 34 percent of adult Italians sampled could not name the prime minister, while only 18 percent could not name the party to which the mayor belonged.[75] A year later another survey by DOXA, the Italian Institute of Public Opinion, showed that 60 percent of adult males in Rome had an accurate understanding of what a *"giunta difficile"* was—despite the fact that the term derived from political jargon and its meaning was not intuitively obvious.[76] Table 4.17 shows that the level of political information or awareness was about the same in Milan and Rome and, in both cases, far above that in Italy as a whole.

One can easily stress the negative qualities of Italian political culture to the point where the continued existence of the political system becomes paradoxical; obviously there are traits in Italian political culture that are functional for system survival or the system would not have lasted for almost a generation. The task of functional analysis is to explain the system's survival rather than its demise.[77]

Thus one must look for some of the more positive or functional elements in Italian and Roman political culture—elements that help to account for system survival. The very high rate of participation in elections has already been noted. This might be discounted as a positive or functional indicator since Decree-Law No. 64 of March 10, 1946, makes voting in Italian elections compulsory: but then massive participation is an indicator at least of a tendency toward universal

73. Joseph LaPalombara, "Italy: Fragmentation, Isolation, Alienation," in *Political Culture and Political Development* ed. Lucian W. Pye and Sidney Verba, (Princeton: Princeton University Press, 1965), pp. 282–329; and Gabriel Almond and Sidney Verba, *The Civic Culture* (Princeton, 1963).

74. P. W. Jackson, *Local Government* (London: Butterworths, 1967), p. 77; Charles R. Adrian, *Governing Urban America* (New York: McGraw Hill, 1969), chap. 4.

75. Pierpaolo Luzzato Fegis, *Il volto sconosciuto dell'Italia: Seconda serie—1956–1965* (Milan, 1966), pp. 787–817; Almond and Verba, *The Civic Culture,* p. 185.

76. Luzzatto Fegis, pp. 808–17. A *"giunta difficile"* was a local-government executive (the giunta) that was "difficult" for the city council to elect because of the necessity for awkward coalition choices.

77. Thus, for example, on many of the performance indicators presented by Bruce Russett et al., *World Handbook of Political and Social Indicators* (New Haven: Yale University Press, 1964), the Italian regime has a quite respectable rating when compared to the other West European nations. Italy ranks fourteenth, and ahead of Canada, the U.S., Austria, Ireland, and Switzerland, on Deane Neubauer's index of democratic development. "Some Conditions of Democracy," *American Political Science Review, 61* (December 1967), 1002–09.

Table 4.16. Turnout in Postwar Elections in Rome*
(Percentages)

| Year | National elections | Provincial elections | Communal elections |
|------|--------------------|----------------------|--------------------|
| 1946 | 80.8 |      | 57.5 |
| 1947 |      |      | 66.8 |
| 1948 | 88.6 |      |      |
| 1952 |      | 85.3 | 85.3 |
| 1953 | 94.1 |      |      |
| 1956 |      | 90.0 | 90.0 |
| 1958 | 95.2 |      |      |
| 1960 |      | 90.2 | 90.2 |
| 1962 |      |      | 87.9 |
| 1963 | 94.8 |      |      |
| 1964 |      | 89.2 |      |
| 1966 |      |      | — |
| 1968 | 91.8 |      |      |

*Source:* Ministero dell'Interno, *Compendio dei risultati delle elezioni comunali e provinciali dal 1946 al 1960* (Rome, 1961), pp. 168–69; *Roma Oggi,* July 1966, p. 9; information supplied to the author by the Ministero dell'Interno, Direzione Generale dell'Amministrazione Civile, Servizio Elettorale.
*The first provincial elections were held in 1952; regional elections (which are not shown) were first held in 1970.

Table 4.17. Level of Political Information in Rome, Milan, and Italy
(Percentages)

Question: Have you ever heard talk about the *"giunte difficili"* in some large cities? Basically, what is that all about?

|                    | Milan | Rome | Italy |
|--------------------|-------|------|-------|
| Informed*          | 60    | 61   | 36    |
| Partially informed | 9     | 3    | 2     |
| Not informed       | 31    | 36   | 62    |
|                    | 100   | 100  | 100   |

*Source:* Pierpaolo Luzzatto Fegis, *Il volto sconosciuto dell'Italia, seconda serie, 1956–1965* (Milan: Giuffrè, 1966), p. 809
*Informed responses included: "Lack of agreement over the new mayor and the composition of the *giunta;* difficulty in creating a council majority; lack of agreement among the center or democratic parties; lack of agreement between the DC, the Center-Left, and the PSI, etc."

compliance with legal obligations![78] There is, in addition, the sizable memberships of the political parties and ancillary groups. Though membership statistics must be taken *cum grano salis* and then some, there is no discounting the fact that the parties in Rome have been successful in mobilizing thousands of supporters as formal party members and activists. In 1961 there were about 1.5

78. In the *Civic Culture* survey, Almond and Verba found only 10 percent of the Italian sample prepared to agree that a person *should* be active in local affairs, as compared to at least 26 percent in the other countries in the survey. Yet the actual rate of participation in Italian local elections in much higher than in any of the four other countries. Given the Italian aversion to being interviewed, one must be prepared to accept actual turnout figures as somewhat "harder" in nature than opinion survey data. It is paradoxical that the nation with the lowest declared sense of local civic obligation should also be the nation (outside of the totalitarian bloc) with by far the highest rate of participation in local elections (p. 177).

million people in the city twenty years of age or older. At about that time the Christian Democrats had around 50,000 party members; the Communists, about 64,000 members (all of Rome province); and the Socialists, 18,000 members (again, all of Rome province). If one adds another 10,000 party members for the six other parties, estimated party membership in the city stood at something over one hundred thousand people. This means that between 6 and 10 percent of Roman adults were party members, at least in the early sixties.[79]

The image of the Roman public as sullen, alienated, and apathetic is also belied by the frequency of protest movements in Roman politics.[80] There are, to be sure, a large number of "passive-fatalists" in the city, especially in the poorer districts, but there are other types of people who are not only aware of their interests but prepared to act on them. For example, as of December 31, 1969, there were over 200,000 pending appeals against city income tax assessments, some going back several years.[81] This ratio of nearly one tax appeal case per taxpayer is surely no mark of fatalistic resignation. Against the master plan of 1962 some 4,365 "observations" or appeals were lodged, nearly half of which were eventually accepted by the authorities. Many of these appeals were collective, so that the number of people involved in protesting the zoning decisions of the new plan was actually much larger. Many collective appeals were lodged by owners of small lots in illegal subdivisions; the city authorities almost invariably agreed to rezone these properties as F1 zones, thus giving them legal status.[82] People in isolated borgate are quite prepared to demonstrate for better facilities, just as the shantytown dwellers periodically agitate for regular housing.[83] Much

79. *Annuario Politico Italiano 1963,* pp. 1262–67; *L'Unità,* January 6, 1970; *Il Messaggero,* September 14, 1957, May 27, 1964; *L'Avvenire d'Italia* (Rome), June 23, 1966.

80. The Crespi-Martinelli survey in a Roman borgata found very low participation rates: 56 percent of the men and 96 percent of the women said they did not participate at all in party or union affairs; 30 percent of the men and zero percent of the women said they participated a little; 2 percent (i.e., one of the 43 men and one of the 47 women interviewed) said they participated a lot. When, however, the same sample was asked about whether they had participated in a recent protest movement to reopen the local elementary school, half the men and about one-fifth of the women said that they had taken an active part in the protest. ("Aspetti del rapporto," pp. 49–50). In the four-district survey, Crespi and Martinelli found few party activists in the two middle-class districts (one out of fifteen interviewees in Montesacro and in Tormarancio), but quite a few in a low income district of the old center (Rione Ponte, eleven out of thirty) and in a peripheral borgata (San Basilio, five out of thirty). "La dinamica," p. 52.

81. *L'Unità,* December 31, 1969.

82. Of the 2,679 observations presented against the 1959 master plan 1,217 came from the inhabitants of twenty-two illegal borgate, who requested rezoning of their settlements as regular, legal city districts. See "Controdeduzioni, 1959," pp. 416–44. The count was made by Prof. Insolera (*Roma Moderna,* pp. 270–71, n. 2).

83. Franco Crespi, "Aspetti del rapporto tra strutture urbanistiche e relazioni sociali in una borgata alla periferia di Roma," *Rivista di Sociologia,* May-August 1967, pp. 5–50. In December 1970 shackdwellers were occupying some of the apartments built in the new model district at Spinaceto and asking for a judicial investigation of the manner in which the other apartments in the district had been assigned. The squatters claimed that many of the apartments, contrary to law, had been sublet, sold, or transferred to relatives of the original owners. *Il Messaggero,* December 1, 1970.

enforcement of building and zoning regulations results from private rather than public surveillance; city offices are frequently visited by delegations of *"frontisti,"* that is, people living across from *("di fronte a")* buildings to which an illegal story has been added. "Frontisti" are quite ready to protest when the addition of an illegal story or the illegal subdivision of an estate blocks their view and reduces the value of their property.

Of course, apathy and the readiness to protest are not incompatible. "Confrontation politics" is an old Italian tradition, serving the need for the dramatic expression of self-interest and, at the same time, reflecting reluctance to routinize sentiment in a framework of persistent organization.

While there is considerable mistrust of authority, there is also a tradition of fearing, respecting, and obeying authority. Studies in the poorer districts of Rome show greater support for the governmental system than for the party system. Part of the authoritarian syndrome that created support for Fascism, both as a strong state and as the destroyer of competitive party politics, survives today in the form of support for public authority, mixed with contempt for the political parties. In the poorer outlying districts the parties are seen as impeding solutions to neighborhood problems, while the city administration is seen as trying to do its best.[84] Thus a measure of support is available in the city for efforts to impose order on the development process, although probably much less than one would find in the cities of central and northern Europe.

The same qualifiedly negative picture probably exists also with regard to the Roman attitudes specifically touching on planning issues. Just as the constituency for effective public regulation of development is weak, at least relatively, so is the constituency for the provision of public facilities and amenities. The lack of parks and recreation facilities in the city is attributable, on the mass level, to the recent urbanization of many inhabitants and their continued association of green with rural misery and of cement with civilization. On the elite level, reduced demand for parks and open space derives from the aversion to nature in traditional Italian upper class culture, in contrast to the cultures of northern Europe.[85] The lack of recreational facilities stems from a general Italian indifference to participatory as opposed to spectator sports. Just as Rome has very few parks, it has very few recreational facilities; it has 0.4 square meters of playing fields per inhabitant, as compared to 4.0 in Amsterdam, 5.0 in Stockholm, and 6.0 in Copenhagen. In 1963 Rome had seven playgrounds with equipment, as compared to Stockholm's seven hundred. The rate of participation in sports in Italy is about one-third the rate in the Netherlands and one-fifth the rate in Sweden.[86]

84. Crespi, "Aspetti del rapporto," pp. 38–39.

85. Italo Insolera, "L'evoluzione del concetto del verde nella cultura urbanistica," *Urbanistica,* May 1966, pp. 18–25.

86. Cederna, *Mirabilia Urbis,* pp. 308–09; *Il Mondo,* February 12, 1963. Sixty percent of the 8,000 Italian communes have no playing fields; Italy has less playing-field area per person than

The question is, however, whether participation rates in sports and the provision of facilities are the results of popular attitudes or the causes: whether, that is, few people participate in sports because there are few facilities open to the public, or vice versa. There is some evidence that Romans are aware of the lack of recreational amenities in the city and increasingly determined to change the situation.[87] The propaganda of recreation and planning groups, the increasing amount of leisure time, the rise in personal income, and the diffusion of "modern" values through television are undoubtedly strengthening the constituency for public facility improvement within the city, although the city's budget sharply limits its capacity to respond. Weakness of demand for public amenities is probably at this point less of a constraint on public action than weakness of supply.

One element in Roman political culture may at the same time be functional for system survival but dysfunctional for system performance—namely, the element of compassion. Roman political culture, for all of its cynicism, isolation, and alienation, is also a compassionate political culture that evokes solidarity with the poor and oppressed against alleged or real oppressors. The compassion that today spares from demolition the thousands of illegally built homes that cover the Roman suburban landscape is the same that once saved the lives of antifascists and Jews in Rome in the days of the Nazi terror.[88]

---

India or Turkey; as of 1963, only five Italian universities had gymnasiums and only one had a swimming pool. These and other impressive figures can be found in the Cederna *Il Mondo* article.

87. Crespi and Martinelli, "La dinamica," pp. 55–56.

88. Thus a district council has "declared war" against the big illegal builders [*"grossi" costruttori abusivi*], that is, those who have built illegal apartment houses with five or six stories, of which there are two to three hundred in that district alone. While filing charges against the big operators, it has recommended leniency for the 1,100 other illegal builders—the *"piccoli" abusivi*—in the district (*Il Messaggero,* December 11, 1970). On the days of the Nazi terror, see the special issue of *Capitolium,* "Roma Città Aperta," June 1964.

# 5

# THE ECONOMICS
# OF ROMAN
# PLANNING

## THE CITY'S PRIVATE ECONOMY

To some economists, Rome is a classic study in urbanization without industriali-zation.[1] Among Italian cities, Rome is indeed not highly industrialized in terms of the percentage of its active population in mining and manufacturing. (See Table 5.1.) In 1961 Rome had only 32 percent of its labor force in industry as compared to 61 percent in Turin, 50 percent in Milan, 43 percent in Genoa, 45 percent in Bologna, 40 percent in Florence; it had a smaller percentage in industry than the major cities of the underdeveloped Italian South like Naples (39 percent), Bari (42 percent), Palermo (36 percent).[2] However, the comparison is somewhat misleading in that the low percentage of the Roman population in industry is partly due to the presence of an unusually large public administrative sector as well as to the lack of industry. If, for the purposes of analysis, the administrative-services sector in Rome is reduced to the 25 percent to be found in the nine next largest cities, then Rome's level of industrialization would be a more reasonable 38.5 percent. Were planners to attempt to give Rome the same percentage of industrial population as in Milan (50 percent), the total population of the city would have to be raised to four million while existing tertiary em-ployment was held constant. Most likely, the tertiary sector would continue to grow and the total population would rise far beyond the four million people considered suitable for a balanced development of Lazio region.[3]

The extent of Rome's industrialization has thus tended to be underrated. It is higher than that of Washington, D.C., which has only 4 percent of its labor

1. F. Gay and P. Wagret, *L'économie de l'Italie* (Paris, 1964), pp. 108–09.
2. "Five Year Plan," p. 37.
3. Ibid., pp. 37–38.

Table 5.1. Distribution of the Active Population in Rome, 1951–1961

| Economic sector | Absolute number | | Percentage | | % variation 1951–61 |
|---|---|---|---|---|---|
| | 1951 | 1961 | 1951 | 1961 | |
| Agriculture | 23,084 | 21,755 | 3.7 | 2.8 | −5.8 |
| Industry | 184,073 | 246,747 | 29.6 | 31.7 | +34.0 |
| Transportation and communication | 49,422 | 66,478 | 7.9 | 8.5 | +34.5 |
| Banking and insurance | 20,229 | 25,358 | 3.2 | 3.3 | +25.4 |
| Commerce and services | 169,973 | 249,543 | 27.3 | 32.0 | +50.3 |
| Public administration | 176,547 | 169,074 | 28.3 | 21.7 | −4.2* |
| | 623,328 | 778,995 | 100.0 | 100.0 | +25.0 |
| In search of first job | 38,250 | 33,469 | 5.8 | 4.1 | −13.1 |
| TOTAL ACTIVE POPULATION | 661,848 | 812,424 | 40.1 | 37.1 | +22.8 |
| female segment | 170,391 | 193,510 | 25.7 | 23.8 | +13.6 |
| Nonactive population | 989,906 | 1,376,736 | 59.9 | 62.9 | +39.0 |
| Resident population | 1,651,754 | 2,188,160 | 100.0 | 100.0 | +32.4 |

Source: "Un programma quinquennale per Roma," *Capitolium,* May-June 1967, p. 37.
*The decline in the public administration sector is partly due to the reclassification of some activites as services in the 1961 census.

force in manufacturing as compared to 39 percent in government employment.[4] The problem of Roman industry is not so much its quantity but its quality. Of the 20,000 industrial firms in the city, only 120 employ 100 or more workers and only four of these employ 1,000 or more workers.[5] Roman industry tends to be small in scale and relatively low in productivity. Another sign of backwardness is the fact that very few firms except for the movie companies produce for the national or international market; almost all serve Rome and its immediate region and lack the expansion possibilities deriving from exports. Roman industry tends, however, to depend on outside sources for its raw materials and semifinished products. The dominant industrial sector is construction and most of the manufacturing sector serves the construction industry. A building slump is thus a major disaster for the city, involving not only firms directly engaged in construction, with relatively low fixed investment, but a large number of firms, with heavy fixed costs, that service the construction industry.

Retarded industrialization in Rome, whether measured in qualitative or quantitative terms, has several causes. What little industry existed in the papal city was eliminated after unification by the superior economic and political capabilities of industry in the North. National government policy after unification sought to discourage industry in the city so as not to provide competition for northern industry, destroy the traditional museum-like character of the city, or create in the national capital a large and turbulent industrial proletariat. Rome, moreover, has no major nearby sources of raw materials or power; it is

4. Homer H. Hoyt, "Importance of Manufacturing in Basic Employment," *Land Economics,* August 1969, pp. 344–49.
5. *Il Messaggero,* April 26, 1968.

distant from the markets of Europe and northern Italy; it has no nearby port. It is surrounded by a depressed agricultural area with little power to purchase its products. Investors do not consider the ethos of the city favorable to the requirements of industrial discipline. They are, in any event, unwilling to invest in Roman industry, given the much greater profitability of investment in Roman real estate.[6]

More recently, industrial development has been discouraged by the scarcity of suitably equipped land within the city, the lack of streets, street lighting, sewers, public transportation, and utilities in the industrial districts, and by the exclusion of Rome from the benefits of national policies designed to stimulate industrial development. The area immediately to the south of the city falls within the jurisdiction of the *Cassa per il Mezzogiorno,* while areas to the north enjoy the benefits of the Law for Depressed Areas of Central and Northern Italy.

In one of many pleas for national financial aid, the mayor of Rome in 1964 argued that Rome was an economically depressed area.[7] Such language was something of an exaggeration since, by some indicators, Rome is one of the most developed and wealthy of Italian economic areas. A study by the Italian Union of Chambers of Commerce identified 260 "economic areas" in the country and marked Rome twenty-third in economic development, following such metropolitan areas in the North as Milan, Genoa, Turin, Bologna, and Florence.[8] Per capita income in Rome province in 1966 was an estimated $1,110, as compared to the national average of $980. In the same year, however, per capita income in the most advanced section of Italy—the Northwest—was $1,420. While Washington is one of the wealthiest American cities, with a median family income in its metropolitan area higher than those of Chicago, San Francisco, Detroit, New York, and Los Angeles, Rome is considerably poorer in per capita income than the industrial cities of the Italian North.[9]

Statistics on provincial per capita consumption of certain commodities, taken as indicators of economic development and prosperity, are rather more favorable to Rome than per capita income statistics might lead one to expect (see Table 5.2).

The paradox between moderately low Roman per capita income and moderately high Roman consumption levels is partly explained by the fact that Rome leads all Italian cities in the number and value of defaulting promissory notes *(cambiali)* (see Table 5.3). During the 1960s, one defaulting promissory note was filed with the courts per year for every three inhabitants of the city.[10]

6. Alberto Caracciolo, "Continuità della struttura economica di Roma," *Nuova Rivista Storica,* January-June 1954, pp. 182–206, July-September 1954, pp. 326–47; Silvio Pozzani, ed., *Roma nuova: la capitale nella vita economica italiana* (2 vols. Milan, 1964); Anne-Marie Seronde, "Le rôle de l'industrie dans la vie de l'agglomération romaine," *Bulletin de l'Associa-tion de Géographes Français,* June-July 1958, pp. 46–60.
7. Amerigo Petrucci, *Un piano per Roma* (Rome, 1966), pp. 91–94.
8. G. Tagliacarne, *260 aree economiche in Italia,* p. 33.
9. "Five Year Plan," p. 39; Edward Banfield, *Big City Politics* (New York, 1965), pp. 10–11.
10. *Corriere della Sera,* May 22, 1964.

Table 5.2. Comparative Consumption Statistics for Leading Italian Cities, 1965*

|  | Expenditures for radio-TV subscriptions (lire) | Expenditures for tobacco (lire) | Expenditures for enter- tainment (lire) | Electric power (kwh) | Readers of Reader's Digest (per 100,000) | Motor vehicles (per 10,000 resid- ents) |
|---|---|---|---|---|---|---|
| Milan | 2,601 | 13,751 | 8,319 | 229.0 | 24.5 | 1,698 |
| Turin | 2,299 | 14,671 | 6,544 | 198.0 | 20.0 | 1,936 |
| Genoa | 2,247 | 16,195 | 7,556 | 185.4 | 23.8 | 1,460 |
| Florence | 2,002 | 16,787 | 8,248 | 159,5 | 16.8 | 1,780 |
| Bologna | 2,234 | 16,654 | 8,325 | 135.9 | 16.5 | 1,765 |
| Rome | 2,199 | 19,718 | 6,979 | 184.7 | 20.3 | 1,793 |
| Naples | 1,431 | 15,382 | 4,265 | 125.3 | 9.5 | 839 |
| Palermo | 964 | 10,968 | 2,961 | 100.4 | 7.8 | 918 |

*Source:* G. Tagliacarne, "I conti provinciali," *Moneta e Credito,* September 1966, pp. 311–13.
*The figures refer to per capita provincial consumption.

Table 5.3. Defaulted Promissory Notes in Leading Italian Cities, 1965

|  | Notes | |
|---|---|---|
|  | Number | Amount (lire) |
| Turin | 175,777 | 12,106 million |
| Milan | 408,913 | 29,453 |
| Genoa | 144,318 | 6,147 |
| Rome | 749,036 | 36,595 |
| Naples | 568,961 | 19,557 |
| Palermo | 239,577 | 7,733 |
| Italy | 4,707,220 | 210,870 |

*Source:* Istat, *Annuario di Statistiche Giudiziarie, 1965* (Rome, 1968), pp. 57–58.

The statistics for city excises on consumption *(imposte di consumo)* tend to substantiate Rome's claim that it is a relatively poorer city than the cities of the North (see Table 5.4). It is generally believed, moreover, that per capita income and consumption figures for Rome are misleading in that the distribution of income and consumption there may be more unequal than in the northern cities.

However this may be, figures from the city income tax show the presence in the city of a large number of families below the level of affluence. In 1969, two-thirds of Roman families earned less than $910 per year and thus were exempt from payment of the city income tax. The distribution of family income, as reported by the city tax assessor in December 1969, is shown in Table 5.5.

But however backward and fragile it may have been, the Roman *private* economy has been much more dynamic and powerful than the local *public* economy in affecting the pattern of postwar urban growth. Between 1951 and 1962, total personal income in Rome province tripled while per capita income more than doubled. The 30,000 cars of 1950 became the 630,000 cars of 1966; the ratio of cars to inhabitants changed from one-to-thirty to one-to-five.[11] The sudden postwar rise in private affluence, private purchasing power, and the

11. "Five Year Plan," p. 43; Pala, "I problemi del traffico di una grande città," p. 25.

Table 5.4. Comparative Consumption Statistics, Rome and Milan, 1966

|  | Rome | | Milan | |
|---|---|---|---|---|
|  | Total | Per capita | Total | Per capita |
| Electricity (kwh) | 485,791,199 | 189.0 | 538,718,481 | 320.7 |
| Cheese and cheese products (100 kgs.) | 257,316 | .100 | 262,682 | .156 |
| Fresh fish (100 kgs.) |  | .573 |  | .687 |
| Fine quality | 18,174 |  | 34,558 |  |
| Common | 129,054 |  | 80,807 |  |
| Horsemeat (100 kgs.) | 41,720 | .0162 | 14,768 | .0087 |
| Veal (100 kgs.) | 69,693 | .027 | 175,168 | .104 |
| Gas (cubic meters) | 259,158,845 | 110.8 | 270,433,322 | 160.9 |
| Butter and butter substitutes (100 kgs.) | 29,011 | .011 | 107,023 | .064 |

Source: Calculated from Ministero delle Finanze, *Imposte comunali sui consumi* (Rome, 1968), pp. 252–59, 324–31.

Table 5.5. Distribution of Family Income in Rome, 1969

| 1969 family income | Number of families | Total family income tax assessed |
|---|---|---|
| below 550,000 (below $910) | 499,000 | exempt |
| 550,000–3 million ($910–5,000) | 232,513 | 6,539 billion |
| 3–10 million ($5–16,000) | 16,134 | 8,256 |
| 10–15 million ($16,000–25,000) | 1,112 | 2,203 |
| 15–20 million ($25,000–33,000) | 536 | 1,570 |
| over 20 million (over $33,000) | 822 | 5,087 |

Source: L'Unità, December 31, 1969.

demand for private consumption goods, together with the pressure from migration, made the task of the planners impossible. Planning development in an era of mass private consumption became much more difficult than it had been when there was less building, less movement, less economic change and social mobility. Sudden affluence in Rome brought with it, almost overnight, massive building and massive congestion. The city could not dominate the process of economic change but only hope "to adapt itself to the logic of private consumption."[12]

Rising wealth increased the effective demand for housing and made possible the diffusion of home ownership in the city. It also made possible the diffusion of automobiles, and thus produced the traffic congestion that has degraded the historic city and bankrupted the public system of transportation. Deficits in public transportation were primarily responsible for deficits in the city budget:

12. Franco Volpi, "La crisi degli enti locali nell'economia dei consumi di massa," *Studi Economici,* September-December 1968, pp. 373–97.

the growth of the private economy has crippled the public economy. The city government has been financially unable to match the rise in private living standards with a commensurate rise or even maintenance of a steady level in community facility standards. Moreover, the predominant position of the building and building materials industry in Roman economic development has made the stakes of planning rather higher than they might have been, had the city possessed a more diversified economy. Too much profit could be derived from the lack of planning, as compared to the profit that might have been derived, through external economies, from a more orderly pattern of development. Land speculation and building were simply too important in the city economy as sources of profit and employment, as compared to manufacturing, especially manufacturing for export.

For the poorer people of the city, especially the immigrants, planning did not lower the price of land but raised it; planning did not combat land speculation but aggravated its consequences. Oligopoly in the land market created high prices in land, which planners, in effect, threatened to raise still higher by restricting the supply of building lots to those which had been legally and properly urbanized. Lots sold under oligopoly conditions were simply too expensive for many thousands of people, if the costs of urbanization were added in. The nature of the private economy, with its sizable and growing number of relatively poor families, facilitated a flourishing black market in building land and the collapse of public control over land use.

But if poverty and the lack of industry in some ways made planning more difficult, they were, in other but perhaps lesser ways, something of a blessing. Lack of industry meant that city planners in Rome, unlike those in Turin or Milan, did not have to cope with the problems of adjusting the reform of city structure to the interests of large established industrial plants. Poverty and the lack of industry were also preserving the historic city: the Rome of 1870 would scarcely have withstood intact the impact of massive industrialization. Luckily, awareness of the value of the historic city came before rather than after its destruction.

The role and location of industry in the Rome of the future remain to be decided. There were some, especially in the Catholic subculture, who feared what industrialization might do to the traditional appearance of the city and the balance of power within it.[13] Catholics saw industrialization, not altogether incorrectly, as synonomous with secularization.[14] Industry would not only "darken the cupolas with factory smoke," it would also strengthen the secular Right (the business conservatives in the Liberal party) and the secular Left (Republicans, Radicals, Socialists, and Communists). In 1957–58, the Catholics

13. Giorgio Bocca, "Roma Capitale," in *Roma Nuova,* ed. Silvio Pozzani (n.p.).
14. The level of religious practice tends to be lower in industrial cities of the North than in the rural areas of Italy, but there are major exceptions such as the northern industrial, but Catholic, cities of Brescia and Bergamo. See S. Burgalassi, in *Il comportamento religioso degli italiani* (Florence, 1968), p. 46.

rejected the CET plan in part because it proposed, or they thought it proposed, to "massify" Rome—to create in the east an industrial Rome that, in its modernity and massiveness, would overshadow and ultimately overwhelm the traditional Catholic city of the west. The Catholics turned against the CET plan and produced a new plan, in February 1959, that banned all heavy industry within the city limits—despite the vastness of its unbuilt territory.

But by 1959 there were few groups, even among the conservatives, that were as hostile to industry as the Catholics. The Christian Democratic council leader might defend the ban on industry as enhancing the spiritual nature of the city, but he was openly contradicted by another Christian Democratic councilman who happened to be the secretary-general of the Union of Lazio Industrialists. The latter denounced the *horror officinalis* or fear of industry among his fellow Christian Democrats, who apparently thought, he said, that Romans, as good Catholics, should stick to living off pilgrimages, jobs in the state bureaucracy, and "expediting" administrative affairs.[15] Even the Monarchists and neofascists criticized the Catholic-Romantic view of the city as no longer tenable. When the Communists threatened to sponsor a winning amendment on the matter, the Christian Democrats relented and accepted a unanimous council resolution permitting heavy industry within the city's six hundred square miles of territory. The Christian Democratic councilman representing Catholic Action abstained.

But after the battle to accept industry within the city was won, where it should be located and how it should be induced to come still had to be decided. Under the wartime law of 1941, an industrial zone had been created in the eastern part of Rome for the siting of strategic industries far from the northern frontier. By 1962, this eastern industrial zone had been only partially utilized; there had been no stampede by Italian industry to build plants in eastern Rome, with its badly congested traffic and poorly serviced industrial sites.[16] Planners in Rome were caught in a major dilemma: on the one hand, they wanted to encourage the establishment of factories within the city to provide employment for some of the huge anticipated population increase; on the other hand, they were equally if not more anxious to create sources of employment *outside* the city, in other parts of Lazio region, in order to break the existing trend toward monocentric development in and around Rome. Encouragement of industry in the rest of the region would cut down on migration to the city, but encouragement of industry within the city would help it to absorb the migration that occurred in spite of regional development efforts.

Location of industrial zones *within* the city, moreover, had a crucial bearing on the pattern of future expansion. Presumably, the intensity and direction of

15. See Comune di Roma, "Council Debates, 1959," pp. 248–55; *Il Messaggero,* May 7, 1959; *L'Espresso,* October 9, 1960.

16. *Il Messaggero,* February 14, 1961; Enrico Camaleone, "Preparare la città-regione," *Capitolium,* July-August 1967, pp. 276–87; Unione degli Industriali del Lazio, *L'industria di Roma e del Lazio: Problemie prospettive 1967–68* (April 1968), pp. 61–80; *Urbanistica Romana,* No. 1 (1968) (*Capitolium,* February 1968).

future expansion would be determined not only by the residential zoning system but also by the pattern of industrial zoning. Emphasis on residential expansion toward the east implied emphasis on industrial zoning in the same part of the city.

Matters were taken out of the city's hands during 1962 when the national government decided to create the Consortium for Rome-Latina Industrial Development under the Southern Development Fund in the towns of the Pontine plains, just south of the Rome city line. Through a technicality, some 3,775 acres of city land, belonging to the Pontine reclamation district, were included in the development area. The Rome master plan presented in June 1962 was quickly revised to create a 2,750-acre industrial zone in the southern tip of the city included in the consortium territory. Thus once again the thrust toward *eastern* expansion was checked by a more powerful counterthrust toward the south and the sea. Just as the master plan contained enough residential zoning to accommodate ample expansion in both east and south, it now contained industrial zoning with the same equivocal pattern of emphasis. It was now even more likely that southern expansion would simply overwhelm the 40–30–15–15 formula.

PLANNING VERSUS LAND ECONOMICS

If the city's postwar growth obeyed any law, it was the law of supply and demand. Rising population and income created a strong demand for new housing and for land on which to build. The supply of building land remained relatively low due to the nature of the public and private economies: because of the weakness of the public sector the city was able to urbanize land only at a very slow pace; because of the strength of the private sector, based on the concentration of landholding, the supply of lots for building could be and was deliberately restricted. When Rome became capital of Italy, most of the land around it was held by a small number of aristocratic families. By 1913, 40 percent of the Agro Romano was still owned by only eleven families—all members of the old papal aristocracy.[17] In the course of time, family interests became connected in intricate ways with corporate interests; the pattern of landholding remained highly concentrated. By 1954, most of the land ripe for development was still held by a few interests, whose individual holdings were sometimes larger than those of the city government itself,[18] as noted in Table 5.6.

The frailty of Italian corporate law and widespread use of dummy corporations make the precise distribution of property around the city difficult to ascertain. But no one has disputed the figures below, as worked out in 1954 by the Communist city council group from the land tax register, and no one disputes the fact of concentrated land ownership. Six private landowners in 1954

17. Prime Minister Giolitti, cited by councilman Natoli, "Council Debates, 1953–54," p. 84.
18. Ibid., pp. 84–85.

Table 5.6. Major Roman Landowners and Their Holdings, 1954

| Landowner | Holding (acres) |
| --- | --- |
| Antonio Scalera | 2,208 |
| Lancellotti Brothers | 1,750 |
| Società Generale Immobiliare (SGI) | 1,685 |
| Sen. Alessandro Gerini | 1,500 |
| Mrs. Isabella Gerini | 625 |
| Count Romolo Vaselli | 605 |
| City of Rome | 1,250 |

*Source:* Comune di Roma, *Decisioni del Consiglio Comunale in ordine alla urbanistica cittadina e al nuovo piano regolatore* (Rome, 1955), pp. 84–85.

held over thirteen square miles of development land, most of which was already zoned for development under the 1931 master plan. In such areas the city was legally required to pay most of the costs of urbanization. As the city gradually installed services, the value of private landholdings around the city grew at fantastic rates. Planning Assessor Storoni estimated in 1954 that the annual capital gains of landowners in Rome due to urbanization amounted to about 100 million dollars.[19] A Christian Democratic senator in 1957 estimated the annual rise in land values around the city at more than 400 million dollars.[20] In 1954, there were six private holdings valued at over 150 million dollars and two additional holdings worth more than 80 million dollars; by 1961, the estimated value of these holdings had doubled.[21] According to still another estimate, the value per acre of the 50,000 acres of raw land suitable for development around the city rose by $1,600 a year between 1952 and 1962; the annual yield from such properties as farms was, in good years, only $80.00.[22] In the absence of an effective system of property or income taxation, most of the gains from increments in land values remained in private hands.

Despite the concentration of property, or perhaps because of it, there was an army of small property owners who bought lots on the fringe in order to profit from the general rise in land values engineered by the large property owners. Large and small land speculators, however, favored different patterns of city expansion and Rome's growth reflected the impact of both types.[23]

Frequently large landholders donated parcels of land to public housing agencies and charitable institutions so that the city government would be under moral pressure to bring out utility lines. When the lines were brought in, the tracts around the newly serviced project and those between the projects and the city proper became much more valuable. Large landholders, therefore, favored leapfrog development—development of land remote from the existing city.

Small property owners, on the other hand, preferred oil-stain expansion.

19. Cited in Della Seta et al., *Il Piano regolatore,* p. 95.
20. Ibid.
21. L. Benevolo, *L'architettura delle città nell'Italia contemporanea* (Bari, 1968), p. 124.
22. E. Sermonti, "Contributo alla conoscenza dell'agricultura nella scelta della localizzazione delle aree a bosco e a parco in Agro Romana," *Urbanistica,* May 1966, pp. 117–19.
23. Siro Lombardini, "La normalizzazione dei mercati delle aree e degli alloggi attraverso la nuova legge urbanistica," *Urbanistica,* March 1963, pp. 7–12.

Continuous, gradual expansion all along the urban fringe gave all property owners nearly an equal chance to make money. Leapfrog development favored the large operators, while oil-stain development created equality of speculative opportunity.

Small operators also preferred lot-by-lot expansion in densely packed districts, with a minimum of space dedicated to streets and public facilities. They preferred expansion by detailed plans, under which the city paid most of the costs of urbanization. The larger operators, on the other hand, were better equipped to handle expansion by large tracts; they could afford to pay a share of urbanization costs and to preserve a larger amount of land for public uses. They preferred expansion by subdivision conventions—a kind of private detailed plan, based on a civil contract between the city and private developers.

Large and small speculators had different perspectives on planning. The principle of selective expansion was extremely threatening to the small operators. They preferred the kind of planning that allowed maximum development of any and all properties around and in the city. Small property owners wanted planning to ratify the decisions made in the private sector for reasons of private economic convenience. They wanted to be able to build all along the urban fringe, in historic, archeological, and scenic sites, and in the historic district. They wanted untrammeled development in the Agro Romano. They also wanted intensive exploitation possibilities in all districts, with a minimum of space devoted to public facilities.

Planners were thus attempting to interfere with the economic interests, hopes, and security of many small property owners. They proposed a plan that would place severe restrictions on property rights throughout the city. Property owners in the central business district were not to be free to renovate their properties as they saw fit; they were not to be free to rent or sell their properties for use as large traffic-generating office buildings; furthermore, they were to face the prospect of declining central values, should the new directive centers in the south and east become more attractive as commercial sites. Landowners in historic, archeological, and scenic sites, such as along the Old Appian Way, were to be prevented from building luxury villas across the landscape. Property owners in partially completed districts were to have their land taken for use as public parks and facilities. Farm owners in the Agro Romano were to lose the right to convert cheap farmland into expensive building lots. Lot owners around the city, especially in the north and west, were not to be allowed to build on their land. Other property owners, those in zones marked for development, would be enormously favored. That there was considerable opposition to the proposals of the planning movement, based on legitimate economic interests, should therefore not be too surprising. The plan seemed to involve immediate and sharp economic losses for many people. And in fact adoption of the plan came only after the great speculative land and building boom in the city had begun to slow down.

Under article 40 of the 1942 Planning Act, the city could not pay compensation, even if it had the funds, for the building restrictions imposed by a master plan. Thus there was no way to make the standards and choices of the plan less damaging and less unacceptable.[24] But even those who were to benefit from planning did not, at least initially, support it. Large operators were less threatened by the principle of selective expansion since they held land almost everywhere and their land was least likely to be "selected out." Large operators could perfectly well survive and thrive under the choices, restrictions, standards, and exclusions that would ruin many small speculators. But the larger operators really preferred a planning operation that made no final choices at all. To them, planning was an opportunity for manipulation. When the planners announced the areas that were excluded from development, the larger operators rushed in to buy up the cheapened land from the small operators. They then used their political influence to unmake the previous choice in favor of another set of choices that would allow them to develop or sell the land previously marked for nondevelopment. The CET plan was rejected in 1957–58 because the large landowners wished to prevent any definitive choices from being made; they wished to perpetuate a system whereby publicly announced zoning decisions would drive down the price of land in certain areas, which the large owners could buy up; the large owners could then use their influence to secure another set of nondefinitive zoning decisions, which would rezone for development the land they had previously bought so cheaply.[25]

The big building contractors, who stood to gain from adoption and implementation of a master plan because of the massive public projects involved, also preferred to fight the CET plan, mostly because their profits from land speculation were ten to twenty times greater than their profits from building. Actual construction became important only as a means of capitalizing land values. Relatively little could be gained by improvements in the quality of construction, design, or technical efficiency, as compared to land transactions. There was thus little incentive for builders to improve their methods or to support efforts to check land speculation, since they themselves were actively participating in the land boom.[26]

During the years of the boom, the city attempted to accommodate the interests of both large and small speculators—in practice, if not in principle. The city accepted and provided for both leapfrog development and oil-stain development. It brought services out to remote public housing projects and also to illegally subdivided borgate and settlements, enriching the owners of surrounding tracts. All around the city it allowed the master plan of 1931 to be implemented with detailed plans that provided little space for the streets and public

24. As amended in Law No. 1187 of November 19, 1968, article 40 reads: "No indemnification is owed for the limitations and restrictions provided for by the general plan or for the limitations and costs involved in the alignment of new constructions."

25. L. Benevolo, "Osservazioni sui lavori per il piano regolatore di Roma," pp. 4–15; see also the private letter cited below, chap, 9, n. 9.

26. Gianfranco Piazzesi, *Corriere della Sera,* May 22, 1964.

facilities required for heavy population densities. Streets in the postwar districts of Rome are as dark and narrow as those in the historic center because the planning offices were unwilling or unable to create districts with higher standards.

Land prices rose steeply both because of speculative maneuvers and because of the city's inability to urbanize land rapidly or to hold prices down through land purchases of its own. The results of heavy and profitable land speculation were serious. The supply of low-cost housing was reduced, since it became more profitable to speculate in land than to build. Rising land prices made it more costly for public housing agencies and city departments to find suitable land for housing and facilities. Given extremely low taxes on unimproved land, there was little tax disincentive to speculation. A great amount of housing was built in the city, but predominantly for the middle and upper income groups. Private housing built for lower income groups became economical, given land prices, only in extremely high-density development.

The boom in construction and land prices, combined with rent controls, created serious inequities as between those people, often quite well off, who enjoyed frozen rents in apartments built before 1947 and those, often much poorer, who were forced to find housing in apartments built after 1947. Similar inequities existed between the owners of older apartments subject to rent controls and the owners of raw land and newer apartments. Rents rose sharply during the boom for those who lived in uncontrolled apartments. Between 1958 and 1961, for example, the rent index for the city (with 1938 standing at 1), rose from 32 to 53.[27]

The Roman building industry, given the seller's market for housing, remained technically backward, poorly organized, and oriented more toward speculation than sound building. Many of the smaller firms had improvised managements and were viable only under boom conditions. Building, as the single most important industry in the city, employing half of the workers in the industrial sector, was a major force in city politics. The long delay in securing official commitment to formulate a new master plan was attributable to the firm determination of city officials not to interfere with the recovery of the building industry, which had been completely paralyzed during the war. In effect, the city government decided to surrender control over development in exchange for the revival of the building industry.

The high price of regularly urbanized land, together with the influx of poor migrants, created a flourishing black market in building lots. Some large owners have connived to have their farms subdivided illegally and sold to poor migrants. The migrants in turn have applied pressure on the city to provide facilities; if and when the city does provide facilities, it plays into the hands of the surrounding landowners. Illegal settlements have arisen on private property

27. Istat, *Annuario Statistico dell'Attività Edilizia e Delle Opere Pubbliche*, 8 (1962), 174.

throughout the city's vast territory. Land is cheaper in these settlements because they are remote from the center, poorly serviced, and illegally subdivided. Generally, the people in these illegal borgate are not too vociferous in demanding services because of their irregular status as owners of homes the city could legally demolish.

A major consequence of the building and land boom was the breakdown of administrative control and integrity. The economic stakes of planning decisions became so high that regular decisionmaking, effective regulation, and impartial law enforcement became very difficult. Speculative pressures generated personal pressures on planning officials and their superiors and disorganized the administration of planning. Continually, the formulators of the master plan in its several versions found that while *they* were deciding matters in one fashion, the building department, with its issuance of permits, was deciding matters in another. Master planners found their own designs constantly being changed without their knowledge or approval. A change of color on the zoning map could mean the gain or loss of a fortune. In times of slower growth and less intense land and building activity, there might have been less pressure on planners and administrators. But rapid change, the pressure for immediate decisions, and the rising stakes of planning decisions were incompatible with undisturbed, impartial, and disinterested plan formulation and administration.

Failure to revise the 1942 Planning Act, moreover, meant that the old penalties, only slightly revalued after the war, remained in force. Thus the maximum fine for illegally subdividing or developing land was $640. Given the land market, this fine was not a major disincentive. Illegally built new dwellings were given the same twenty-five-year exemption from property taxation as legally built dwellings. Illegally built dwellings were frequently built with subsidies from the state. Only in 1967, with Law 765 (the "bridge-law"), were penalties raised to significant levels and tax exemptions removed from illegal structures.[28]

By 1967, however, the building and land boom had come to an end. The end of the boom was a shock to most of the population and generated considerable resentment. Middle-class Romans had grown accustomed to buying apartments and selling them five years later at double the price.[29] Contractors had grown accustomed to such high levels of return that 30 or 40 percent was considered rather poor. Peasants migrating from central and southern Italy had grown accustomed to finding ready employment in an industry that concentrated more on speculation in land than on skilled, efficient production for its profits.

There were radically different concepts of who was to blame for the slump, and what was to be done about it. The conservative parties denied that the crisis was due to saturation of the housing market or the rising price of housing and land; they fixed the blame on the policies of the local and national governments, on proposals for new national planning legislation, on measures like Law 167,

28. Ministero dei Lavori Pubblici, *Legge 6 agosto 1967, N. 765*, pp. 86–88.
29. Gianfranco Piazzesi, *Corriere della Sera*, May 22, 1964.

on adoption of the master plan of 1962, and on similar "mortifications" of private initiative. The fault, said the conservatives, lay with the Center-Left coalition and with the public authorities. These arguments were not without effect in a city of many builders and very many speculators. There was a veritable reserve army of aspirant speculators, who, disappointed in their hopes for a "killing" in the sale of their apartments, were to flock to right-wing opposition parties in 1964 and after.

The Left, particularly the Communists, blamed the crisis partly on the private land "monopolists" and partly on the government. The Communists said that the Center-Left (Christian Democratic–Socialist) coalitions in power nationally and in Rome since 1962 had identified the speculator-enemy, but simply refused to take the necessary strong action through new regulatory legislation and public housing programs. Arguments that the Center-Left coalitions were well-intentioned but ineffectual found a ready response among building workers and immigrants, who flocked to the Communists and to the PSIUP (Partito Socialista Italiano di Unità Proletaria), a Maoist group that split off from the Socialist party in 1964.

The crisis in the building industry fed opposition to the new master plan. The predictions of the summer of 1962 that the plan would cripple the building industry seemed to be coming true. (But planners could reply that the crisis in building was nationwide and therefore could not be attributed exclusively to the master plan of 1962, which applied only to Rome.) In 1964, about five hundred small building companies in Rome went bankrupt. Land investors now feared that the city might expropriate them at less than market value. Building and apartment speculators rather suddenly found no buyers, even though high interest payments had to be kept up.[30]

It is sometimes argued that the best or only time to formulate and adopt a master plan is during building recessions, rather than during building booms. In recessions, it is said, there will be relatively few pressures on the planners because the stakes of decisions will be very low. No one will much care about the outcome; planning will interfere with fewer private goals and plans. Immediately after the war, building construction in Rome was at a standstill and the land market was inactive. Since war damage in the city had been slight as compared to what happened in many other Italian cities, there was no prospect

30. Builders blamed the crisis on the new master plan; the lack of government subsidies for housing; the lack of savings available for investment in housing; the rigidity of housing prices due to high sunk costs, particularly in land (Unione degli Industriali del Lazio, *L'Industria di Roma e del Lazio: Problemi e prospettive 1966–67*, p. 66). Others tended to blame builders for having concentrated on and saturated the market for expensive housing. City statistics (*Notiziario Statistico Mensile*, February 1967) showed that 68 percent of the dwellings built between 1963 and 1966 were of the *popolare* or low-cost type and nearly thirteen thousand of these remained unrented or unsold as of 1966. There was thus a backlog of low-cost housing available in the city, although perhaps at prices that were only relatively *"popolare."* As of March 31, 1966, 26 percent of the dwellings completed between 1963 and 1966 remained unsold or unrented.

of a massive reconstruction effort in sight. According to the "recession theory" of planning, this would have been a good time to make a new plan.

Unfortunately, periods of building recession in Rome are not propitious for planning for two reasons. First, the lack of employment opportunities in the city and the relative importance of the building industry mean that the city government will be more anxious to stimulate recovery in the building industry than it will be to make and enforce master plans. Recessions give precedence to building over building well. Planning is seen as a disturbance rather than a stimulus to private building enterprise. Building workers in the city are an important social constituency whose employment needs take priority over planning needs. Second, during recessions there seems to be little impetus to plan: planning problems have low salience compared to social problems. There is little ongoing activity to be coordinated. The effects and costs of nonplanning are not evident. Given the lack of impelling pressure to plan, city governments in Italy have been quite content to postopone planning decisions—involving many unpleasant choices—to a later time. When eventually they begin to plan, it is usually during a building boom and the pressures on planners to make what they consider "bad" plans are strong. It is probable, also, that plans made during a recession will not reflect or be supported by social and economic realities once the cycle swings upward; with the upward swing, the plan is likely to be ignored or swept under.

Nor do recessions seem to be particularly favorable to plan *implementation*. The master plan of 1962 was adopted just as the boom was coming to an end. Pressure on the city government to modify the stringent choices and standards in the new plan increased with growing unemployment in the building industry and the growing number of bankruptcies among Roman contractors. By 1965, Mayor Amerigo Petrucci, who as planning assessor had guided the new master plan through the council debates late in 1962, was announcing with pride that the city had held the line on the new plan, saving it "from dangerous modifications and deteriorations that might have profoundly altered its substance or have prejudiced particular solutions adopted as extreme remedies in situations already compromised when the plan was passed."[31] Given the building slump, it was apparently a major achievement not so much to carry out the great projects of the 1962 plan as to defend the plan's most elemental standards.

THE COLLAPSE OF THE PUBLIC ECONOMY

Most of the benefits of the postwar economic and population boom in Rome were captured by the private economy, while most of the costs fell upon the public economy. The costs of urban development were as considerable as the benefits. By 1969, the city's finances reached a state in which interest payments on the city's two billion dollar debt absorbed 71 percent of operating revenues.

31. *Il Tempo,* December 31, 1965.

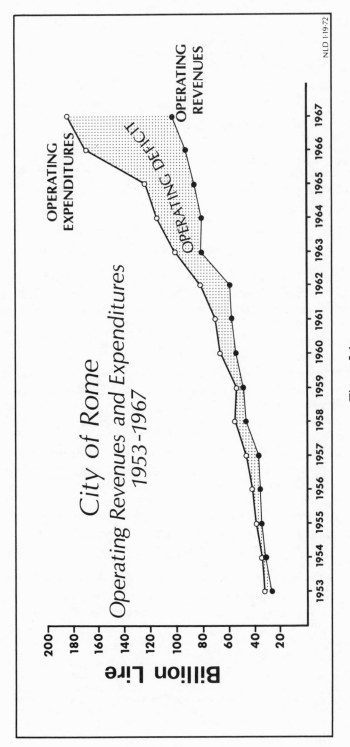

Figure 5.1

Table 5.7. Rome City Tax Revenue Sources, 1956, 1966

|                                              | 1956<br>% | 1966<br>% |
|----------------------------------------------|-----------|-----------|
| Consumption duties                           | 42.8      | 34.4      |
| Family income tax                            | 14.9      | 13.6      |
| Business and professional income tax         | 13.1      | 13.0      |
| Building lot capital gains                   | —         | 1.6       |
| Other taxes                                  | 2.5       | 2.1       |
| Tax on occupation of public property and signs | 3.5     | 3.3       |
| Improvement assessments                      | 3.3       | 8.6       |
| Service charges                              | 3.3       | 2.8       |
| Land and building surtax                     | 4.1       | 7.6       |
| Farm income                                  | 0.1       | 0.1       |
| Shares in state taxes                        | 12.4      | 12.9      |
|                                              | 100.0     | 100.0     |

Source: "Un programma quinquennale per Roma," Capitolium, May-June 1967, p. 55.

The city had to borrow not only to pay for capital investment but to pay the salaries of city employees. The cost of providing services and infrastructure for the city's booming population—even at very inadequate levels—had simply exhausted the public economy.

The problem was not that revenues did not rise as fast as per capita income; actually, they rose faster. During the period of the economic boom, 1956–66, per capita income rose at an annual rate of 7.6 percent, while per capita revenues rose at an annual rate of 6.1 percent. Unfortunately, per capita expenditures during the same period rose at a rate of 15.6 percent. Current expenditures already exceeded current revenues by 30.5 percent in 1957; in 1966, they exceeded revenues by 125 percent.[32]

Even before the economic and demographic boom of the late fifties, city revenues were insufficient to cover operating expenses. (See Figure 5.1.) Though operating revenues rose, they did not rise fast enough to close the already existing gap. About 70 percent of city operating revenues have come from taxation, relatively little from state grants-in-aid (7 percent), property income (10 percent), and service charges (7 percent).[33] Taxes have simply not yielded sufficient revenues to cover mounting expenses. The relative importance of various city taxes is shown in Table 5.7.

Consumption duties ("imposte di consumo"), falling mostly on items of necessity such as food, clothing, and utilities, still constitute the largest single source of city tax revenue. Indirect taxes now constitute 47 percent of total tax yield, as compared to 55 percent in 1956.[34] The relative unimportance of the

32. "Five Year Plan," pp. 54, 65.
33. Rome's financial crisis is only part of a nationwide crisis in local finance, described in Associazione Nazionale dei Comuni Italiani, La finanza locale oggi (Rome, 1966), and Camera dei Deputati, Esame dello stato della finanza locale in Italia (Rome, 1967).
34. Summaries of the major revenue sources and expenditure objects for all Italian cities with more than 100,000 people are contained in the national statistical yearbook, Annuario Statistico Italiano.

property (land and building) tax in Rome as compared to American and British cities should be noted.

Tax yields in Rome tend to be much lower than in northern Italian cities. This is partly because the city has a poorer tax base; and partly, perhaps, because, as Table 5.8 seems to indicate, it does not apply as much tax pressure on the public.

If Rome taxed its citizens in proportion to their income at the same rate as Milan, per capita receipts from the family income tax in Rome would double, as they would also, it should be said, in Turin, Genoa, Palermo, and Naples.[35] As noted, two-thirds of the city's families are exempted from payment of the city income tax because they earn less than $900 per year. Many of these exempted households are headed by government employees or former government employees, enjoying, if that is the word, the ungenerous salaries and pensions of the Italian state. Others are poor, unskilled migrant families. Tax yields are also low because of tax evasion and litigation. About one out of every two city assessments is challenged in court. In 1966 there were some 268,324 tax appeals pending in the courts, 201,527 of them involving the city income tax.[36] The city has had particular problems with wealthy taxpayers, particularly movie stars, who establish residences for family-tax purposes in neighboring communes so as to escape higher assessments and rates in the city. This is one of the reasons why per capita taxation rose only 4.6 percent between 1956 and 1966 as compared to the rise of 5.8 percent in per capita income.[37] Tax evasion is a major problem, reducing the yield of the city income tax by several million dollars each year.[38] Evasion results from the understaffing and inefficiency of the city tax offices as well as traditional Italian attitudes concerning taxation.[39] In addition, the city's

Table 5.8. Comparative City Tax Pressure in the Largest Italian Cities

|  | *(A)*<br>*Percapita city*<br>*income tax*<br>*(1965)* | *(B)*<br>*Percapita pro-*<br>*vincial*<br>*income* | *(A/B)*<br>*Percapita city income tax as* %<br>*of provincial/percapita*<br>*income* |
|---|---|---|---|
| Rome | 3,577 lire | 568,120 lire | 0.63 |
| Milan | 11,605 | 792,345 | 1.46 |
| Genoa | 5,273 | 653,025 | 0.81 |
| Turin | 5,907 | 681,488 | 0.87 |
| Bologna | 6,457 | 592,436 | 1.09 |
| Naples | 1,973 | 354,869 | 0.56 |
| Palermo | 1,956 | 314,138 | 0.62 |

*Source:* Camera dei Deputati, *Esame dello stato della finanza locale in Italia* (Rome, 1967), pp. 349–65.

35. Camera dei Deputati, *Esame dello stato, 1,* 53.
36. "Five Year Plan," p. 56.
37. Ibid., p. 55.
38. Mario Bosi, "Il problema finanziario odierno di Roma," *Studi Romani,* October-December 1968, p. 476.
39. *L'Unità,* December 31, 1969. Tax yields are also lower than they might be because of the

large number of diplomatic, government, religious, and charitable institutions enjoy varying degrees of immunity from personal and property taxation.

The city receives relatively little aid from the national government. The national government, to be sure, directly pays for and administers several services that in other countries are frequently municipal, such as police and fire protection, public education, and welfare. However, the city has some financial and administrative responsibilities even in these areas. State aid to the city in the period 1956–66 averaged 8 million dollars per year, or about 8 percent of city operating revenues.[40] Under Fascism, state aid to the city was very generous; it was tied to migration rates. Since the war, the state has been willing to provide the city with aid at about half the prewar rate, but without reference to migration rates. The state now makes an annual grant to the city of $16 million to cover the city's ceremonial and other expenses as national capital.[41] The state has assumed the cost of building the Rome subway system, and since 1967 it has taken over most of the cost of school construction. But the city still has heavy financial burdens. Rather than give the city new sources of revenue, such as larger shares in state taxes or grants-in-aid, the state has preferred to grant only additional authority to borrow money. Thus the city now has a 2.2 billion dollar debt and an annual burden of interest payments that absorb almost all the city's operating revenues.[42]

The city is not free, of course, to impose taxes or to exceed national maximum rates of taxation unless specifically authorized to do so by national law. Its tax powers are closely defined by the national authorities, as are its powers to borrow and to spend. The city's budget, once adopted by the city council, must go to the Ministry of the Interior for approval. The ministry, which approves all the city's important financial transactions, makes heavy use of its authority to change any item in the city budget. The ministry has tried to hold the line on city spending while putting pressure on the city to raise taxes; in 1964, for example it increased taxes in the city by six million dollars, while cutting spending by more than fifty million dollars. In so doing it reduced the anticipated deficit from $150 million to $80 million dollars.[43] The city may legally appeal these decisions to the President of the Republic or to the Council of State but does not, since no such appeals have ever been successful.

City revenues are low also because of the uneconomic prices charged by the city transit companies and the low service charges of the city funeral and gar-

division between the assessing agency and the collection agency: property assessments are made by the state financial offices while most of the proceeds go to the city. Under the terms of the bill on local finance submitted to Parliament in 1970, Rome and all other cities will cease to have any important tax assessment and collection activities at all. The city will derive its revenues from shares in state taxes assessed and collected by the state. On the somber implications of the general reform bill for Rome city finances, see *Il Messaggero,* December 18, 1970.

40. "Five Year Plan," pp. 55–56.
41. Bosi, "Il problema finanziario," p. 464.
42. *Il Messaggero,* June 25, December 18, 1970.
43. Ibid., Jan. 28, 29, 1965.

bage services.[44] Profits from the city water and power company are completely erased by the deficits of the city transit and milk companies. The city bus company loses 10 cents per passenger carried; the city milk company loses 6 cents on every liter of milk it manages to sell.[44] There are obvious political obstacles in the way of raising transit fares, service charges, and milk prices.

In the 1953–54 city council debate on the new master plan, there was general agreement that a new tax was needed to combat land speculation and allow the city to recoup some of the capital gains it was creating through public investments. It was hoped that a new and stringent tax on building land would lower land prices, discourage illegal building, make for more compacted development in zones closer to the center and more easily urbanized, and improve city finances.[46] The city council voted to petition Parliament for such a law. A series of bills was presented to Parliament, beginning in 1954, but conservative opposition, particularly of the Liberal party and the *Coltivatori Diretti*—an aggressive group of small farmers attached to the dominant Christian Democratic party—stalled action for almost ten years. When the new tax law was finally approved it had been so amended as to be of little use in either curbing land speculation or improving city finances. The procedures under the law (Law No. 246 of March 5, 1963) are cumbersome. To recoup some of the spectacular capital gains of the preceding decade, the law permitted taxation of gains occurring during the ten years before the city adoption of the tax. In 1966, however, the Constitutional Court declared the provisions on retroactivity to be in violation of constitutionally protected property rights. Instead of an expected yield of some 10 million dollars in 1964, the first year of the tax yielded only some 2 million dollars; it was hoped that it would yield at least that much in succeeding year, thus contributing 1.6 percent of city revenues.[47]

The tax on increments in land value has yielded much less than improvement assessments *("contributi di miglioria")* and sewer assessments, which rose from about $160,000 in 1956 to $950,000 ten years later.[48] Unfortunately, improvement assessments have never covered a major proportion of the city's actual urbanization costs. Quite often, city tax assessors arrive with improvement assessment statements only after apartments have been built, sold, and occupied. By that time the subdivider responsible for payment of the assessment may be difficult to find. About 80 percent of all improvement assessments are litigated, thus raising the costs of collection and reducing the net yield.[49]

44. Bosi, "Il problema finanziario," pp. 475–76.
45. Ibid., p. 471.
46. "Council Debates, 1953–54," pp. 20–22. For general background, see G. P. Cassio, "Vicende di un'imposta sulle aree fabbricabili," *Città e Società*, July-August 1966, pp. 77–84.
47. F. Forte, *La strategia delle riforme* (Milan, 1968), pp. 390–93; Charles K. Cobb, Jr,. and Francesco Forte, *Taxation in Italy* (Chicago, 1964), pp. 261–51; "Five Year Plan, "pp. 56–57. Note that the national system of income taxation was little more effective in taxing speculative gains than the local system. Direct taxes on income still constitute only a minor portion of the revenues of the Italian state.
48. "Five Year Plan," p. 55.
49. Cobb and Forte, *Taxation in Italy,* pp. 260–61, 350.

The city does have a tax on income from land and improved property, but the tax has been relatively unimportant as a source of revenue. The yield from the tax on buildings has been low because of the 25-year exemption granted to all new buildings and because of rent controls on most older buildings. Assessment remains in the hands of state finance offices. The relative unimportance of real estate taxation in Rome has major consequences for planning. Real estate valuations, which play such a large role in American city planning and municipal finance, play a much less important role in Italy. Planners in Italy do not have to be greatly concerned with the tax consequences of their zoning decisions. But on the other hand, tax policy is not readily available as a planning tool.

The view of city finances from the expenditure side is no brighter than it is from the revenue side. Heavy migration into the city from the neighboring regions and migration from the inner city outward have forced the city government into large infrastructural expenditures. The cost of urbanizing a square meter of land was estimated by the review *Mondo Economico* in 1961 as follows:[50]

$4.45 for city public services (streets, street lighting, schools, markets, administrative centers);
 1.85 for provincial and state public services;
 1.55 for transportation, telephone, and health installations
$7.85

This excluded any of the costs of public housing or housing subsidies or the general costs of master plan implementation. The cost of "primary urbanization" for each new room under the Law 167 program has been estimated at $160, with a similar sum required for "secondary urbanization" costs. Every time the city issues a building permit in unurbanized areas, in effect, it obligates itself to spend $160 for each room to be built.[51] The unplanned pattern of growth has raised the costs of providing necessary services and, in fact, delayed the process of actual installation. In the developments scattered in various parts of the city's six hundred square miles of territory—which is five times larger than the former County of London and three times larger than the former Department of the Seine—buildings are being sold and occupied long before the installation of streets, sewers, and utility lines. When the city eventually proceeds to bring in the basic services, costs have risen because of the rise in land prices, the frequently irregular pattern of development, and scatteration itself. Delay in bringing in services has been one way that the city has coped with burdens far beyond its financial capacity.

Delay in servicing new residential sections has meant that, in addition to its

50. *Mondo Economico,* December 30, 1961.
51. Giovanni Astengo, "Il costo dell'attesa," *Urbanistica,* Aguust 1964, pp. 2–4.

two billion dollar visible debt, the city has accumulated a vast, if difficult to quantify, "invisible debt" of unmet service demands. Coping with the visible debt alone has become increasingly difficult. In 1950, the city debt, which wartime inflation had practically eliminated, amounted to little more than one million dollars; by 1958 it had risen to about 230 million dollars; by 1970, it reached 2.3 billion dollars! The year before it had reached the psychological threshold of one trillion lire.[52] Unfortunately, much of this debt has been incurred to cover operating expenditures rather than capital improvements. As of 1968, about two-thirds had been borrowed in order to cover the operating losses of the city transit companies; 15 percent had gone for investments in the municipal companies; and only 20 percent into public works.[53]

For Rome, as for many other cities, public transit company deficits have become a source of financial disaster. In 1965 alone, one of the city bus companies, Azienda Tramvie ed Autobus (ATAC) incurred a $25 deficit for every man, woman, and child in the city.[54] In that year, ATAC and the other city transit company, Società Tramvie e Ferrovie Elettriche (STEFER), lost over seventy million dollars, or 60 percent of the total municipal government deficit. Deficits were caused by rising labor costs, the proliferation of private motor vehicles, rising operating costs due to congestion, and the continuation for political reasons of uneconomical lines between the center and distant settlements out in the Agro Romano.

City expenditures have also increased because of the relative inefficiency of city departments and companies, which often have excess personnel, hired for party patronage purposes, and managements that are not productivity-oriented or quick to adopt modern techniques. Some portion of city spending went for unneeded personnel at the same time that badly needed new staff could not be hired.[55]

The state of city finances has had a disastrous effect on city planning. The city has not had the funds to provide or maintain decent facility standards throughout the city. It has not had the funds to carry out the programs implied in the new master plan, such as the rehabilitation of slums in the historic center and the borgate, the installation of needed facilities, or the building of the eastern axis and the new directive centers. It has not had the funds to carry out widespread expropriation of land in zones marked for development to provide for stricter surveillance of building activities in the Agro and in the city center. It has not had funds to conduct an important low-cost housing program, or to build sewers, schools, playgrounds, streets, and aqueducts where needed. It has

52. Bosi, "Il problema," p. 469; *Il Messaggero*, December 1, 1970.
53. Bosi, p. 469.
54. *Il Messaggero*, May 12, 1967.
55. Thus for example, the national government allowed the city to create a new economic development department, provided no new staff was hired; for several years it forbade the hiring of new policemen and sanitation workers.

not had funds to maintain a prestigious and highly qualified planning staff or to pay for a competent, respected staff for building regulation. In sum, it has not had public funds to use as a means of shaping urban development.

Under these conditions the city authorities became objects rather than subjects—the victims of urban development rather than its protagonists, shaped by economic forces rather than being able to shape them. The city possessed too little economic power of its own to prevail against the weight of groups and structural tendencies opposed to the public direction of urban development. Planners urged the city to become a major economic force itself in the land and housing markets and in the general process of economic development. But the city was unable to shake the domination of private economic forces until the recession of 1962–63, when the thrust of private development began to diminish. Even then the city was not able to reverse existing development patterns, but only to establish a stalemate between private economic forces and the planning movement.

Although the Left was particularly adamant in seeking solutions to planning problems that enlarged the role of the public authorities, they could not really claim or demonstrate that public authorities used their existing powers well.[56] There was some irony in the fact that the Left, in opposition, was more favorable to enlarged public control than the Right, which actually held the reins of government. Laissez-faire policies for the conservatives derived, at least in some cases, not so much from a desire to defend economic privilege as from a realistic assessment of how bad any policies, however effective and appropriate in other settings, would be if attempted in Rome.

There was no traditional foundation in Rome for a predominant public role in land or housing. While cities in northern Europe are major landowners, sometimes owning more than half their entire territories, Italian cities, including Rome, have very small landholdings.[57] In 1954, as noted, the commune of Rome owned some 1,250 acres of land—about 0.03 percent of the city's territory. Around the turn of the century northern European cities carried out large-scale purchases of rural acreage for future development; this policy of advance acquisition has been essential in permitting public guidance of the development process. Advance acquisition—the formation of communal land domains— never became an important practice in Rome or other Italian cities. Under article 18 of the 1942 Planning Act, cities may expropriate land in areas zoned

56. Ironically, the Left was particularly hostile to the one example of successful *public* enterprise in Rome—the operation at EUR.

57. This was true even in Communist-controlled Bologna, where, in the fifties, the city government sold off its landholdings in order to maintain a balanced budget! (See Mario Dezmann, "Mancini docet anche a Bologna," *Il Ponte,* April 1966, pp. 443–47.)

for development by a master plan. Compensation to be paid must not include increases in land values resulting from the adoption of the master plan. The city is required to urbanize the land expropriated and then resell it to the original owners at a price that covers some, but only some, of the costs of urbanization. Article 18, however, has never been used by any Italian city, including those governed by the Communists.

More recently, Law 167 (April 18, 1962) required all large Italian cities to formulate ten-year programs of land acquisition for low-cost housing. Up to half the land acquired may be resold to private developers for the building of low-cost housing and commercial centers; the rest is to be given to public housing agencies. The plan adopted by the city in 1963 and approved by the Ministry of Public Works in 1964 calls for the taking and clearance of 12,000 acres of land in various sections of the city, enough to house 700,000 people during the period 1964–74. Of the 12,000 acres, 1,250 were to be donated by the city and 1,000 by public housing agencies; over 10,000 acres were to be expropriated *at 1961 market value prices* from private owners.

The Law 167 scheme is designed to be self-financing. The proceeds from the sale of urbanized land to private residential and commercial builders are to pay for the condemnation of more land. Thus much of the estimated forty million dollars required for land purchases and site preparation is to be recouped, as each set of Law 167 districts is sold. Most of the residential expansion of the city is to be accommodated in the seventy-four Law 167 districts, located in accordance with the 1962 master plan expansion directives. The Law 167 program is to be the city's major technique to break the existing pattern of scattered, lot-by-lot, unserviced development in favor of a new pattern of expansion by preserviced, large districts, located in accordance with an overall development plan. The Law 167 scheme is also designed to coordinate the location and activities of the several public housing agencies that hitherto have built in scattered fashion on the cheapest land available. Public housing is now to have better land, with better facilities, in the midst of different types of housing. In 1965, the Italian Constitutional Court declared unconstitutional the compensation provisions of Law 167; a new act, Law 904 of July 21, 1965, modified those provisions. Even so, litigation has prevented the taking of *any* private land for the Law 167 scheme and so far only one district, has been started, Spinaceto, which will eventually house 26,000 people.[58]

Given the difficulties of public operations in the land market, the city seems to have gone back to the much easier practice of allowing and regulating expansion

58. See Marcello Girelli, "Il piano per l'attuazione della legge 167 a Roma," *Urbanistica*, March 1964, pp. 85–87; Carlo Crescenzi, "Il piano di zona Spinaceto e l'attuazione della 167," ibid., December 1965, pp. 85–87; Bruno Zevi, *L'Espresso*, March 7, April 11, 1965; *Roma Oggi*, December 1968; Paolo Luzzi, "La '167' del Comune di Roma," *Città e Società*, January-February 1967, pp. 63–71; Valeria Erba, "Alcuni esempi di applicazione e attuazione della legge 167," *Città e Società*, July-August 1970, pp, 46–53.

through private subdivision contracts. In 1967 the city council approved seven subdivision conventions, authorizing residential developments for about 120,000 people.[59] Subdivision conventions have the great advantage for the city of placing the financial burden for urbanization on private developers. In exchange for financial relief, however, the city has to surrender some of the initiative in determining the time and location of development. New subdivision controls now in effect may allow the public authorities to retain a greater measure of control over subdivision quality than has been possible in the past. Under the "Bridge-Law" of 1967, all subdivision permit applications for all Italian cities must now be approved by the Ministry of Public Works or its regional offices. Whether centralized controls will actually improve the quality of Italian subdivisions remains to be seen.

Public operations have played a very minor role in the housing market. Public housing and publicly subsidized housing amounted to only 20 percent of all housing built in the postwar period in Rome, despite the large number of state employees eligible under the special state employee housing program, Istituto Nazionale Case Impiegati dello Stato (INCIS). In 1966, only 12 percent of Roman dwelling units were publicly owned; about 360,000 people lived in them. In the period 1963–66, only 10 percent of the dwellings built in the city were public, as compared to the 4 percent built by cooperatives, 36 percent by private individuals and corporations, and 50 percent by private construction companies.[60] The failure to provide an amount of low-cost public housing comparable to that in the cities of northern Europe was national rather than strictly Roman. Italy has had a relatively small public housing program as compared to West Germany, Sweden, Britain, or even the United States.[61] Law 1460 of November 4, 1963, was supposed to launch a major new national effort in low-cost housing, mostly in the form of mortagage assistance to purchasers of low-cost housing. The GESCAL (Gestione Case per Lavoratori) program was launched the same year, providing for 160 million dollars annually in public low-cost housing. But appropriations for subsidized housing have been small and spent with unbelievable slowness.[62] Between 1951 and 1961, 17.4 percent of total investment in housing came from the state, accounting for 19 percent of the rooms built.[63]

Public action in the housing field was too small to have a major limiting effect on the rise in housing prices, especially after 1960, following rising prices of labor and land. But even had there been a larger public housing effort, there is little reason to believe that the housing agencies would have lent their institutional resources to the purposes of the physical planners. Public housing

59. *Roma Oggi,* December 1967, p. 6.
60. *Notiziario Statistico Mensile,* February 1967, p. 11.
61. Paul Wendt, "Post-World War II Housing Policies in Italy," *Land Economics,* May 1962, pp. 113–33.
62. Francesco Forte, *Saggi sull'economia urbanistica* (Naples, 1964), pp. 296–301.
63. Marcello Vittorini, *Pianificazione urbanistica e politica edilizia* (n.p., n.d.), p. 168.

agencies in Rome have not traditionally been the willing instruments of the city's planning policies. In Rome, as in the other Italian cities, there have been several such agencies, each operating under different laws, each acting under a different supervisory authority, each serving a different clientele. Each public housing agency has been accustomed to act much like a private operator in the choice of building sites and to react much like a private operator to coordinating efforts by the city or the Ministry of Public Works. The city has had no direct authority over public housing agencies, which have been reduced to the status of field agencies of various national ministries. The city itself was authorized by law to enter the public housing field; thus, while it could not coordinate the activities of the housing agencies it might have competed with them. But lack of financial resources removed the city from the competition. Law 167, passed in 1963, for the first time gave the city a hold over the sectorial planning of the housing agencies. Under this law the public housing agencies were forced to surrender their landholdings to a common pool and to work out a common program of action under the leadership of city authorities and in accordance with the city's master plan.

There was an important cooperative movement in the housing field, but it operated quite differently from the cooperative movements in northern Europe. The building cooperatives that have flourished in the city have often involved wealthy individuals who used programs of assistance to build luxury dwellings, rather than the low-cost housing intended by the pertinent legislation. There was no cooperative *movement* as such but a plethora of individual cooperatives, with nine to twelve members, building apartment houses in completely scattered fashion all over the city. Thus the building cooperative movement in Rome, unlike the cooperative movement in northern Europe, was neither an instrument for social advancement of the working classes nor an instrument for a more compact and orderly development process.[64] Rising rents led the national government in 1963 to impose rent controls at 1961 levels on much of the housing built between 1947 and 1963 and to extend existing controls on housing built before 1947. The 1963 rent controls expired in 1966. More severe inflation in rents and housing prices followed, while funds actually appropriated for public housing were somehow not being spent. A series of squatter occupations of unoccupied private and public housing led the national government in September 1969 to reimpose rent controls and ban evictions in the major Italian cities until 1972 and to announce still another major new public housing program. Under the Five Year Plan voted by Parliament in 1967, public investment was to have accounted for 25 percent of the total investment in housing in the period 1967–71; the actual figure reached in 1968–69 was only 8 percent. The housing shortage became a major issue in the nationwide labor agitation of late 1969.[65]

64. Ibid., pp. 169–70.
65. *Il Messaggero,* September 12, 1969.

Rent controls were not, however, a particularly equitable device for containing housing prices or for promoting the achievement of planning goals. Rent controls protected some lower income groups, but also many wealthy families. They allowed landowners to profit from development at the expense of property owners. They discouraged maintenance expenditures and accelerated the deterioration of buildings in the historic center. They did not get at the root causes of inflated rents: land speculation, inefficient building methods; lack of public housing, and high construction costs.[66]

The most recent public intervention in the urban development process has taken the form of economic development planning—at the local, regional, and national levels. Local economic planning has taken the relatively modest form of the city's Five Year Plan (1967–71) for its proposed capital investment or rather its capital investment requirements. The plan does attempt to coordinate the various sectors of city government activity, but it does not in itself give the city government any greater control over the development process. The plan may help to convince the national government that Rome is making serious efforts to put its financial house in order. If it leads to greater state aid, it will have served an important purpose and given the city greater economic means of controlling development. Otherwise the Five Year Plan will merely serve to show the discrepancy between what the city is doing and what it ought to be doing.

At the next highest level, the region, a development plan has been in gestation for several years, sponsored by the cities and provinces of Lazio region and by the national Ministry of the Budget and Economic Planning. A regional development plan was adopted in 1969 by the Regional Economic Planning Committee for Lazio, established in 1965 by the Ministry of the Budget. The committee includes the presidents of the five provinces in Lazio, as well as the mayors of the five provincial capital cities, including Rome. Ideological, political, and local rivalries have paralyzed any effective action that the committee might have taken on the evolving development plan. The plan seeks to promote the more balanced development of Lazio region, to reduce rural exodus and migration to Rome, and to prevent the concentration of industrial development along and near the coast south of Rome. But the effort, sponsored mostly by the Socialists, to create different "poles of attraction" for Lazio and southern migrants, has come up against Christian Democratic disinclination to interfere with "natural" economic processes. It has also pitted the drive of the leftist inland towns of the *Castelli Romani* for greater economic development against the interests of the more conservative Christian Democratic coastal towns. It is hoped that the regional council elected in June 1970 will be able to reconcile these differences in a way that relieves some of the pressure on the regional and national capital.[67]

66. Diego Cuzzi and Enrico Fattinanzi, "Edilizia residenziale: prospettive 1970," *Tempi Moderni,* Winter 1968, pp. 75–82.
67. *Il Messaggero,* July 13, 1969.

*National* economic planning, if effective, would presumably have a much greater impact on the city than any regional or local plan. The national Five Year Plan, adopted in 1967, was designed to redress some of the North-South differences that have produced massive internal migration, congestion in the northern industrial cities and in Rome, and abandonment of costly but now underutilized infrastructures in the South. If national planning is successful, demographic pressure on Rome and the northern cities should be eased, and more funds may become available from the national government to enable Rome and other large cities to reduce the large "invisible" debt of unbuilt facilities and to help cover the deficits of public transportation. As of 1970, implementation of the first national economic plan does not seem to have had any noticeable effect on the city's problems. Migration from the South continues, while there has been no important rise in the amount of state aid.

### ECONOMICS AND PLANNING PERFORMANCE

Economics did not have a major impact on the *style* of planning, nor did economic analysis. The master plan was formulated by planners trained in architecture and engineering rather than in economics. Economists became active in planning efforts for Rome only after the master plan was adopted and attention turned to regional and national economic planning. Economics had a good deal to do with the *power of planners* in Rome: planners and the city government wielded relatively little control over the conditions in the land and housing markets that were determining the pattern of city growth. The pattern of expansion desired by the planners, moreover, involved perceptibly serious economic losses for many people; the alleged economic benefits of their planning proposals seemed, in contrast, remote and uncertain. Economics also affected *environmental amenity:* the distribution of income between private and public spenders favored private spenders, or some of them. Consequently, increasing affluence financed the achievement of private consumption goals rather than the goals of public planning policy. Adoption of a new plan had to wait until the end of the building boom, when profits had been taken, and the resistance of the larger interests had become less intransigent. But the facts of economic life continued to plague the planners even after the master plan was finally adopted; by this time the city had barely the ability to make its interest payments and pay its employees; its ability to pay for implementation of the master plan was practically nil.

# 6

# THE
# MACHINERY
# OF GOVERNMENT

Despite its status as national capital, Rome has the same institutions for urban government as other Italian cities and towns.[1] Its city government, the commune of Rome, is one of the 8,000 communes into which Italy is divided. As a *commune,* Rome lies at the base of a three-tiered system of subnational government, consisting of 20 regions, 92 provinces, and 8,000 communes. The organs of government at each level are much the same (see Table 6.1): a representative assembly, directly elected by the people (the Lazio Regional Assembly, the Rome Provincial Council, the Rome Communal Council); a collegial executive, elected by and responsible to the assembly (the regional giunta, provincial deputation, and municipal giunta); and a chief executive, also elected by the assembly (the regional president, provincial president, and mayor).

Rome is the capital not only of Italy but also of Rome province (1,546 square miles) and of the region of Lazio (6,669 square miles). Lazio region includes five provinces: Rome, Viterbo, Rieti, Latina, and Frosinone. Rome province consists of 114 communes, including the commune of Rome. For various reasons, Lazio regional government and the regional governments in most of the rest of Italy were not established until 1970, despite the provisions of the republican constitution framed in 1948 after the fall of Fascism. According to the constitution, regional governments are to be given a large number of powers presently exercised by the national government. The whole field of *"urbanistica"* or city planning is one of the most important matters devolved upon the regional governments, although regional legislation in this field, as in the others delegated

1. The institutions of Roman city government are described by Giuseppe Chiarelli, "Rome," in William A. Robson, *Great Cities of the World* (London: Allen and Unwin, 1957), pp. 514–46. (A third edition is in press.)

Table 6.1. Regional, Provincial, and Communal Government Organs

| Territorial jurisdiction | National government representative | Representative assembly | Collective executive | Chief executive |
|---|---|---|---|---|
| Italy | Minister of the Interior | Parliament | Council of Ministers | Prime Minister |
| Lazio region | Government Commissioner | Lazio Regional Assembly | Lazio regional giunta | President of Lazio region |
| Rome province | Prefect | Provincial Council | Provincial deputation | Provincial President |
| Commune of Rome | Mayor | Communal Council | Communal giunta | Mayor |

to the region, will be subject to the terms of a national "framework-law" for each substantive matter. The Lazio regional government will also be given the tutelage power over provincial and communal government now exercised by the Ministry of the Interior and its representatives in the field, the prefects. Had the constitution of 1948 been implemented immediately, the tutelage powers of the Ministry of the Interior and the planning powers of the Ministry of Public Works might well have passed to a Lazio regional government twenty years ago; the outcomes of Roman planning struggles might have been different.

The results of the first Lazio Regional Assembly elections in June 1970, however, suggest that the difference might not have been great. As Table 6.2 shows, it would presumably have been possible for the same conservative forces that controlled the Ministry of the Interior and the Ministry of Public Works to have controlled the supervisory agencies of Lazio region.[2] However that may be, Lazio region was not created until June 1970; and thus the national ministries remained key actors in Roman planning for most of the postwar period.

Rome province has a forty-five-man council elected under a complicated system of proportional representation and the single-member-district system. There is a rural bias in the orientations of the Rome provincial council, as with provincial councils throughout the country. The council and its executive giunta are seen by the rural communes as their representative against the big city, that is, the provincial capital. Provincial elections are consequently of greater importance in the rural areas than in the cities and of greater importance to the politicians of the small communes than to those of the city.

The province does not possess very significant legal powers or very high

2. That is to say, a centrist or Center-Right coalition, dominated by the Christian Democrats, would have been possible and likely in Lazio region. Lazio region has, after all, been the stronghold of the same conservative Christian Democratic faction, led by Giulio Andreotti, that has dominated postwar Roman politics. On the nature and policies of the Andreotti faction, see Giampietro Dore, "Correnti e gruppi nel Partito Popolare Italiano e nella Democrazia Cristiana," *Battaglie Politiche,* April 6, 1957, pp. 3–6, and Giancarlo Mura, "Correnti e gruppi nella storla della D.C. romana," ibid., pp. 7–11. (*Battaglie Politiche* was the voice in Rome of the *"basista"* faction.)

standing as a government authority. It functions mainly to maintain various state field offices; to collect certain taxes; to maintain a network of rural highways; to subsidize various kinds of public works; to operate institutions for the blind, deaf mutes, illegitimates, and the mentally ill; and to maintain a public health laboratory.

For various reasons, the province has had only slight importance in the planning process. For one thing, it has no authority under the Planning Act of 1942 to formulate master plans with legal effects on property rights. Only communes and the national government may make legally binding plans. Rome province attempted to formulate its own advisory development plan in 1956, but its appropriations for this purpose were vetoed as illegal by the prefect of Rome, representing the Ministry of the Interior.[3]

Rome city officials do not defer much to the opinion of provincial officials. The city has more than one-third of the province's area and three-quarters of its population. The city's budget, poor as it is, is more than ten times the size of the provincial budget and more than ten times the combined budgets of the other 113 communes in the province.[4] The city's leaders are not the subordinates of the province's leaders within their respective parties, but at least coequals.

Table 6.2. Elections in Lazio Region, 1963–1970

| Party lists | Percentage of Valid Votes | | | |
| --- | --- | --- | --- | --- |
| | National (1963) | Provincial (1964) | National (1968) | Regional (1970) |
| Communists | 25.5 | 25.7 | 27.6 | 26.5 |
| Proletarian Socialists | — | 2.6 | 3.2 | 2.6 |
| Socialists | 12.0 | 9.5 | — | 8.8 |
| Socialists-Social Democrats | — | — | 13.0 | — |
| Social Democrats | 5.8 | 7.8 | — | 7.6 |
| Republicans | 1.9 | 2.4 | 2.5 | 3.7 |
| Christian Democrats | 33.5 | 31.6 | 34.6 | 33.2 |
| Liberals | 8.2 | 8.2 | 7.5 | 5.8 |
| Monarchists | 1.9 | 1.9 | 2.2 | 1.3 |
| Neofascists | 10.0 | 9.1 | 8.2 | 10.2 |
| Others | 1.2 | 1.2 | 1.2 | 0.3 |
| Valid votes | 100.0 | 100.0 | 100.0 | 100.0 |

Source: Rinascita, June 12, 1970, p. 7.

3. Il Paese, November 23, 1952. (The Rome province office for a regional master plan included such outstanding planners as Piccinato, Zevi, Quaroni, and Ridolfi.) This veto reflected a general policy of the Ministry of the Interior contrary to provincial ventures in the planning field. In the early postwar years the ministry saw planning primarily as zoning, and zoning power belonged either to the communes or the state. After planning came to be seen in terms of economic development in the late fifties, the ministry again denied any provincial jurisdiction, ruling this time in favor of the Chambers of Commerce and Industry controlled by the ministry of that name. Only after 1962 were the provinces allowed to enter the planning field. See Andrea Villani, Le strutture amministrative locali (Milan, 1968), 2, 45–47; Robert Fried, "Administrative Pluralism and Italian Regional Planning," Public Administration (London), Winter 1968, pp. 375–91; and Questitalia, March 1962, pp. 38–40.

4. Istat, Bilanci delle amministrazioni regionali, provinciali, e comunali: Conti consuntivi anni 1953 e 1954 (Rome, 1956), pp. 40, 42, 290–91.

During most of the postwar period, that is, until 1962, the province was under left-wing control while the city was under rightist control. Rome province, with its little rural "Stalingrads," was considerably to the left of Rome city. Since 1962 both city and province have been under the control of the same parties. Intraparty factionalism now plays the same role that interparty differences used to play in creating city-province tensions.

While the commune resembles the American city, the province, the American county, and the region, the American state, there is no figure in American local government comparable to the prefect.[5] The prefect is a state functionary, appointed by and responsible to the Ministry of the Interior and the national cabinet—one to each province. He may be a career official of the Ministry of the Interior or a political appointee: the cabinet is free to choose practically anybody it wishes to serve as prefect. It is also free to dismiss a prefect from the government service at a moment's notice. Such dismissals occurred, for example, after the fall of the Fascist regime. Every postwar prefect of Rome has been a career official, usually chosen near the end of a distinguished career.

The prefect is the representative in the province of the national government. As such, he is in charge of important negotiations between the national government and the major political and social figures of the province. He is responsible for keeping the national government informed as to the state of provincial affairs. He is in charge of the national police forces stationed in the province and responsible for the maintenance of public order and safety. He is responsible for transmitting to the national government the demands and petitions of individuals, interest groups, and local officials. He is the coordinator of relief in the event of disaster and a mediator of most provincial labor conflicts. He is required to certify the legality of all decisions made by the city council, giunta, and mayor of every commune in the province and by the provincial council and executive as well. All such decisions must be submitted to the prefecture before they can come into effect. The prefect has ten days in which to challenge their legality. He has a general right to inspect the operations of municipalities, the province, and public charitable institutions.

The prefect of Rome, while enjoying a socially prominent post, has rather less influence and importance than his colleagues in other provinces. He may be the representative of the national government in the province, but since the national government is located in Rome it has little need here for representation. The supervisory power over local government enjoyed by his colleagues is, with regard to the city of Rome, centralized directly in the Ministry of the Interior. The same applies to the direction and supervision of the police. The provincial police chief, a national official called the *Questore,* who in other provinces reports to the prefect, reports in Rome directly to the Ministry of the Interior.

5. Robert Fried, *The Italian Prefects* (New Haven, 1963).

The prefect is far more influential with respect to the lesser entities of the province: the other communes and the province itself. At least until 1962, the policy of the national government was to make life as difficult as possible for local governments—provinces or communes—under left-wing control. The prefects were the principal instruments of this policy and they systematically harassed leftist local officials while closing more than one eye to the activities of local governments under centrist or rightist control. Since Rome city was under centrist and rightist control, it was given a fairly free hand, while the provincial government and the "Red" communes in the province were subjected to all manner of legal obstructionism.

The prefect is charged with enforcing the terms of the 1934 Provincial and Communal Act which, among other things, permits him to request the dissolution of the city council when it cannot comply with its responsibilities under the law. If a city council in Italy cannot or will not comply with its legal responsibilities, including the election of a mayor and giunta and the adoption of a budget, the prefect requests the national government to dissolve the council and to appoint a prefectoral commissioner to run the city. This has happened twice, and almost happened several other times, in postwar Rome. In 1946 and again in 1961 the parties on the Rome city council could not form a majority coalition and the council was dissolved. The powers of the council, as well as those of the mayor and giunta, were transferred to the hands of a prefectoral commissioner, whose term of office under law is three months, extendable to six months.

Roman experience with government by prefectoral commissioner has not been happy. While, to some politicians, dissolution of the council and appointment of a commissioner is preferable to being forced into an unwanted coalition, to others it represents postponement of the inevitable and a stasis in city policy-making. The incentive to compromise is somewhat reduced by the knowledge that the council can be dissolved, while the parties wait and see which way national political trends are going. Dissolution also means, however, the risk and expense of new elections. The prefectoral commissioner is usually a member of the prefectoral corps of the Ministry of the Interior—that is, a career bureaucrat trained in the supervision of local government. He is not a local party leader or prominent citizen. He is not usually in a position to take important decisions without some support from national and local party leaders. He is supposed to be an agent of the national government and subject to its orders, at the same time that he acts on behalf of the commune. It was, therefore, expected that the prefectoral commissioner governing Rome in 1962 would adopt the new master plan drafted under the sponsorship of the Ministry of Public Works, not only because of his previous understandings with that ministry but because of his position as agent of the national government. Prefectoral commissioners had adopted master plans for Florence, Venice, and Naples just shortly before. It was therefore astonishing to all concerned when the prefectoral commissioner of Rome refused, for reasons still unknown, to sign the new master plan in June

1962 and thus forced the plan to be adopted by emergency decree of the national government.[6]

The prefecture of Rome, located in the same palace as the elected provincial government, does not itself carry out any planning for the province or the city. Unlike the prefecture of Paris, the prefecture of Rome has no operating responsibilities in the field of planning, except for the issuance of decrees of expropriation for public utility.[7] Thus, despite the prefectoral system, Rome, unlike Paris, has its own locally elected executive; unlike Washington, it has its own locally elected council. Rome therefore enjoys a high degree of political if not legal or financial autonomy.

The fragmentation of government authority, both vertically as between levels of government, and horizontally among units at the same level, has implications for the level of planning effectiveness in Rome.

Horizontal fragmentation has been relatively unimportant. The vast size of the city has permitted suburbanization to take place within the city limits. While this has been an advantage, it has also meant that the city, unlike Milan and Turin, has been unable to pass on to suburban communes the costs of urbanization within the metropolitan area. The communes around the city were brought into the Roman planning process only at the last moment, primarily as a stratagem to postpone a final decision on the Rome master plan. Under Ministry of Public Works sponsorship, Rome and forty neighboring communes worked out an "intercommunal plan" for the metropolitan area in 1960, but none of the forty local authorities has ever formally adopted the plan.[8] Failure to adopt the plan has not prevented Rome from adopting its own plan and forging ahead on its own. Despite its own vast territory, however, Rome is still dependent on its neighbors for recreational facilities and for the success of its master plan. Romans badly need the recreational facilities available only in the hill towns to the southeast of the city; if demographic pressure on the city from migration is to be eased, Rome's neighbors must become rival centers of attraction. Hopefully, Lazio Region may be more willing and able to protect Rome's interests in its region than the city itself or the national government has been.

The vertical fragmentation of power, as between different levels of government, has been more important in affecting planning in the city. The basic governmental actors in the Roman planning process have been, on the one hand, the city and its departments and, on the other, the national government and its field offices. There are no special districts for education, transit, recreation, water supply, or sanitation with jurisdiction over the city. Even the intermediate

6. Giulio Tirincanti, *Il Messaggero*, June 11, 1962; Benevolo, *L'architettura delle città nell'Italia contemporanea*, pp. 100–06.

7. See the elaborate planning mechanisms described in the *Bottin Administratif 1969* (Direction Générale de l'Aménagement Urbain, Direction de l'urbanisme, Service Technique de l'Aménagement), at pp. 662–64.

8. See chap. 4, n. 21.

levels of government between the city and the national government have not
been very important in planning. The province has played little role in planning,
and the region, just created, none at all. The city has thus had to share its planning authority with agencies of the national government, but not to any great
extent with any other governmental institutions. The role of the national government in Roman planning will be discussed in the following chapter.

THE CITY GOVERNMENT

Compared to the structural forms of American city governments, the governmental system for Rome is simplicity itself. There are only two important
organs: the city council *(consiglio comunale)* and the executive organ called the
giunta *(giunta municipale)*. The giunta consists of the party leaders elected by
the majority coalition on the council and headed by the mayor *(sindaco)*. The
members of the giunta, called assessors *(assessori)* are like cabinet ministers;
individually they direct the work of the city departments; collectively they
formulate policy for the city, subject to the approval of the city council. Just
as in parliamentary cabinet government at the national level, the mayor and
giunta are elected by and responsible to the city council, not the electorate. In
accordance with the theory of legislative sovereignty and ministerial responsibility, municipal authority lies in the hands of the majority coalition on the
council and that coalition's leaders in the giunta. If the giunta fails to maintain
a working majority on the council, convention requires it to resign, again
following the norms of parliamentary government as applied to the local level.

There are no independent commissions or boards to interfere with council
and giunta control over municipal policy. While there are numerous boards in
charge of various municipal institutions—such as the *Teatro dell'Opera,* the
transit companies, and the water and power company—personnel appointments,
budgets, and policies are determined by the municipal council and its leaders.
There is no independent commission for planning or any other purpose. Nor
does the council have to share its powers with the local electorate: Italian law
does not require or permit the use of the referendum as a form of citizen participation, except for the municipalization of utilities.

The council, with its eighty members elected at large by proportional representation, possesses, in theory at least, basic policymaking authority in city
government. It elects from its own members the giunta and mayor; it passes the
city budget; it votes on all important appointments and financial transactions;
it adopts the city building, fire, health, and market codes; it determines the city
tax rates; it adopts the master plan, detailed plans of implementation, and
variances; and it votes on all subdivision conventions. Under existing law,
many minor questions and all major questions of city government require
council action. The council even elects the 240 members of the twelve councils
that now represent the various city districts.

Table 6.3. Distribution of Seats on the Rome City Council, 1946–1971

| Party | Initials | 1946* | 1947 | 1952 | 1956 | 1960 | 1962 | 1966 | 1971 |
|---|---|---|---|---|---|---|---|---|---|
| Communists | PCI | (16) | (15) | (12) | 20 | 19 | 19 | 21 | 21 |
| Proletarian Socialists | PSIUP | | | | | | | 1 | 1 |
| Socialists | PSI | 30{ (6) 28 | (10) | (4) | 9 | 10 | 10 | 6 | 7 |
| Actionists | | (3) | (1) | | | | | | |
| Labor Democrats | | (2) | (1) | | | | | | |
| Social Democrats | PSLI,PSDI, PSU | | 3 | | 3 | 3 | 5 | 8 | 8 |
| Republicans | PRI | 6 | 5 | 3 | 1 | 1 | 1 | 1 | 3 |
| Radicals | | | | | 1 | 1 | | | |
| Christian Democrats | DC | 17 | 27 | 39 | 27 | 28 | 24 | 26 | 24 |
| Liberals | PLI | 4 | 1 | 6 | 3 | 3 | 6 | 9 | 3 |
| Monarchists | PNM,PDI PMP,PMI PDIUM | 5 | 4 | 3 | 6 | 3 | 2 | 1 | — |
| Common Man | UQ | 17 | 8 | | | | | | |
| Neofascists | MSI | | 3 | 8 | 10 | 12 | 13 | 7 | 13 |
| Independents | | 1 | 1 | 1 | | | | | |
| | | 80 | 80 | 80 | 80 | 80 | 80 | 80 | 80 |

Source: Ministero dell'Interno, Compendio dei risultati delle elezioni comunali e provinciali dal 1946 al 1960 (Rome, 1961), pp. 168–69; Ministero dell'Interno, private communication to the author, for the 1962 and 1966 elections; L'Unità, June 17, 1971.
*In 1946 and 1947, the parties of the Left formed the Blocco Popolare; the share of each party in the resulting BP city council delegation is not easily ascertainable. The discrepancy between the total of party seats and the total of BP coalition seats is due to the presence on the BP list of independents.

The length and substance of the list of council powers is formidable, but the council, like Parliament, its national counterpart, has not been a very powerful institution. Decisions as to how the council's powers shall be used have been made not by the council itself but by party leaders in the giunta and in the outside party executive committees. Most council decisions are foregone conclusions; the council votes as the leaders of the majority parties decide. Members of the party delegations on the council are consulted before important decisions are made by party leaders, but they are expected to follow whatever course the leaders finally choose. In all the parties, the provincial or city committee of the party has the unchallenged right to dictate orders to the party delegation on the council and in the giunta.

The major function of most councilmen, then, is to present themselves at council meetings when important decisions are to be made and to vote the party line. It is extremely rare for a councilman to vote against his party; disciplinary proceedings and expulsion are the likely consequences of such behavior. Most of the eighty councilmen pursue occupations that require attention and time that might otherwise go into attendance at council meetings. The council meets in the evening, that is, the second half of the normal Roman working day, which runs, as noted, from 9:00 A.M.–1:00 P.M. and 5:00 P.M.–8:00 P.M. The result is that council meetings are called off and adjourned for lack of a quorum quite regularly.

Active participation in council affairs is discouraged by the facts of strict party voting. Councilmen of the opposition parties know beforehand that the outcome is already decided. Councilmen of the majority are bound by strict party discipline and a prudential desire not to compete with the party leaders in the giunta. Then, too, it is difficult for the ordinary councilman, absorbed in business, professional practice, parliamentary duties, or the tasks of party and union management, to stand up to a member of the giunta who is much more deeply involved in city affairs and backed by an expert bureaucratic staff.

Council participation is not completely an exercise in futility, especially for the opposition parties, who do most of the work of the council and who probably draw the greatest benefits from its existence. Council meetings allow the opposition to attack the giunta, to secure information, to force the giunta to defend itself, and, finally, to demonstrate the expertise and present the policies of the opposition. Council meetings give the opposition a platform from which to reach the public—to the extent that what they do and why they do it is reported in the press. Much of the time, however, reporting in the Roman press is so biased that council debates serve only to allow party representatives to perform representational acts for the edification and delight of the party faithful who read the party press.

It is generally advantageous to the majority and its giunta to avoid council debates. They do not need council meetings to secure attention in the press; press conferences can be more easily manipulated than council debates. But the giunta simply cannot avoid appearances before the council because council votes are required by law on most matters, even matters of detail. The rules of the council give the opposition the right and possibility of criticism. They also allow the opposition and "alienated" members of the majority to pry information from the giunta through interrogations and interpellations and to use the same devices for the purposes of harassment.

The impact of the council on policy is difficult to assess. Council influence is exercised primarily through the rather powerful council committees. In the privacy of council committee meetings, discussion of issues is much less partisan than in debates on the floor of the council chamber. In committee, the governing parties may make concessions to the opposition without losing face and the opposition parties may participate in decisionmaking without becoming overtly committed or appearing to "join the system." In committee, also, department heads (assessors) can keep in touch with informed councilmanic opinion. The planning committee of the city council has played an important role as watchdog of the city's planning policies. It was the planning committee of the city council that in 1963–64 examined and ruled on the 4,365 appeals lodged against the 1962 master plan. It was again the city council planning committee that in 1970 rejected several detailed plans proposed by the city planning departments because they would have allowed further development in already highly congested districts and allowed residential development of areas marked for parks and schools.[9] The committee system is thus a structural device that promotes interparty consensus and allows for some checks and balances, despite the rigidities of the party system. The norms of floor debate tend to highlight the polarized aspects of the Roman party system; by pitting majority against minority, these norms make mutual concessions very awkward, if not impossible. The norms of committee deliberation permit a less Manichean and partisan handling of issues.

The council has had greater impact on policy during periods of détente between majority and opposition. In the early 1950s and in the period after 1962, majority-minority relations were relatively civil and many issues were settled through compromise. In periods of détente, the giunta normally accepts some of the amendments offered by the opposition from the floor and the opposition does not use its ability to obstruct. In a period of tension, such as 1958–60, on the other hand, relations between the giunta and the opposition are barely civil; the opposition does little but oppose; and the giunta systematically rejects any proposals or amendments from the opposition. Comity between majority and minority is obviously related to the type of coalition constituting the majority in different periods. When the governing coalition is centrist and excludes both extremes of the party spectrum, consensual relations are more likely. The giunta can maintain a kind of equidistance between the extremes and accept proposals from either extreme without becoming tainted. When the governing coalition includes one of the extremes, as during the period of the Catholic-Fascist alliance (1958–60), the opposition is broad, united, and bitter, since one extreme is in power. Relations can be more consensual when both extremes share pariah status.

The Communists, who have been in the opposition since the resignation of the Resistance-based giunta in 1946, have made the most of their opportunities as an opposition party. Through assiduous attendance, specialized competence, talented leadership, and accumulated experience, the Communists have never lost their position as *the* opposition force in the city and more than once have influenced the course of city policy from the opposition benches. Through questions and speeches, sometimes reported in the nonparty press, the Communists have been able to reach a larger audience than through their own press. They have been able to force the giunta to explain and justify its decisions and to embarrass it into halting or postponing awkward and unpopular decisions.

Both majority and minority, however, are under strict party discipline. Occasionally there is a maverick who systematically opposes party policy in debate; but mavericks stand with their party when the votes are counted, or leave the party. Elective officials, whether mayor, assessor, or councilman, are viewed as delegates of their respective political parties. Party committees deter-

9. *Il Messaggero*, June 26, 1970.

mine coalition policy. They determine who shall be elected to the council and to the giunta—at least they determine who shall be on the party list and how the preference votes of the party apparatus shall be distributed among the members of the list. They determine the basic interparty agreements on whcih the council and giunta coalitions are based. They write the campaign platforms ("programs"), which presumably constitute the basis for action by their delegations in the city government.

Councilmen do not have much discretion. If their party is in the majority, one out of three of them will be in the giunta; the role of the remaining two-thirds will be to acclaim, applaud, and defend the policy of the giunta—not to make policy or attempt to govern. One or two of them, with a strong personal following and the organizational means of ensuring that they are renominated by the party and receive enough preference votes, may essay the role of *enfant terrible,* provided that they always rejoin the party fold when the votes are counted. Opposition councilmen cannot make policy, at least directly, nor can they, on their own, even decide when and what they shall oppose. Decisions to accept or oppose proposals that involve matters of principle are made by outside party organs, not by council delegations. The more controversial the issue, the less likely that council delegations will be left with the decision. Only routine matters are decided by the party delegations in the giunta and the council. But once the majority parties have negotiated an agreement and the giunta has presented its proposals based on that agreement, the majority in the council will faithfully vote for those proposals. There are no cases, apparently, in which the council majority has revolted against the giunta. Party discipline, reinforced by the lack of secret balloting, is a universally accepted norm of councilmanic behavior.

The fact of party power is uncontestable. What is more difficult to determine is the weight that party delegations from the giunta and the council have inside their parties. Relations between outside party committees and party members in government seem to be far from unilateral, since many members of the giunta and council are powerful and independent figures within their party and not subject to outright dictation. Sometimes the provincial party secretary may also be, simultaneously, the leader of his party's council delegation or a member of the giunta; this can reduce the tension between party executive committees and party delegations in government that exists in spite and because of the supremacy of the party executive outside government. Tension may also be reduced by a division of labor between outside party and party-in-government, whereby the former concentrates on patronage and the latter on policy. Party committees outside have seldom been contented for long with that particular formula.

The *giunta municipale* resembles the Council of Ministers in the national government. It is composed of fourteen assessors, plus the mayor, its chairman. It is elected by the council, following the election of the mayor, for a five-year term, the term of the council. The mayor delegates authority over the various city departments to the members of the giunta in a pattern that varies from giunta to giunta, and even from year to year. Actually the allocation of departmental portfolios is decided not by the mayor personally but by the interparty negotiations that lead to the establishment and maintenance of the giunta. Just as the prospective members of the national majority coalition bargain over ministerial portfolios, their local branches argue over departmental assignments in the city government. The council merely ratifies the results of the interparty negotiations.

A position in the giunta, or rather, as assessor in charge of a particular department or group of departments, may carry considerable power. In the city planning politics described in this book, the planning assessor *(Assessore all'Urbanistica)* often played a decisive role in shaping decisions within his assigned jurisdiction. Individual assessors, like cabinet ministers, derive their influence from their departmental status, their factional and party standing, and their personal prestige. It does not follow that the giunta, which brings together all the assessors, achieves power equal to the sum of its individual members; for the particular sources of influence that make the individual strong may make the giunta weak—unable, that is, to come to any decision because of the party, factional, and personal rivalries within it. The giunta may be reduced to ratifying the proposals of each assessor in his field for fear of otherwise initiating interparty, interfactional, or interpersonal warfare.

With one short-lived exception, all postwar giunte have been coalition giunte, just as all postwar council majorities have been coalition majorities. (See Table 8.1.) The giunta, like the national cabinet, is designed to be sufficiently representative of the assembly majority to be able to commit that majority to the courses of action it has taken or proposes to take. If the giunta loses its majority in the council it is expected to resign, although legally it has a five-year term of office and can be forced to resign only by a dissolution decree of the national government. As has been seen, concepts and conventions of parliamentary cabinet government are generally applicable. The giunta represents the city council in the intervals between the two annual sessions of the council, exercising general supervision over the city departments and, in cases of urgency, exercising the powers of the council itself. Most matters discussed in council are discussed first in the privacy of the giunta and then presented by the giunta to the council for its consideration. The giunta is responsible for executing council decisions and for summoning the council into session.

Giunta members may be and have sometimes been members of Parliament, dividing their energies between Montecitorio and Palazzo Madama, where the Chamber and Senate respectively sit, and their city offices. There are always some city councilmen who also sit in Parliament or in the provincial council. Only the mayor is required to serve the city alone: since 1957 he has been forbidden to be both mayor and member of Parliament.

Between 1870 and 1888 the national government appointed the mayor of Rome, and mayors of all other Italian cities, from among the members of the city council. Between 1888 and 1925 the mayor was elected by the city council itself. When the council was unable to agree on a candidate or unable to function for some other reason, it was dissolved and the city was placed under the control of a commissioner appointed by the national government. In Rome this happened several times: in 1890, 1907, 1913–14, and 1923–25.[10] In 1925, under the Fascist dictatorship, the city was for the first time given special administrative arrangements. It was placed under what amounted to a permanent commissioner, the governor, who absorbed the powers of the former council, giunta, and mayor, as well as some powers of the national government and the province. In November 1944, after liberation of the city by the Allies, the *Governatorato* was abolished in favor of the pre-Fascist mayor-giunta-council system. A mayor appointed by Allied Military Government, Prince Doria Pamphili, held office until the first elections were held in November 1946. When the council elected in November could not agree on a choice for mayor, the council was dissolved and the city was placed under a prefectoral commissioner *(commissario prefettizio)*, appointed by the national government. The commissioner, Prefect De Cesare, governed Rome from December 1946 to November 1947. The council was able to elect a mayor in 1947, and again in 1952 and 1956. However, after the elections of 1960, it was incapable of producing a majority and the city again came under a prefectoral commissioner. This second postwar *commissario* remained in office from July 1961 to June 1962. Since the elections of June 1962, the council has been able though often only barely able to agree on a mayoral candidate, that is, on a majority coalition formula. Table 6.4 shows the vicissitudes of postwar executive leadership in Rome.

Unlike dissolutions of the national parliament, which are immediately followed by new elections, dissolution of Italian city councils can lead to rule of a commissioner appointed by the national government for long periods of time— sometimes two or three years. There is no way to force the Council of Ministers to hold elections in those cities whose councils have been dissolved. The cabinet often postpones elections, either to allow the parties to negotiate a majority coalition before going to the trouble and expense of holding new elections, or to allow its friends in the city concerned to increase their prospects of winning.

The mayor is both the chief executive of the city and an official of the national government. As chief executive of the commune, he directs the work of the city departments, the giunta, and the council. He is the city's legal representative and signs contracts approved by the council and giunta. He sees to the enforcement of all city ordinances, and he issues various kinds of certificates and licenses, such as building licenses.

10. Comune di Roma, *Una legge per la capitale* (Rome, 1957), pp. 221–24.

Table 6.4. City Executives in Rome, 1946–1971

| Mayor or Commissioner | Party | Date of appoint-<br>ment or election | Date of resig-<br>nation | Days before<br>election |
|---|---|---|---|---|
| Prefectoral Commissioner<br>De Cesare | — | Dec. 28, 1946 | Nov. 4, 1947 | — |
| Salvatore Rebecchini | DC | Nov. 5, 1947 | May 27, 1956 | 24 |
| Umberto Tupini | DC | July 2, 1956 | Dec. 27, 1957 | 36 |
| Urbano Cioccetti | DC | Jan. 10, 1958 | May 20, 1962 | 14 |
| Prefectoral Commissioner<br>Diana | — | July 10, 1961 | June 10, 1962 | — |
| Glauco Della Porta | DC | July 17, 1962 | March 10, 1964 | 37 |
| Amerigo Petrucci | DC | March 11, 1964 | Nov. 11, 1967 | 1 |
| Rinaldo Santini | DC | Dec. 21, 1967 | March 19, 1969 | 38 |
| Clelio Darida* | DC | June 30, 1969 | June 12, 1971 | 120 |
|  |  | Oct. 3, 1971 | — | 105 |

*Source:* Commune of Rome.
*Mayor Darida resigned on the eve of the June 13, 1971, city elections. He was reelected mayor by the city council on August 7, but refused to be sworn in by the prefect until October 3. Four months were required before he could secure an effective governing majority on the council. The new city giunta, composed only of Christian Democrats, was elected on October 19.

Within the sphere of local government and as far as legal powers are concerned, the mayor's authority is great as applied to individual cases, but much weaker in determining general policies and regulations: here the legal authority belongs to collective bodies—the giunta and the council. The mayor's ability to affect general decisions derives from his political rather than his legal position. And the political position of the mayor of Rome has not been very strong. None of the postwar mayors, for example, has been master of his political party. All postwar mayors have been members of the Christian Democratic (DC) party. All have had to contend either with a powerful factional machine that dominated the DC and the DC men on the council, in the giunta, and in the mayor's office (1954–61); or with an unstable multifactional situation within the DC in which no individual possessed great unilateral control (1947–54, 1961-present).

Despite his modest legal and party position, his unique status and visibility may make the mayor the single most powerful person in the government of the city. No other individual is in quite the same position to influence the entire range of official decisions; no other individual has the same necessary involvement in all important decisions. The mayor has the ability to focus and divert public attention. The public, which is unaware of his limited legal and party positions, considers the mayor responsible for what the city government does or does not do: the city executive is called the "Rebecchini giunta" or the "Cioccetti giunta," thus conferring upon the mayor a certain amount of personal prestige. Periodization in the postwar political history of the city is still based on changes in mayoral administrations. Certainly no decisions of any importance are taken by the city without the mayor's participation, or when the mayor is out of town.

The form of the city's government is in itself no obstacle to effective planning. The electoral law, providing for at-large election of the council, probably eliminates a considerable amount of interdistrict logrolling that election by wards might entail or require. The simplicity of the city's governmental system makes decisionmaking and action relatively easy, provided that enough interparty agreement exists to allow the structures to operate. There are no checks and balances, no organs with separate and independent constituencies, no independent citizens' commissions to cloud the responsibility of the council and the giunta. At-large elections may even reduce the political risks of some kinds of planning decisions which, by relocating people, affect the balance of power within particular parts of the city.[11]

### PLANNING AND THE ROMAN BUREAUCRACY

Planning Rome has been difficult less because of the structures of policymaking than because of the structures of administration.[12] The structures of policymaking have been simple and action-oriented, at least if we compare them to policymaking structures in American cities, with their numerous independently elected executive officials, independent boards and commissions, checks and balances, separated constituencies, and separated powers. Responsibility for policymaking in Rome is clearly defined and concentrated: policy initiative belongs to the giunta, while policy discussion and acceptance lie with the city council. But the structures of administration in Rome have been able to provide neither competent policy advice nor efficient and faithful policy execution. Administrative deficiencies must bear some of the blame for the delay in adopting a new plan, the degradation of the Roman environment, the lack of sophisticated and broadly representative plans, and the poor record in achieving planning goals.

Like many Italian cities, Rome has been unable to build a strong, talented, reasonably honest, and effective planning apparatus. The offices charged with current plan enforcement and with forward master planning have reflected, in magnified degree, the general defects of Roman and indeed Italian public administration. In the city planning agencies, just as in most city agencies and national ministries, one finds the same set of stifling, paradoxical traits: overstaffing and understaffing, legal formalism and corruption, overspecialization and technical incompetence, overcompliance and lack of responsiveness. The defects of the state bureaucracy are aggravated in the city bureaucracy by the financial problems of the city, which keep city employees in a perpetual state of agitation and anxiety. In recent years, employees have never been sure that the city would be able to pay next month's salary. The city's ability to compete with the private sector for educated and talented personnel has been nullified by the city's financial woes and by the boom in the private economy. The city's competitive disadvantage has been especially severe in the case of technical person-

11. Cf. George S. Duggar, "The Relation of Local Government Structure to Urban Renewal," *Law and Contemporary Problems,* Winter 1961, pp. 62–69.
12. Though note the qualification to this statement in the last paragraph of this section.

Table 6.5. Distribution of City Employees

| Unit | Number of employees |
|---|---|
| Mayor's Office | 157 |
| General Secretariat I Directorate | 162 |
| General Secretariat II Directorate | 253 |
| General Secretariat III Directorate | 20 |
| Technical Communications Service | 354 |
| City Attorney's Office | 79 |
| Comptroller's Office | 367 |
| Personnel Dept. (I) | 508[a] |
| Real Estate Dept. (II) | 413 |
| Tax Dept. (III) | |
|     Direct taxes | 616 |
|     Consumption taxes | 1,046 |
| Public Works Dept. (V) | 1,043 |
| Utilities Dept. (VI) | 146 |
| Police Dept. (VII) | |
|     Delegations | 530 |
|     Traffic police | 2,482 |
| Health Dept. (VIII) | |
|     Public health | 1,227 |
|     Funeral services | 259 |
| Education and Welfare Dept. (IX) | 3,614 |
| Antiquities and Fine Arts Dept. (X) | 245 |
| Food and Markets Dept. (XI) | 352 |
| Supplies Dept. (XII) | 278 |
| Beaches and Agro Romano Dept. (XIII) | 327 |
| Traffic Dept. (XIV) | 177 |
| Planning and Building Dept. (XV) | 487 |
| Entertainment, Sports, and Tourism Assessorate | 17 |
| Electoral Service | 311 |
| Sanitation Service | 5,676[b] |
| Parks Service | 1,008 |
| Zoo | 97 |
| Milk Company | 1 |
| Billposting and Publicity Service | 155 |
| TOTAL REGULAR CITY EMPLOYEES | 23,010 |
| Water and Power Company | 3,612 |
| Transportation Company | 12,657 |
| Milk Company | 1,338 |
| TOTAL MUNICIPAL UTILITY EMPLOYEES | 17,607 |
| TOTAL CITY EMPLOYEES | 40,617 |

Source: Comune di Roma, Ufficio Statistica e Censimento, Bollettino Statistico, April 1966, p. 68.
a. Of whom 210 actually in service in the Department; 298 on loan to other departments.
b. Of whom 5,583 on annual contract (servizio in economia).

nel, and this has had particularly unfortunate consequences for city planning administration.

The city employs about 23,000 people in the regular city departments and about 18,000 people in the city-owned enterprises. There are fifteen *Ripartizioni* (departments), six *Servizi* (services), some miscellaneous other units, and three major municipal companies for public transit (ATAC), water and power (ACEA), and milk *(Centrale del Latte.)* The city is the sole stockholder in a fourth enter-prise, STEFER, which operates the subway system and a network of suburban trolley and bus lines. Departments, services, and companies are grouped to-gether for purposes of political direction and supervision by one of the eighteen assessors in the city giunta. Table 6.5 shows the major subdivisions of the city's administrative system and the relative importance of each division in terms of employment.

Each of the city departments is managed by a permanent, politically neutral set of officials, recruited on the basis of open, competitive examinations. Beneath the white collar level are the city workers *(salariati)* who are hired without ex-amination. (See Table 6.6.) The tables of organization are rigidly controlled by the Ministry of the Interior, which makes authoritative suggestions as to how the city administration is to be organized and reorganized. Only the lower levels of the city service are accessible to party patronage, but even at this level workers once hired are not fired when there is a change in administration. Given the rigi-dity of the tables of organization and de facto recognition of employee tenure rights, there is relatively little room for the operation of the spoils system. Party and personal connections do, however, play an important role in promotions and other aspects of personnel management, at all levels.

The city bureaucracy has thus displayed considerable continuity of personnel, both leading and subordinate, a continuity that even the events of 1943–44 did not appreciably interrupt. Major prewar administrative officials survived the purge of 1944–45 and served far into the postwar period. Some important figures who were purged in 1944–45 were later reinstated. The war severely disrupted Italian education and the civil service examination system, already damaged by the growing interference of the Fascist party. As a result, thousands of employees were admitted into the city bureaucracy who lacked the usual prerequisites of training and competence. The war also lowered standards of integrity within the administration, an integrity already badly weakened by twenty years of dictatorship. Two decades without a free press and without political competition bred habits of corruption and arbitrariness that could not easily be shed. The

Table 6.6. Rome City Payroll, 1959 and 1964

|  | 1959 | | 1964 | |
|---|---|---|---|---|
|  | Number | Expenditure (billions of lire) | Number | Expenditure (billions of lire) |
| Salaried employees |  |  |  |  |
| On the rolls | 4,227 | 7.1 | 5,988 | 14.9 |
| "Temporary" | 924 | 2.0 | 1,350 | 2.8 |
| Wage earners |  |  |  |  |
| On the rolls | 11,633 | 12.1 | 14,124 | 26.0 |
| "Temporary" | 3,222 | 3.1 | 1,065 | 1.6 |
| Total | 20,006 | 24.4 | 22,257 | 45.3 |

*Source: Annuario Statistico della Città di Roma, 1964,* p. 296.

fall of Fascism, the subsequent two military occupations, plus the chaos of the war and immediate postwar period, destroyed whatever regularity, discipline, and order had previously existed in the city offices. The general level of efficiency and effectiveness in the city bureaucracy has remained rather low during the postwar period.

The city has suffered a handicap in recruiting the best available talent for service in its higher ranks because of the unfavorable stereotype that city enjoys, especially in the North and Center. Curiously, the attractions of Rome that makes it so desirable an assignment within the state bureaucracy do not seem to help the city in recruiting for the municipal service. The national prestige of the Rome city bureaucracy is not as high as it might be. For some reason, the bureaucracies in the northern cities, such as Milan or Turin or Bologna, enjoy higher reputations despite the greater competition in the North from private enterprise.

A separate Planning Department *(Ripartizione XV—Urbanistica ed Edilizia Privata)* was detached from the Public Works Department *(Ripartizione V)* in 1957. It is a permanent organization, composed of regular city functionaries and employees, created in the 1930s for the implementation of the master plan of 1931 and the building code of 1934. The Planning Department, which has basically the functions of a building and safety department, has been responsible for processing applications for building permits and for administering the existing ground rules for development, rather than designing new rules. Its performance in enforcing existing rules has been almost totally unsatisfactory.[13]

The Planning Department has not been able to curb widespread illegal building activities, including subdivisions in the Agro Romano and alterations in the historic center. It has allowed major projects to be built without authorization. It has allowed private construction companies to move trolley tracks, demolish landmarks, and subdivide land in reclamation districts. It has often provided legalization after the fact, granting permits for already completed projects. It has not enforced the terms of permits, when duly applied for and issued, and has not regularly checked to see whether permit specifications have been met. Most illegal building in the city has taken the form of violating building and subdivision permit conditions. Disorganization and corruption in the department have frequently allowed private operators to secure revision of their permits in order to legalize their faits accomplis. Overwhelmed by the flood of permit applications, the department has tended to act only on those applications backed by political influence. Interminable waiting for permit applications to be processed could be avoided if the applicants had *"santi in paradiso"* (literally:

13. Some of the administrative problems of Roman planning are discussed in the report of Planning Assessor Enzo Storoni, contained in "Council Debates, 1953–1954," pp. 6–22, and in the report of Planning Assessor Amerigo Petrucci, "Riordinamento degli Uffici del Piano Regolatore, dell'Urbanistica e dell'Edilizia Privata," mimeographed (1963?).

"saints in paradise"), that is, high-level patrons in the parties, the church, or in business. Action could also be obtained through bribery.[14]

Perhaps more serious, the department authorized projects that violated laws and regulations. One of the major forms of "illegalism" in the city's development was thus an "official illegalism," in which the enforcement agency conspired to subvert the rules it was charged with enforcing. The department designed detailed plans to implement the master plan of 1931, not on the basis of any overall scheme of implementation but on the basis of pressures from private developers. Its detailed plans almost invariably raised the permissible density levels above those allowed by the master plan. But master plan specifications for facilities were followed, even though they were no longer appropriate for the newly raised densities. Thus the department is responsible for the narrow, dark, and winding streets, the lack of parks and facilities, and the general lack of amenities in the legally built districts of postwar Rome. The department also sponsored the same intensive development in the rebuilding of older districts under variances to existing detailed plans.[15]

As the new master plan was being formulated, the department continued to apply the standards of the old plan, interpreted in a fashion as favorable as possible to private developers. It failed to notify the master planners of ongoing building activities that were filling sites the planners assumed were vacant and available for facilities. On many occasions the department seemed to be deliberately sabotaging the master planning operation by permitting building on such sites. While the route of the eastern axis was being designed, the department issued permits directly on the routes selected by the master planners.[16] Officials in the department, in fact, were very lukewarm about the master planning operation; they were generally skeptical about the newer planning theories being taught in the university and being applied to the new master plan.[17]

They worked under extremely difficult physical conditions, packed into tight quarters, with no physical barriers between them and the public and no facilities for the orderly filing and protection of documents. Extreme disorder within the offices made all sorts of irregularities a matter of course. A relatively small professional staff had to design detailed plans and process thousands of permit

14. The literature on the defects of the Rome City Planning Department is abundant. See, inter alia, the verdict of the court in the *L'Espresso* defamation trial, "Tribunale di Roma, Sezione Quarta, Sentenza del 29 mese di dicembre [1956] . . ." (typescript); the Storoni report in "Council Debates, 1953–54," pp. 6–22; Leone Cattani, *Urbanistica romana: una battaglia liberale in Campidoglio* (Rome, 1954); *Il Messaggero,* May 10, 1962, December 17, 1963, October 31, 1964; *L'Espresso,* December 11, 1955, January 22, April 8, 15, 1956, December 6, 1962, December 15, 1963, March 7, 1965; *Notiziario dei Costruttori Romani,* November 1966, pp. 14–16.

15. Italo Insolera, "La capitale in espansion," in *Roma: Città e piani,* pp. 140–44; Vittorini, *Pianificazione urbanistica* p. 42.

16. Della Seta, *Il piano regolatore di Roma,* p. 90.

17. Benevolo, "Le facoltà di architettura," pp. 15–34. Benevolo makes it clear that *most* Italian universities were extremely unsympathetic to the newer planning approaches.

applications. Conditions in the department were denounced by Planning Assessor Storoni in 1953, but as the building boom took shape and, at the same
time, the master planning operation threatened to impose new limitations on
development and building, conditions in the offices grew even worse. Pressures
on the department increased with each new master plan, as development norms
grew more restrictive, reducing development possibilities nearest the urban
fringe and lowering allowable building volumes in all legal expansion zones.
Restrictions on development and building reduced the supply of land and
housing, raised the prices of legally available land, and created enormous
economic incentives to violate the law. Ten thousand building permit applications flooded into the department just before the 1962 master plan went into
effect, as applicants sought to enjoy the broader development and building
possibilities allowed under previous norms.[18]

Part of the blame for the poor performance of the Planning Department
can be attributed to the small size of its staff and its lack of equipment. For the
surveillance of building activities throughout the six hundred square miles within
the city limits, the department in 1954 had three building inspectors, equipped
with one jeep.[19] By 1963 the inspection force had been augmented by the allocation of seventy members from the *Corpo dei Vigili Urbani* or city police force;
this was less than the nine hundred-man staff estimated by the corps as necessary to provide effective surveillance for a city as large as Rome.[20] The city
police force is responsible only for the enforcement of city ordinances, not for
general law enforcement. The latter, in Rome and throughout Italy, is the
function of two national police agencies, the Ministry of the Interior's Public
Security Guards and the Ministry of Defense's Corps of Carabinieri. Under the
Planning Act of 1942, the national police forces were not authorized to aid in
the enforcement of building and zoning ordinances; this responsibility was left
entirely up to the city. The *Corpo dei Vigili Urbani,* with fewer than 2,500 *vigili,*
can spare relatively few men for building regulation since it is responsible for
enforcing all city codes, including and primarily the traffic code, as well as for
delivering official notices, catching stray dogs, inspecting markets, and the like.[21]

Part of the blame for poor performance lies also with the institutions with
supervisory responsibility for city performance. The courts, including the regular courts and the Council of State, tended to interpret the Planning Act of
1942 in such a way as to minimize the city's right to deny building permit applications and to suspend or demolish unauthorized construction.[22] The investigating magistrates, moreover, seem to have been slow in detecting the ram-
pant corruption within the Planning Department. Only in 1963 did these magis-

18. Petrucci, "Riordinamento," p. 6.
19. "Council Debates, 1953–54," p. 7.
20. *Il Messaggero,* December 29, 1963.
21. *Annuario Statistico della Città di Roma: Anno 1964* (Rome, 1969), p. 342.
22. Petrucci, "Riordinamento," pp. 7–9.

trates, the Italian equivalent of the district attorney's office, launch an investigation into Planning Department corruption. Indictments were returned against leading department officials in 1966 for having permitted the construction, in violation of the building and zoning code, of a development with twenty apartment houses on Monte Mario. The sites involved were not zoned for development; the apartment houses were built with an unlawful number of stories.[23] The Ministry of the Interior, responsible for the *administrative* supervision of Italian local governments, did not use its vast powers of investigation to curb illegalities in Roman planning, as it did in Naples, Agrigento, and Palermo, though there is no reason to believe that conditions in those southern cities were any worse than they have been in Rome.[24]

Part of the blame for poor performance must also fall upon the city Building and Planning Commissions, which are required to determine, on the basis of reports from the Planning Department, whether building permit applications conform to the building code (Building Commission) and to the master plan (Planning Commission). Despite its name, the Planning Commission *(Commissione Urbanistica)* is not much like institutions of the same name in the United States. It is composed of thirty-six members; half of them represent city and state agencies; half are experts designated by the engineering, planning, and architectural associations. One member is designated by the Property Owners' Association. There are no general representatives of the public, as on planning commissions in the United States. The commission reviews important applications for building permits, as well as proposed detailed plans of implementation. It may be overruled by the city giunta or council. Its decisions are not public and it has no access to public opinion; it publishes no reports; it does not prepare the capital budget. It acts in quasi-judicial fashion, rather than as an agency for debate or deliberation. It is an internal, almost private, advisory organ of the city government. Its activities and decisions are never reported in the press. It cannot set planning policy in conflict with the desires of the politically responsible planning assessor, giunta, mayor, or council. The system of responsible party government precludes the possibility of independent policymaking organs that might detract from the full responsibility of the political executive.

Even without independence, the Planning Commission is an important actor in the planning process because it is the day-to-day interpreter of the master plan and a major guardian of plan norms. While it played no role in formulating the new master plan, it performed rather poorly its function as guardian of the master plan of 1931, allowing the Planning Department to issue detailed plans, variances, and building permits that violated the none too restrictive standards of that plan. The commission, composed of extremely busy city functionaries

23. *Il Messaggero*, March 26, 1966.
24. On its investigations in Palermo, see Michele Pantaleone, *Antimafia*.

and private professionals, appears simply to have ratified most proposals laid before it by the Planning Department.[25]

Another reason for the ineffectiveness of the Planning Department is the massive scale of the illegal activities it is supposed to curb, combined with the lack of strong popular support for law enforcement. Department indulgence toward powerful real estate operators has really not been much greater than its indulgence toward the small illegal builders in the suburbs—migrants, white collar employees, and workers—who simply could not afford to build on legally subdivided land. The number of subdivisions mounted as the price of lots in duly authorized tracts rose and as it became clear that the city could not or would not take strong action against illegal subdividers. There is considerable sympathy for those who have bought small, illegally subdivided lots in the suburbs, who have paid for their lots and possess clear title to them as acreage, and who have proceeded to build illegally on them on the basis of promises by the subdividers of impending city approval. Action to demolish the illegally built structures is widely regarded as unfair since this punishes the victim rather than the fraudulent subdivider. Demolition of illegal structures, whether houses in the countryside or additional stories in the historic center, goes against strong Italian traditions regarding *ius aedificandi* (the right to build on one's property), the sacredness of *"la casa,"* and the destruction of wealth. An unwritten law forbids the demolition of any structure once it has been roofed, whence the pressures on the Planning Department to tolerate illegal building and the pressures on the master planners to incorporate the "spontaneous" subdivisions in the master plan.[26] As of the late sixties, there were about 150 illegal subdivisions around the city, most of which have been legalized in the new master plan. Attached to these illegal subdivisions are some five hundred shantytowns, which, of course, are slated for eventual demolition. The number of illegal subdivisions and shantytowns continues to grow.[27]

A Special Office for the New Master Plan (Ufficio Speciale Nuovo Piano Regolatore or USNPR) was established in 1953 to help formulate a new master plan, leaving the administration and implementation of the existing 1931 plan in the hands of the Planning Department. USNPR was to be a temporary office, composed of private professional planners hired on annual contract; like many temporary offices, it has made itself sufficiently indispensable to acquire de facto if not de jure permanency. The planners in USNPR were mostly drawn from the academic world and private consulting firms. The relations between them and the planning administrators in Planning Department have not been mutual-

25. I. Insolera, "L'Istituto del Regolamento Edilizio," *Urbanistica,* October 1959, pp. 311–13; *La Giustizia,* October 20, 1953; Giulio Tirincanti, *Il Messaggero,* March 22, 1962.

26. Accordingly, most illegal building takes place at a furious pace at nighttime so that by dawn the new structure has a roof to protect it, both from the elements and from the law.

27. The February 1969 issue of the city newsletter, *Roma Oggi* (pp. 1–9), contains pictures and descriptions of *fifteen* illegal subdivisions under investigation by the city authorities.

ly supportive. USNPR planners are future-oriented, concerned with the defects
of the existing system, and staunch believers in master planning. Planning
Department functionaries have been much more concerned with practical problems of plan administration, building regulation, and subdivision control;
they were less critical of the traditional planning policies about which they knew
a great deal and skeptical about the need for a new plan. They resented the
budget and attention received by the Special Office and were as uncooperative
with the office as they could be.

The Special Office, with about a dozen planners, has had the thankless task
of attempting to mediate between the "realistic" values of the bureaucratic-
political world of city government and the idealistic values and demands of the
professional city planning movement. It has had to contend with the skepticism,
inefficiency, and sabotage of the Planning Department, on one flank, and the
lack of support from fellow professionals in the Institute of Planners. When first
established in 1953, the Special Office seemed destined to play the dominant
role in researching and designing the new master plan. In 1954, however, the
major role in design was given to the prestigious members of the CET and the
Special Office was relegated to the role of research and drafting. The CET and
the Special Office worked together on reasonable terms in dealing with the
Grand Commission and in working out the new plan. When in 1958 the CET
was disbanded and its plan rejected, the Special Office became the principal
source of technical advice to the conservative planning coalition; its relations
with the professional planning movement deteriorated rapidly as it became, at
least in the eyes of outside planners, the instrument of the speculator "counter-
revolution." The Special Office designed the master plan adopted by the city
council in June 1959—a plan almost universally condemned by the professional
planners. The Special Office accordingly lost all standing with the professional
planning movement; when the latter regained control of the master planning
process in 1962, it brought in a set of progressive planning consultants from the
outside, the Committee of Five, to design a new version—the third—of the
master plan. The resulting 1962 plan was in many ways a reversion to the 1957
CET plan; one of the prominent members of the CET, Professor Luigi Piccinato,
a Socialist, became the leading member of the Committee of Five in 1962. By
1962, however, good working relations between the progressive planning consultants and the Special Office had become impossible. During the formulation
of the 1962 master plan there were frequent conflicts between the two groups
and threats of mass resignation. Eventually two separate reports were prepared
on the plan, one by the Special Office, one by the Committee of Five. A single
official map and a single set of norms were, however, agreed upon.[28]

28. On the Special Office, see Mario Manieri-Elia, "L'attività dell'Ufficio Speciale per il
Nuove Piano Regolatore," *Urbanistica*, October 1959, pp. 164–68; Petrucci, "Riordinamento";
and Mario Coppa, "La lunga strada per il piano di Roma," *Urbanistica*, March 1965, pp. 16–
17. On the conflict between the consultants and the Special Office, see also *Il Tempo*, May 20,
21, 1962; *Il Paese*, June 8, 1962; *Il Messaggero*, July 10, 1962.

Once again, just as in 1931, a new plan was designed and presented by an ad hoc drafting committee, the Committee of Five, which then was disbanded, leaving control of implementation in the hands of the permanent bureaucracies. In effect, a policy designed by and for progressives was entrusted to the mercies of conservative administrators. Progressives were fully aware of the dangers involved and accordingly placed great stress on the need to create new planning institutions to administer the new plan. The Left and the professional planners secured from the giunta in December 1962 a pledge to create a new Permanent Planning Institute and to reform the existing city planning offices, the Planning Department and the Special Office. The Permanent Planning Institute was to be a progressively oriented research outfit; the reformed planning offices were to become more honest, efficient, and enlightened. The exact division of labor between the permanent institute and the planning offices was not precisely defined.

The creation of new planning agencies has been held up by several things, including a jurisdictional conflict with Rome province. In 1963, Rome province joined with the other provinces of Lazio in creating their own regional economic research institute, thus to some extent preempting the field. The mayors of Rome, in any event, have been concerned lest any new planning agency diminish the autonomy of the city and particularly the power of the mayor's office. The new research institute proposed by the Socialists is supposed to have metropolitan and even regional scope; it might become a powerful center for planning that would rival and perhaps outweigh the city administration in determining policy for the city. The city might not have sufficient control over what the institute proposed. Christian Democrats have been wary of creating the new institute, both because it is so obviously desired by the Socialists and by the progressive planners and because it might create trouble between the city and the provincial branches of the Christian Democratic party itself. Creation of the new institute has also been held up by the number of unresolved issues concerning what it is to do, how it should be organized and controlled, and how it should be fitted into the structure of general governments at the local, provincial, and regional levels. The national government, for its part, does not seem greatly disturbed by the lack of a new research institute for Roman planning; it has regularly vetoed appropriations for that purpose in the city budget. The existing city planning offices, needless to say, are not anxious to be displaced by the new institute. Thus the administrative structure for Roman planning remains unaltered.[29]

With the aid of conservatives in the Christian Democratic party, conservative planning interests have been able to prevent the reform of the planning offices and the creation of the new planning institute. Conservative forces have retained at the administrative level *some* of the power they lost in 1962 at the policy level.

29. For the background to the permanent institute, see *Il Messaggero*, December 28, 1961; for background on the vetoes, see ibid., September 17, 1963, January 28, 29, 1965. The administrations elected in July 1962, April 1964, July 1966, December 1967, and August 1969 have all pledged themselves to create the Permanent Planning Institute, without success.

Christian Democrats have kept control over both the Planning Department and the Special Office since 1962. For the formulation of the Law 167 housing scheme, the Socialists refused to use the planning offices and instead created a new planning staff in the Real Estate Department under a Socialist assessor. The Planning Department continues to process building permit applications as inefficiently as before: the average time required for permit issuance is 514 days.[30] Of course, by the time permits are issued, market conditions may have changed considerably. Enforcement of the zoning and building norms of the new master plan continues to be plagued by the lack of a final and definitive version of the official map and regulations. In its absence, the Planning Department has continued to design detailed plans and approve development contradicting the norms of the new master plan. Thus, the city council's own planning committee was recently forced to veto several proposed new detailed plans designed by the Planning Department because they sanctioned further development in already congested areas *(Viale Marconi)* and on sites marked for public facility construction.[31]

The Special Office is still responsible for translating the generalities of the 1962 master plan into more specific functional and areal plans. It has been able to begin this translation only recently, having been deeply involved in a long series of lower level operations: the practical drafting of 70 zone plans for the Law 167 program in 1963; the processing of 4,365 appeals against the 1962 master plan and of 1,877 appeals against the Law 167 program in 1963–64; the formulation of the first Biennial Implementation Program (1965–66); the preparation of the General Variance of October 17, 1967, and the processing of the resulting appeals.

Only in 1966 did the work of translating the 1962 master plan into specifics begin. Rough plans for the "conservationist" rehabilitation of the historic center began to appear in 1966, and for the eastern axis, the new directive centers, and the Agro Romano, in 1968.[32] The Special Office, however, still employs only architect and engineer planners—no economists, sociologists, or other experts in social-economic research. It has made use of the Antiquities Department, the Statistics Office, and university planning experts, but it still operates largely without reference to community preferences or social scientific advice.

In the absence of new research facilities, some of the initiative for plan implementation and plan revision has been taken by the private planners, working for the most part voluntarily. An impressive scheme of parks and recreational facilities for Rome was elaborated by an INU commission and presented to the public in 1966.[33] INU planners were given the cooperation of a large number of

30. *Notiziario dei Costruttori Romani,* November 1966, pp. 14–16.
31. *Il Messaggero,* June 26, 1970.
32. See *Capitolium,* September–October 1968 (eastern axis); special edition, 1968, "La Carta dell'Agro Romano"; September–October 1966 (historic center).
33. *Urbanistica,* May 1966.

city departments and national agencies. Many kinds of specialists were brought into the planning process, including archeologists, planners, recreation experts, and ecologists. While various agencies and professions were willing to cooperate in formulating the new plan, implementation has been a slow and difficult process, involving the actual mobilization of resources for the goals agreed upon in the plan.

Conflicts among planning agencies and groups have not made it easy for the planners to coordinate the work of other city and national agencies. Presumably one of the major purposes of master planning is to provide a common frame of reference for the large number of actors in the development process. The Grand Commission gave formal representation in the city planning process to numerous public organizations, local and national, in the hope that a commitment to a common scheme could be achieved. To many of the city departments the master plan was an annoying and possibly threatening interference in their autonomy. Though all departments could see the virtues of coordinating investment and activities, many were skeptical about the effectiveness of a master plan as a coordinating device. The Public Works Department, for example, found that when it built to existing master plan specifications, the resulting infrastructures were inadequate; the detailed plans implementing the master plan, or variances modifying the master plan, invariably raised densities beyond the load of the infrastructure it had built. Though it was preferable on many grounds, including public health, to install water and sewerage *before* development, it was, in practice, unwise; there was no way of knowing beforehand just how much development was going to occur. Thus Public Works came in with facilities after, rather than before, people were actually living in a district.

The process of adjusting sectorial plans to the master plan has been difficult though not impossible. The tendency has been for the traffic, public housing, sewerage, water, parks, school, utilities, and public transportation sectors to produce plans of their own, with at least lip service to the master plan. A permanent coordinating committee of department heads, established under the planning assessor's chairmanship in 1963, has had some success in seeing to it that the various sectorial plans and annual programs overlap with the intentions and priorities of the master plan. Coordination is also enhanced by a gradual shift toward largescale expansion in the form of large private subdivisions, Law 167 districts, and detailed plans. Various city departments seem to have found it convenient to have the new master plan for their own planning purposes. The city planners, in return, have usually been willing to modify the master plan to take into account the needs of the various sectors.

But the city departments were more willing than able to help implement the master plan. They suffered from the same lack of effectiveness as the city planning offices. They had low budgets, poor morale, little modern equipment, and old-fashioned methods. They tended to be overstaffed at the lowest levels and to lack technically qualified people in the higher ranks. The Parks Department *(Servizio Giardini)* employs 1,100 gardeners but no landscape architects; it has no planning unit.[34] The Sanitation Department uses old trucks and equipment; it collects garbage daily from each apartment because the apartment houses in the city have no garbage chutes or facilities for storing garbage. The streets are cleaned by street sweepers, while council appropriations for new equipment are regularly vetoed by the national government. Refuse collection is increasingly costly, given the congestion on the city streets and a doubling in the amount of refuse to be collected.[35]

Given the *administrative* situation, one may well wonder whether it made any difference at all what kind of planning policies were adopted during the years of the boom or even since. The available administrative structures were incapable of enforcing restrictions on building. Whether they would have or could have enforced a newer, stricter set of zoning regulations and building restrictions is doubtful. Existing agencies were simply too weak to cope with the "anarchy of production." The regulatory agencies of the national government, notably the superintendent of monuments, showed no greater regulatory capability than the city agencies. The superintendent of monuments is charged with enforcing the regulations protecting historic, artistic, and scenic resources under 1939 laws. The superintendency in Rome, as in other parts of Italy, has simply lacked the staff for the purposes of surveillance and the political support necessary to resist the demands of influential people who wish to develop properties in areas of historic or scenic importance, as along the Old Appian Way.[36]

Of course, much alleged administrative inefficiency in Rome really masks a considerable ability on the part of Roman bureaucrats to interpret and apply the implicit, rather than the explicit, policy of the city's leaders and leading groups. By explicit policy is meant the formal declarations, resolutions, and decisions of the city council and giunta, as well as the programmatic declarations of the governing parties, and even the opposition. By implicit policy is meant the actual policies that political groups want to have enforced and the way in which they want them enforced. It is not necessarily cynical to suggest that political groups

34. Vittoria Calzolari Ghio, "Roma, luglio 1966; nuovo piano regolatore nuovo amministrazione, nuovo verde?" *Italia Nostra,* May-June 1966, pp. 32–42.

35. Carlo Rosato, "Il servizio di nettezza urbana di una grande città: problemi e soluzioni," *L'Impresa Pubblica,* November-December 1967, pp. 9–18.

36. For documentation on the ineffectiveness of the superintendents of monuments, see the papers presented to the first national conference of *Italia Nostra,* Rome, November 18–20, 1966; the issues of the *Italia Nostra* bulletin since 1956; and Alfredo Barbacci, *Il guasto della città* (Florence, 1962). The interventions of the superintendent in Rome have been sporadic and controversial. In September 1969, for example, the superintendent vetoed a Traffic Department program to build nine underground parking lots in and around the historic center on grounds that this would increase the traffic burden of the old center; the leading newspaper of Rome, *Il Messaggero,* which is on the side of the progressive planners and conservationists except in questions involving traffic regulation, denounced the superintendent for condemning Rome to be a dead city (September 12, 1969). The superintendent's office was itself denounced for building a new ticket building on the Palatine in October 1965. (*Paese Sera,* October 30, 1965). A recent series in *L'Espresso* (February-March 1970) discussed the difficulties under which the superintendents operate.

and leaders have private opinions as to what is the public interest, opinions not for publication. The greatest gap between explicit and implicit policy usually occurs in the areas of (1) social reform and (2) regulation. The ineffectiveness of Roman administrative agencies in planning may well reflect their considerable talent in administering the implicit, rather than explicit, planning policies of the city's elites.

GOVERNMENT FORM AND PLANNING PERFORMANCE

A well-received idea in the literature on planning is that major planning achievements are more likely under a dictatorship, with its concentrated power and immunity to the pressures of heterogeneous and shifting interests. Experience in Rome before the war under Fascism and since the war under democratic forms of government would suggest the need for a less simplistic comparative generalization. Did the change of regime from dictatorship to pluralistic constitutional democracy at the national and local levels produce less effective planning?

By one criterion, certainly, there was a spectacular difference—the *time* it took to formulate and adopt a new master plan. Mussolini installed the drafting committee for the 1931 master plan on April 14, 1930, with orders to produce a plan by October 28 of the same year—the eighth anniversary of the Duce's accession to power. Six months later a plan was duly presented. By Royal Decree No. 981 of July 6, 1931, the plan became law. Thus in little over one year a plan was designed, adopted by the city authorities (the governor), and approved by the national government. The postwar city giunta approved the formulation of a new plan, in principle, in October 1951; debate began in the city council in December 1953; in May 1954, the Grand Commission and the CET were appointed to formulate the actual plan. The decree of the President of the Republic promulgating the new master plan of Rome appeared in the *Gazzetta Ufficiale* of February 11, 1966—over a decade later. Fascism made the city planners run on time.

Formulation and adoption of a new plan under a democracy were much more timeconsuming. Democratically responsible officials were loath to impose regulatory curbs on urban development and postponed making choices and restrictions until the latest possible moment. Under existing financial and legal conditions they could not compensate the losers, but the losers could withdraw support from them by voting for and contributing funds to the opposition parties. Nor was there any mass pressure for a new plan; if anything, public opinion seemed to support a policy of laissez-faire. Then, too, planning was a new kind of issue in a new political system: it was not at all clear what the stakes were, how the public felt, or what the various forces were after—what they stood to gain or lose. Democracy made it rather easier than before to block *any* initiative, not only a new plan: resistance to proposals was now legitimate, likely to be supported by one or more political parties and newspapers, and more embarrassing to city officials.

Delay was due in part to the combination of democracy and a controversial, risky policy area, in part to the combination of democracy and a highly competitive but badly fragmented party system. The parties in postwar Rome were new; their clienteles were not stable; they found it difficult to collaborate with each other in stable governing coalitions. Some stability has been achieved through immobilism, particularly in the planning field—a field that would otherwise be extremely disruptive. Democracy and a fragmented party system at the national level added further sources of instability to local sources.

By other standards the contrast is less stark. Fascist planning *style* was a good deal less comprehensive than the postwar democratic style. The Fascist plan of 1931 was obviously not the product of a broadly representative decisionmaking process, involving a large number of agencies, parties, and groups. It was the work of twelve architects, engineers, and city officials working privately under the chairmanship of the governor of Rome. The planners did attempt to interrelate various aspects of city life into a coherent scheme, but only engineering, architectural, and legal concepts and techniques were brought to bear. There was no attempt to place city planning in a regional setting. Nor was the 1931 master plan, in spite of secrecy and dictatorship, particularly coherent: it proposed to allow and encourage oil-stain expansion and at the same time to shift the center of the city toward the east.[37]

The postwar plan was so long in coming because it was not imposed on the city but adopted by officials responsible to the voters of the city. It followed years of debate in the city council, the press, and during election campaigns. It was freely adopted by a locally responsible city council, rather than decreed from on high by the national government. The final plan is perceptibly an attempt to reflect and adjust a wide range of interests, including those of the lowest economic groups in the borgate. It zones the entire city territory rather than just the central nucleus, as in the 1931 plan. The 1962 plan goes beyond the city territory, in fact, to take regional needs and possibilities into account.

The professional planning movement took organized shape in the National (Fascist) Institute of Planners (INU) in 1929. One of the founders of the Institute, architect Marcello Piacentini, was rapporteur for the master plan of 1931. INU members were active in designing the many public works projects of the regime and its new towns in the Pontine marshes and the African colonies. Yet the *impact of professional planners* was blunted by the resistance of national agencies, such as the Italian Railways, to the planning proposals of merely local functionaries; by sharp divisions within the planning movement over basic professional principles; by the hostility of property owners to many of the regulatory aspects of planning; by the conflicts of interest and shifting patterns

37. Ludovico Quaroni, "I problemi del Piano Regolatore di Roma," pp. 96–97.

of influence within the coalition of interests and ideologies that constituted the Fascist regime; and by the inconsistent values and goals of the planning movement and of individual planners. Despite its acceptance of the planning movement as legitimate and compatible with its totalitarian ideals, Fascism did not provide planners with a stable and secure power base. Because city planning was defined as technical rather than political, it was debatable. What made the movement acceptable to Fascism was its "nonpolitical" nature, but because it was nonpolitical it was also vulnerable, that is, open to criticism and resistance. Planning proposals were thus subject to much the same kind of opposition under Fascism as under postwar democracy. (Of course, opposition under the postwar democratic regime was justified for precisely the opposite reasons. Postwar democrats defined city planning not as technical but as political, and therefore debatable.) The Fascist regime did enact the Planning Law of 1942, still the basic enabling act the in planning field. But the 1942 law came much later than similar laws in northern Europe; it was adopted extremely reluctantly and only after wartime bombardment made reconstruction a major policy problem. The necessary implementing *Regolamento* was never issued. Fascist commitment to the new planning legislation was never put to a test.[38]

With regard to *goal achievement,* the same dictatorial power that permitted the Fascists swiftly to make a plan allowed them, just as swiftly, to unmake the plan and ignore it. The firmness and continuity of purpose of which the regime boasted were not evident in Roman planning. As seen in chapter 2, the regime rather blithely and almost systematically ignored its own plan in deciding on major projects. It carried out, fortunately, few of the clearance projects proposed in the 1931 master plan and derived from that plan few of the projects that it actually carried out. Ironically, between 1925 and 1943, under the Fascist regime, the city had six different governors. During the preceding period, 1899–1920, it had had only four mayors, while during the subsequent eighteen years, under the democratic system, it would have only five mayors. There was apparently no greater executive stability under Fascism than under the competitive party system, nor was there the unity or continuity of will to make for more coherent planning.

The Fascist *Governatorato* was no better able to repress illegal building in the city than postwar democratic governments. The 1931 master plan banned all development outside of the plan perimeter, without city authorization. Nonetheless a large number of illegal settlements and shantytowns appeared in the Agro, to which the governor in 1935 was forced to give official recognition.[39] The number of illegal settlements continued to grow, especially with the massive immigration to the city during the thirties and the start of the war. The Fascist government was just as incapable of repressing illegal subdivision and building as it was of enforcing the laws banning migration to the city.

38. Benevolo, *L'architettura delle città,* pp. 167–80.
39. Crespi et al., "Aspetti del rapporto," pp. 13–23.

In one respect the Fascist regime was much more favorable to Roman planning effectiveness than the postwar governments. It granted an annual subvention of $100 million dollars (at 1958 rates of exchange) to the city for the purposes of plan implementation.[40] The importance to Mussolini of Rome as his imperial capital accounted for the generous financial aid he provided for the city and for the interest he took in Roman planning. Yet the benefits of this spending for the city's amenity are difficult to measure. Fascism emphasized monumentality rather than amenity. It carried out a number of clearance projects in the historic center and relocated the former residents in isolated borgate under the watchful eyes of the police but hidden from the highways on which the tourists passed. Thousands of former residents of the historic center found themselves settled far out in the country, without employment opportunities, and living in housing with only collective sanitary, washing, and drinking facilities. The impact of Fascism on general living conditions is perhaps measured by the index of crowding, which fell from 1.49 persons per room in 1921 to 1.41 persons per room in 1931, only to rise again to 1.49 in 1943.[41] The postwar period has seen the index drop to 1.1 persons per room.

The establishment of democracy brought with it a process of rapid economic growth. It also gave the lower classes greater political muscle in the form of aggressive Communist and Socialist parties. But democratic rules did not place the parties of the lower classes in the majority. The establishment of democracy did not ipso facto revolutionize the structure of Roman society. It gave free expression to a structure of social influence not very different from that which dominated—at least in tone—the prewar city.

40. Comune di Roma, *Una legge per la capitale* (Rome, 1957), pp. 149–50.
41. Comune di Roma, Uffiico Speciale Nuovo Piano Regolatore, *Piano Regolatore Generale, Raccolta di Graffici Allegati alla Relazione* (Rome, 1957).

# 7

# NATIONAL
# POLITICS AND
# ROMAN PLANNING

THE IMPORTANCE OF NATIONAL POLITICS AND POLICY

Italy is a centralized, unitary state,[1] whence the importance of national policy for urban performance. The city of Rome derives its legal powers and its very existence as a legal entity from legislative acts of the national government. Whatever discretion the city enjoys in managing its affairs is discretion granted and removable by *lo Stato*—the national government. Unlike American cities, Rome has no city charter adopted by vote of its citizens. Its form of government, boundaries, and legal authority are determined by national law and decree. The powers of the city government are those delegated to it by national law and they are exercised under sometimes penetrating and absolute national controls—legislative, fiscal, administrative, and judicial. What the city does and how well it does it ultimately depend on what it is stimulated, allowed, or helped to do by the state.

The city's general organization and legal powers derive from the Provincial and Communal Acts of 1915 and 1934; its tax powers derive from the Local Finance Act of 1931; its planning powers derive from the Urban Planning Act of 1942. Under these laws, every decision of any importance by city government officials is subject to the detailed examination and revision of national government officials. The thousands of deliberations of the city council and the giunta must be transmitted to the prefecture for review of their legality. All important decisions—budgets, plans, ordinances—are subject to ministerial approval and revision. The city thus must get ministerial approval before it can establish a new city department, increase the size of the traffic police force, build underground garages, create a planning institute, or increase its tax rates. The

1. Accordingly, when the term "state" is used in this book, it refers to the Italian *national* government.

national government may have occasion to intervene even more drastically in the city's affairs. If the city fails to carry out its legal obligations, if it fails for example to adopt a budget, the prefect may appoint a commissioner to perform the required act. If the city council is unable to elect a mayor and giunta, the council may be dissolved and city government powers transferred to a prefectoral commissioner appointed, again, by the prefect. The council may be dissolved for "serious reasons of public order" or for failure to meet its legal obligations. Mayors may be suspended or even removed on the same grounds. Thus the national government in Italy has much tighter control over local government than do American state governments.

It would be incorrect, however, to see city policymaking as dominated by national policymaking, for intergovernmental relations in Italy are marked as much by bargaining and interpenetration as by hierarchy. Even under Fascism, certain discretionary powers were lodged at the local level and removed from supercession by national officials. With the restoration of constitutional democracy, much of the dominance of the national government over local governments became theoretical rather than actual; the national government could not intervene in the affairs of cities without regard for the consequences, electoral and otherwise. Tutelage over local government is fundamentally a regulatory activity of the national government and subject to the foibles of regulatory administration in all democratic regimes. Fear of adverse reaction has made the national government somewhat hesitant to use its legally unlimited powers of supervision and control. In the case of Rome, the national government is dealing with a city government controlled by a powerful and autonomous Christian Democratic party faction, closely tied to eminent figures in the Catholic church. A city government with this kind of protection and patronage possesses a good deal of de facto autonomy.

The dramatic interventions of the national government in city affairs—the dissolutions of the city council in 1946 and 1961—were both necessitated by the inability of local political forces to agree on a governing coalition for the city. It is the action or inaction of local forces that determines whether the national government can legally intervene in city affairs. Usually the problem has been, at least in the case of Rome, not to avoid national intervention but to secure the right kind of national intervention, namely, financial aid. More often than not the national government, with regard to both regulatory tutelage and financial aid, has pursued a policy of nearly absolute laissez-faire: no strings, and no aid.

The role of the national government in Roman planning is very important but not all-important. National officials have always been intimate participants in Roman planning, as well as amused or despairing informal participants in the city's everyday life. The "urban crisis" in Rome is not an abstraction for national officials, who can see for themselves how well the city is working—at least in the middle-class districts. But however disturbed they may be personally about conditions in the capital, as *national* officials they are unable to do very much about them, for Italy as a nation is very unsympathetic to the plight of its national capital. "Anti-Romanism" prevents the national government from doing very much to rescue the city from its financial abyss. In dealing with the city, the national government finds its policies of regulation constrained by the city's legal and political autonomy, and its policies of financial support constrained by the city's unpopularity.

NATIONAL POLITICS AND PLANNING STYLE

National politics and policy had an impact on both the representativeness of the planning process in Rome and the scope of planning—an impact that worked, on the one hand, through formal legal and administrative rules and decisions and, on the other, through the changing balance of political forces at the national level.

National "constitutional" policy had crucial or potentially crucial importance for Roman planning. The constitution of 1948 would have had a much greater impact if Parliament had proceeded to enact the required implementing statutes. Under the constitution, authority over the whole field of urban government and urban planning was to be transferred from the national government to a set of regional governments. Had the regional governments been established, Roman planners and officials would have worked under the supervision and guidance of Lazio regional authorities rather than under the national Ministries of the Interior and of Public Works. The Lazio Regional Assembly would have been authorized to pass regional planning laws, within the bounds set by the national constitution and a national "framework-law" in the planning field. Until 1970, Parliament was unwilling either to create the regional governments or to adopt a framework-law for their guidance in the various fields of their competence. Thus the pre-Fascist and Fascist arrangements with regard to both local government tutelage and urban planning remained in effect. Constitutional guarantees of freedom of movement were likewise not implemented until 1961 when Parliament abrogated the 1931–39 laws prohibiting internal migration.

The constitution of 1948 has been much more important, even if in an indirect way, in sanctioning and organizing constitutional democracy in Italy. Roman planning outcomes were substantially different under the Republican constitution of 1948 than they had been under the Fascist dictatorship. The 1948 document created a democratically elected national government, highly sensitive to public opinion and therefore reluctant to adopt a new planning law. The national government was constantly torn between instincts of conservation and demands for reform, and was threatened, electorally if not physically, by the existence of strong antidemocratic sentiment on the Left, the Right, and in the Center. The Fascist dictatorship could adopt whatever policy for Rome it wished and could plan the city by fiat, although, by definition, there was nothing that could hold it faithful to the terms of any policy or plan it adopted.

Under postwar constitutional democracy, policy and planning for the city had to be adjusted to national public opinion and the national balance of power among the several political parties, as well as to the opinions and forces that prevailed within the city. Regular, open, and free competition for power within the city was possible only within the framework of national constitutionalism. A dictatorship at the national level would not have tolerated a local democracy any more than a constitutional government would have permitted a dictatorship in the city. Roman democracy owed its existence and survival to Italian democracy.

The constitution also legitimized and protected democratic participation in the planning process. Fascism had idealized hierarchy; the new regime idealized consent, equality, and widespread participation. It also legitimized the concepts and practices of pluralism, opposition, and compromise. The planning process in Rome reflected an effort by all political forces to apply some notion of democracy to the problem of planning. Few saw democracy in populistic terms— terms that implied the right of the people to make policy for the city directly by means of a referendum or terms that implied the need to consult popular and group preferences *before* adopting a plan. Most saw democracy as the competition of political elites for mass support and as a method of making decisions by consensus and compromise, rather than by majority or minority imposition. National and local democracy meant, if nothing else, that Roman planning— both the formation of new plans and the administration of existing ones—would benefit from the aggressive and generally constructive criticism and opposition of the Communists. There is no doubt that the quality of postwar Roman planning was enhanced by the presence in the city of a powerful, technically competent, and alert Communist opposition party.

Democracy, while permitting the existence of an astringent opposition, also placed in power a set of conservative forces that were much less committed to planning and possibly less committed to democracy than the Communist opposition. The power of the church in postwar Italy has derived from its ability to swing votes throughout the country. All the national forces, except the Radicals, were willing to accommodate the church's desire for a friendly city government in Rome, and dominant forces in the church during the fifties preferred a rightist-oriented government. The formation of the Catholic-neofascist alliance in the city in 1957–58 marked also the triumph of forces opposed to effective planning. When in 1960 an attempt was made to establish the same alliance at the national level in what was a clear and present threat to the republican constitution, the resulting riots throughout the peninsula made it clear that what was permissible in Rome was not viable in the rest of Italy. The threat to the republican regime struck an unexpectedly strong protective reflex and released a wave of progressivism that carried with it a new national and local coalition formula (the Catholic-Socialist alliance) and a new deal, if not a new order, in Roman planning. The master plan of 1962 owes its paternity to the "constituent" response of the street demonstrators of 1960.

The representativeness of the planning process was also affected by the terms of the Planning Act of 1942. Strangely enough, the act, though adopted by a fascist dictatorship, was rather easily adapted to the purpose of democratic planning. Primary responsibility for planning even under the Fascist system lay with the local authorities—local dictators *(podestà)* under Fascism, local councils under the republic. The procedural requirements for planning, even under Fascism, contained democratic elements. Plans once adopted had to be put on public display. Interested groups and individuals were given the legal right to present written objections. The local authorities were required to answer each of the objections and might recommend acceptance or rejection of them by the Ministry of Public Works, when it reviewed the plan. Though fascist in origin, the Planning Act of 1942 did not really cramp the democratic style of postwar Roman planning.

The act, to be sure, did provide for central powers of review and approval of locally adopted plans. Plans could not come into legal effect unless promulgated by the head of state on recommendation of the minister of public works. The ministry could refuse to approve a plan; it could send a plan back to the local authorities with recommended changes; or it could approve a plan with conditions. But the ministry could not make basic changes in the plan without the consent of the city, and thus could not nullify the basic planning policies desired by the local community.

The Planning Act of 1942 defined planning in physical and regulatory terms. There were to be three kinds of plans under the act: regional plans *(piani territoriali di coordinamento)*, prepared directly by the Ministry of Public Works; intercommunal plans, formed by groups of neighboring communes having common planning problems; and local master plans *(piani regolatori)*, adopted by individual communes. All plans were designed to regulate land use by means of zoning and building regulations and the power of eminent domain. Previously, Italian master plans covered development only in the existing built-up urban core and the neighboring fringe; large amounts of city territory might remain immune from planning, as they did under the Rome master plan of 1931. Under the 1942 act, master plans had to regulate development throughout the city. The plan had to indicate the major circulation facilities and the locations of public services. It had to "specify the characteristics and regulations to be observed" in building within each zone. The master plan was to be implemented in stages by the formulation and promulgation of detailed plans *(piani particolareggiati di esecuzione)* for each renewal project, public works project, or new residential district. In conformity with the master plan, detailed plans specified the location of roads and facilities, the exact buildings subject to renovation, the volumes and heights of new structures, and the design of new lots. Detailed plans listed the specific properties to be affected and the specific public expenditures to be made. Urban expansion was to be guided by public authorities by means of detailed plans. Under article 18 of the planning act, a city might even expropriate properties in zones marked for expansion, urbanize them, and resell them to private interests. Or it could simply design the subdivision, expropriate only the area needed for public services, and install the facilities, leaving the rest to private developers. The assumption was that zoning and building regulations, supplemented by the power of eminent domain and the power to install facilities, would be sufficient to permit the local authorities to guide the process of urban development and redevelopment.

Master planning was thus to be an exercise in design and regulation. The economic-financial aspects of planning were seen as incidental to the purposes of land use control. Those formulating a master plan would have no use for social or economic analysis; they would not be required to prepare a financial plan or even a rough estimate of the costs involved in their plan, except when they proposed that the city carry out compulsory land purchases in areas of expansion. Financial commitments did not need to be specified except at the detailed plan stage, when specific properties were to be taken for public services. Thus the report on the 1962 master plan contains no information on possible costs of implementation or on implications of the plan for the city's economy.

The legalistic conception of master planning inherent in the Planning Act of 1942 thus shaped the nature of the Rome master plan adopted twenty years later. The master plan was already designed in its essentials in July 1962 when a regional economist, Professor Glauco Della Porta, was elected mayor. Mayor Della Porta does not seem to have played any role in the final formulation of the plan between July and December 1962. Only after 1962 did the city begin to engage in capital programming and development planning, presumably under the influence of Mayor Della Porta but also in imitation of the more progressive Italian cities. Milan adopted its Five Year Plan in 1962; Rome was not able to produce a Five Year Plan until 1967. This plan was the first major effort to coordinate the investment policies of the city departments.

The Planning Act of 1942 does not establish any means for the systematic review of public building and investment plans to ensure their conformity with the master plan and building codes. It is true that national agencies, except for those in defense, are required to submit their works projects to the Ministry of Public Works to ensure that they conform to the master plan and code. But even in the planning act itself there is a provision allowing the Ministry of Corporations (now Industry and Commerce) to locate new industrial plants wherever it wishes. The Ministry of Public Works, supposedly *the* coordinator of planning, has been unable in the postwar period to prevent the emergence of a large number of operating agencies and planning authorities not subject, in practice, to its coordination.

The ministry is among the oldest ministries of the Italian state and has, for some time, together with the other traditional ministries, been considered inefficient, slowmoving, and old-fashioned. The tendency during the postwar period has been to create agencies outside the regular framework of Italian public administration, to plan and carry out the most important new development programs. Though the traditional ministries retained nominal powers of supervision, funds and energy flowed into powerful and autonomous new agencies, such as GESCAL for public housing; the *Cassa per il Mezzogiorno* for southern development; CONI (the Italian National Olympic Committee) for sports and recreational facilities; and the land reform agencies. New ministries were created with responsibilities in the physical planning field, such as the Ministry of Health (hospitals), the Ministry of Transport, and the Ministry of Defense (airports). Some of the older line ministries also has planning responsibilities, such as Agriculture (land reclamation) and Public Instruction (school construction). Powerful public corporations were created, such as ENI, the oil and natural gas company, and IRI, the state holding company that controls a large number of Italian firms and exercises great influence over the location of industry through the country.[2]

The Ministry of Public Works was in no position to coordinate the activities of this growing number of powerful and independent agencies. The Planning Act of 1942 assumed that the ministry, through its regional plans ("territorial coordination plans"), would be able to coordinate all the activities of government agencies that affected land use throughout the country. In the early fifties, the ministry began to sponsor the formulation of regional plans for the government agencies, but soon gave up the attempt. Only since 1965, with the emergence of regional economic development planning sponsored by the rival Ministry of the Budget, has the interest of the Ministry of Public Works in regional physical planning revived.[3]

If the Ministry of Public Works, with its statutory powers of coordination and its status as an agency of the national government, has been unable to provide coordination among the various state agencies, one cannot expect the city of Rome, with its inferior legal position and its merely local status, to have had much success in attempting to do the same kind of thing through its master plan.[4]

The city council sought to provide ample representation for the dozens of

2. Benevolo, *L'architettura della città*, pp. 167–71. At the first congress of the *Italia Nostra* society in 1966, Prof. Renato Bonelli made clear the supervisory impotence of the Ministry of Public Works:

The State Railways, the Ministry of Telecommunications, the Ministry of Defense, the port authorities, the National Electricity Board, and other important agencies continue to build facilities on arbitrarily chosen sites. Hospitals, sanatoriums, schools of every type and dimension, office buildings, sports facilities, courthouses, prisons, cemeteries, churches, and parish centers are being built anywhere, often in scenic zones protected by use restrictions or in the heart of historic centers; they are being built everywhere except where they were supposed to go under the existing master plan.

Renato Bonelli, "Principi, Metodi e Strumenti della Tutela, "*Relazione Gernerale*, Part 3, mimeographed.

3. Fried, "Administrative Pluralism," p. 383.

4. Article 29 makes the ministry responsible for ensuring that public works executed by state agencies are in accordance with the city master plan and building code. Agencies are required to submit building plans to the ministry for its approval.

agencies involved in the city's development when it established in 1954 the Grand Commission. Of the eighty-three original seats on the Grand Commission, six were occupied by city assessors, fourteen by city councilmen, nine by city functionaries, and fifteen by the architect-engineers on the Building and Planning Commissions. Fully thirty seats went to *national* ministries, agencies, and field services. Most national ministries were represented, as were most city departments. Representatives of the national ministries were among the most active participants in the commission's debates and took a leading role in opposing the master plan drafted by the CET in 1957. After the Grand Commission was dissolved there was no longer any forum for the representation of ministerial interests and viewpoints. Ministerial representatives, of course, were in a privileged position on the commission, for if it failed to take into account some vital interest of theirs the plan could be changed when it came to the national government for approval. The role of the Ministry of Public Works representatives on the commission was particularly strange: they were consultants to the city and formulators of the city's plan and, at the same time, those who would later be responsible in the ministry for reviewing and criticizing the plan.

As already noted, the constitution provided for the creation of regional governments to assume responsibility, among other things, for urban and regional planning. Under the Planning Act of 1942, however, the Ministry of Public Works had authority and responsibility for preparing regional plans, and did establish regional planning committees in various parts of the country, including Lazio in 1951–52. But no regional plans were ever presented and promulgated, partly because this might have seemed an infringement on the prerogatives of the still to be created regional governments. Thus master planners in Rome did not have the benefit of a regional plan, with its set of parameters and working hypotheses.

Instead of supporting the city's master planning, regional planning actually became a means of sabotaging it. One of the major arguments for rejection of the CET plan in 1957–58 was that it did not derive from a regional plan or even an intercommunal (metropolitan area) plan. Conservatives, who in the early fifties had opposed the idea of regional planning, turned to regional or rather intercommunal planning as a means of preventing, at least for a time, the adoption of a master plan for the city alone. They argued that there was a logical relationship among plans at various levels: that regional plans should derive from an overall national infrastructural plan; that intercommunal plans should derive from regional plans; and that local master plans should derive from intercommunal plans. Acceptance of this "Chinese boxes" argument postponed adoption of a local plan for a profitably indefinite period, especially since under the 1942 Planning Act no intercommunal plan could be adopted without the *unanimous* consent of all communes involved.[5]

5. On the interrelationships between communal, intercommunal, and regional physical planning, see the volumes published by the Istituto Nazionale di Urbanistica, *La pianificazione*

In 1958 the Ministry of Public Works sponsored an intercommunal plan for the Rome area, including Rome and forty surrounding communes. The province was also allowed to participate. An unofficial draft intercommunal plan was presented in 1960; unlike the master plans adopted in 1959 and 1962, it was accompanied by a series of volumes on various aspects of life in the Rome metropolitan area, indicating the basis for the choices made in the plan itself. Curiously, the intercommunal plan was formulated *without significant controversy* by planners representing both Communist and Christian Democratic communes—and this during a period of maximum interparty tension in Rome city politics as well as in national politics.[6] The intercommunal planners reached conclusions that confirmed the choices made earlier by the CET, particularly with reference to the pattern of expansion. The master planners of 1962, whose numbers included one of the intercommunal planners, could now claim that their choices were derived from choices, or at least conclusions, reached at a higher level by those with a broader areal overview.

The emergence of regional economic planning committees sponsored by the Ministry of the Budget in 1965 reminded the Ministry of Public Works of its own neglected responsibilities in the regional planning field. In 1966 an agreement was reached between the Ministry of Public Works and the Ministry of the Budget, providing for cooperative planning at the regional level. The Ministry of Public Works appointed a new committee to draft a physical plan for Lazio later that year; the Regional Economic Planning Committee for Lazio refused to accept the plan it produced, mostly because the minister of public works, a Socialist, had appointed only Socialist planners to the plan committee. The Regional Economic Planning Committee was headed by Mayor Petrucci of Rome, a Christian Democrat.

### NATIONAL POLITICS AND PLANNING ECONOMICS

The Planning Act of 1942 did not provide national financial assistance for urban planning. In fact, it stipulated that if a city refused to make a master plan, the Ministry of Public Works could step in, make the plan, and charge the costs to the city involved. The Italian government has made no grants to local authorities for planning purposes, nor has it generally provided any financial incentives for cities to plan, relying rather on regulatory powers. Between 1954 and 1961 the ministry ordered each of 645 communes to make a plan; as of 1963, only sixty-five had complied. As of the same date, only twenty-seven of the ninety-two Italian provincial capitals had formulated and secured national approval of a master plan.[7] By 1968, only 139 communes out of some eight

---

*regionale* (1953) and *La pianificazione intercomunale* (1957), and more recently, the March and October 1967 issues of *Urbanistica.*

6. Ideological conflict did, however, become a major factor in the much more important intercommunal planning operations in Milan and Turin. See the October 1967 issue of *Urbanistica* on those operations.

7. See the survey published in the March 1963 issue of *Urbanistica.* The impotence of the

thousand had submitted to the laborious process of producing a master plan and securing approval for it from the national government.[8] Reliance on regulatory powers alone, without financial assistance programs, has not proved successful. Likewise, the 1939 acts to conserve historic, archeological, artistic, and scenic resources, which rely exclusively on the use of police powers and contain no provision either for national financial aid or for compensation, have not worked well.[9]

Far from supplying aid to the city for planning purposes, the national government has used its powers over the city budget to veto appropriations for planning. In 1964 it vetoed an appropriation by the Rome city council for the creation of a permanent planning institute, to which the city has been committed since 1962. Since the city is utterly dependent on the national government for the funds, or at least the borrowing authority, with which to implement its plans, the level of its activity cannot be assumed to indicate the level of its interest.

The national government has given Rome some financial help. It directly provides many of the basic services that are provided locally in other countries, and is financing and managing the construction of the new Rome subway system, although the city will have to provide the rolling stock and equipment. In 1967 the national government assumed the full cost of school building construction; in public education, the city is now required to pay only custodial salaries and maintenance expenses. Since 1967 the Ministry of the Treasury has been supplying periodic emergency grants to help the city pay its employees.

At the same time, however, the national government is responsible for much of the city's failure to meet the sharply rising demand for public services, while national policies have themselves been responsible for the internal migration that has created the growing demand. The national government has been unable to cope with the problem of reforming local government finance, so closely is that problem tied to the problems of general tax reform, regional government finance, and the reform of Italian public administration. The major reason for the gap between rapidly rising private wealth and living standards and slowly rising public wealth and community facility standards is that the cost of providing community facilities has fallen largely on local governments. While the revenues of the national government have kept pace with the rise in per capita

---

Italian Ministry of Public Works should not be exaggerated. In the Soviet Union, where presumably planning is taken more seriously, nearly half of the 1,700 cities did not have the required general plan, as of 1961. "The general plan for Volgograd [formerly Stalingrad] was approved only in 1962, i.e., 17 years after the end of the Second World War." See Timothy Sosnovy, "Housing Conditions and Urban Development in the U.S.S.R.," in U.S. Congress, Joint Economic Committee, *New Directions in the Soviet Economy,* 89th Congress, 2d Session (Washington: Government Printing Office, 1966), pp. 531–68.

8. Emilio Vega De Luca, "Politica territoriale e crisi dell'amministrazione dei lavori pubblici," *Città e Società,* January-March 1968, pp. 31–36.

9. See the papers presented to the 1966 *Italia Nostra* congress and also Alfredo Barbacci, *Il guasto delle città.*

income, local revenues have not. The local share in total public revenues fell from 55 percent in 1955, before the economic boom, to 44 percent in 1963 at the crest of the boom. If 1938 revenues are used as an index of 100, state revenues in 1963 reached 306, while local revenues remained at an index of 161. However, if local revenues lagged between 1951 and 1966, local expenditures did not. Per capita *state* revenues increased by 463 percent and per capita state expenditures by 375 percent; *communal* per capita revenues increased by 413 percent, while per capita communal expenditures increased by 563 percent. While national revenues rose faster than local revenues or local spending, local spending rose faster than all three. A great expansion in the production of public goods and services took place during the boom, but at the local rather than the national level, although much increased local spending went for interest payments rather than investments. Over half the total local debt of eight billion dollars accumulated as of 1964 had been incurred to pay operating expenses, rather than for capital improvements.[10]

Italian local governments, especially that of Rome, have been caught in a circle involving inadequate revenues, chaotic urbanization and building, inadequate but costly infrastructure, and enormous indebtedness. It is hard to tell whether it was the Planning Act of 1942 that caused the disaster in local finance or the Local Finance Act of 1931 that caused the disaster in local planning. A better system of local finance might have made the planning act more workable and vice versa. The planning act required some means of compensating those who stood to lose by negative zoning decisions. The only way, without a compensation scheme, to adopt an acceptable zoning scheme under the act was to formulate a master plan that minimized the number of losers, by providing for maximum private development possibilities and minimum space for public facilities. But a pattern that allowed for maximum private development—both of the oil-stain and leapfrog variety—was also a pattern that spelled financial disaster for the city, which was forced then to service developments on all sides and in all parts of the city territory. The only kind of plan that was politically acceptable and reasonably equitable was the kind that would bankrupt the city that adopted it.

If a compensation scheme was needed to make negative zoning workable in Britain, where the civic culture is strong, one can imagine the workability of negative zoning without compensation in Italy, where the civic culture is not strong. Regulatory planning is an attempt to secure public policy goals without paying for them. It has been no substitute for eminent domain, taxation, or the development of positive incentives as planning techniques.[11] But the financial techniques presuppose that local authorities and/or the state are willing and able to pay for them, which is not the case in Italy. In Rome, even the minimal

10. Associazione Nazionale dei Comuni Italiani, *La finanza locale* (Rome, 1966), pp. 13–23.
11. William F. Whyte, *The Last Landscape* (New York, 1969).

costs of regulation—an adequate police force and a helicopter to patrol the Agro Romano—seem beyond the financial means of the city.

Local finance has had a direct and negative impact on planning effectiveness. The normal method of expansion under the Planning Act of 1942 was to have been through detailed plans rather than private subdivision contracts; private subdivisions were a permissible but not the preferred method of expansion. While master plans are usually drawn at a scale of 1:10,000, detailed plans are drawn at a scale of 1:500. In conformity with the master plan, they indicate precisely the location and layout of roads and facilities; the actual parcels to be expropriated; the volumes and heights of new buildings; and the subdivision of land into lots. Under the detailed plan mechanism, the city decides which land is to be developed; it pays not only the designing costs of the detailed plan but also most of the urbanization costs. Detailed plans have to go through almost the same arduous procedure of review and promulgation as the original master plan.

In practice, very few Italian cities have ever issued any detailed plans, usually for financial reasons. Private subdivision conventions require private developers to pay a larger share of urbanization costs, in theory at least. Most Italian cities in the postwar period expanded through private subdivision conventions. Subdivision contracts do not require publication, the collection of and reply to appeals, or submission to the Ministry of Public Works. They are cheaper for the city; they allow the local authorities to give private developers what they want without the possibility of censure from above.

Generally, in Rome as in the rest of Italy, subdivision conventions have worked very badly from the planners' point of view. Not only have they permitted the private developers to dictate the pace and pattern of city development, they also in practice have allowed private developers to evade their urbanization responsibilities. The terms of subdivision contracts have tended to be very generous to private developers, by allowing heavy densities and little allotment of space to public services. But local authorities have found it impossible to enforce the terms even of these very generous contracts.

In Rome, many new districts were built on the basis of subdivision contracts outside the perimeter of the 1931 master plan. Those regularly authorized as of 1963 covered 2,925 acres of land. *Unauthorized* subdivisions in Rome, as of the same date, covered some 6,250 acres: At the same time large areas covered by detailed plans remained unbuilt, preference going to private subdivisions.[12]

The bridge-law of 1967, recognizing the importance in practice of subdivision contracts, made some basic changes in the 1942 Planning Act, requiring for the first time ministerial approval of all such contracts and laying down minimum nationwide standards to be observed in subdivision contracts throughout Italy. It also stiffened the penalties for illegal subdivision and increased the authority of the ministry to intervene directly against them.

12. Fiorentino Sullo, *Lo scandalo urbanistico: storia di un progetto di legge,* p. 135.

Financial reasons were also responsible, at least in part, for the inability of local authorities to use their powers of eminent domain under Article 18 of the planning act in areas of future expansion. First of all, the compensation they were allowed to pay under article 38 was not "to take into account increments of value directly or indirectly attributable to the approval of the master plan and its implementation." This meant that local authorities would have to pay low acreage prices for land that actually had enormously higher market value; no local authority was prepared to take such drastic action.[13] Italian law regularly provides for the application of eminent domain, with compensation *below* "fair market value." The 1865 Expropriation for Public Utility Act provided for compensation at market value where public facilities were concerned. The 1885 Act for the Renewal of Naples allowed, for the first time, compensation at *less* than market value; this formula has been used in a long series of special laws dealing with such matters as public housing, the master plans of particular cities, school construction, slum clearance, and railway rights of way. The result is that different rates of compensation can be paid for similar land, depending on which law is invoked to justify condemnation. Some owners have their land taken at less than market value, in some cases at acreage value, and witness at the same time a sharp rise in the value of neighboring parcels. A widespread feeling that the normal operation of "the law" is unjust is not entirely due to *incivisme,* especially since the powers of eminent domain have frequently been used, though not necessarily in Rome, for purposes of political discrimination and intimidation.[14]

The Local Finance Act of 1931 allowed city governments to collect improvement assessments *(contributi di miglioria)* to help defray the costs of urbanization. But assessments were applicable only to improved property, could amount only to a maximum of 30 percent of the cost of the improvement or 15 percent of the increase in property value due to the improvement. For various reasons, as already seen, these assessments have been difficult to collect. The gap between expenditures on public works and improvement assessments for Rome is shown in Table 7.1. The Local Finance Act also allowed the city to impose sewer charges after sewers have been constructed and improvement assessments on them have been paid. As Table 7.1 shows, sewer charges provide some measure of return to the city for its investments.

Table 7.1. Public Works Expenditures vs. Improvement Assessments in Rome, 1959–1964
(in lire)

|  | 1959 | 1962 | 1964 |
|---|---|---|---|
| Expenditures on new public works | 5,635,511,000 | 8,895,485,000 | 7,306,303,000 |
| Improvement assessments | 219,774,000 | 554,587,000 | 724,147,000 |
| Sewer user charges | 1,794,063,000 | 2,883,024,000 | 3,321,706,000 |

Source: *Annuario Statistico della Città di Roma. 1964,* pp. 297–99.

13. Ibid., p. 140.
14. Ibid., pp. 105–06.

The Local Finance Act was amended by Law 246 of March 5, 1963, which instituted a tax on increases in the value of building lots and attempted to increase the yields from improvement assessments. As noted in chapter 5, the tax on building lots has not become a major source of city revenue, partly because of adverse court decisions. Unless the national government takes more effective steps to raise local revenues and halt the disastrous practice of borrowing to meet current operating expenses, there is little prospect for any kind of effective planning in Rome or other Italian cities. Unfortunately, the national government is concerned for the state of its own finances and tends to attribute the collapse of local finance to poor management practices at the local level.[15]

## NATIONAL POLITICS AND TIME COSTS

Was the national government responsible for the long time it took for Rome to prepare and accept a new master plan? Was it responsible for some of the costs of the delay? Some answers to these questions are quite clear. It was national law and national administrative pressure that forced the city to commence the planning process. The Planning Act of 1942 stipulated that existing master plans, such as the Roman plan of 1931, would be valid only until 1952, at which time, if they were not replaced by new plans, all zoning and building regulations would expire. By that time the Ministry of Public Works was to have seen to it that new plans were ready to take the place of old or nonexistent plans. National law thus made planning vitually compulsory, although some of the urgency was reduced by Law 504 of April 20, 1952, which extended the expiration date to 1955. In 1955, Parliament again saved the day by extending the validity of existing plans until such time as new plans were promulgated.

The planning act authorized the Ministry of Public Works to publish lists of communes required to adopt new plans. Rome appeared on the first such list, which was published by the ministry in 1954. Under the terms of the Slum Clearance Act of that year, Rome was given two years—until 1956—in which to adopt a new plan; if it failed to do so, the Ministry of Public Works was authorized to formulate a plan for the city at the city's expense. The ministry was given authority to extend the deadline by two years—until September 1, 1958.[16]

By September 1958, however, the situation in Roman planning and the relations between the city and the Ministry of Public Works had changed dramatically. In the early fifties the city, albeit reluctantly, took the necessary steps toward the formulation of a new plan in compliance with national law and ministerial policy. The giunta committed the city to the formation of a new plan

15. See, for example, Minister of Finance Preti's testimony before the Chamber of Deputies Internal Affairs Committee on February 3, 1967; Camera dei Deputati, *Esame dello Stato, 1*, 375–81.
16. On the instability of deadlines in Roman planning, see INU, *Roma: Città e piani*, p. 292, n. 1.

in October 1951.[17] After the 1952 elections one of the members of the giunta was given the new title of planning assessor *(Assessore all'Urbanistica)* and responsibility for the planning activities formerly in the province of the (city) public works assessor. In 1953 the Special Office for the New Master Plan was created, and later that year debate began on the new plan in the city council, based on a lengthy, well-prepared report of Planning Assessor Storoni.[18] In 1954, the council unanimously laid down general policies for the plan and appointed the CET and the Grand Commission to formulate a plan in accordance with its general policies.[19] The CET and the Grand Commission worked on the plan for more than three years, with representatives of the Ministry of Public Works taking a leading part in commission debates. By November 1955 a compromise had been reached on the pattern of city expansion.[20] There were no commission meetings between March and October 1956; during this time elections were held, which brought in a new mayor and a new planning assessor. In February 1957 the commission approved a rough sketch of the new circulation scheme. On November 15, 1957, the complete draft of the CET's plan was presented to the Grand Commission by the new planning assessor.[21] Presumably the commission would examine the plan and formulate a compromise resolution of approval and turn the matter over to the city council for final adoption by the 1958 deadline.

Instead, rather abruptly, a motion condemning the CET plan completely was presented to the Grand Commission by Lt. Col. Giuseppe Amici (Ministry of Defense-Air), director of construction at Fiumicino International Airport. Amici's motion to reject the CET plan was signed not only by the usual conservative critics of the CET on the commission but also by the representatives of the Ministry of Public Works, who had hitherto sponsored the compromise resolutions that allowed the CET to continue its work. The ministry now openly came out against the CET and its plan.[22]

17. The giunta report is contained in Leonardo Benevolo, "Le discussioni e gli studi preparatori al Nuovo Piano Regolatore," in INU, *Roma: Città e piani,* pp. 205–10.
18. The Storoni report is contained in "Council Debates, 1953–54," pp. 6–22.
19. The unanimous council resolution is contained in "Council Debates, 1953–54," pp. 210–13, and in Benevolo, "Le discussioni," pp. 232–33.
20. The 1955 compromise resolution can be found in "Commissione Generale," 2, 114A–F.
21. The CET report is contained in Comune di Roma, Ufficio Speciale Nuovo Regolatore, *Relazione al Piano Regolatore Generale* (Rome, 1957), with an *Appendice,* a *Raccolta di graffici,* and *Note tecniche integranti gli elaborati graffici del P. R. Generale.* The CET zoning map is reprinted in *Roma: Città e piani,* facing p. 272.
22. The Amici resolution against the CET plan is contained in "Commissione Generale," 3, 95–101, and also in *Roma: Città e piani,* pp. 258–59. At the same time that Col. Amici was working *with* Minister of Public Works Togni against the Rome master plan, the two were fighting a furious battle for jurisdictional control over construction of Fiumicino airport. A parliamentary investigation into the building of the airport in 1961 uncovered the fact that Col. Amici, in addition to his official responsibilities in the Ministry of Defense, had between 1945 and 1961 founded and run five building societies and seven real estate corporations. See Atti Parliamentari, Camera dei Deputati, III Legislatura, Doc. No. XI, pt. 2, Commissione Parlamentare d'Inchiesta sulla costruzione dell'aeroporto di Fiumicino, *Relazione* (December 23, 1969). See also Piero Radice, "Fiumicino e dintorni," *Il Ponte,* January 1962, pp. 23–28.

The change in ministerial policy on the Rome master plan followed the replacement as minister of public works of a liberal Social Democrat, Giuseppe Romita, generally favorable to progressive planners, by a right-wing Christian Democrat, Giuseppe Togni. A man of authoritarian and conservative tendencies, who was alarmed at the leftist tendencies among Italian city planners, Minister Togni was sympathetic to the evolution of the Christian Democratic party in Rome and in the nation toward an alliance with the Right and extreme Right. The Catholic-neofascist alliance in Rome was based on a secret agreement to reject the CET plan and (eventually) to formulate a plan more favorable to private interests.[23]

Under Togni, the ministry became a silent accomplice in the rejection of the CET plan and the promotion of a conservative plan. The September 1958 deadline came and went without ministerial reaction. The ministry agreed to the city's proposal for the formation of an intercommunal plan and allowed the city to draft a new master plan—a master plan that left open or evaded most of the basic choices that planners thought had to be made. The giunta's plan, or "nonplan,"·as the opposition called it, was adopted by the city council in June 1959 and submitted to the Ministry of Public Works for approval in January 1960. It lay in the ministry for almost two full years. (Under the Bridge-Law of 1967 the ministry is given a maximum of one year in which to examine master plans.) Togni lost his post as minister of public works in the upheaval of the summer of 1960 and was replaced by Benigno Zaccagnini, a middle-of-the-road Christian Democrat somewhat more sympathetic to the city planning movement but hesitant to make any move with regard to the by then notorious affair of the Rome master plan. The ministry refused to act on the 1959 master plan until after the Rome city council was dissolved on July 10, 1961, and the city was placed under a prefectoral commissioner, Prefect Francesco Diana. Prefect Diana, in turn, appointed engineer Alberto Bianchi, a ranking functionary of the Ministry of Public Works and secretary of the Superior Council of Public Works, to be his subcommissioner for planning. The superior council was responsible for drafting the ministry's position on the Rome master plan. If it now sent back the plan to the city for revision, the council's own secretary would be

23. The terms of the pact, leaked by a dissident Social Democratic faction, were reported as follows:
1. Cioccetti will be elected mayor on the second ballot and will make no political declaration.
2. The MSI (neofascists) will vote favorably on the budget and the giunta will maintain its present tripartite composition.
3. The Grand Commission will be dissolved in order to permit presentation of a master plan providing for expansion of the city exclusively toward Via Cassia [the north] and toward the sea.
4. The project for the Hilton Hotel shall be approved as soon as possible.
5. The opinion of the MSI will be decisive in the choice of the site for the Olympic Village.
6. The giunta shall collaborate with the Association of Roman Contractors, the president of which enjoys the complete confidence of the MSI.
7. Villa Torlonia will be subdivided.
*Avanti!* January 14, 1958; *L'Espresso,* April 24, 1960.

in charge of revising the plan on behalf of the city government. Thus revision of the Rome master plan would be kept within the ministerial family.

But even when finally issued in November 1961, the ministry's ruling on the Rome master plan was a masterpiece of ambiguity that sought to achieve a "centrist" stance on the plan by combining equal measures of praise and criticism. The ministry returned the plan to the "local" authorities (the prefectoral commissioner and his subcommissioner for planning) for revision and adoption before June 18, 1962, the new deadline for action. Under the 1955 law on safeguard measures, local authorities, after adopting a master plan, were authorized to turn down building permit applications that conflicted with the new plan's provisions, even before it was promulgated as law.[24] This power lasted for only three years; since the master plan had been adopted by the Rome city council in June 1959, the safeguard measures would expire in June 1962. If no new plan were forthcoming the city would be legally obliged to approve all building permit applications in accordance with the old master plan. The speculator's impossible dream would become possible. The ministry, by taking two years to act on the plan, had left the city with only six months to carry out the required revisions.

A new minister of public works, this time a left-wing Christian Democrat, Fiorentino Sullo, replaced Zaccagnini in February 1962. Under Sullo, who was the first minister of public works in a cabinet based on Socialist support, the ministry swung to the left. Instead of allowing the Rome plan to be revised by the conservative Special Office for the New Master Plan under the direction of a functionary of his own ministry, Sullo asked Prefect Diana to appoint a committee of five progressive planning consultants to work out a revision of the 1959 plan along progressive lines. The revision of the giunta plan—that is, the design of the master plan of 1962—was carried out in only three months. It was presented to Prefect Diana for signature on June 8, 1962. In the morning of June 9, Diana worked out with his aides a press release announcing adoption of the new master plan. At 5:30 in the evening, the release drafted that morning was recalled and a new statement issued to the press, announcing that Prefect Diana refused to adopt the new master plan. What caused the commissioner to change his mind the day before election of a new council and thirteen days before expiration of the safeguard norms, we do not know.[25]

Minister Sullo responded to the crisis by securing from the Italian cabinet an emergency decree that adopted the master plan of Rome on behalf of the city and that gave the newly elected city council six months in which to examine the

24. Law of December 21, 1955, No. 1357.
25. See the hour-by-hour reconstructions of the events of June 9 in G. Tirincanti, *Il Messaggero*, June 11, 1962, and Benevolo, *L'architettura della città*, pp. 100–06. For Prefect Diana's explanation, see his report to the Rome city council (July 12, 1962), cited in *Informazioni Urbanistiche*, April-August 1962, pp. 17–19. While Prefect Diana adduces many good and weighty reasons for not approving the master plan, he does not explain why these reasons suddenly became cogent during the day of June 9.

plan and adopt its own version. The Rome city council adopted the new plan on December 18, 1962. Immediately safeguard norms based on the new plan went into effect, permitting, though not requiring, the mayor of Rome to refuse permits for buildings in violation of the 1962 plan. The city did not complete the processing of the 4,365 objections to the new plan until February 1965, over two years later. This time, national government agencies acted relatively swiftly; they completed their examination in ten months, permitting the president of the republic to sign the plan on December 16, 1965, two days before the expiration of the safeguard norms. Following the rule that little in Roman planning flows smoothly or follows in a predictable direction, the presidential decree itself did not appear in the *Gazzetta Ufficiale* until February 11, 1966. Anxieties about the financial implications of the plan in the Court of Accounts *(Corte dei Conti)* had to be assuaged before it would register the decree and allow it to come into effect.

Under the bridge-law of 1967, procedure for plan approval has been simplified and standard deadlines set for each stage of the planning process. When ordered by the ministry to plan, communes now have three months to name their planners, then twelve months to adopt a plan; they must submit a plan to the ministry within twenty-four months after being ordered to plan. Unless given an extension by the ministry, the prefect, after giving the city council thirty days to act, must step in and appoint a commissioner to carry out the planning obligations of the commune at its own expense. If the ministry returns a plan to a commune for revision, the commune has 180 days in which to act, or again, the prefect, after giving the council another thirty-day period of grace, must appoint a commissioner.

The Ministry of Public Works, which formerly *might* intervene to impose a plan on a city that refused to adopt one, now *must* intervene to do so: national supercession, formerly discretionary, is now mandatory. All communes ordered to adopt a master plan since 1954 were required to do so by March 1, 1968. The prefectures now have ninety days in which to veto council planning deliberations on legal or financial grounds. The Ministry of Public Works has one year in which to examine plans submitted to it. Had these deadlines been in effect in the early fifties, a master plan for Rome might have been promulgated in 1957 or 1958 rather than in 1965–66. It is difficult to believe, however, given the existing nonplanning climate, that any deadlines, however precise and peremptory, would have been enforced.

What of the national government's responsibility for the *costs* of delay? Was it responsible for the breakdown of land-use controls, for example? Under the Planning Act of 1942, the Ministry of Public Works had the power, if the city refused to act, to suspend construction of or demolish any structures built without regular city permits and to annul any permits issued by the city in violation of its own master plan. The ministry could not demolish structures built in violation of the city *building* code. The bridge-law of 1967 extended ministerial powers to cover building code violations, but it fixed a five-year statute of limitations for demolition proceedings. Demolition is still not mandatory. So far as is known, the ministry has never intervened to demolish illegally built structures. As Minister of Public Works Sullo stated to the Chamber of Deputies (October 23, 1962), "Faced with such powerful interests, the administrative offices are defenseless: the laws give them important sanctions, it is true, but since they cannot see and check on everything, to exercise those powers would be a form of discriminatory treatment."[26]

In practice, the field services of the Ministry of Public Works and the Ministry of Public Instruction have found it impossible to enforce the laws regulating building. The most fully documented case of failure is that of the Sicilian city of Agrigento where a full investigation was ordered by the Ministry of Public Works in 1966, following an earthslide that destroyed a large number of buildings erected illegally in a famous site, the Valley of the Greek Temples. Investigators found that of the 20,000 rooms built in Agrigento between 1955–65, 8,500 had been built without authorization; of these, 3,500 had been built in areas zoned for parks, industry, and agriculture. Forty percent of the volume built in that period was illegal. Field services of the state were powerless to combat the coalition of city officials, a huge number of small entrepreneurs, and complaisant architects and engineers. The breakdown in land-use controls, in fact, was nationwide and the Ministry of Public Works, facing this broad challenge to its authority, was no more successful in responding than was the commune of Rome in responding to the same challenge within its local jurisdiction.

### NATIONAL POLITICS AND THE POWER OF PLANNERS

The power of professional planners in Rome varied almost directly with the policies of the national government, particularly those of the Ministry of Public Works. These phases in the relationships between the Ministry of Public Works and the professional planners of INU reflect roughly the major phases in the general political evolution of postwar Italy, as shown in Table 7.2.

The Minister of Public Works has usually reflected the general political orientation of the cabinet. Given the strong progressive tendencies within the post-

Table 7.2. National Politics and Planner Power, 1949-Present

| General national political tendency | Relations between Ministry of Public Works and Planners Institute (INU) | Period |
|---|---|---|
| Centrism | Mutual support | 1949–57 |
| Center-Right | Mutual hostility | 1957–60 |
| Neo-centrism | Partial rapprochement | 1960–62 |
| Center-Left | Mutual support | 1962– |

26. Cited in Sullo, *Lo scandalo*, p. 53, n. 1.

war Italian city planning movement, relationships with the national government and the ministry have been best when the national government is middle-of-the-road or left-of-center. Relationships between INU and the ministry should be close; after all, the ministry is "the planner's ministry," charged with carrying out the basic Planning Act of 1942. In 1952 the ministry established a Bureau of City Planning *(Direzione Generale dell'Urbanistica)* and a special Planning Section (VI) of the Superior Council of Public Works *(Consiglio Superiore dei Lavori Pubblici* or CSLP), for advisory purposes. In the field, the planning bureau had only small staffs attached to the regional purveyors of public works; operating responsibilities under the Planning Act lay with the 8,000 communes, not with the ministry's field services.[27] INU was the natural constituency for the planners in the ministry; ministerial representatives sat by right on the national directive council of INU. The president of section VI of the CSLP was on the INU executive committee, just as INU members were consultants for the CSLP. Ministerial representatives, including the director general of planning and the president of section VI, were leading participants in the work of the Grand Commission, generally playing the role of technical advisers rather than advocates. They played a major part in the elaboration of the compromise resolutions that marked successive stages in the commission's deliberations. As participants in and supporters of the Rome master plan operation, they reflected the general policies of Minister of Public Works Giuseppe Romita (1954–57)—a strong backer of the planning movement, who in 1954 issued the decree requiring one hundred Italian cities, including all provincial capitals, to proceed forthwith to comply with their obligations under the Planning Act of 1942—that is, to formulate and adopt master plans.

But as already noted, in July 1957 Romita was replaced by Giuseppe Togni, a right-wing member of the DC party. Under Togni the ministry swerved to the right and relations with INU became cool and at times something worse. The Italian city planning movement by the late fifties was becoming increasingly disillusioned with the ineffectiveness of existing planning institutions, policies, and practices. At the INU national conference in 1957 on the preservation of rural and urban scenic resources, many planners took the government to task for not pursuing a more vigorous conservation policy. Minister Togni who considered such criticism improper on the part of a professional society so closely tied to government circles, attempted without much success to swing INU somewhat closer to the Italian business community.[28] In Rome he was able

27. The *Direzione Generale dell'Urbanistica,* with its 187 employees in Rome and in the field, including clerks, has virtually collapsed under the weight of its new responsibilities under the 1967 bridge-law, according to Emilio de Luca, "Politica territoriale e crisi dell'amministrazione dei lavori pubblici," *Città e Società,* January-March 1968, pp. 31–36. On the background of the *DG Urbanistica* (Bureau of Planning), see the INU volume, *La pianificazione intercomunale,* pp. 517–47.

28. *Avanti!,* November 12, 1957; *L'Unità,* January 22, 1960; *Quest'Italia,* December 1958, pp. 38–41. INU had some protection in that its president, Adriano Olivetti, head of the type-

to bring city planning more in to line with the desires and needs of private enterprise by helping to defeat the CET plan and produce the giunta plan of 1959, the indeterminacy of which made it attractive to private operators in the city. But Togni was replaced as minister in the summer of 1960, before a conservative master plan for Rome could be finally promulgated.

Togni's replacement as minister, Benino Zaccagnini, attempted to heal the growing rift between the ministry and the planning movement. He openly recognized the failure of the Planning Act of 1942 and agreed to sponsor the formulation of a new general planning act on the basis of a planning code worked out by INU in 1960. Zaccagnini in June 1961 sponsored a national conference of the Christian Democratic party on urban planning reform and invited prominent liberal Catholic planners, architects Michele Valori and Leonardo Benevolo, both active in the struggle against the conservative version of the Rome master plan, to be the principal speakers. Under his guidance the Superior Council of Public Works in February 1961 rejected a master plan for Venice that progressives considered disastrous. But the general stance of the ministry during this period (July 1960-January 1962) was middle-of-the-road "watchful waiting"; it was during this period that the church, the DC party, and the Socialists were deciding whether or not to launch the "opening to the left," the Catholic-Socialist alliance. Until it became clear that this alliance was going to take place, any zealous reformism would be hazardous. The ministry's verdict on the conservative Rome plan was, as noted, a triumph of equivocation; it pleased the conservatives by approving the plan in general; it pleased the progressives by requiring some amendments to the plan along progressive lines. On the basis of this ministerial opinion, the scope of revision could be narrow or broad, depending on whether revision lay in the hands of conservatives or progressives.

The formation of the first Center-Left cabinet in Feburary 1962 was a triumph for the progressive planners. The cabinet was formed on the basis of interparty agreements providing, among other things, for a new planning act. Privately, the parties agreed also to see that the Rome master plan was revised along progressive rather than conservative lines.[29] The new minister of public works, Fiorentino Sullo, was (then) a left-wing Christian Democrat, leader of a faction in the party, the so-called *"Base,"* which was close in its social and economic ideals to the Socialists and thus a natural bridge between the DC and its new Socialist ally. Sullo brought to the ministry ideas on planning reform as advanced as any advocated by progressive elements in INU and in the Socialist party. These ideas were incorporated in a new bill on urban and regional planning, which was drafted at the same time that the revision of the Rome master plan was being carried out, also under Sullo's sponsorship. The new urban planning bill and the new Rome plan were both presented in June; both were

writer firm and great supporter of the planning movement, had been elected to Parliament and his tiny group's support was needed at the time to keep the cabinet in power.

29. B. Zevi, *L'Espresso,* June 3, 1962.

victories for the planning movement, especially the new planning bill. Ironically, the Rome master plan, less satisfactory to the progressives, went on to become law, while the Sullo planning bill, because of its progressiveness *(dirigisme)*, went down to defeat.[30]

The Sullo bill differed from a bill prepared by his predecessor in three essential respects: it gave a major role in physical planning to the regional governments; it tied physical planning very closely to the emerging new system of national and regional *economic* planning; and it placed major reliance on a new system of public ownership of land in expansion zones. The Sullo bill accorded well with the commitment of the Center-Left government to create, finally, the regional governments and launch a major national economic planning effort. But the provisions on public ownership of land proved to be explosive: conservatives mounted a highly successful national campaign to convince Italian public opinion that the Center-Left government was about to abolish private property in land and housing. On the eve of the national elections in April 1963, Minister Sullo and his bill were openly disowned by his own party, the Christian Democrats. The bill was never allowed to come before the cabinet for discussion and Sullo was dropped from the cabinet later that year. But if unsuccessful in promoting new national planning legislation, Sullo did succeed in securing from the cabinet and Parliament the decree-law that saved the planning situation in Rome.[31]

Sullo's successors as ministers of public works were no more successful than he in securing a basic reform of the 1942 Planning Act. Socialists Giovanni Pieraccini and Giacomo Mancini each presented a new general bill, but neither was able to secure parliamentary approval, despite the fact that each succeeding version of the bill made greater and greater concessions to conservative opinion. Only after the disastrous and scandalous landslide in Agrigento in the summer of 1966 and the floods in Florence and Venice later that year was sufficient support available for some legislative reform in the planning field. This took the form not of a totally new system of planning, as proposed in the INU, Zaccagnini, Sullo, Pieraccini, and Mancini bills, but rather a tightening up of the penalties for violations of planning laws and regulations. The maximum fine for violating a building code is now $1,600; for building or subdividing without a permit, six months in jail and up to $3,200. When demolition of illegal structures is not feasible, a fine in the amount of the value of the illegal structure may be imposed. The new regulatory authority conferred on the ministry and the local authorities may have some useful effect since the climate of opinion in recent years seems to

30. Sullo, *Lo scandalo*.
31. The same cabinet meeting that approved the decree-law for emergency promulgation of the Rome master plan also approved the nationalization of the Italian electric power industry. Ironically, the private electric power companies, such as Edison, used their compensation funds to buy real estate in Rome, thus adding the force of powerful northern financial interests to the already strong speculator coalition (*L'Espresso*, July 1, 1962).

have become more favorable to public regulation. As the "boom psychology" recedes, there are probably better prospects of regulation than during the frenzy of the fifties and early sixties.

If the planners have not won a new general reform, they have won important national victories in the form of Law 167 on low-cost housing; the bridge-law of 1967; the ministerial investigation into the events at Agrigento; and a gradual strengthening of ministerial determination to enforce the law. Planners in Rome have benefited from these national advances and also from particular national actions in Rome. These include approval and promulgation of the master plan; the rezoning "in the pre-eminent interests of the State" by the Ministry of Public Works of the entire Appian Way district as a public park; the rejection in 1967 by that ministry of a proposed private subdivision at Capocotta along the coast, which would have further reduced the already limited amount of free public beach in the city. Thus, since 1962, planners in Rome and in Italy have enjoyed the general moral support of the national government and occasionally more specific forms of support.

Most of the support the Ministry of Public Works has been able to give the planning movement during the postwar period has been moral, for the ministry itself has had little power to provide any other kind. Immediately after the war the ministry was deeply involved in the problems of recovery and reconstruction, rather than forward planning. Once recovery was completed by the early fifties, the ministry was simply overwhelmed by the torrential pace, scale, and intensity of development. It was also overwhelmed, as we have seen, by the emergence of a large number of dynamic programs impinging upon its jurisdiction but under independent control, such as the public housing program of the Ministry of Labor (INA-Casa, later GESCAL); the public works programs of the Southern Development Fund; the reclamation projects of the Ministry of Agriculture; the school building programs of the Ministry of Public Instruction; the railway building plans of the State Railways and Ministry of Transport; the investment programs of the great public corporations, ENI and IRI, and the Ministry of Public Enterprise *(Partecipazioni Statali)*. Many of the newer programs were given to public corporations freed from the stifling, ineffective procedures and controls that continued to be applied to the older line ministries. The ministry even had difficulty in controlling the operation of ANAS, the State Highway Corporation, which lay under its supervision at least nominally. Within the ministry itself, the planning bureau was only one of several bureaus and far from the largest or strongest.

In practice, the ministry could not effectively supervise the local planning authorities—the communes—or effectively coordinate the activities of the major national agencies. In this respect it was just as ineffective as was the other major regulatory agency in the planning field, the Ministry of Public Instruction, which is responsible for protecting the Italian natural, historical, monumental, and artistic heritage. Both Public Works and Public Instruction were incapable of resisting unrelenting pressure from all parts of the peninsula for lax enforcement of the Conservation Acts of 1939 and the Planning Act of 1942. While INU attempted to strengthen the regulatory resolve of the Ministry of Public Works, the *Italia Nostra* society, founded in 1955, attempted to bolster the conservation efforts of the Ministry of Public Instruction and its local superintendents of monuments. But these small, overlapping groups were no match for the almost universal spirit of resistance and indifference to planning throughout the country. Functionaries at all levels in both ministries were forced to accommodate private demands for minimal regulation and maximum development, given the "anything goes" spirit of postwar reconstruction and the "economic miracle," when the historic cities and villages of Italy became, in a sense, boom towns on the frontiers of economic growth.

# 8

# PARTY POLITICS:
# POLARIZATION VERSUS
# MULTIPARTISANSHIP

## A POLARIZED PARTY SYSTEM

Policy for the city of Rome is *not* made in the following ways, typical of patterns of policymaking in other urban governments. It is not made by a dominant party and then imposed on the city government, which would be the Soviet pattern and that of American cities with powerful party machines. It is not made by committees of the national legislature, which would be the predominant pattern for Washington, D.C. It is not made by the interaction of a national bureaucrat (prefect) and a locally elected council, as in Paris. It is not made by the interaction between mayors (or managers), councils, and commissions, as in many U.S. cities. It is not made by the president of the republic and his deputy, as in Mexico City. Rather, it is made by the process of interparty transactions characteristically found in the multiparty urban political systems of Western Europe.

The Roman party system, however, is not typical of all urban multiparty systems. Together with its parent national party system, it would undoubtedly be classified as a "nonworking" or "polarized" multiparty system in contrast to the "working" or "nonpolarized" multiparty systems of northern Europe.[1] Dominant views of the Italian national party system stress its ideological fragmentation, "extreme pluralism," lack of bargaining and compromise, growing alienation and extremism, and—as a result of these—"immobilism and ineffectiveness in policy."[2] Polarization, if measured and defined by the electoral

1. Giovanni Sartori, "European Political Parties: The Case of Polarized Pluralism," in *Political Parties and Political Development,* ed. Joseph LaPalombara and Myron Weiner (Princeton, 1966), pp. 137–76.
2. Gabriel Almond and G. Bingham Powell, *Comparative Politics: A Developmental Approach* (Boston, 1966), pp. 111–12.

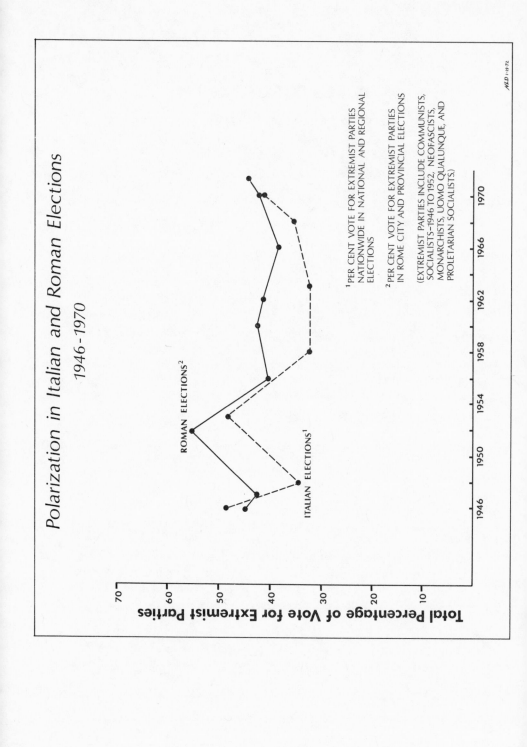

Polarization in Italian and Roman Elections
1946 - 1970

Total Percentage of Vote for Extremist Parties

70  60  50  40  30  20  10

1946    1950    1954    1958    1962    1966    1970

ROMAN ELECTIONS[2]

ITALIAN ELECTIONS[1]

[1] PER CENT VOTE FOR EXTREMIST PARTIES
NATIONWIDE IN NATIONAL AND REGIONAL
ELECTIONS

[2] PER CENT VOTE FOR EXTREMIST PARTIES
IN ROME CITY AND PROVINCIAL ELECTIONS

(EXTREMIST PARTIES INCLUDE COMMUNISTS,
SOCIALISTS–1946 TO 1952, NEOFASCISTS,
MONARCHISTS, UOMO QUALUNQUE, AND
PROLETARIAN SOCIALISTS.)

NLD 1·1972

strength of extremist, antisystem parties, has, if anything, been even worse in Rome city politics than it has in Italian national politics, as can be seen in Figure 8.1. Extremist parties of Left and Right have generally won about 40 percent of the vote in Rome city elections (see Figure 8.2). Rome has had not only a powerful Communist party, winning about one vote in four, but also an unusually powerful neofascist party, the MSI, which wins between 10 and 15 percent of the city vote. In addition, each of these parties has usually had the aid and comfort of other "antisystem" parties. Even the more moderate parties in and around the center have been sharply divided among themselves by differences in tradition, clientele, and policy. Given this degree of polarization, one would expect to find in the operations of this party system immobilism, instability, ideological confrontation, irresponsible opposition, and lack of accomplishment. One would expect narrow majorities, transient coalitions, and periodic breakdowns. It is likely also that such a system or subsystem of parties would be incapable of mounting a successful master planning operation, and of undertaking and completing long-term programs of great complexity, technicality, comprehensiveness, or cost—and master planning is generally seen as involving all of these.

Polarized political party systems would seem to possess few attributes favorable, on a priori grounds, to the mobilization of support and coordination necessary to assert control over the process of urban development. Political, social, and ideological fragmentation make it less likely that any agreement can be reached on how a city should develop, if it should, or that there will be any predisposition to comply with any agreement or plan that is somehow made. Polarization makes it difficult for planners to be responsive to a wide range of groups, whose goals are likely to be antagonistic and incompatible where they are not competitive. Polarization means that resistance to planning will be widespread, intense, and intransigent: any agreed-upon plan will be viewed by large sectors of the community (or so-called "community") as illegitimately imposed by factious political enemies. Groups will be hesitant to aid planners in making predictions by revealing their values and intentions with regard to urban development; they will be hesitant also to accept the information provided by other groups as truthful, neutral, objective, or sincere. Ideological perspectives will introduce rigidities into the planning process: such perspectives will be unreceptive to the notion of flexible planning, provisional goals, and the use of feedback to meet unanticipated problems of change, evolving values, modified preferences. Ideological perspectives will also induce party leaders to identify the public interest with their party program, the "public" with the party faithful, and citizen participation with consultation of the party rank and file. Absolute value orientation will mean contempt for, indifference to, or suspicion of social science as a tool for social action, as a means of generating objective information, and as a technique for predicting trends and analyzing policy proposals. Fragmentation will also make it difficult to coordinate the activities of public agencies and private operators: the centrifugal effects of conflicting institutional

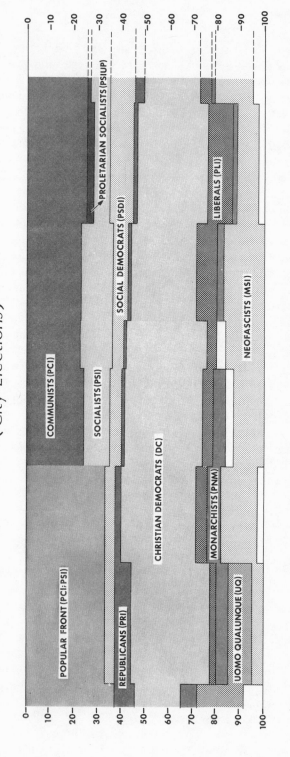

Figure 8.2

loyalties will be magnified by ideological, partisan, and factional cleavages. Finally, fragmentation will make it difficult for any coalition that manages to agree upon a plan to remain in power long enough to give it some form of implementation or to maintain sufficient cohesion to mobilize the support and resources needed to carry out the plan.

To what extent does this polarization model delineate the pattern of Roman policymaking, at least in the planning field?

### POLARIZATION AND ROMAN PLANNING

The polarization model correctly describes many aspects of the style of postwar Roman planning. It makes intelligible, first of all, the sharp conflicts that emerged among, and within, the parties over planning goals and techniques. Party differences in ideology, social constituency, interest group connections, and coalition policy made for literally "polarized" perspectives with regard to planning.

The right-wing parties (neofascists, Monarchists, Liberals) saw planning as a possible threat to legitimate private economic interests. They wanted a plan that would maximize the freedom to utilize and exploit private property rights and that confirmed existing development tendencies.[3] The master plan of 1959 was tailor-made for their purposes. It reinforced the existing monocentric pattern of city expansion and confirmed the vested rights of property on all sides of the city. It postponed to a later date the definition of expansion zones, except toward the southwest, beyond EUR, where private interests had already begun important subdivisions.

The Communists wanted an entirely different kind of master plan. As the right wing correctly charged, the Communists saw the master plan as an instrument in the Roman class struggle. To the Communists, the plan would be a means whereby the dominant property interests preserved or extended their hegemony over city affairs or it would be an instrument whereby the progressive forces of the city destroyed, once and for all, the economic and therefore political power of the "urban latifundists." Against the overwhelming power of the speculators, the Communists argued, no plan would be effective that did not expropriate the major landholdings around the city at rural acreage prices. The Communists rejected the 1959 master plan as no plan at all. They saw many good points in the 1962 master plan, particularly its restrictions on redevelopment in the historic center; its subway scheme tangential to the center; and its

3. See "Council Debates, 1962," remarks of councilmen Aureli, D'Andrea, Teodorani, Nistri, Greggi, Pompei, Turchi, Petronio, Cini, De Totto, Crocco (!), De Marsanich, Bozzi; "Council Debates, 1959," remarks of councilmen Guglielmotti, Benedettini, Greggi, Bozzi, Aureli, Lombardi, and D'Andrea; planning commentary in the newspapers *Il Tempo, Giornale d'Italia, Il Globo, Il Secolo, Il Quotidiano* (until 1962), *Il Messaggero* (until 1959), *L'Osservatore Romano* (until 1962).

efforts to break the pattern of oil-stain growth through the eastern axis and directive centers. But, said the Communists, without wholesale expropriation of the giant real estate interests and incorporation of the Communists into the the governing coalition, there would not be sufficient political power to ensure that eastern development—the part of the plan supported by the Left—would actually take place. And unless the power of the speculators was broken, it would not be possible to enforce the plan's rather stringent restrictions on building and development. Because the plan did not attempt to destroy the great property interests, the Communists voted against it.[4]

Both conservative and Communist planning policies were electorally sound. Most of the costs of existing laissez-faire "planning"—actually nonplanning— (that is, inferior services) were paid by the lower income groups that voted Communist, while most of the benefits of that policy (that is, speculative profits) went to the groups that voted for the Right. A plan that profoundly altered the development pattern of the city would require restrictions on and higher taxes for the clientele of the rightist parties: as such, it was a painless proposal for the Left.

The Socialists shared all of the Communists' dislike for the master plan of 1959 and many of their apprehensions about the plan of 1962. But they staked their party's electoral fortunes on the hope that, as a partner in the governing Center-Left coalition with the Christian Democrats, they would have sufficient power to see that the better features of the 1962 plan were implemented. They agreed with the Communists that the speculative interests were still powerful in the city, but they hoped through their new power in the city government to be able to reverse existing lasissez-faire policy and establish some minimal public direction of urban growth. If the new plan were administered by the existing city planning department, they felt, it would be under heavy pressure from the speculators. Only the establishment of a new permanent territorial planning institute, with broad regional, political, and technical representation, would guarantee that the plan would be interpreted, implemented, and revised in a progressive manner.[5]

The Christian Democrat party, as the pivotal party of the center, the senior party in any governing coalition, the government party par excellence, and the party of the church, had distinctive needs in the planning field. As a government party it was rather more reluctant than opposition parties, such as the Communists, to endorse new plans involving radical change and stringent regulation. As a Catholic party of the Center, with a socially heterogeneous clientele, the

4. It is quite possible and even likely that the Communists voted *against* the plan in order to save and legitimize it. Communist support for a measure makes it electorally difficult for moderate parties to vote for that measure; Communist support for the moderates is in itself disquieting. Thus the Communists have often followed in Rome what one might call a reverse "kiss of death" strategy—opposing those measures they wish to see passed. See "Council Debates, 1962, pp. 99–107, 143–55, 216–31, 439–42.

5. "Council Debates, 1962," pp. 127–30.

DC party had to balance the property interests of its financial supporters with the social needs of some of its voters. Catholic social doctrine, which tended to stress social needs, was less influential in shaping party policy than an electoral strategy designed to capture the entire Center-Right spectrum of the Roman vote. Typically, more attention was paid to questions of social theory by minority opposition factions within the DC than by Catholic administrators in power. But even Catholic administrators had ideological stakes to protect. Though politically dominant in Rome and Italy since 1946, the Catholics have been only the largest minority force; despite their uninterrupted success at the polls they have continued to act as a culturally defensive minority group, suspicious of other groups in Italian society. On key issues of ideology, such as divorce, for example, Catholics have been in a minority.

Perhaps the single most important party in the postwar struggle over the master plan was a small, electorally insignificant, and shortlived party, the Radicals, who elected one councilman in 1956, Cattani, on the Radical ticket and three councilmen in 1960 on the Socialist ticket. But if the Radicals, even before they split apart in 1962, never became an important electoral force, they did have a deep effect on the nature and evolution of Roman, and Italian, politics. When the Liberal party in the early fifties determined to become the party of conservative Italian business interests, its left wing split off to form the Radical party. The Radicals aimed to transform Italy into a modern, democratic, secularized, welfare state, modeled after the countries of northern Europe. To do this, they proposed legislation that would implement the more progressive features of the 1948 constitution, destroy or regulate monopolistic tendencies in Italian business, modernize and decentralize the Italian bureaucracy, and curb the growing influence of the clergy in Italian life. Through the Radical weeklies, *Il Mondo* and *L'Espresso,* the Radicals reached far beyond their own ranks to shape the policy positions of all Italian progressive forces. The Radicals, more than any other party, created the progressive position and the progressive coalition on the Rome master plan; they created *"una coscienza urbanistica"* or awareness of planning problems among all the parties of the Left and Center-Left. Radical campaigns against corruption in Roman city planning and against land speculation aroused sufficient public interest to direct the attention of the more powerful leftist parties toward planning themes. As the Socialists turned from a program of revolutionary maximalism toward a program of democratic social reform, they found in Radicalism an entirely appropriate and readymade set of themes and positions. Thus the radicalized Socialists in Rome, by the late fifties, had adopted planning themes as the major element in their party's program and insisted upon master plan concessions in their negotiations with the Christian Democrats as a precondition for a Catholic-Socialist alliance.

But if the Radicals helped to create the progressive position on planning, they tended to disrupt the coalition of parties that might put their program

across. For they combined attacks on administrative corruption, land speculation, and monopoly, with attacks on the clergy. Conservative planning groups
were able to argue successfully that Radical attacks on planning abuses were
merely another form of anticlericalism; that Radical attacks on real estate
speculation by church-owned corporations, such as the *Società Generale Immobiliare,* were aimed less against real estate speculation than against the
church. Progressive Catholics who attacked land speculation could be and were
criticized as aiding and abetting the enemies of the church. Conservatives could
exploit the anxieties and defensive attitudes of the Catholic world to protect
conservative economic interests. Catholics were prepared to believe that their
secularist opponents, especially those on the left, wished to use the master plan
for ideological purposes—to damage the church and advance the cause of secularism. They were (and are) prepared to believe that the progressive planners'
emphasis on eastern expansion reflected a desire to create a secular Rome in
the east as a challenge to the authority of the Vatican and the prestige of the
historic center. They could point to examples of deliberately anticlerical planning in the city's history, especially in the early decades of united Italy, when the
streets in an entire district adjacent to St. Peter's, Prati, were so laid out as to
give no view of St. Peter's, and when deliberately provocative statues were
erected to Giordano Bruno and Giuseppe Garibaldi.[6] They were prepared to
believe that the housing designs for the new Law 167 housing projects were
ideologically motivated. To secularist observers and sophisticated Catholic
planners these suspicions seemed fantastic, but to many in the Catholic camp
they seem real enough.[7]

Radical attacks on the church were a major cause behind the rejection of the
CET plan in 1957, the formation of a Catholic–neofascist alliance in 1958, and
the passage of a new master plan in 1959. After the city council passed the new
master plan in June 1959, the Christian Democratic council leader declared:
"The mobilization of all the atheistic and anti-Catholic forces against the plan
just adopted is an indirect confirmation that it corresponds to the true interests
of Rome."[8] But by late 1960, the cause of clerico-fascism had been discredited
and the church itself, under the influence of Pope John XXIII, began to assume
a less intransigent and isolationist ideological posture and to work toward
greater understanding with secular and Protestant forces. It became ideologically

6. On *"urbanistica anticlericale,"* see the article by Luigi Bellotti reprinted in *Battaglie
Politiche,* December 1, 1957, pp. 16–18.
7. *Avvenire d'Italia,* April 11, 1965. Catholics were subjected to conservative propaganda on
planning issues, such as the headlines in *Il Globo,* organ of the Italian General Confederation of
Industry, which described the Spinaceto project in headlines and subheads such as the following
(June 15, 1965): Spinaceto, City of Error; The Quarter of the Dead Souls; Realized In
Accordance with Marxist Criteria; The New Center Annuls the Individual in the Mass and
the Society in the Crowd; Intolerance for Housing Will Lead to Intolerance for the Family;
The Neurosis Will End in a Subversive Charge on Which the Communists Are Counting.
8. *Il Popolo,* June 25, 1959.

possible for Catholics to collaborate in common planning and even governing coalitions with secularist forces of the Left. The latter for their part, especially the Socialists, were ready to exorcise Radical anticlericalism in the interests of concrete social progress.

But even in the new Center-Left or Catholic-Socialist alliance, each party preserved its own distinctive outlook on planning matters. The Socialist party demanded rapid implementation of the master plan of 1962, especially of the provisions on the eastern axis and directive centers. They pressed for the establishment of the Permanent Planning Institute, which would transfer control over plan implementation from the conservative city Planning Department to progressive forces. They urged adoption of major programs of public land acquisition and public housing. They insisted that the city commit itself to specific programs of plan implementation in accordance with progressive requirements.

The Christian Democrats, for their part, were anxious to accommodate and enlist the support of private enterprise. They were hesitant to create a Permanent Planning Institute if this meant losing control over city planning policy to outside forces. Their basic planning policy was designed to meet the needs and interests of a socially diversified electoral clientele. This they accomplished by a policy of thoroughgoing equivocation in planning matters. In election campaigns and in city council debates, Christian Democrats were outspoken on *both* sides of every planning issue. Left-wing Christian Democrats supported progressive positions, while right-wing Christian Democrats echoed all the themes of the neofascist–Liberal conservative opposition. In the end, always, right-wing Christian Democrats obeyed party orders and voted for compromise resolutions worked out with the Socialists, aware, perhaps, that between the general resolutions of the council and daily administrative practice there was an all-important cesura. The city Planning Department has been in the hands of a Christian Democratic assessor since 1960. Control of planning at the administrative level and equivocation on planning issues have given the Christian Democrats the freedom of maneuver necessary to please their heterogeneous but basically conservative supporters and at the same time to preserve their shaky coalition with the Socialists.

The polarization model accounts for the difficulties involved in trying to devise a plan, or any policy, that is satisfactory to all parties in Rome or even some of them. It also accounts for the prevailing attitudes concerning facts and values. Ideological perspectives have made it difficult, if not impossible, for the parties to accept a common set of facts, to accept any information relevant to planning as neutral or objective, or to accept the advice of professional experts as unbiased. Professional advice or professional "information" is accepted only if the ideological connections of the professional are clearly established and vouched for. Thus, the only experts with any credibility are those attached to the various parties, who advance their information and proposals from a clearly disclosed position.[9] When teams of professional planners were created for master planning purposes, in 1954 and again in 1962, there was careful concern to pick an expert from each of the major subcultures in the city. Where the connections between experts and subcultures are not overt, they are assumed to exist and discounted in advance.

The impact of ideological polarization on planning style is not entirely negative. If it makes agreement and reconciliation difficult, it also helps to ensure that a diversity of perspectives will actually be represented in the planning process. Under conditions of greater consensus there may be less tendency to seek out and give articulation to the full diversity of values in the community, and in some situations consensus may be more of an assumption than a reality. In a polarized community there is little inclination to assume consensus. Then, too, ideology as such is not a negative force because ideology provided much of the impetus and drive behind the movement to establish a new master plan for the city. Without the ideology of the planning movement, as supported by Socialist, Catholic, and Radical doctrines of public regulation of economic life, there would have been no planning campaign to begin with. Third, these ideological justifications for public control over economic life were bonds of unity among the parties, not just causes of disunity: even right-wing parties, including and especially the neo-fascists, had doctrinal reasons to support attempts to shape urban growth through public policy. It was the Mussolini regime, after all, that had sponsored the Planning Act of 1942, with its provisions that profoundly modified traditional concepts of property rights. Even earlier, it was the Liberal regime under the Savoy monarchy that in the Expropriation for Public Utility Act of 1865 provided cities with authority to regulate building and land development; thus Liberals and Monarchists had ample historical justification in subscribing to postwar planning effort. Ideology could be an integrative as well as a disruptive force in postwar Roman planning. Though it may interfere with planning to the extent it produces rigidly held and disparate values, it can also supply the fervor and commitment to goals that make for effective planning. Ideology may provide the symbolic underpinning, the mystique, that helps to get a plan adopted and implemented.

The polarization model is useful, even indispensable, in making intelligible the turns and twists, advances and reverses, settlements and surprises that have continued to characterize the planning process in postwar Rome. The polarization model explains not only the improbability of reaching agreement but also the fragility and transience of agreements reached. The model accounts quite satisfactorily for the instability of party coalitions in the city and the periodic breakdowns of the coalition system itself. Twice in the postwar period, in 1946 and 1961, the parties have been unable to form a majority coalition; on both

9. On the other hand, sometimes the only expertise of the supposed "expert" is his representativeness from a partisan or factional point of view. See Alberto Predieri, "Il pseudoesperto come politico di 'serie C,' " *Il Mulino,* May 1968, pp. 406–08.

occasions the national government has had to dissolve the council and appoint a prefectoral commissioner to govern the city in lieu of elective organs of government. This kind of temporary bureaucratic rule has not, of course, been available at the national level.

Since the war the city has been governed by a series of rather disparate coalitions (see Tables 8.1, 8.2), each with its own distinctive planning policy. Coalition instability has meant instability also in planning policy. Each new coalition tended to reverse the planning policies of its predecessor. The shift from the CLN coalition in 1946 to a prefectoral commissioner and Center-Right coalition ended attempts at reversing Fascist planning policies in the city; progressive planners were removed from the city's planning bodies; laissez faire became the

Table 8.1. Coalition Types in Postwar Roman Politics and Planning

| | Communists | Socialists | Radicals | Republicans | Social Democrats | Christian Democrats | Liberals | Uomo Qualunque, Monarchists | Neofascists |
|---|---|---|---|---|---|---|---|---|---|
| The Right | | | | | | | | ▓ | ▓ |
| The Extreme Right | | | | | | | | ▓ | ▓ |
| The Center-Right | | | | | | ▓ | ▓ | ▓ | ▓ |
| The Center | | | | | ▓ | ▓ | ▓ | | |
| The Center-Left | | ▓ | ▓ | ▓ | ▓ | ▓ | | | |
| The Left (1958-1960) | ▓ | ▓ | ▓ | ▓ | ▓ | | | | |
| The Extreme Left (to 1956) | ▓ | ▓ | | | | | | | |
| The Anti-Fascist Resistance | ▓ | ▓ | ▓ | ▓ | ▓ | ▓ | ▓ | | |
| The Center-Left Partisan Planning Coalition | | ▓ | ▓ | ▓ | ▓ | ▓ | | | |
| The Center-Right Partisan Planning Coalition | | | | | | ▓ | ▓ | ▓ | ▓ |
| The Multipartisan Planning Coalition | ▓ | ▓ | ▓ | ▓ | ▓ | ▓ | ▓ | ▓ | ▓ |

Table 8.2. Coalitions in Postwar Roman Politics

1944–46 Antifascist (Committee of National Liberation) coalition, from extreme Left to Center-Right (Communists, Socialists, Christian Democrats, Liberals).

1946–47 Prefectoral Commissioner

1947–52 Center-Right coalition (Christian Democrats, Liberals, *Qualunquisti*), excluding the neofascists.

1952–56    Center coalition (Social Democrats, Republicans, Christian Democrats, and
           Liberals).
1956–60    Center-Right coalition (Republicans, Social Democrats, Christian Democrats,
           Liberals, Monarchists, neofascists; the Republicans withdrew in 1957, the
           Social Democrats, in 1958).
1961–62    Prefectoral Commissioner
1962–      Center-Left coalition (Socialists, Social Democrats, Republicans, Christian
           Democrats).*

*In 1971, the mayor and giunta were elected by the Center-Left coalition on the city
council, but only Christian Democrats were represented on the giunta.

dominant city policy with regard to planning. With the formation of the Center
coalition in 1952, progressive planners were restored to influence and the city
made a firm commitment to formulate and adopt a new master plan. The shift
in 1958 to the Center-Right, including the extreme Right, had drastic consequences for planning: the plan elaborated by the progressive planners of the
CET was summarily rejected; the CET and the Grand Commission were dissolved;
and a new master plan based on a completely different set of concepts and
assumptions was formulated and adopted. When the Center-Right (Catholic-
neofascist) coalition gave way to the Center-Left (Catholic-Socialist coalition)
in 1962, the conservative plan adopted in 1959 was summarily rejected and a
new plan, based on the radically different ideas of the CET, was adopted.

The fragility of postwar Roman party coalitions has also been a major factor
in impeding the implementation of the master plan adopted in 1962. The
Center-Left coalition between 1962 and 1966 had no absolute majority on the
council and had to rely on one Monarchist vote for the passage, by a vote of 41
to 39, of the master plan in 1962. Subsequently, in 1963 the Center-Left was
strengthened when a former Rome province federal secretary of the neofascist
Movimento Sociale Italiano (MSI) resigned from the MSI and was accepted into
the Christian Democratic ranks, providing a much needed extra vote. The
coalition was again endangered early in 1964, when the Proletarian Socialist
party (PSIUP) split off from the left wing of the Socialist party (PSI). One member
of the PSI delegation went over to the PSIUP; the Center-Left majority dropped
back to only 40 out of 80 seats. The Center-Left compensated for this by
utilizing the votes of "independent" Monarchists. Thus in its first four years
the Center-Left had a very uncertain existence. The elections of 1966 gave the
parties of the Center-Left a majority of 41 out of 80, to which was added in the
course of time the regular services of "independent" Monarchists and former
Monarchists. The narrowness of the coalition's majority made adoption of
any major project difficult, if not impossible, except when the coalition was
willing to accept the votes of the Communist delegation. This was the case for
the passage of the Law 167 program in 1963.

But just as important as the narrowness of the governing coalition's majority
was internal conflict within the coalition. The Center-Left coalition contained
within it extreme right-wingers like councilman Greggi (Catholic Action),
councilman Cini (a realtor), and councilman Pompei (the former neofascist leader),

as well as ardent social reformers among the left-wing Christian Democrats and the Socialists. In council debates on almost all planning matters, right-wing Christian Democrats echoed the viewpoints of the right-wing opposition parties, openly attacking the compromises worked out with the Socialists, and announced that they would vote for these compromises only because of party discipline.[10] The center of gravity within the Christian Democratic party was still where it was when the party had been a member of the coalition with the neofascists. The same people who had worked with the neofascists were now working with the Socialists. Right-wingers completely identified with the previous conservative coalition continued to be reelected, even if they lost something of their former influence within the party. The year 1962, and the opening to the Left, had marked a watershed in the postwar political history of the city. The change was far from revolutionary—the basic structure of interests and power remained as before—but symbolism and atmosphere changed radically. Socialist entry into the government of the city isolated both extremes, transforming the political situation. It called forth a new political rhetoric in favor of planning and progress from the DC. It brought the center of gravity in city politics from near extreme Right to the center point and perhaps slightly, but very slightly, left of center—certainly not as far left as under the Nathan administration of 1907–13. The center of gravity had been shifted, moreover, by the intervention of external forces, notably the national Christian Democratic party and national DC leaders such as Minister Sullo, with the at least tacit permission of the Vatican.

But there were still strong ties between the DC and the Right. Conservative economic interests were still very powerful; the larger interests had rather easily accommodated themselves to the new course and been accommodated in return. The great real estate fortunes were still very much intact and continued to provide financial and moral assistance to the conservative elements in several parties, not merely those on the Right. As in the national government, the conservative segments of the Center-Left coalition dictated the pace and direction of any reform.

Lack of progress in implementing the new master plan has not been a major embarrassment to the DC, given the conservative characteristics of its electorate. The DC has paid and is still paying a price in votes, not for any new policies or new plan but simply because it has brought the Socialists into the government.

10. Councilman Agostino Greggi was a former president of Catholic Action Youth in Rome who won fame by instituting and winning a civil proceeding in 1957–1958 against the publishers of the wall posters advertising Anita Ekberg and Brigitte Bardot films. With his subsequently large following in Catholic Action and later in rightwing business circles, Greggi became one of the leading DC politicians in the city. In 1963 he secured election to Parliament where he became the only member of the DC party to vote against the Moro cabinet in December 1963. He received the fourth highest number of preference votes on the DC list in the 1966 city elections. Though he has two degrees, one in law and one in engineering, Greggi's influence in planning decisions derived much less from his personal talents than from the weight of those he represented.

The DC's major problem is to maintain the Socialist alliance with minimum loss of votes on its right. The alliance itself is a major concession to progressive demands, apart from any policy innovations that might result. The DC can perfectly well go slowly in plan implementation and in this way both have its cake and eat it too. Reformist elements in the DC continue to be weak. The triumph of the Center-Left has not meant the triumph within the DC of the leftist factions that had identified themselves with and fought for that formula. The progressive formula is being realized under conservative auspices.

The Socialists in Rome, and in the nation, have been too weak to impose much change on a city government hardened in the ways of conservatism. They are the junior partners in the coalition. Compared to the Christian Democrats, who have been governing the city since the War, the Socialists until recently had no governmental experience, no connections and sympathies in the city bureaucracy. They had no experience in drafting and putting through a program of reform. If the DC electorate could be contented with a modicum of progressivism, the same was not true of the Socialist voters and rank and file who needed to see the concrete results that justified abandonment of the party's traditional and comfortable role in the opposition. The Socialists have a much greater need than the DC of showing concrete gains and programmatic achievements—but they do not have sufficient strength themselves to bring about those gains and achievements. They derive relatively little support from the Social Democrats, who lack any strong reformist impulse, or from the Republicans, who hold only one seat on the council.

Characteristically, the major reformist force within the Center-Left coalition, the Socialists, has been weakened by severe internal factionalism. The left wing of the party split off in 1964. When, in 1966, the Socialists and Social Democrats agreed to form a unified party, factional disputes within Socialist ranks became even worse. Less than three years later, in the summer of 1969, the unified Socialist party split in two, but both Socialist parties agreed to continue their collaboration in the Center-Left coalition.

The Communists have claimed, not without reason, that without them no major reform—political, administrative, or social—is possible. The Communists have had a large share of the talent, the aggressiveness, the organized following among the forces of change in Rome, which means that their exclusion from power brings about relative stasis in city government. Polarization has made it impossible for the parties of the Center-Left, particularly the Christian Democrats, to collaborate with the Communists. The Christian Democrats fear that, just as their alliance with the Right in 1958–60 gave enormous prestige and power to the Communists, any alliance with the Communists would create space for a powerful antisystem, anticommunist movement on the right. Accordingly, when Center-Left proposals receive Communist support, the Christian Democrats take pains to make it clear that Communist support is unwanted, unneeded, and coincidental.

Some forces within the Christian Democratic and Socialist parties favor a "dialogue" with the Communists, but most people in those parties are against such a shift. There are divergencies within the coalition on many other points and endless quarrels over the distribution of government patronage. Problems of coordinating the action of various city agencies are magnified by questions of partisan and factional power and prestige. Thus the polarized nature of the party system has been a major factor in delaying the adoption and implementation of the Rome master plan and it has helped to produce sharp fluctuations in the power of planners in city policymaking.

### MULTIPARTISANSHIP AND ROMAN PLANNING

But if the polarization model accounts for many of the difficulties in Roman planning, particularly those involving *Kulturkampf,* it does not lead us to expect or help us to understand those elements of the Roman party system that have made for compromise, cooperation, and achievement. Given the polarization model, it seems little short of miraculous that for several years after World War II there was considerable consensus among the Roman parties on planning issues. As late as 1957, decisions on a new master plan were based on unanimous interparty agreements, negotiated in typical marketplace fashion. Even after the consensus broke down in 1958, the parties in Rome showed a remarkable ability to submerge ideology and partisanship in the interests of arriving at practical agreements. The polarization model of the Roman, and probably the Italian, party system rightfully stresses the sensitivity of Roman parties to matters affecting subcultural prestige and survival, but it does not indicate their capacity for mutual accommodation and peaceful coexistence.

Much of city decisionmaking in the planning field and other fields has taken the form not of ideological confrontation but *multipartisanship.* Many decisions have been made through bargaining, negotiation, and even rational discussion of the issues. Antagonistic forces have, in fact, been able to work together in many areas on several issues, although on others conflict has been frontal and frequently even physical. Quantitatively, consensus decisionmaking has been the rule rather than the exception. The overwhelming number of council deliberations are made unanimously; party battles and disputes are preserved for relatively few questions.

For more than ten years after the war, planning decisions were made in accordance with the multipartisan rather than the polarization model. In the first few postwar years the parties shared a common, resounding lack of interest in city planning, as compared to the immediate, pressing problems of recovery. Such problems as relieving hunger, restoring electricity and gas, and relocating refugees housed in schools and barracks seemed a good deal more important to the parties than rather abstract and idealistic issues of city planning. Planning is primarily oriented toward growth and development, and there was little growth or development to plan. If anything, planning seemed a threat to recovery and was therefore to be avoided.[11]

The party system itself was new. It did not consist of organizations long accustomed to each other or to dealing with the city's problems. The parties had never dealt with master planning before, or with any other aspect of city government. Those who were now in the top political offices were new to city government. The parties were not familiar with the significance, especially the political significance, of planning under democratic conditions, because the city had not formulated a plan under such conditions for nearly half a century. Planning held unknown penalties and rewards for the parties, especially since party loyalties were not yet stabilized and the stakes of control in the city were high. Planning involved difficult choices among competing interests, without the legal or financial possibility of compensating the losers. Thus, all parties were rather reluctant to begin the master planning process and it was only the pressure of national law and administration that forced them to begin. Without the prodding of the Ministry of Public Works and the imminent expiration of the master plan of 1931, the parties in Rome would undoubtedly have agreed to take the low road of piecemeal variances rather than the high road of master planning. Once embarked upon the course of master planning, the parties for several years found it possible to maintain a common stance on planning issues, to make planning decisions on the basis of multipartisanship rather than polarization.

Multipartisan policymaking occurs because it has advantages for both governing parties and opposition parties. It allows a governing party, without a fixed council majority coalition, to stay in power without having to commit itself to a possibly compromising choice of coalition partners. Thus the DC party in 1946 and 1961, when torn between choosing partners on the left or the right, appealed for an all-party coalition; this would have allowed it to avoid making a choice of partners. Multipartisanship allows governing parties to spread the risks of unpopular decisions. In return for relinquishing their monopoly of formal decisionmaking authority they secure some immunity from attack at the next elections. It places the governing parties in a stronger position when competing with the leaders of other cities for aid from the national government. It permits the governing parties to give some deference to the norms of democratic due process. In Italian thinking, *colpi di maggioranza,* or the brute use of majority power to ignore and override opposition criticism, violates those norms. Multipartisanship permits governing parties, especially in a centrist coalition, to maintain communications and relations with the opposition parties. The arithmetic of coalition building requires that parties be brought together in a majority coalition which retains many ties with the parties left outside. It is particularly difficult for a centrist coalition to be strongly opposed to either

11. See the interview with Mayor Rebecchini in *Il Paese,* April 1, 1951.

extreme, for such a coalition tends to include within it elements sympathetic to both excluded extremes.

Multipartisan policymaking also has advantages for opposition parties. They choose not to oppose for several reasons. They wish to avoid the charge of *"opposizione preconcetta,"* "preconceived opposition" to any and all government proposals, regardless of merit. They hesitate to vote against "distributive" proposals that benefit the city generally or some segment particularly, such as raises for city employees or neighborhood projects. They want to benefit from the distribution of government patronage. All parties in Rome receive a share of seats on the boards of municipal companies and of the Opera House, and vote these appointments on the basis of reciprocity norms; this form of converting opposition into support has been known in Italy since the nineteenth century as *trasformismo.* Opposition parties may want to keep the door ajar for future eventualities. The postwar period has witnessed all types of party coalition in Rome and in Italy; all party combinations have occurred at one time or another and therefore none can be ruled out a priori. Thus it is prudent for opposition parties occasionally to pull their punches so as to maintain their "availability" for future combinations. They also may want to enjoy a share of power over city policy. The Communists have not been in the giunta since 1946; the neofascists have never been allowed in the giunta. For such parties, multipartisan policymaking is an opportunity to relieve the frustrations of opposition by helping to make policy for the city. Opposition parties want to demonstrate loyalty to the city as against other cities or the national government; they frequently join in unanimous resolutions of protest against cuts in the city budget made by the national government or against anti-Rome polemics in the northern newspapers.

Multipartisan policymaking occurs also because it is feasible, as well as good party strategy and tactics. On most questions that come before the city council there is no particular disagreement among the parties. There is no quarrel, for example, over the need for more school buildings, higher city employee salaries, greater state aid, more hospital beds, more public libraries, more parks, more drinking water, or more efficient public transportation. Thus, once it was clear that by law the city was going to have to produce a new master plan, all the parties were prepared to agree that a new master plan would be desirable. No party wanted to challenge the desirability of an up-to-date master plan, of more orderly development, and of civic improvement. Then, too, since they are powerful and semiautonomous, the parties have been fairly free to determine what they will define as a partisan question and what they will define as a nonpolitical question appropriate for handling through multipartisanship.

Multipartisanship exists because norms are available to legitimize it. Such norms imply that local government is or should be "nonpartisan" or "nonpolitical" and that many issues concern technical efficiency or city welfare, not party politics. Opposition parties can legitimize their participation in multipartisan policymaking by defining issues as nonpolitical. They can also legitimize

208                                                    PLANNING THE ETERNAL CITY

their support for compromise proposals by asserting that whatever is good in
these proposals results only from their participation.

It is advantageous for both the government and opposition parties to engage
in multipartisan decisionmaking, for some things they have in common. One
is a common fear of the electorate's *qualunquismo:* a strong contempt for all
political parties. In much of the electorate there is a latent condemnation of all
the parties and a preference for a strong, authoritarian government. The parties
are seen as impeding government solutions to problems.[12] Multipartisan collaboration is a defensive reaction of the parties to a distrustful environment and
an attempt to make the party system minimally effective, if not quite legitimate.
Opposition and government parties are tied together also by factionalism.
Factions, while disruptive *within* parties, are a major source of integration
*between* parties. Within most parties there are elements in sympathy with forces
in other parties; some factions, in fact, may have more in common with other
parties than with elements within their own party. Factions thus constitute
bridges between and among the parties—a set of informal coalitions that cut
across party lines and mitigate interparty conflicts.

Another factor making for multipartisanship in the Roman party system is
the existence of a semidominant, "catch-all" center party. Such a party tends to
be an integrating factor within the system: all the parties relate to it, as the
natural senior party in any governing coalition, and through its factions it
attempts to maintain relations with them all. For such a center party, alliance
with one extreme, as in the Catholic–neofascist alliance of 1958–60, is "unnat-
ural," strongly disturbing, and, in the nature of things, of short duration. More
normal is alliance with parties around the center, excluding both extremes as
pariahs. For centrist alliances, multipartisanship is a means of keeping the
majority coalition intact by treating both ends of the spectrum with equal respect
while excluding them from formal power.

Multipartisanship can also occur because, though each party tends to have a
distinctive social base and ideology, the congruence between principles, clientele, and party is far from perfect. Thus all parties in Rome share a belief in the
necessity of some measure of public regulation of business. Then, too, there are
many powerful sets of values or principles, such as leftism, conservatism, antifascism, anticommunism, and civic patriotism, that tie together several parts of
the political spectrum. The electoral clienteles of the parties also tend to overlap.
The polarization model implies a greater amount of sociopolitical segregation
than actually exists in Rome. Table 8.3 shows the imperfect correlation between
party voting (1960) and social characteristics in the various districts of the city.[13]

12. See, for example, the attitudes of borgata residents tapped by Franco Crespi in "Aspetti,"
cited above, chap. 1, n. 11.
13. The social characteristics of the districts are derived from the 1951 census, as presented
in "Popolazione e territorio," while the voting data by districts are taken from *Momento Sera,*
June 8, 1962. For other analyses of Roman voting patterns, see Mattei Dogan, "La stratifica-

Table 8.3. Imperfect Correlation between Party Voting and District Social Traits, 1960*

|  | University graduates | Persons/ room | Apartments with central heating | Apartments with bathrooms | Public employees | Building workers | White collar employees |
|---|---|---|---|---|---|---|---|
| Communist vote (%) | −.88 | .92 | −.78 | −.76 | −.65 | .70 | −.83 |
| Socialist vote (%) | −.65 | .64 | −.48 | −.39 | −.56 | .47 | −.54 |
| Social Democrat vote (%) |  | −.36 | .51 | .67 | .38 |  | .61 |
| Republican vote (%) |  | −.36 |  |  |  | −.56 |  |
| Christian Democratic vote (%) | .56 | −.16 | .45 | .37 | .65 | −.58 | .57 |
| Liberal vote (%) | .88 | −.80 | .82 | .69 | .32 | −.39 | .58 |
| Monarchist vote (%) | .58 | −.62 | .42 | .51 |  | −.56 | .48 |
| Neofascist vote (%) | .70 | −.73 | .64 | .71 | .50 | −.46 | .73 |

*Correlations below 95% probability have been omitted.

There is no Roman party with a socially homogeneous clientele, except perhaps the Liberals—the party of the wealthy professional, bureaucratic, and business class. All the other parties have low-income, middle-income, and upper-income supporters; northern, central, and southern supporters; and native and immigrant supporters. Each party, to be sure, has a social center of gravity and its position on the left-right spatial scale approximates the position of its clientele in the ladder of Roman society. Nonetheless, rather than being strictly divisive as the polarization model would suggest, the parties have also been "aggregative" and "integrative"; they have all attempted to make a broad rather than a narrow appeal and to mobilize as many individuals and groups as possible—at least within the broad sectors of Right, Left, and Center. Roman parties have sought to capture very large groupings as their clienteles—all conservatives, all Catholics, all workers, all the poor, all the middle classes. Factionalism within the parties has served as a kind of structural adaptation to each party's drive to mobilize groups on both of its flanks. The considerable overlap among the parties, not dealt with by the polarization model, explains the relative ease with which leaders migrate from party to party. It also explains the fierce competitiveness of the Roman party system: parties are not content to mobilize a narrow segment of society; they carry out raids on their neighbors' clienteles quite as ruthlessly and systematically as do parties in a two-party system.

Multipartisan policymaking is most likely to prevail when: (1) a centrist coalition is in office, (2) the issues are distributive, rather than regulatory or redistributive, (3) the issue is relatively new, (4) the stakes are not very clear or apparently high, (5) "decisions" can take the form of ambiguous resolutions, with sufficient provisos, exceptions, and emendations to satisfy all

zione sociale dei suffragi," in *Elezioni e comportamento politico in Italia* ed. Joseph LaPalombara and Alberto Spreafico (Milan, 1963), pp. 407–74, particularly pp. 473–74; Giorgio Braga, *Il comunismo fra gli italiani* (Milan, 1960), pp. 70–76; and Giuseppe Glisenti, "Esame analitico dei risultati elettorali romani," *Cronache Sociali,* October 31, 1947, pp. 4–7.

qualms, (6) the goals of the groups are (in Bertrand Russell's term) "compossible," satisfiable through logrolling, the addition of claims, and haggling,[14] and (7) there are some unifying general themes, such as preservation of the historic center and defense of the city against the outside world.

Multipartisanship in one policy area may actually occur simultaneously with extreme polarization in other policy areas. The period 1953–57, when the parties were collaborating on the master plan, was one of acute ideological, social, and political tensions and warfare, particularly between the Communists, on the one hand, and the church, the national government, and the neofascists, on the other. This was a period of acute cold war in Italian politics, but it did not prevent multipartisan policymaking on the city level and probably in some areas on the national level.[15]

While multipartisanship prevailed, planning was likely to result in a somewhat flexible, open, and ambiguous plan, containing many points of compromise, though based on some common theme such as preservation of the old city. Plans were likely to be additive rather than selective: to incorporate the more or less contrary preferences of a diversity of groups, rather than reflect the more narrow choices of a few. Fortunately for planners, perhaps, master plans are divisible public goods: they can be designed so as to please a variety of people. The master plans of 1957 and 1962 are quite discernibly products of logrolling among the warring Roman subcultures. In a sense such plans are temporary armistices—pauses that permit the contenders to catch their breath before commencing a new round of competition and negotiation. In this, the master plan designs of 1957 and 1962 resemble the unanimous council and commission resolutions of the early fifties: their very vagueness and catholicity permit the planning process to proceed to the next stage.

### THE FRAGILITY OF MULTIPARTISANSHIP

Multipartisanship, while it exists to some extent at all times in Rome, is fragile as a way of making major controversial decisions. It may occur, but it is easily upset and replaced by partisan polarization.

Partisan policymaking is encouraged by the need of parties and governing coalitions to compete for support in fiercely competitive elections; by the at-

14. Bertrand Russell, *Human Society in Ethics and Politics* (New York: New American Library, 1962), p. xiv. The distinction between distributive, regulatory, and redistributive issues was made by Theodore J. Lowi, "American Business, Public Policy, Case Studies, and Political Theory," *World Politics,* 6 (July 1964), 677–93.

15. The systematic study of Italian politics, as of American politics, has hitherto concentrated on the presumed *inputs* of policy—voting, political culture, interest groups, political parties, the social origins of legislators—rather than on the outputs of the policymaking process. We have little idea of how the presumed inputs of the system mesh with the actual outputs. Knowledge of the system's outputs, apart from such admittedly important areas as land reform and economic planning and development, is spotty. Thus whether and to what extent multipartisanship has functioned at the national level remains a mystery.

tachment of individual parties to particular social groups and ideologies; and by the development of strong solidarities within the parties as "interest groups" or "clans" or "sects" in their own right. Partisan policymaking may be a response to partisan behavior by rival and enemy parties. It is legitimized by the norms of democratic competition, which call for a clear differentiation between a responsible governing coalition and the opposition, and for clear differentiation in the stands and positions of the various parties. Polarized policymaking tends to become general when the centrist party can no longer stay in power without the aid of an extremist party of the right or left.

Multipartisan policymaking in planning (and other fields) broke down in 1957 for several reasons. The electoral law for the 1952 elections had awarded the Center coalition fifty-three out of eighty council seats, that is, two-thirds of the council, though it had achieved a plurality of only 41.8 percent of the vote. With so many seats on the council, the Center coalition remained viable between 1952 and 1956 and multipartisan policymaking was feasible. The controversial electoral law for the 1952 elections was repealed, however, for the 1956 elections and, though its share of the vote rose from 41.8 to 42.5 percent, the Center coalition was returned with only thirty-four seats. The Christian Democrats were faced with the problem of enlarging their coalition to include one extreme or the other. On the left, the Socialists who had broken with the Communists after the Khrushchev report and the Soviet invasion of Hungary were willing to cooperate, but they were still identified with the Popular Front alliance and tied to the Communists in hundreds of local governing alliances as well as in the labor movement.

The Christian Democrats had to choose between alliance with the Socialists—"Marxist atheists" and close allies of the Communists—and alliance with the neofascists, who were extremely deferential toward the clergy as well as being violent anticommunists. The Christian Democrats chose the neofascists of the MSI, who insisted as an alliance precondition on a strong shift to the right in planning policy. In this they were seconded by speculator interests close to the church and the DC party. Multipartisanship was also being undermined by the emergence of an anticlerical crusade, led by the Radical party, which denounced the power and policy of the church in Italy and accused Christian Democratic leaders in Rome of improperly favoring the speculative activities of Catholic business interests. The Vatican, with its power to lay down coalition policy for the Christian Democrats, was alarmed by the support given by the Communists and the Socialists to the progressive planning movement and to the compromise plan of 1957. In the goals and values of the progressive planning movement, conservatives in the church came to see a new and dangerous form of anticlericalism.

Under these conditions, the centrism that had provided the political base for multipartisan planning collapsed. Incorporation of the neofascists into the governing majority drove the antifascists out of the coalition. Roman politics polarized into two bitterly antagonistic coalitions—clerico-fascist and anti-fascist—utterly intransigent, unwilling to compromise, full of mutual hatred and contempt. Under these conditions multipartisan planning became impossible.

To buy neofascist support, the Christian Democrats agreed to reject the CET plan and to adopt a new plan—a plan that omitted most of the features desired by the progressives. The multipartisan coalition broke down during the preparations for the 1960 Olympic games in Rome. Characteristically, the new clerico-fascist coalition that refused, on June 4, 1959, for the first time, to celebrate the Allied liberation of the city, also refused to erase Fascist slogans from the facilities to be used during the Olympics. The new sports facilities were located in the north, west, and southwest—exactly where the progressive planners wished to discourage development. Progressive planners were excluded from influence both over current facilities planning and over master planning for the future.

Exclusion of the neofascists from the governing coalition (or more precisely from the council majority, since no MSI member had actually been brought into the giunta) later in 1960 after the Olympics, and the formation of the Catholic-Socialist coalition in 1962, made possible a partial, but only a partial, return to multipartisan planning and policymaking. By this time the Socialists had become less identified with left-wing extremism and were viewed more as a centrist party than an extremist party. Members of the new Center-Left coalition had contacts and sympathies with both extremes—the DC with the Right, the Socialists with the Communists. Thus one of the Christian Democratic leaders in the giunta was Dr. Pompei, former provincial federal secretary of the MSI. The Socialists, for their part, were still tied to the Communists in jointly run labor unions and they had very similar electoral clienteles.

The master plan of 1962 produced by the Center-Left coalition was the typical product of multipartisanship—a bundle of compromises, containing many features desired by the Right, such as expansion toward and beyond EUR, as well as features desired by the Left, such as the eastern axis. In multipartisan fashion the governing coalition accepted floor amendments from both extremes. Nonetheless, the return to multipartisanship was only partial. In the end, even after the concessions made to all points of view and all points of the compass, the master plan was carried by a vote of 41 to 39, rather than unanimously. By this time the stakes of planning were much clearer than they had been in the early fifties. The master plan had become the most important single theme in city politics and the major element in Christian Democratic and Socialist propaganda. Multipartisanship may, in fact, be possible only for new issues. Once an issue has become partisan, as master planning became after 1957, it may be too difficult, as the Italians say, to remake its virginity.

# 9

# ROMAN
# PLANNING
# INTERESTS

Like the Roman party system, the Roman interest group system could be generally described as a case study in "extremist" or "polarized" pluralism. Joseph LaPalombara has documented the tendency for Italian interest groups to be "isolative and nonbargaining," "rarely in communication with each other," and parts of "mutually exclusive ideological aggregations."[1] Postwar Roman planning provides ample evidence for this, but it also suggests that despite subcultural cleavages considerable group bargaining and accommodation can and do take place. An understanding of Roman politics and policymaking requires the use of two models: the model of *fazione,* or polarized pluralism, but also the model of *combinazione,* or moderate pluralism.[2]

The *fazione* model depicts a political system in which:[3]

1. Group demands tend to be latent, diffuse, particularistic, affective, ideological, rigid, ambiguous, deceptive, radical, and incompatible.
2. Groups use illegitimate channels to articulate these demands, such as violent demonstrations, personal connections, secret contacts.
3. Government decisionmakers cannot formulate responsive policies, given the rawness, incompatibility, unintelligibility, and contradictory nature of the demands being made.

1. Joseph LaPalombara, *Interest Groups and Italian Politics* (Princeton, 1964), p. 249, and "Italy: Fragmentation, Isolation, Alienation," in *Political Culture and Political Development,* ed. Lucian Pye and Sidney Verba.
2. *Fazione* is a synonym for "sect," while *combinazione* is a synonym for *negozio* or bargaining.
3. The *fazione* model draws heavily on the polarization model elaborated by Gabriel Almond and G. Bingham Powell in *Comparative Politics,* pp. 90–91.

4. Many interests are not represented in any stable fashion, but find sporadic articulation in sudden outbursts of violence; participation rates in associational life are low.
5. Participation by institutional interest groups tends to be high, if covert.
6. There is little cross-group communication flow; communications remain within subcultural aggregations.
7. Subcultural groups exist to organize the entire social life of their members, with unions, schools, newspapers, professional associations, political parties, recreational clubs, etc., isolated from those of the other subcultures.
8. In policymaking, the same coalition makes all decisions and rejects proposals and amendments from opposition groups.
9. Policies are impositions on opposition subcultures, which are without legitimacy and likely to be ignored or resisted.
10. There are strong pressures toward a dualistic confrontation along the lines of major ideological confrontation.
11. There is considerable cynicism, mutual hostility, and mutual intolerance.
12. Within the subcultures, parties dominate interest groups or interest groups dominate parties.

The model of *combinazione* politics and policymaking depicts a different type of system in which:

1. Group demands tend to be specific, instrumental, pragmatic, flexible, clear, and negotiable.
2. Most interests are organized in stable associations.
3. There is some overlap in associational memberships.
4. Group demands are articulated openly, peacefully, and through legitimate, formal channels.
5. Policymakers make decisions through bargaining and compromise.
6. There are different coalitions for different issues.
7. There is considerable cross-group communication flow through a variety of channels, including channels regarded as neutral.
8. Policies, as compromises, are more easily administered, though they take longer to adopt.
9. There is some mutual independence among groups, parties, and institutions, which allows individuals and groups to choose from a variety of positions, roles, and affiliations.

The politics of fazione matches the politics of polarization among the parties, while the politics of combinazione matches the politics of multipartisanship. To understand postwar Roman group politics requires the same dualistic model needed to understand postwar Roman party politics. Roman groups, just as Roman parties, have had two modes of interaction: one of mutual accommodation, the other of ideological confrontation and intransigence. The evolution of phases in group and party modes coincided. In both cases there was a period of accommodation (multipartisanship and combinazione), which lasted until 1957. This was followed by a period of intense polarization and fazione, culminating in the nationwide confrontations of the summer of 1960. The dangers of polarization and fazione having become abundantly clear during that summer, Roman and Italian politics reverted partially to multipartisanship among the parties and combinazione among the groups.

Unlike Roman parties, Roman interest groups do not struggle for power in a formally institutionalized system of competition, nor do they display as much uniformity as political actors. Group participation varies from the open, constant, specialized, almost legislated participation of the professional planners (INU) to the usually discreet *démarches* of the church and the land speculators. Compared to the parties, the groups as a whole are uninterested in city politics. They intervene sporadically and often privately, keep their oligarchical internal affairs quiet, and act publicly through proxies, whether journalists, professional experts, or party politicians.

The combinazione model describes fairly well the behavior of Roman interest groups in the planning process up to 1957. Until that time they seemed generally favorable to the formation of a new master plan and prepared to work hard at finding a generally acceptable design. The formulation of successive resolutions on the new plan—those of October 1951, May 1954, November 1955, and June 1957—involved normal political bargaining and compromise. Groups put forth proposals and time and energy were spent working out compromises satisfactory to all forces and interests. Between 1951 and 1957 bargaining was the normal method of decisionmaking or policymaking in the planning field, with such typical outcomes as the 40-30-15-15 formula for expansion. Did this formula perhaps have some relation to the fact that the Left, which wanted eastern expansion, had about one-third of the electorate; the Center, which wanted southern expansion, had 40 percent of the vote; and the Right which wanted northern and western expansion, controlled about 25 percent of the vote?

The all-group coalition based on the politics of combinazione was possible because there are many things that work toward combinazione rather than fazione. Ideological or subcultural fragmentation makes bargaining more difficult, to be sure, but also more imperative, for groups that have mortal enemies need allies more desperately than ever. Inter-ideological or cross-ideological coalitions are the only safe form of protection.[4] Coalition is still prudent in Italian politics, for no group by itself can achieve security. Then, too, overlapping group membership, while not so common as in the United States, exists

---

4. The Fascist party was a defensive coalition of Liberals, Socialists, Nationalists, and Catholics held together by bonds of mutual interest and charisma. See Alberto Aquarone, *L'organizzazione dello stato totalitario,* (Turin, 1965), p. 299.

to a politically significant degree. If many groups are ideologically segregated in Rome, others are not.

Professional planning societies, for example, have successfully united in common cause both Liberals and Communists, Catholics and anticlericals, Socialists and conservatives. The cleavages in Italian society are to some extent intersecting rather than congruent. This is why many Italian interest groups deliberately avoid overt commitment to an ideology or party and why they actually attempt to escape from ideology in order to associate on the basis of professional, regional, economic, religious, or cultural interest. In addition to the dominant pattern of ideological segregation, there are many rival sets of interests that can be and are successfully organized.

Ideological segregation is the aspiration of fanatics, but it has never been completely achieved. The parochial, apolitical, familistic nature of Italian political culture makes such ideological commitment and permeation of society impossible.[5] Ideological segregation has also been incomplete because of the complex pluralism of Italian society: there are large numbers of people— economic, professional, cultural, and bureaucratic elites, especially—for whom ideological segregation is a handicap in the achievement of their economic, professional, cultural, and bureaucratic goals. Many of these elites are consequently prepared to submerge their differences and to bargain in order to get their jobs done. Political culture surveys show that Italians admire more than any other quality the ability to do a job well.[6]

As has been seen, ideology and class lines do not coincide. Middleclass groupings adhere to a variety of causes—neofascist, Monarchist, Liberal, Catholic, Radical, and Social Democratic. The lower classes are far from homogeneously Marxist; they give significant support also to the Catholics, Monarchists, and neofascists. Every social grouping seems to contain a diversity of outlooks on issues of public policy. Catholics do not have identical attitudes in social and economic matters, or even on religious matters, as the reactions to Vatican Council reforms have made clear. While it is a divisive force in Italian politics, the church is also a source of social integration, bringing together a variety of social, political, professional, and cultural forces. The Marxist world is not much more homogeneous than the Catholic world, suffering sectarian division into several varieties and subspecies of socialism and communism. The anticlericals, for their part, are also scattered among several classes, high and low, and several parties, left and right.

Some interest groups are anxious to grow and bring in all kinds of people, to enlarge the roster of their allies and supporters, to expand their appeal. Such

5. Interviews in a Roman borgata in the early 50s did not, for example, reveal the "appropriate" attitudes toward the church and religion on the part of many Communist sympathizers. See Hadley Cantril, *The Politics of Despair* (New York, 1962), p. 114.

6. Arend Lijphart, *The Politics of Accommodation: Pluralism and Democracy in the Netherlands* (Berkeley, 1968), p. 146; (Table 22).

aspirations force them to play down divisive themes and to search for unifying ones, such as "the unity of the working class," or "fidelity to the church," or anticommunism. In postwar Roman planning, then, interest group leaders were talented in the art of compromise as well as in the art of intransigence. Neither complete expediency nor complete rigidity was a normal state.

If there are forces that lead to and sustain intergroup cooperation, there are others that make such cooperation difficult, if not impossible. As the labels on the Roman parties make clear (Monarchists, Republicans, Liberals, Communists, and so forth), there are a number of distinctive sociopolitical traditions in the city that animate a set of mutually hostile and mutually suspicious social and political forces. The fazione model may not be all-explanatory but it is still indispensable. History has divided Romans into several factions, each with distinctive loyalties and symbols and each with a sense of betrayal. To older cleavages along clerical-anticlerical lines have come newer ones: fascists vs. antifascists, monarchists vs. republicans, bourgeois vs. Marxists, and nationalists vs. internationalists. A rationalistic culture, at least at the elite and middle levels, has encouraged an ideological rather than pragmatic orientation toward politics—a search to be "coherent" rather than effective. A Catholic culture has accentuated the dogmatic approach to politics on the part of both "believers" and "anti-believers." Separate subcultures have emerged, each highly defensive, each striving for a complete, self-sufficient community of the faithful. Thus in Rome there are separate labor unions, parties, planners' associations, building cooperatives, newspapers, schools, youth groups, women's groups, for each of the major subcultures. Indoctrination in a subculture involves learning a version of the past that stresses group betrayal, persecution, and provocation. From this comes a tendency in all groups to search beneath the appearance of issues for their "real" content—that is, the inevitable implications they have for subcultural survival.

It is not surprising, then, that all-group coalitions, based on the politics of combinazione, are fragile and easily break down. Thus bargaining over city planning policy can easily degenerate (or rise) to the level of Kulturkampf.

The all-group coalition supporting multipartisanship in planning broke down in 1957 under the weight of Radical attacks on corruption in the Rome city government—attacks that had as targets the Christian Democratic administration in Rome and the church-owned real estate company, SGI.[7] The clergy interpreted attacks on the Rome DC, on the SGI, and on Roman planning administration as salvoes in a war against religion generally and against the church in particular. The church redefined conflict over planning in Rome as meaning not a conflict of negotiable interests but another episode in the struggle between secularism and religion. In December 1957 the Radical weekly, L'Es-

7. On the growing anticlerical-clerical tensions of this period, see Norman Kogan, *A Political History of Postwar Italy* (New York, 1966), pp. 91–92; and Domenico Settembrini, *La Chiesa nella politica italiana, 1944–1963* (Pisa, 1964), pp. 371–416.

Table 9.1. The Conservative vs. Progressive Coalitions

A. *The conservative planning coalition in Rome (1957–62)*
  1. Professional planning groups
       URIA (Union of Roman Engineers and Architects)
  2. Conservative press
       *Il Tempo* ("independent" Liberal-Fascist)
       *Il Giornale d'Italia* ("independent" Liberal-Fascist)
       *Il Secolo* (Neofascist party)
       *L'Osservatore Romano* (semiofficial Vatican)
       *Il Quotidiano* (Catholic Action)
       *Momento Sera* (Catholic "independent")
       *Il Popolo* (DC party)
       *Il Globo* (Confederation of Industry)
  3. Conservative business groups
       Landowners (unorganized)
       ACER (Rome Building Contractors Association)
       APER (Rome Property Owners Association)
       Union of Roman Industry *(Confindustria)*
       Provincial Agrarian Union
       Provincial Federation of Small Farmers *(Coltivatori Diretti)*
       Union of Roman Merchants
       SGI and other real estate corporations
  4. Religious groups
       Vicariate
       Catholic Action
       Most religious orders
       (also Catholic interest groups such as *Coltivatori Diretti* and SGI)
  5. Conservative parties and factions
       Christian Democratic party (DC)
            *"Primavera"* faction
       Liberal party (PLI)
       Monarchist parties
       Neofascist party (MSI)
  6. Institutional interest groups
       Ministry of Public Works: Urban Planning Bureau and Section; ANAS (State
            Highway Corp.)
       Ministry of the Interior
       Ministry of Defense: Civil Aviation Bureau
       Ministry of Agriculture: Provincial Agrarian Inspectorate
       Ministry of Merchant Marine: Maritime Domain
       CONI: Italian Olympic Committee
       INCIS (State Employees Housing Agency)
       EUR
B. *The progressive planning coalition*
  1. Professional planning groups
       Union of Catholic Technicians (UCIT)
       *Italia Nostra* preservation society
       IN/arch (progressive architects)
       INU (National Planning Institute) and its Lazio section
       SAU (interideological architect and planner society, 1960)
       UIA (International Union of Architects)
  2. Leftist and moderate press organs
       *L'Unità* (Communist party)
       *Paese* and *Paese Sera* (paracommunist)
       *Avanti!* (Socialist)
       *La Giustizia* (Social Democrat)

Table 9.1.  (Continued)

*Il Mondo* (Radical weekly)
*L'Espresso* (Radical weekly)
*Il Messaggero* (moderate-conservative)
3. Leftist parties
   Communists
   Socialists
   Social Democrats (in theory)
   Republicans
   Radicals
4. Left factions in the Christian Democratic party
   Fanfani faction
   *Base* faction
5. Progressive interest groups
   UDI (Union of Italian Women, Communist)
   Building workers union (Communist)
   UGC (Union of Catholic Jurists)
   ACLI (Catholic workers association)
   Rome Chamber of Labor (Communist)

*presso,* was found guilty of claiming, without sufficient proof, that the SGI had corrupted Roman planning officials.[8] *L'Osservatore Romano,* in its praise of the court decision on January 13, 1958, denounced Radical attacks on land speculation and the SGI as a pretext for attacks on the Vatican itself, which was the principal shareholder in SGI. In a speech to the parish priests of Rome on February 19, 1958, Pope Pius XII himself defended the SGI against Radical charges. It was just at this time that the Christian Democrats in Rome were joining the revolt against the CET version of the new master plan.

The all-party coalition split into two hostile coalitions: a progressive planning coalition, which defended the CET plan presented in December 1957, and the conservative planning coalition, which rejected that plan and secured the adoption of a new one in June 1959. Table 9.1 shows the components of each coalition.

During the next three years, 1958–60, interest groups in Rome displayed the rigid, uncompromising intransigence ascribed to them in the fazione model. In this period ideology colored everything, even the points of the compass. Eastern expansion was seen as favoring the East in the cold war; it was said to

8. The lower court found that SGI had subdivided a reclamation district without notifying the Ministry of Agriculture from which it was receiving grants and without asking city permission; had built several buildings without a permit; had in the course of construction moved trolley tracks, without requesting permission, etc. (See Tribunale di Roma, Sezione Quarta, Sentenza del 29 mese di dicembre [1956] . . . , pp. 23–33, 43–49, of the typescript.) The verdict said: "SGI was accustomed to carry out works on its own initiative knowing full well that, in all probability, they would be approved either because already carried out or because among the functionaries of the Commune of Rome there existed a certain acquiescence and subservience in the face of large corporations or persons connected with them" (p. 22). The lower court found evidence of SGI influence, but no evidence that substantiated *L'Espresso* charges of corruption; it nonetheless dismissed the case against *L'Espresso.* The appellate court, more logically, reversed the decision of the lower court and found the editors of *L'Espresso* guilty of defamation.

have been chosen by the Communists because it demonstrated loyalty to the Soviet Union. Support of expansion to the west, which Mussolini had favored, and where the Vatican was located, became in contrast a sign of loyalty to the Atlantic community. City planning had become a means of demonstrating ideological *cum* international sympathies.

Even in this period (1957–60), however, neither side was monolithic. The attempt to convert the planning struggle into a Manichean confrontation of world views was never completely successful. The unity of the Catholic front was conspicuously broken by the Union of Catholic Technicians, which included in its leadership some of the most prominent Italian city planners. The union denounced the 1959 master plan and worked with the Left to secure its revision.[9] Conservative hostility to the CET plan derived from rather different concerns. Among Ministry of Public Works functionaries, opposition to the CET plan stemmed from a professional preference for flexible planning and a deep concern to preserve the historic center. Among small Roman contractors, hostility to the CET plan arose from a desire for complete anarchy and from a contempt for the whole governmental process. Two of the leading participants in the revolt against the CET plan, moreover, Minister of Public Works Giuseppe Togni and Lieutenant-Colonel Giuseppe Amici, the director of construction at Fiumicino International Airport, while united against the CET plan, were at the same time involved in a bitter struggle for jurisdictional control over construction of the airport.[10]

During this period the Socialists maintained a constant willingness to come to terms with the Catholics. The giunta, for its part, Liberals and DC included, did not as a rule describe the plan in ideological terms at all but in technical terms. The giunta plan, it was constantly said, was no more than an extension of the CET plan, with some modifications; it would eventually be revised "in the light of" the objective information about regional trends discovered in the formulation of the intercommunal plan.[11] In the language of most responsible politicians

9. Clelio Darida, *Rinnovamento,* January 1958, pp. 1–2; *Tecnica e Uomo,* February 1958 (published also in *Il Quotidiano,* February 18, 1958). In July, Catholic planners wrote privately to the national leaders of the Christian Democratic party, protesting against the alliance with the neofascists and against the planning situation the alliance had brought about. "The present situation appears to the objective observer to be determined exclusively by the massive intervention of economic groups (Società Generale Immobiliare, Talenti, Gerini, Lancellotti, Vaselli, etc.), who see in the Rome Master Plan an obstacle to their financial game and property speculations [*"aggiottaggio fondiario"*]. This is the cause of the veto [of the CET plan.]" Letter dated July 18, 1958.) See also Mario D'Erme, "L'ombra di Villa Chigi sulla vita della città, *Rinnovamento,* January 1958, and L. Benevolo, "Il Piano Regolatore di Roma," *Italia Nostra,* January-February 1958, pp. 1–4.

10. Piero Radice, "Fiumicino e dintorni," *Il Ponte,* January 1962, pp. 23–28.

11. See the record of the 1959 council debate on the master plan in "Council Debates, 1959". See also the resolutions of the Rome DC executive on the master plan published in *Il Popolo* on February 16, 1958, July 4, 1958, February 14, 1960, and November 25, 1961. Although the intercommunal plan was formulated during the height of ideological confrontation in Roman politics, the transcript of the deliberations reveals no trace of ideological conflict, despite the fact that participants came not only from conservative Rome, but also from the "Red" suburbs of Rome province.

and bureaucrats, planning remained a technical, nonpolitical, completely non-ideological matter. Ministry of Public Works officials, including Minister Togni himself, never discussed the plan in ideological terms. Nonetheless, he and other conservatives worked to extend the clerico-fascist alliance from the Rome city council to the national Parliament. This coalition formula tended to convert every policy issue into a crusade either against communism or fascism.

When the attempt was made in the summer of 1960 to set up a Center-Right (Christian Democrat-neofascist) coalition on the national level, the resulting nationwide riots showed how dangerous the formula was for conservative interests. Bipolarity in Italian politics tended to favor the Communists. Moderates on both sides of center took alarm and began to work toward a more polycentric political system. Ideological intransigents in the Catholic, Radical, and Socialist camps were bypassed in favor of compromisers willing to work out an alliance between the Catholics, secularists, and Socialists. The church was forced to reconcile itself to the inevitability of an alliance between Catholics and Socialists—an inevitability deriving from the arithmetical distribution of party power in the country and Parliament. Had the DC retained its 1948 level of parliamentary support in the subsequent national elections of 1953 and 1958, there would not have been the violent conflict over alliances and the instability of the 1950s, with its possibilities for authoritarian inversion. The church under Pope John began to move toward a more flexible strategy of opposition to communism, just as it developed a more accommodating attitude toward Protestantism and secularism. The Socialists, for their part, were evolving toward a policy of gradual reform. Both Catholics and Socialists retained distinctive symbols, ideas, and loyalties, but both developed a more tolerant or resigned attitude toward diversity. At the same time even the Radicals began to applaud the growing liberalism of the church, which made clerical intervention in politics less of an issue: in fact, the authority of the clergy was now going to be needed and used to bolster the alliance with the Socialists both in Parliament and in Rome.

Disavowal by the church nationally and in Rome of the proposed alliance with the Right was an essential ingredient in the victory of the progressive planners in Rome. The shift of the church allowed the Christian Democrats to ally themselves with the Socialists, both nationally and locally. A broad centrist coalition of groups emerged to dominate Roman planning. This new coalition was, to be sure, extremely heterogeneous; included in its ranks were Catholics and secularists, Marxists and moderates. The very diversity of the new coalition, while an obvious source of weakness, was also a source of strength. There were elements in the new Center coalition that neither political extreme wished to attack or could easily attack. The Communists could not, after all, claim that a coalition including the Socialists was a coalition of the reactionary bourgeoisie; nor could neofascists and Liberals claim that a coalition that included archconservative Christian Democrats—that is, their own former allies—was a coalition of the subversive Left.

Table 9.2. Group Coalitions in Roman Planning since 1962

1. Conservative opposition coalition
     Liberal party
     Monarchist party
     Neofascist party
     ACER (Builders Association)              Accommodative conservative groups:
     Confindustria                           UCR (Union of Rome Builders)-large builders
     Il Tempo                                USNPR (Special Office for Master Plan); City
     Il Giornale d'Italia                    Planning Department
     Il Secolo
2. Centrist supporting coalition
     Christian Democratic (DC) party
     Social Democratic party (PSDI)
     Republicans (PRI)
     Socialists (PSI)
     Ministry of Public Works
     Vicariate
     Union of Catholic Technicians
     Union of Socialist Technicians
     INU & Urbanistica
     Il Messaggero
     Il Popolo
     Avanti!
     L'Espresso
     Il Mondo (to 1965)
3. Leftwing opposition coalition
     Communists (PCI)
     Proletarian Socialists (PSIUP, formed 1964)
     L'Unità
     Il Ponte, L'Astrolabio

The formation of the Center-Left party coalition paved the way for the reemergence in Roman group politics of a relatively moderate pluralism, in which a broad, internally divided center coalition once again placed both extremes in opposition roles. The new lineup of coalitions in planning after 1962 is shown in Table 9.2. Note that in delineating the group coalitions in Roman planning, parties, interest groups, newspapers, weekly magazines, and government departments have been included on an equal plane of importance. The evidence suggests that no single category of actors dominated the Roman political or planning process.

Organized interest groups do not seem to have dominated the process, manipulated the other actors, or determined by themselves the shifts in the city's planning policies. Certainly much of postwar planning politics in the city seems to have been a battle between progressive planning groups and conservative planning groups, as ranged in the coalitions delineated above. The difficulties of planning the city certainly derived from the relative weakness of proplanning groups as compared to antiplanning groups. Antiplanning groups were powerful enough to postpone plan adoption until 1962 and they have had some part in blocking implementation of the plan adopted in that year. A pivotal role in reversing the balance of power among the political forces in the city was played by another interest group, the church, certainly the most powerful single interest group in Rome and in Italy. The church exercized very tight control over the Christian Democratic branches in the city, just as the confederations of industry and agriculture exercised considerable influence over the right-wing parties, which they financed. But were the parties, which apparently dominated Roman policymaking and planning, merely the agents of interest groups?

Possibly the most crucial test of this hypothesis occurred during the city election campaign of 1952. Disturbed by the apparent growth of communism in recent elections, Pope Pius XII urged the formation of a general anticommunist coalition that would keep Rome safely in the hands of those sympathetic to the church. The pope, it was said, preferred to have Soviet troops in St. Peter's Square rather than have the Rome city government fall under leftist control.[12] The proposal, which would in effect have allied the centrist parties with the parties of the extreme Right, became an issue in Italian national politics. After considerable anguish, Prime Minister DeGasperi, though a staunch antifascist, agreed to the formation of the Center-Right coalition in Rome. But if the Christian Democrats were compelled to go along with the papal proposal, their secularist allies were not. The Social Democrats and Republicans, both left-of-center secularist parties, threatened to bring down the national cabinet if the coalition with the Right was formed in Rome. Faced with this threat the Vatican withdrew its proposal. The lesson in 1952, as in 1960, was that even if the Vatican had complete control over the DC party it did not control the secularist allies the DC party has needed to stay in power. If the church forces the DC party to turn to the right-wing parties for support, it drives the moderate progressives into a coalition more or less dominated by the Communists. Thus the power of the church over the Italian party system as a whole is much less than its power over the leading Italian political party.

The influence of real estate speculators on the Roman political and planning process has also been very great, due to the fortunes accumulated by the speculators, their willingness to use their wealth for political purposes, and their ties to other influential institutions such as the church. But even with these and other resources, the speculator groups have not automatically been in a position to dictate policy to the political parties, to other interest groups, to the city government, or to the national agencies involved in Roman affairs. After 1960, Italian national politics began to shift leftward, with the inclusion of Socialists in the governing coalition—an event that the speculators probably deplored but were unable to prevent. They subsequently began to lose *some* of their considerable influence over Italian and Roman politics. Where formerly their

12. For the background of this most famous episode in postwar Roman politics, see Manlio Del Bosco, "La Chiesa ed il partito," *Il Mondo,* October 20, 1965; *La Giustizia,* February 16, 1952; *Avanti!,* May 22, 1952; *Il Tempo,* April 17, 1952; Maria Romana Catti De Gasperi, *De Gasperi uomo solo* (Milan, 1964), from which the pope's reported phrase is taken, p. 327; and Giulio Andreotti, *Concretezza,* August 14, 1965.

power in the city had been almost unlimited, at least in matters of concern to them, they now had to contend with Center-Left coalitions in which anti-speculator forces were fairly strong. By late 1962, when the Center-Left coalition in Rome, backed by the Center-Left coalition in the national government, was about to adopt the master plan, the speculators found themselves bargaining with the parties of the Center-Left, not dictating to them. The Center-Left parties were now in a position to exchange greater development rights for campaign contributions.[13] With the national and local shift in party alliances, the speculator groups were placed on the defensive. Their defenses, needless to say, have been very strong. Nonetheless, after the "opening to the Left" the speculators needed the ruling parties as much as the ruling parties needed speculator campaign contributions. The DC, which had been generously financed by the real estate lobby, was far from being completely dependent on that particular interest group or on any private interest group, except for the church. The DC has made much of its opportunities as a "professional" governing party, nationally and locally, to secure jobs and financing from public agencies. Thus in Rome the DC has used two agencies, *Ente Nazionale Protezione Infortuni* (ENPI) and *Opera Nazionale Maternità ed Infanzia* (ONMI), as sources of party patronage.[14] Patronage from public agencies gave the governing parties a measure of independence from private economic interests. The power of the speculators now depended on their (considerable) ability to compete openly for public support against the forces favorable to planning.

On the other side of the economic fence the parties were even stronger. The building unions of the city, grouping about 25 percent of the building workers, might have been under some pressure from employers and speculators to oppose progressive demands for stricter building standards. In their own right the unions might have seen in the planning operation, generally, a threat to employment in the industry. But the major unions were solidly controlled by the Communist and Socialist parties, with the result that the unions adhered to the progressive planning line at all times.[15]

13. The insertion of large numbers of G4 zones, allowing luxury, low-density development of rural acreage, is reported to have been the result of these transactions between the real estate interests and the parties of the Center-Left.

14. These agencies, designed respectively to inspect elevators and assist mothers and children, have been used as sources of jobs and favors by the dominant DC factions in postwar Rome. (See *Agenzia Radicale,* July 23, 1965). For his alleged official misconduct as Rome commissioner for ONMI, former mayor Petrucci was arrested in 1968, on the eve of parliamentary elections. (*Il Messaggero,* January 21, 1968). Factional rivalries within the DC party were widely believed to have been responsible for the arrest. On the allocation of patronage among individuals and factions in the DC party, see Cesare Zappulli, "E l'ora della dosimetria," *La Nuova Tribuna,* November 1966. On DC party finance, see Stefano Passigli, "Italy," *The Journal of Politics,* November 1963, pp. 718–36; *L'Espresso,* January 31, 1965. According to *L'Espresso* (p. 3), "almost half the expenses of the [national] DC, amounting to about five billion lire [eight million dollars] until recently were provided by the building land market, partly through direct operations, partly through the generous contributions which private contractors or land dealers made to the provincial organs of the party in exchange for favors, immunities, master plan changes, etc. With the crisis in building, and real estate, this source of finance has dried up."

15. Marco Cesarini Sforza, *Il Mondo,* April 10, 1962.

## THE GROUP IMPACT ON PLANNING PERFORMANCE

The balance of power among interest groups in Rome favored the opponents of planning, who were able to use their power to delay final adoption of a master plan until 1962. The long delay resulted, however, not only from the blocking power of the antiplanners, but was inherent in the sheer number, weight, and diversity of institutional interests that had to be discovered and adjusted in the planning process. Italian planners, who are not as a rule particularly tender in their judgments of planning performance in Rome, will admit that, at least among Italian cities, Rome has a uniquely difficult set of interests to be accommodated and regulated through planning.[16] Time was thus required for the city to examine the vast number of appeals against the master plans it adopted. Examination of 2,766 appeals against the 1959 master plan took, it is true, only six months, probably because the 1959 master plan put off so many zoning choices to the future. Examination of the 4,365 appeals against the 1962 plan, a plan that made many of the difficult choices evaded by the 1959 plan, took a good deal longer—nearly two years.

Interest groups were given a formal and legitimate role in the planning process under the terms of the Planning Act of 1942. Fascism did not object to participation by community groups in the formulation of master plans, since by 1942, of course, most interest groups were in the hands of loyal Fascists. But fascisticized or not, all affected interests were given the legal opportunity to present general criticisms of new master plans, once the plans were adopted by the local political authority. Planning decisions could be criticized, presumably, only because city planning was seen as the nonpartisan, nonpolitical, basically technical adjustment of conflicting private and public interests. Strictly speaking, only public institutions and labor-management ("syndical") organizations were authorized to present observations on adopted master plans; private individuals and firms were supposed to wait until the formulation of detailed implementing plans before presenting their criticism. In a 1954 circular, the Ministry of Public Works "amended" the 1942 act by reinterpretation in order to allow the presentation of private observations at the master plan stage.

Under article 9 of the 1942 act, the criticisms presented were supposed to concern the general character of the master plan rather than how it affected specific interests. But few groups or individuals cared very much about the general principles of the plans adopted in 1959 and 1962. The ad hoc board set up to review appeals against the 1959 plan noted that:

> Of all the [2,766] observations, only thirty were presented by public bodies and the associations contemplated in the [1942 Act, Article 9]. Of the observations presented by private parties, 54 deal with questions of a general character relating to the contents of the Master Plan or to the criteria followed in the solution of the various planning problems. Prevalent in the others is the

16. A. Cederna, *Il Mondo*, November 21, 1961.

desire of the authors to protect only their own particular interests, formulating proposals that are barely or not at all concerned to coordinate private utility with the general utility of the collectivity.[17]

In the postwar period, of course, interest groups once again became autonomous; their participation could thus contribute a great deal to the representativeness of the planning process. The prewar set of fascisticized interest groups was replaced after the fall of Fascism by a multitude of interest groups, with allegiances to a variety of political, cultural, and ideological viewpoints. Since a much wider variety of viewpoints could now be articulated, planners and politicians could have a much more accurate view of community preferences than under Fascism. But, unfortunately, the polarization of the postwar Roman interest group system has made it unlikely that any one plan could be responsive to community preferences.

The polarized nature of the Roman interest group system tends to lessen its usefulness to the planners as a means of reducing resistance to their decisions; for polarization means that the communication of group preferences and intentions is highly and deliberately distorted. Different groups belong to different political worlds and restrict their communications to other members of their world. Ideological segregation impedes the flow of information needed by the planners to adjust conflicting interests and ideals. The planning profession itself is fragmented by the same sectarian tendencies. Each group tends to work through the parties, associations, media, and professional experts belonging to its own world. Within each world other groups are depicted with inaccuracy, perceived with fear, and judged with bigotry.

Ideological segregation and the lack of a political no-man's land has meant a dearth of reliable information about group preferences and intentions. Rome has been a community with a vast "credibility gap" among its groups and between groups and government. The lack of civic trust produces and is reflected in the lack of reliable information as to what groups and individuals genuinely prefer. In such a community the most characteristic form of political communication is the anonymous letter.

Romans feel freer to express their opinions in anonymous letters than in opinion surveys and they send large numbers of such letters not only to public authorities but also to the press, as a kind of public confessional. Flora Antonioni, a prominent journalist, has written:

> The "anonymous letter complex" still pervades our spirit and our life. Fear, an ancient fear with remote roots in the foreign dominations that for centuries controlled our land; the subtle taste for a *carbonarismo* which has become part of our blood; and the inevitable mental deformation provoked by more than twenty years of dictatorship have reduced us to the condition

17. Comune di Roma, "Controdeduzioni, 1959", p. 1.

of "the most untruthful people in the world." Camorras and mafias are only the ramifications of a natural state of mind, of a legitimate defense, of a profound distrust of the law and of the constituted authorities.

Moreover, the misunderstood sense of hierarchy—a hierarchy based on slaves subordinated to each other and dominated by the one on top—overshadows our existence; but often the one who stands at the top is afraid of those below and for different reasons fears retaliation.[18]

Enormous guile and energy must be devoted in this skeptical society to getting one's version of the facts accepted. In a society where one is guilty until proved innocent, in the courts and before tax examiners, and where one is never telling his real opinions but only conforming and dissimulating, only anonymous letters permit one to express the truth. Thus the police will not act on tips that are not presented to them in the form of a *"lettera anonima."*[19]

Italian political culture has for a long time sanctioned and suggested the necessity for deception and *furberia* in political communications between individuals, groups, and government. In such a culture, the rational man takes no ideological claim at face value, nor even any expression of self-interest. In such a culture, secrecy is cherished as a political strategy and resource by individuals, groups, and government agencies. Planning efforts are hampered by the refusal of many government agencies to supply needed information. The tax assessment process assumes that no person, if mentally healthy, presents a true return. The notion of "objective" information or information useful for an "objective" community purpose, such as planning, is not widespread.[20] No statement of preference, therefore, can be taken at face value. When the Communists say they are against the 1962 plan, this means they are really in favor of it. When the Communists say they prefer eastern expansion on "technical" or "natural" grounds, this means that they are camouflaging a scheme to build a Marxist paradise in the eastern suburbs. Honest declarations of preference and intentions are discouraged by considerations of prudence, by the general atmosphere of skepticism, and by the fact that, to many segments of the community, the declared preferences and intentions will undoubtedly seem illegitimate.

Then, too, communications are distorted because of the domination of interest groups by political parties or by other interest groups. The labor unions are subject to party domination. The professional groups are subject to infiltration by parties, interest groups, and government departments.

The Ministry of Public Works early in 1962 reportedly put considerable

18. *Il Messaggero,* December 10, 1961.
19. Ibid.
20. The city assessor in charge of conducting the 1971 census operation in Rome declared that fear of the tax collector had induced may Romans to falsify their 1971 census returns. Few Romans, he said, were willing to admit that their apartment had a bathroom; "nobody has two bathrooms, and almost everybody moves around not in cars but on foot." The margin of error in the 1971 census was expected to exceed the 30 percent considered normal by census officials. (Cited in the *Los Angeles Times,* November 9, 1971.)

pressure on the INU planning group in Rome to accept a conservative plan, implying that any sacrifice in collective principle would be more than compensated for by individual career satisfactions.[21] Speculator groups have made great efforts also to capture the INU and other planning groups, rounding up sympathetic architects and planners to take over meetings and conventions. Speculators were successful in taking over one Roman planning association, the Istituto Nazionale di Architettura (IN/arch) in 1965, but failed in a similar attempt to win control at the INU national convention that year.[22] The Communists have organized assemblies for the discussion of planning issues in various districts—not for an impartial examination of the issues, of course, but to build support for the party's predetermined position. The Roman press suffers from the same debilitating division into ideological worlds and domination by "outside" interests—parties, business groups, the church. For a rounded view of city politics, one has to read a dozen dailies and several weeklies. Even then it is not always clear for whom these organs speak—whose preferences they are, in fact, articulating.

A final distortion of the communications process occurs because of the lack of general awareness of planning issues and the seeming absence of general preferences on those issues in the public at large. No official effort was made at any stage of the planning process to inform the public about the plan, apart from the legal notices posted from time to time on buildings throughout the city. It was taken for granted, perhaps rightly, that although most people would be very aware of how planning proposals affected their property, few would care to formulate any general preferences for the city as a whole.

On the other hand, it is hard to think of any significant segment of the population to which some form of interest articulation was not available. Communist organizations may have provided more vigorous representation of the very poor, particularly, the interests of the borgate inhabitants, than similar groups have in American cities. Any group that wished to could present an observation on the plans of 1959 or 1962 without particular cost or reprisal; interest representation seems to have been both broad and free. There were probably many fewer groups active in the planning process than would have been the case in an American city—particularly neighborhood and conservationist groups—but this may reflect the relatively undifferentiated social complexion of the city. It should be noted that the 2,766 appeals of 1959 and the 4,635 of 1963 did not represent *all* the interested people but only those with a grievance. Many other thousands undoubtedly followed events but were either not adversely affected or, in any case, affected enough to protest. The observation stage did allow groups and

---

21. *Il Messaggero,* February 7, 1962.

22. *Paese Sera,* April 20, November 20, 1965. More recently, a surprise attack by student groups forced the immediate adjournment of the 12th national congress of INU in Naples (November 14–16, 1968). The students asserted that the members of INU were *"INU/tili"* and refused to allow the convention to be held. See Giovanni Astengo, "Relazione generale introduttiva: venti anni di battaglie urbanistiche," *Urbanistica,* September 1969, pp. 45–52.

individuals with ideas to come forward with their reactions and with some prospect of having an impact. The ministry accepted about seven hundred of the appeals against the 1962 plan.

Ideological segregation in communications was only a partially fulfilled aspiration of pure sectarians. There was actually a good deal of communication among various parts of the political elite, if only because the enemy press has to be read to be answered. Events were perceived and depicted in the various sectors in a reasonably convergent form. There were many communication bridges: party factions, independent newspapers such as *Il Messaggero,* professional groups such as INU, and occasional interideological conferences on the plan such as those sponsored by IN/arch, INU, and *Italia Nostra*. What the major groups in the city wanted became clear in the course of time, after a number of surprises. By 1962, when the final plan was made, it was abundantly evident to all groups which accommodations had to be reached and accepted.

REAL ESTATE INTERESTS

The economic operators involved as actors in the planning process in postwar Rome included two key groups: the landowners and the builder-developers. About ten groups controlled most of the land suitable for development, and most of these were old aristocratic families related to each other by ties of marriage and business. The exact size of particular holdings is not easy to determine, since many of the owners worked also through dummy corporations. SGI, the Vatican-owned corporation, stopped publishing figures on its land operations and holdings in 1954.

The power of the speculators derived from their ability to subsidize parties and party factions, including parties left-of-center after the rightist parties began to lose their influence. They could afford to hire good lawyers and economists and to bribe the daily and weekly press.[24] Their opponents lacked these financial resources. The speculators were almost ostentatiously nonpolitical, for the most part, and accused the planners of having political motivations in attacking them.[25]

23. See *Urbanistica Romana,* No. 2 (1966), "Decreto di approvazione del Piano Reoglatore Generale del Comune di Roma" (*Capitolium,* March 1966).

24. The speculators managed to corrupt even the planning reporter of the paracommunist morning newspaper, *Il Paese,* who throughout the spring of 1962 denounced the progressive planners in vitriolic terms. (See *Avanti!,* May 26, 1962).

25. The major exception was Senator A. Gerini who was both a powerful politician in the Rome DC and perhaps the wealthiest landowner in the city. He was particularly active in the campaign to open up the land around the Old Appian Way for development and seemed on the brink of success when in 1962 the Center-Left took power, in Rome and nationally. In 1963, Gerini was given a hopeless senatorial district to run in and lost his seat in the Senate. In 1965, the Italian government decided to condemn the entire Appian district for conversion into a public park. On the vicissitudes of the Appian district (and of Marquis Gerini), see A. Cederna, *I vandali in casa,* pp. 137–250; and Cederna, *Mirabilia Urbis,* pp. 393–448; Italo Insolera, "Vicende del parco Appio," *Casabella,* April 1964, pp. 37–41; and *Capitolium,* March 1969.

The speculators seemed absolutely convinced that the city and the city government belonged to them. They felt themselves very much the group in power,
the establishment, free to pursue their interests and follow their opportunities
as ruthlessly and fully as their influence allowed. Their motivations were strong,
given the millions of dollars in development values that the status quo annually
awarded them at little risk, effort, or expense. What they were doing, moreover,
was usually legal, justified by the norms of capitalist competition and condemned by people whose good faith (in more than one sense) they doubted.
The politicians had no strong objections, except in public. The spirit of the
economic boom, following wartime catastrophe and postwar revolutionary
terror, reinforced a consciousness of the sanctity of property rights—justifying
even rapacity—which the general population seemed to share.

Speculators could not be indifferent to planning decisions that might injure
them greatly without adequate, or indeed any, compensation. Nor were they
stoic enough to see some property owners enormously favored while they themselves suffered deprivations. Maintaining close ties with the city officials was
an inevitable defensive strategy to ensure that rivals and enemies did not turn
public policy against them. Most planning decisions were discretionary and
fundamentally arbitrary, at least in the eyes of planning officials, who found
political "pull" as good as criterion as any for judging among competing interests. Officials were reluctant to enforce regulations that they felt unfairly inflicted
economic injury without compensation.

The speculators did not organize for political purposes because they did not
need to and because it would have been imprudent to have done so. They
possessed as individuals as much weight as they would have had formally united.
They did not require the services of a lobbyist when they could act discreetly,
personally, and directly themselves. It was prudent for them not to organize
because, organized, they would constitute a much more visible target than if
they remained anonymous, shadowy figures in the background. If they needed
organization, the Rome Builders Association (Associazione Costruttori Edili
di Roma, ACER), provided its services willingly and free of charge.

Though their economic interests lay in having a supply of cheap land, and
though they might accordingly be expected to oppose the speculators, the Roman
builders became the speculators' strong and faithful allies. At every stage the
builders endorsed and promoted the planning policies of the speculators, despite
the theoretical conflict of interest between them. One reason was that, under
conditions of scarcity, builders could pass the cost of land along to the housing
consumers—the buyers of apartments who expected, in turn, to pass the cost
off to the next buyer in what seemed to be an eternal round. Relations between
the builders and speculators were strengthened by the fact that many builders
became active land speculators as well as builders, while speculators invested in
building companies. Builders, moreover, were dependent on a relatively few
suppliers of land. The marginal builders in particular, of whom there were a
great many, depended on a speculative market for survival since their inefficiency

would not permit them to survive under normal conditions. Many builders were new to the industry and had little experience or technical competence. Many were not used to financial success. Neither established nor marginal operators had much respect for the political process.[26]

Some builders—the serious ones, with scruples—opposed the CET plan because they had legitimate fears about the manner in which the city was likely to administer a master plan with restrictively high standards. Doing business with the city had not given them an elevated conception of the honesty and competence of city officials. A preference for laissez-faire and a nonrestrictive master plan stemmed in their case not from inordinate belief in private virtue but rather from fear of official discrimination, extortion, or ineptitude.

Thus the builders joined the revolt against the CET plan and became supporters of the giunta plan, though even they criticized the plan for "diffused indeterminacy of its norms of implementation" that "left too many measures up to the discretion of the technical and administrative organs in charge of the plan."[27] In its observations on the 1959 plan, ACER criticized several things: the restrictions on development in the historic center and in archeological zones; the standards for green space in the new districts, which reduced the amount of land available for building; and the restrictions on bulk, density, and height. Its criticisms were based on what it felt to be economic "realism," which it opposed to the "idealism" of the planners.

When the national government promulgated the 1962 plan by decree the builders turned to direct action. They were valuable allies to the speculators because of their crucial role in the city's economy; building is, after all, the only major industry in the city and its troubles can affect the entire city economy. ACER decided to fight the 1962 plan in the labor market; it cut wages and threatened to shut down the industry if the plan's standards were not revised downward to permit greater profits and more indiscriminate building. ACER hoped that pressure on the building workers—who passed for the "proletariat" in Rome—would touch the parties of the Center-Left in a vulnerable point. It predicted that the new plan would provoke a recession in the Roman building industry; a recession, in fact, did develop after the plan was adopted, but it was part of a nationwide slump rather than only a Roman problem. Early in 1963, ACER led a coalition of property owners, real estate corporations, religious orders, and conservative newspapers against the proposed new urban planning legislation of the national government. They persuaded masses of small property owners and prospective owners that this bill, introduced by Minister of Public Works Sullo, was going to nationalize ownership of all apartments and housing. On the eve of the April 1963 elections, the DC party disowned both the bill and Minister Sullo, as we have seen.[28]

ACER democratically adopted a policy that sought to protect the interests of

26. On the attitudes of the real estate interests, see M. C. Sforza, *Il Mondo*, March 13, 1962.
27. "Controdeduzioni, 1959," p. 9.
28. *L'Espresso*, December 11, 1966; Sullo, *Lo scandalo*, pp. 7–25.

its most marginal members rather than those of its largest members such as SGI. SGI did not need the extremist tactics of ACER to defend its interests, which the 1962 plan did not really threaten, while hundreds of small builders required nothing less. Large builders were less opposed to the 1962 plan than smaller ones because the plan favored them a good deal more and because the worsening recession did not threaten their existence. Within ACER, the larger, more viable, more technically competent and efficient firms, and those firms that worked primarily on public contracts, gradually adopted a more accommodating attitude to the plan: they could meet the standards of the new plan and still operate profitably. Marginal firms remained violently opposed; they could not operate on the scale demanded by the plan nor expect to land contracts for the major public projects proposed.[29] ACER resorted to a lockout late in 1963, which resulted in rioting and bloodshed and was condemned by the national builders' association (Associazione Nazionale Costruttori Edili, ANCE). After calling off the lockout ACER seceded from the parent association. The larger firms seceded in turn from ACER to form a new builders' association, the Unione Costruttori Romani (UCR), which rejoined ANCE and attempted to reach a modus vivendi with the Center-Left. UCR's strategy of accommodation also included a quiet attempt to reduce the intransigence of the planners' organizations by boring from within. One of them, IN/arch, was successfully taken over in 1965 by conservative architects and engineers, but similar efforts in INU in 1965 and 1966 failed. Early in 1966 the two builders associations reunited to form UCR-ACER, which adopted a conciliatory program strongly in favor of reforming city planning administration and carrying out the public works projects proposed in the 1962 plan. By 1966 some builders were ready to admit that land speculation and chaotic building had been unfortunate for the city, especially because they had crippled municipal finances. All builders, however, remained skeptical about the wisdom and feasibility of the building norms and zoning restrictions contained in the plan.[30]

PUBLIC AGENCIES

As the national capital, Rome was destined to be the victim of whatever the ministries and agencies of the national government decided to do with their practically unlimited rights to build what they wanted where they wanted. Under the Planning Act of 1942 the city lacked authority to subject the agencies of the national government to its regulations on zoning and building. Article 29 of that act left it to the Ministry of Public Works to see that the national government agencies respected some order, presumably that established by the city and sanctioned by the ministry, in locating their activities within the capital. Public enterprise proved no less difficult than private enterprise to subject to a

29. *Il Messaggero*, October 4, 1963.
30. *L'Espresso*, February 28, 1965.

planning order—and no less determined to act in accordance with its own definition of the public interest. Public agencies possessed a nearly absolute conviction of their right to disregard externally imposed or determined directives concerning their real estate decisions. They were, it appeared, determined to show that public enterprise, no less than private enterprise, should and could be free.

A major planning problem for the city thus arose not only from the anarchy of private speculators but also from the anarchy of public operators. Inspection of the "observations" to the plans of 1959 and 1962 reveals no significant difference in the attitudes of public and private operators as far as planning was concerned. Public operators, no less than private operators, were concerned to protect and enhance their particular interests and displayed a uniform lack of concern for the city's planning problems.

The city government attempted to cope with the problem of coordinating the physical plans of central government ministries, para-state agencies, and the two sets of foreign embassies, by providing formal representation for many of them on the Grand Commission in 1954. Most government departments and para-state agencies harbored only a general desire that the plan should allow them to pursue their own real estate interests, unencumbered by zoning and building restrictions. Few of the agency representatives played any role at all on the Grand Commission; but those few who were active tended to side with the conservatives. In their behavior the various ministries did not show much respect for the consensus principles of the 1954–57 period, preferring to act much as any private corporation in choosing where to build and locate. They joined with private interests in seeking to develop the historic center with new office buildings, although some were willing to locate at EUR. They frequently chose locations in the northwest, just where the planners sought to discourage further development.

The public housing agencies, most of them state agencies, also rejected the idea of decentralization or at least the idea of selective expansion; they built projects in the west and along the Via Cassia in the north. Public housing agencies, however, accounted for relatively little of the building in the city; just as they were not a major resource for implementing the plan, they did not pose a major problem in coordination. They could do little damage, from the planners' point of view, just as they could be of little help.[31]

The two sets of foreign embassies behaved much the same as Italian agencies, whether state, para-state, or local. The behavior of the embassies, ministries, and religious institutions tended to convert the city into a collection of extraterritorial compounds, or rather to reduce the city to its medieval baronial anarchy, without the fighting.

There was nothing uniform about the policies of these "institutional" groups

31. *Il Messaggero*, March 14, 1961; Italo Insolera and Mario Manieri-Elia, "Tre anni di cronaca romana," *Urbanistica*, March 1964, pp. 41–42.

in the planning process, except for this universal insistence on freedom to look after their own property interests. Most of the agencies were interested in the plan only as it affected the property interests of the agency and those of the building cooperatives of agency employees. The Ministry of Posts and Tele-communications, for example, insisted on building a major new installation in the heart of the old city, a few steps from Trevi Fountain. It abandoned its original project for a new Palace of Telecommunications, with 4,400 square meters of office space, after criticism from the city, the Order of Architects, and Parliament. It settled for a north-south coaxial cable telephone amplification center on the site of a seventeenth-century convent, which it demolished. The center—which it agreed to build with seventeenth-century-style walls—had to be located on that particular site, ministry technicians insisted, because this and only this was the "telephonic baricenter" of Italy.[32]

Economic motivations—a search for cheap land—turned public housing agencies into defacto supporters of leapfrog development. Clientele relations turned the Ministry of Agriculture's provincial agrarian inspector into an enemy of the CET plan, which reduced the development possibilities of land in the Agro and fired the wrath of farm organizations. Religious zeal may have accounted for the Italian Olympic Committee's proposal in 1955 to build a sports stadium on top of the catacombs opposite the church *Domine Quo Vadis?* in the Old Appian Way. Catholic Action gave its complete backing to the project, which was to be built in homage to Pope Pius XII and to be used during the Olympics of 1960. After protests in most of the press, including right wing organs like *Il Tempo* and *Il Giornale d'Italia,* the Vatican announced that it would not insist on the idea.[33]

Neither technical reasons nor reasons relating to Italian political culture help explain the freewheeling activities of the foreign embassies in the city, which have generally claimed the extraterritorial right to violate the master plan. The Soviets, as already mentioned, showed complete indifference to city planning decisions when they built housing for embassy employees within the grounds of their private estate, Villa Abamelek, in violation of master plan regulations designed to minimize further development within the few remaining old Roman villas.[34] The French provided another example of extraterritorial behavior when they built their *Lycée* in Villa Strohl-Fern, at the eastern end of Villa Borghese, despite the master plan's ban on building there and designation of the land as a future park. The unanimous protest of the city council addressed to the French Minister of Culture, André Malraux, seems to have been in vain.[35] Generally, the Italian Foreign Ministry has not been successful in using its good offices to defend the city's master plan.

32. Cederna, *Mirabilia Urbis,* pp. 186–88, 222–23, and *I vandali in casa,* pp. 43–52.
33. Cederna, *I vandali,* pp. 225–48.
34. Cederna, *Mirabilia Urbis,* pp. 317, 390, 480, 496; Paolo Monelli, *La Stampa,* January 31, 1965.
35. Cederna, *Mirabilia Urbis,* pp. 385–90.

In at least one sense institutional groups are not, however, free to do what they will. They can be fairly certain that any major project affecting historical, scenic, or archeological values will be denounced in most of the press and will involve the violator in a polemic to defend its reputation for civility and good will.

## THE CHURCH

The most important interest group constellation in the city was undoubtedly the one that centered on the church. But the church, though such an intuitively obvious and identifiable organization, has been singularly amorphous as a political actor, at least in postwar Roman planning politics. The church in Rome has at times seemed a most pluralistic hierarchy, a congeries of organizations, a loosely connected network of personalities. The number of ecclesiastical institutions in the city by itself has made difficult the appearance, not to mention reality, of monolithic unity.

The Diocese of Rome, which includes only part of the city and excludes Vatican city state, has a population of over 2,350,000 people, over 90 percent of whom have been baptized Catholics. The diocese is administered by nine cardinals, sixteen bishops, 400 secular and 412 religious priests, in some 135 parishes. Within the city there are 25 pontifical academies, 46 seminaries, 53 ecclesiastical colleges, 61 confraternities, and 95 miscellaneous religious bodies. There are also 178 male orders living in 650 houses, and 372 congregations of sisters living in 770 convents. These form altogether a community of over one hundred thousand priests, nuns, brothers, and seminarians.[36] Most work in the international activities of the church, but some of them also perform pastoral duties in a ceaselessly growing city. To these must be added the central organs of the church—the Roman Curia—and the offices of the papacy itself. Catholic interests in Rome have also been articulated through a host of lay organizations and through several Catholic newspapers, ranging in authority from *L'Osservatore Romano* to *Momento Sera*. The pope, as bishop of Rome, has administered his uniquely vast diocesan interests through the *Vicariato,* which is thus the church office most deeply involved in city affairs.

Where the church stood in planning politics has not always been clear, partly because the Catholic world has seldom spoken with one voice in planning matters. Nonetheless, a fairly distinct line has existed at any given time to which most Catholic spokesmen and actors have adhered. The church, along with most conservative groups, sponsored the formation of the new master plan and designated a representative of the vicariate to sit on the Grand Commission in 1954. It is safe, in fact, to assume that the entire master planning process would never have been launched without church approval, given the great power of the vicariate over the Rome branch of the Christian Democratic party. During

36. F. X. Murphy, "Rome", *New Catholic Encyclopedia* (New York, 1967).

the next couple of year (1956–57) the representative of the vicariate subscribed to the planning compromises gradually evolved on the Grand Commission.

The attitude of the clergy began to shift when Mayor Rebecchini and the Christian Democratic administration were accused by the Radicals and Communists of showing favoritism toward the Vatican-owned real estate company, the *Società Generale Immobiliare*. In December 1957 the representative of the vicariate signed the resolution hostile to the CET plan. At this point the church was placing itself on the side of the conservative planning interests and providing the support necessary to reject the CET plan and lay the foundations for adoption of the giunta plan of 1959.

The church remained with the conservatives until the critical events of the summer of 1960, when it began to move toward the other side. By late 1960 the Christian Democratic mayor of Rome found it possible to admit that the giunta plan of 1959 was not, after all, infallible but could stand some revision. In the elections of November 1960, the Christian Democratic councilman who had declared the master plan of 1959 to be a triumph against atheism was defeated by the discreet efforts of the church itself.[37] From this point on, reports on Roman planning in *L'Osservatore Romano* and in other Catholic newspapers like *Il Quotidiano* (belonging to Catholic Action) changed drastically from polemical defense of the conservative case to a tone of matter-of-factness and a stance of neutrality. By 1962 it was clear that the church was giving quiet support to the Center-Left planning operation and holding conservative Catholics in line in the defense of progressive solutions. On July 28, 1962, *L'Osservatore Romano* defended the new plan against charges that it was going to create a slump in the Roman building industry.[38]

The following five factors account for the evolution in church policy toward the plan.

*1. Papal Policy.* Church policy in the city is set in the first and last instance by the pope, as head of the church and as bishop of Rome. Even since 1870, when they relinquished responsibility for temporal government, the popes have continued to delegate some of their diocesan responsibilities to a vicar general—a practice begun at least as early as 1198. Pope Pius XII was, however, a well-known practitioner of centralized administration; no discordant line could be expressed by Catholic leaders in the city without papal toleration or approval. He took a great personal interest in Roman affairs, having been born and raised in one of the most distinguished Catholic families of the city. Under Pope Pius XII the church in Rome pursued a highly conservative course. The prelates he appointed to direct the vicariate were archconservatives who used the influence at their command to make life difficult for liberal elements in the church, to tie the Catholic world to social and economic conservatism, and to wage war on

37. *Il Messaggero*, November 10, 1960.
38. *L'Osservatore Romano*, July 28, 1962.

what were considered the three major enemies of the church in the city—the Communists, the Free masons (including Rotarians), and the Protestants.[39]

Clement Cardinal Micara, born in Frascati in 1879, was vicar general between 1946 and 1965 and he became not only the dominant church figure for the city but one of the small group of five powerful cardinals—the so-called *"pentagono vaticano"*—who dominated the Curia in the last years of Pius XII's pontificate.[40] Cardinal Micara molded the Roman clergy into a powerful electoral force. On the eve of every election, *L'Osservatore Romano* calls upon faithful Catholics to vote in united fashion for the Christian Democrats.[41] The parish clergy were made responsible for mobilizing the faithful and directing the network of the 225 Catholic Action civic committees during campaigns. Through detailed electoral analysis, the performance of the parish clergy in elections was closely examined, compared, and evaluated. These efforts met with some success, considering that the DC vote has generally reached 30 percent of the total, while church attendance has dropped to an estimated 23 percent of the same adult population.[42] The 1948 elections marked the clergy's greatest triumph, unmatched since then: the DC in Rome won 51.2 percent of the vote. Concerned to maintain DC control in the city against a possible leftist advance, Pope Pius in 1952 asked Prime Minister DeGasperi directly, that is, through the Secretariat of State, to constitute a DC-Right alliance for the coming elections. The DC alliance with the neofascists in Rome that eventually came about in 1958 had thus been legitimized at the highest levels.

As his special deputy to supervise elections in the city, Pope Pius in 1948 had appointed Monsignor Fiorenzo Angelini who was also central ecclesiastical assistant for Catholic Action Men. Together with Professor Luigi Gedda, the lay president of Catholic Action Men, Msgr. Angelini launched a general effort to provide the church with a more conservative and reliable political instrument than the DC in the form of the civic committees—the political action committees of Catholic Action. The elections of 1948 were rightly regarded as a triumph as much for the civic committees, Msgr. Angelini, and Prof. Gedda as for the DC party. Msgr. Angelini's access to Pope Pius made him one of the most powerful figures in Rome city politics. He obtained the support and became a

39. The *Bollettino d'Informazione* published by the *Ufficio Catechistico* kept the clergy informed about the activities in Rome of the Communists, Freemasons, and Protestants. See, for example, the issue of December 1954.

40. Carlo Falconi, *Il pentagano vaticano* (Bari, 1956).

41. What the vicariate actually says is the following (*L'Osservatore Romano*, June 8, 1966): "In the imminence of the local elections, both in the city and the province, the Vicariate reminds all Catholic voters of their duty to exercise the right to vote with a sense of social responsibility and mature wisdom, keeping in mind the grave civic, moral, and religious problems connected to that right, and keeping in mind how the dispersion of votes may prejudice their efficiency."

42. Silvio Burgalassi, *Il comportamento religioso degli italiani*, p. 53. Angelo Cardinal Dell'-Acqua, Vicar of Rome, complained in October 1970 that only about one-third of the Romans attend Sunday Mass (*Los Angeles Times*, October 28, 1970).

patron of the leading Roman politician, Giulio Andreotti, a member of the Italian cabinet, almost uninterruptedly, since 1946. In 1955, with the backing of Catholic Action and Andreotti, Msgr. Angelini launched a campaign to build outside the city the Pope Pius XII International Center. This would house the headquarters of the conservative Movement for a Better World, headed by a Jesuit, Father Lombardi, brother of the Rome council majority leader who was later to hail the 1959 master plan as a blow against atheism. The center was designed and built by the same engineer from the Defense Ministry who was to head construction of Fiumicino Airport and who was to lead the revolt against the CET plan. Pope Pius himself inaugurated the center in 1956.[43] Thus some of the leading actors in Roman planning politics were closely associated with the Vatican.

In 1957, Msgr. Angelini was again appointed by Pope Pius to prepare and direct the election campaign for 1958. Cardinal Micara had for some time been ailing and was unable to take a very active part in diocesan affairs. Msgr. Angelini was apparently a major figure, together with Giulio Andreotti and Cardinal Micara, in the formation of the Catholic-neofascist alliance in December 1957 in Rome.[44]

Msgr. Angelini's great papal patron died in October 1958. The new pope, John XXIII, did not for some time make any change in church policy with regard to the city. Elected with something of a commitment to decentralize church government after the extreme centralization of his predecessor, Pope John allowed the existing ecclesiastical authorities in Italy a much freer hand. Paradoxically, the result was a sharp swing to the right in church policy under a rather progressive pope. Decentralization allowed the conservatives and reactionaries among the Italian clergy to sponsor a general rightward evolution within the DC. Cardinals Micara and Traglia, vicar and deputy vicar of Rome, were outspoken supporters of the Tambroni attempt in the spring and summer of 1960 to establish nationally the same clerico-fascist coalition that had existed for two years or more in Rome city government. But the riots of 1960 discredited the clerico-fascist formula as dangerous and laid the basis for a gradual shift of church policy in the other direction.

By the election of November 1960, the church was cutting its political ties to the neofascists and even ordering the parish priests of the city not to oppose the progressive candidates on the DC ticket.[45] But it was not yet prepared to accept an alliance of the DC with the Socialists. While the church allowed the first Center-Left giuntas to be formed in Milan and Genoa early in 1961, it forbade a similar alliance in Rome. A 1961 article in the *Information Bulletion of the Vicariate*, "Notes on The Present Political Situation," asked whether "the desired opening to the Left . . . would not fatally lead to the breakdown of the

43. *L'Espresso*, January 14, 1962.
44. Falconi, *Il pentagano*, p. 147.
45. *L'Espresso*, November 6, 1960.

political unity of all Catholics. Do we want to arrive at this?" A major figure in
the vicariate, its secretary, Msgr. Maccari, was quoted as saying in July 1961,
"Before making the Center-Left in the city of the Pope, you'll have to pass over
my dead body.[46] (Msgr. Maccari had just been appointed the general ecclesiastical president of Italian Catholic Action.) An opening to the Left in Rome
against the opposition of the deputy vicar and secretary of the vicariate in the
summer of 1961 was out of the question and the city council was dissolved.

Promulgation of the encyclical *Mater et Magistra* in July 1961 marked the
first implicit commitment of the church to a more progressive course in Italian
politics. By updating the social doctrine of the church, the encyclical provided
doctrinal underpinning for a political alliance between Catholics and Socialists.
After the church, late in 1961, dropped its opposition to a Center-Left alliance
in Italian national politics, there was no longer any possibility of opposing it
in Rome—a local arena where the stakes were, after all, somewhat smaller.
Permission to work with the Socialists that had been denied in mid-1961 was
granted to the Rome DC six months later.

Though not a Roman by birth as was Pope Pius XII, his predecessor, nor
Roman by long residence as is his successor, and although a decentralizer, Pope
John was not unaware of city affairs and even of the less decorous aspects of
city life, making frequent visits to the poorest parishes, the city jail, hospitals,
and orphanages. He continued the practice of receiving members of the city
giunta in audience. On one of these occasions, January 6, 1963, as the city
officials were about to leave, Pope John called Mayor Della Porta over and
according to the account in *Il Messaggero,*

> thanking the city for its homage, asked about the details of the city's problems
> of development. Mayor Della Porta cited statistics to demonstrate the com-
> plexity of the problems due to incessant growth. At the end of his recital,
> Pope John urged the officials to continue their efforts on behalf of the popula-
> tion and offered "his modest assistance as Bishop" in overcoming certain
> obstacles that seemed to be impeding the achievement of the goals which had
> been outlined to him. There are those who affirm that the "modest assistance"
> did not remain a mere promise.[48]

Pope John's successor in June 1963, Pope Paul VI, continued his predecessor's
policy with regard to the city and emphasized the Vatican's support for the new
progressive course of city government under the Center-Left by making, on
April 16, 1966, the first official papal visit to the Campidoglio since 1847.[49] This
was no small contribution to the prestige of the Center-Left giunta. Pope Paul
VI, unlike Pope John, had become a Roman by over twenty years of residence,

46. *Bollettino d'informazione del Vicariato,* January-February 1961; *L'Espresso,* July 9, 1961.
47. *L'Espresso,* July 9, 1961.
48. *Il Messaggero,* June 4, 1963.
49. *Roma Oggi,* May-June 1966.

and was inevitably more interested and involved in Roman affairs. His support
for the progressive side in Roman politics went back at least to 1952 when, as a
papal aide, Monsignor Montini had been the leading opponent in the Curia of
the proposed DC–neofascist alliance in Rome.[50] For his resistance to the rightist
line, Monsignor Montini had been "exiled" to Milan as archbishop in 1954. He
returned in 1963 to a Rome that had become much more congenial in spirit.

2. *Social Interests.* Church policy on the master plan was determined by the
major shifts in the personnel and policies of the papacy. No new pope, however,
could eliminate the traditional social attachments of the papacy to the Roman
aristocracy. One hundred years after the end of the temporal power, the papacy
retained some of the traits of monarchy including some form of obligation to
the court aristocracy. One hundred years after the end of the temporal power,
the pope continued to receive the Roman patriciate in annual audience.[51] The
papacy in some ways behaved as a government-in-exile which was at the same
time, strangely enough, in power. It continued the ways of the papacy when it
was the temporal government of the Papal States, while at the same time exercising a universal magistracy. In this respect the church seemed torn between
the concrete demands of security—involving reliance on old and sure supporters,
including Roman aristocrats—and newer forms of support. One of the reasons
that the church sided with the conservatives on planning issues was that many
prominent Catholic laymen were engaged in speculative activities and many of
the speculators were "good Catholics," prominent in church circles.

3. *Economic Interests.* Real estate has been a traditional form of church investment and the church is the largest landholder in the city after the national
government. Directly and indirectly, the church owns much of the improved
real estate in Rome and much of the land suitable for development. It has had
large economic stakes in the planning conflict. Its development-land holdings,
direct (through the Sacred Congregations, Pontifical Works, and chapters of
the Roman cathedrals) and indirect (through the hundreds of orders and
institutions), were estimated in 1958 at approximately 58 million square meters,
or about 23 square miles, and valued at several million dollars.[52]

50. Falconi, *Il pentagono vaticano*, p. 76.
51. Pope Paul ended the practice in 1968, when he stripped the Roman nobility of all its
privileges in the Vatican and opened the way for Italian and non-Italian commoners to be
named members of the pontifical court. The pope abolished the title of "prince" in the papal
household and decreed that henceforth no offices in that household would be hereditary. Roman
nobles fought hard against the abolition of such privileges as having Vatican City license plates,
which gave exemption from extremely high Italian taxes on gasoline. They also lost the right to
buy tax-free goods at the Vatican commissary. (*Il Messaggero,* March 29, 1968.)
52. See the careful study by Enrico Mantegna in *Il Mondo,* March 12, 19, 26, April 2, 1957,
based on examination of the *catasto rustico.* The study *excluded* all land with improvements
(churches, schools, convents, hotels, clinics, movie houses); all land held by persons and corporations not obviously connected with the church; all land held by Vatican-owned corpora-

The figure includes only landholdings held by identifiably church-related institutions; it excludes all land held by church-controlled real estate companies, such as SGI and Beni Stabili, and all land with any form of improvement; SGI in 1957 held over eight million square meters in its own right.[53] Fifteen million square meters of the holdings were within the perimeter of the 1931 plan. Relatively few of the holdings were in the name of the Holy See itself as compared to the religious orders and institutes.[54] Church holdings lay in all directions, on all sides of the city, especially along the consular highways—Via Trionfale, Via Aurelia, Via Portuense (in the west); Via Ostiense (in the south); Via Tiburtina, Via Casilina, and Via Tuscolano (in the east).

Marxists have attempted to explain the behavior of the church toward the plan in terms of its joint economic interests with the land oligopolists and northern industrial investment corporations. Vatican funds were invested in real estate, finance, utilities, and banks, and its representatives sat on the same boards with the representatives of the great industrial and financial interests, developing a community of outlook, interest, and policy. Thus the revolt against the CET plan, it is argued, involved a joint action by the church and the speculators, based principally on the profit motive; because the CET plan threatened the economic interests of the church it was rejected. The only flaw in this explanation is that the CET plan did not threathen the economic interests of the church or of church-related institutions such as SGI. The plan presented in November 1957 provided for ample development of church land; given the wide distribution of church holdings this was inevitable. Some religious orders had land that was not included in expansion districts or zoned for maximum development, but whether their protests within the church determined a general policy of opposition to the plan is not clear. Nor is it clear to what extent there was any central management of all ecclesiastical property matters, rather than complete decentralization in the hands of each order and institution. The evidence suggests a pattern of decentralized property management in which the individual church institution had to defend its own property interests under the general protection of the church.[55]

The central church itself held controlling interest in SGI, the largest development and construction firm in the city and in Italy, with operations in several

---

tions, such as SGI and the Istituto Beni Stabili; and all land in Vatican city. The Mantegna data were brought up to date in *Paese Sera,* April 2, 1958, which also provided a rough sketch of Vatican holdings around the city.

53. Cederna, *Mirabilia Urbis,* pp. 37–41.

54. Falconi, *Il pentagono vaticano,* pp. 155–69.

55. One of the members of the committee of five consultants who drafted the 1962 master plan acted as the informal representative of church-related institutions and secured general protection for those interests in the plan. But a large number of these institutions found it necessary, nonetheless, to register objections to the resulting plan. See Comune di Roma, *Controdeduzioni alle osservazioni sul nuovo Piano Regolatore Generale di Roma adottato dal Consiglio Comunale in data 18 dicembre 1962: Deliberazione della Giunta Municipale N. 984 del 24-2-1965* (Rome, 1965) (henceforth, "Controdeduzioni, 1962"), passim.

other Italian cities and in several cities abroad.[56] SGI was a major element in the land oligopoly and became a major component in the conservative planning coalition that campaigned againt the CET plan, beginning with its 1957 annual report. SGI had been the favorite target of the anticlerical weekly, *L'Espresso*. During and after the SGI-*L'Espresso* libel suit in 1956, *L'Osservatore Romano* was an outspoken defender of SGI, *not*, of course, on financial grounds but on religious grounds: SGI, it said, was being attacked because of its connection to the church. Pope Pius' defense of SGI in his speech of February 18, 1958, undoubtedly aided conservatives in the church, in SGI, and in the DC who favored alliance with the neofascists and rejection of the CET plan.

If the church itself in acting against the CET plan was not necessarily acting solely on the basis of the profit motive, many religious orders were. The orders were among the most active land speculators in the city and among the strongest opponents of zoning and building restrictions in general.[57] The economic explanation of planning stands may be more valid in the case of the orders than in the case of the Curia, where ideological and political factors were also important.

The shift of the church position in 1960 was accompanied, apparently, by a shift in Vatican economic policy. *L'Espresso*, to which one may or may not lend credence, reported late in 1960 that the Vatican was no longer as interested as it had been in real estate investment and, having made handsome profits in real estate, was now turning toward industrial investment to profit from the economic boom.[58] In June 1969 the Vatican announced that it was selling about 5 percent of its holdings in SGI, but denied that the sale represented an effort by the Vatican to escape payment of Italian tax on stock dividends. Hitherto the Vatican had enjoyed exemption from this tax. The value of Vatican holdings in SGI before the June 1969 sale was estimated at about 120 million dollars.[59]

*4. Ideology.* Church social doctrine condemned real estate speculation—"land usury" (*usura fondiaria*) as Pope Pius called it in 1953—but for various reasons the doctrine was difficult to apply in practice. The opportunities for impecunious church-related organizations were so great, and the line between legitimate

56. On SGI, see Cederna, *I vandali*, pp. 404–12, and *Mirabilia Urbis*, passim; the reports on the *L'Espresso* trial in the Roman and Italian press, July–December 1956, and the sentence of the court on December 29, 1956; *Time*, November 28, 1969, p. 96; *Paese Sera*, April 11, 1958; Angelo Conigliaro et al., *Pradoni della città* (Bari, 1958), pp. 11–15; Nino Lo Bello, *The Vatican Empire* (New York, 1968), chap. 7; Giovanni Grilli, *La finanza vaticana in Italia* (Rome 1961), pp. 127–30.

57. Sullo, *Lo scandalo*, pp. 22; see also the numerous observations presented against the 1959 and 1962 plans by religious orders in the "Controdeduzioni, 1959," and "Controdeduzioni, 1962."

58. *L'Espresso*, November 9, 1960.

59. *The New York Times*, June 21, 1969. According to a report on Vatican finance in *Time* (January 25, 1971), the Vatican has sold "two-thirds of its 15% interest in Immobiliare" to the Gulf and Western corporation as part of a general plan to diversify its investments.

investment and illegitimate speculation so difficult to discern, that few could resist the temptation to make some money by playing the land market. The logic of papal encyclicals, moreover, had a greater impact on Catholic intellectuals than on Catholic businessmen or on Catholic politicians, who had their own distinctive standards and preoccupations. Then, too, some elements in Catholic ideology—those relating to the defense of the church itself against secular attack—carried greater emotional freight than the elements relating to social policy, so that even Catholic intellectuals were prepared to see in Radical attacks on speculation a masked attack on the church itself. Ideology was thus available to justify different and contradictory courses of action—for or against the CET plan, the giunta plan, and the 1962 plan—depending on whether anticommunism and clericalism were emphasized, or social progressivism.

Catholic doctrine, with its concept of the social function of property, legitimized planning efforts though it tended to place more stress on private property rights than most professional planners in Italy were willing to do. There was a strong tendency within the church under Pius XII and his successors for lesser authorities and laymen to interpret away the more advanced social pronouncements of the papacy, to adopt, with William F. Buckley, a *"Mater sed non magistra"* attitude toward nonconservative church social doctrine.[60] The social constituency among the Catholics of Rome for the progressive interpretation of church policy was relatively weak, as compared to northern Italian Catholic communities with their Catholic labor unions and cooperatives. The dominant elements in the church and the DC party stressed the anticommunist and antisecularist themes that linked the Catholic world to the social and economic elites. Supporters of progressive reform were a minority force in the Rome DC party and the clergy, most of them from the poor suburban parishes.

Pope Pius himself, in his speech of February 19, 1958, defined the planning issue as basically a battle between the church and her secularist enemies. He urged the Roman clergy and the faithful

> to keep watch over the good name of Rome and to prevent, as much as you can, a small number of denigrators from carrying on with impunity their work of devastation in hopes of transmuting the sacred face of the *Urbs* into a new, as they call it, secular, or almost pagan face, trying as hard as they can to cancel from the sentiments and customs of the people the glorious traditions of the fathers.[61]

*Il Mondo,* the journal of highbrow anticlericalism, replied:

> As honest secularists that we profess to be, we have never fought real estate speculation only or essentially because we thought that those involved were mostly militant Catholics. We have fought against misgovernment by the

60. *The National Review,* July 29, 1961.
61. *L'Osservatore Romano,* February 20, 1958.

City of Rome without thinking about the fact that those responsible lead exemplary Christian lives by going to mass, taking the sacraments of religion, joining processions and taking part in other kinds of pious functions. What we want to say, formally, is that we are far from identifying the "glorious traditions of the fathers" cited by the Pope with the civic misconduct perpetrated by the sons and nephews.[62]

*5. Political Considerations.* For obvious reasons, the church is an immensely powerful institution in the city. Another period of papal exile in Avignon is not needed to demonstrate the importance of the papacy in the life of Rome: the attention it brings to the city in the world media; the tourists, pilgrims, and seminarians it attracts; the prestige its presence in the city confers.[63] The city knows to whom it owes its survival and immunity during World War II; in gratitude, the city council in 1950 unanimously bestowed on Pope Pius the title of *Defensor Civitatis.* The special and deep interests of the church in Roman affairs are given formal recognition in the Lateran Pacts and the Italian constitution.[64]

The church is powerful as the sponsor of the Christian Democratic party, which has controlled all national governments and Rome's giuntas since the war, and has held about 40 percent of the seats in the national parliament and about 30 percent of those on the Rome city council. After a period of physically violent anticlericalism in the immediate postwar years at both national and local levels, the non-Catholic parties became very respectful of church interests in the city, and allowed the DC to pursue policies in Rome that they would not tolerate in other places.

One consequence of church power was the fact that neither the city nor nation-

62. *Il Mondo,* January 21, 1958.

63. "I asked an experienced American news correspondent in Rome what the composition of his file was, and he replied, 'Sixty-five percent Vatican, 30 percent Sophia Loren, 5 percent all the rest, including politics and government.' " John Gunther, *Twelve Cities* (New York, 1969), p. 116.

64. Article 1, Par. 2 of the Concordat between the Holy See and Italy (February 11, 1929) reads: "In consideration of the sacred character of the Eternal City, the Episcopal See of the Supreme Pontiff, centre of the Catholic world, and goal of pilgrimage, the Italian Government will be careful to keep Rome free from anything which should be inconsistent with such character." (John J. Wuest and Manfred C. Vernon, *New Source Book in Major European Governments,* Cleveland: World Publishing Co., 1966, pp. 597–98). Under article 7 of the postwar republican constitution, the Lateran Pacts still govern the relations between the Italian government and the Catholic church. This might have caused trouble, had the leftists won electoral control over the city government in the early postwar elections. The papacy might conceivably have invoked its prerogative in order to remove a leftist coalition from power in the city. As it is, the clause has caused trouble only once, in 1965, when attempts were made to ban presentation of the Hochhuth play, *The Vicar,* in Rome. Catholics felt that presentation of the play was offensive in the light of the gratitude shown by the people of Rome to Pius XII in the rally on June 5, 1944, the day after Liberation and in the unanimous award to Pius XII of the title *Defensor Civitatis.* Anticlericals, however, interpret the new constitution as incorporating only those features of the Lateran Pacts that are not incompatible with the rights granted in other parts of the constitution, such as freedom of speech.

al government could easily regulate the largest set of private property owners in the city. Religious institutions became responsible not only for much of the land speculation but also for violations of zoning and building regulations, and they sometimes felt very much above the law. The SGI-*L'Espresso* trial in 1956 provided dramatic proof that church-related organizations did not need to corrupt the city government at all but were automatically given favorable treatment and immunity.

But if some members of the clergy attempted to use their power to extend, so to speak, the limits of extraterritoriality, the church as a whole felt rather insecure. The church was quite aware of its presence in what was in some ways a very hostile environment. Anticlericalism was and is a powerful force in Italy and Rome and the church was prepared to find it disguised in many different forms and shapes, including a proposed new master plan. Since 1870 the church had lived through the Liberal regime of 1870–1922, rather openly based on anticlericalism, and the Fascist regime of 1922–43, whose totalitarian impulses provided but a poor guarantee for the Lateran Pacts of 1929. After the fall of Fascism, there had been a wave of anticlerical terrorism in the North and a violent anticlerical campaign in Rome itself that had partly determined the decision of the Rome DC party to discontinue its wartime collaboration with the Left in 1946. In postwar elections Roman voters have given less than one-third of their votes to the party of the church. Most of the remaining two-thirds have gone to occasionally or constantly anticlerical parties. Only the neofascists have tried to compete with the DC for the favor of the Catholic electorate on the basis of fidelity to the church. Secularization, moreover, has made strong inroads in the city, reducing the level of church attendance to about one-third or one-quarter of what it might be. Rome is much less "Catholic" than many cities of the Northeast, such as Brescia, Bergamo, Trent, or Verona, where the Catholic party receives two-thirds of the vote and church attendance is a majority phenomenon.

Even the Catholic faithful in Rome have to be sermonized on the right and duty of the clergy to intervene in politics; standard sermons are read in all parishes condemning the admittedly widespread belief that such intervention is not legitimate.[65] Many of the boldest statements in favor of the clergy's right to exercise community leadership are reactions to such doubts.[66] Hierarchy remains more of an aspiration than an achievement. Thus even in the period of greatest ideological tension, 1957–60, it was impossible for the church to create

65. *Bollettino del Clero Romano*, October-November 1957, pp. 377–80.
66. Borgata residents expect the parish priest to be active in securing action from government officials and providing letters of recommendation, rather than in giving voting instructions. (Crespi "Aspetti," p. 40.) In one central district survey, 59% of the people objected to any intervention of priests in politics, with greatest hostility (84%) among the executives *(dirigenti)* and least (56%) among the workers. See Alfredo Fasola-Bologna, "Il ruolo del sacerdote nelle aspettative della popolazione di una parocchia romana," *Rivista di Sociologia*, January-April 1968, pp. 69–88.

and maintain a united front. Progressive Catholics refused to be intimidated by the threat of sanctions from the Holy Office and kept alive the links between the Catholic world and the Left.[67]

The church then has powerful reasons for fearing isolation and attack and in part reacted to the CET plan in these terms. The CET proposals for eastern expansion, eastern directive centers, and an eastern axis seemed a rather naked attempt by the secularists to create a new and modern city in the east as a *"contraltare"* or "counter-altar" to the traditional Catholic city in the west. Industrialization was feared for similar reasons. Churchmen were particularly prone to hold the *"romanista"* concept of the city, which sees Rome as an historico-religious monument, as an achievement, not a problem.[68] The Italian church, in particular, still suffers from a fear of cities in general, seeing in urbanization the major cause of declining religion. Only since 1961 has the Catholic world begun to accept urbanization as inevitable and in some ways positive, and begun to formulate a Catholic action program for the cities that includes city planning.[69]

67. The dissident Catholics were able to resist the pressure from the Holy Office only by securing the protection of a sympathetic Dominican friar.

68. On the *"romanista"* concept of the city, see the denunciations by Cederna in *I vandali in casa,* passim, and *Mirabilia Urbis,* passim.

69. Robert Fried, "Urbanization and Italian Politics," *Journal of Politics, 29* (1967), 505–34. The church became the only rival to the Communist party in providing leadership and assistance to the inhabitants of the new suburban districts; the city and the national government played practically no role in assimilating migrants and organizing community self-improvement projects. Thus 84 percent of the playing fields in suburban Rome have been provided by the parish churches. See Gianni Cagianelli, "Giovani della periferia," *Capitolium,* May-June 1967, pp. 194–213. The church has had just as much difficulty in coping with the rapid growth of the city as the city government. Central parishes in Rome have ten or more priests, while outlying churches have two or three priests to serve twenty thousand or more parishioners. In large U.S. cities there is one priest per 1,200 parishioners, while in Rome there is one priest per 4,000 parishioners. (G. Bocca, "Quattro aspetti dell'espansione romana," *Roma Nuova, 1,* 167.) The diocese, which covers only the central portions of the city's territory, has expanded from 57 parishes (1901) to 232 parishes (1966), only 43 of which are in and near the old city. (*Avvenire d'Italia* [Rome], February 3, 1966). According to Pier Giorgio Liverani, the ratio of priests to population is now one per 11,000 ("Chiese e Parocchie nella Roma d'oggi," *Capitolium,* October 1965, pp. 460–69).

# 10

# EVALUATING

# AND COMPARING

# ROME'S PERFORMANCE

## THE COSTS OF DELAY

In the Introduction, several criteria were set forth by which to evaluate performance in the city planning field. These criteria will be applied in this chapter in order to evaluate planning in Rome and to compare planning in Rome with planning in other Italian cities.

The first criterion is the length of time required to adopt a plan. By this standard Rome's performance rating is quite poor. From the time when the Rome branch of the National Planning Institute (*Istituto Nazionale di Urbanistica* or INU) first proposed, in 1950, that a new plan be drafted, sixteen years passed before the city secured an officially approved plan. This was fifteen years after the city government had officially agreed to draft a new plan. It was twelve years after the Italian Ministry of Public Works ordered all major Italian cities to draft and adopt new master plans. Only in 1966 did Rome have its new plan, and in the years before 1966 there was much growth in Rome to regulate. As Planning Assessor Petrucci said during the council debates on the plan in December 1962:

Any mediocre plan whatever, adopted in 1952–53, would have been better than allowing for more than a decade the continued implementation of the Master Plan of 1931. . . . Unfortunately we have seen the effects of implementing that Plan since the end of the War; these are the years that have seen the emergence and consolidation of overgrown quarters with abnormal dimensions, with excessive densities, without essential services or schools or green, with massive, anonymous, overpowering buildings, which do no honor to our city and which permitted exceptional profits for private operators.[1]

1. "Council Debates, 1962, p. 247.

How does the Roman performance in master planning compare with that of other Italian cities? As noted in Chapter 1, it is hard to make satisfying comparisons of municipal performance, especially in the planning field, if only because there is little consensus on what good planning performance is and how it might be measured. Then, too, cities face different challenges and have different resources to deal with them. The nearly saturated territory of Milan, the massive industrial complexes of Turin, the islander-mainlander conflicts and sinking level of Venice, the crumbling subsoil of Naples constitute unique challenges to the master planners of each city.[2] The major Italian cities have widely different population densities to deal with, as shown in Table 10.1. The reader will keep these cautionary remarks in mind when considering the following attempts at intercity comparison.

Table 10.1. Comparative Populations and Densities of Leading Italian Cities, 1961

| City | 1961 population (thousands) | 1961 area (sq. km.) | 1961 density (persons/sq. km.) |
|---|---|---|---|
| Bologna | 444,872 | 140.7 | 3,161 |
| Florence | 436,516 | 102.4 | 4,262 |
| Genoa | 784,194 | 238.4 | 3,289 |
| Milan | 1,582,534 | 181,8 | 8,707 |
| Naples | 1,182,815 | 117.3 | 10,086 |
| Palermo | 587,985 | 158.8 | 3,704 |
| Rome | 2,188,160 | 1,507.6 | 1,451 |
| Turin | 1,025,822 | 130.1 | 7,881 |
| Venice | 347,347 | 199.8 | 1,107 |

Source: 10° Censimento della Popolazione, 15 ottobre 1961, vols. 2, 3, passim.

Table 10.2 compares the leading Italian cities' planning performance in terms of the time they have taken to secure an officially approved plan. There is a sharp contrast between cities like Milan, which began to formulate a new master plan immediately after the war, adopted the new plan in 1950, and secured national approval for it in 1953—before Rome had even established its Grand Commission—and cities like Naples, which secured a new plan only in the late sixties. The speed with which Milan acted and the earliness of its action are fully in keeping with the city's reputation as the best governed city in Italy. Bologna also has a reputation for good government—a reputation that is upheld by the relative speed with which it, too, formulated and adopted its new master plan. Genoa and Turin were somewhat slower but both managed to secure nationally approved plans by 1959. At the next level of performance are cities like Venice, Florence, and Rome where the planning process ran much

2. On the planning problems of Milan, see the special issue of *Urbanistica*, March 1956; Cederna, *I vandali*, pp. 308–51; *Il Mulino*, May 1969, pp. 537–41; and *Urbanistica*, October 1967, pp. 16–64. On Turin: *Urbanistica*, October 1967, pp. 66–115 and Giancarlo De Carlo et al., *La pianificazione territoriale urbanistica nell'area torinese* (Padua, 1964) (bibliography, pp. 101–02). On Venice: *Urbanistica*, January 1967 (special issue), and "La 'cultura delle citta' oggi in Italia, con riferimeno all'esperienza di Venezia," *Quest'Italia*, July 1961, pp. 10–25.

Table 10.2. Time Absorbed in Plan Formulation and Adoption in Major Italian Cities

| City | Drafting began | Council adoption[a] | National promulgation | Years between drafting and promulgation[b] |
|------|---------------|---------------------|----------------------|--------------------------------------------|
| Bologna | 1952 | 1955 | 1958 | 6 |
| Florence | 1949 | *1958* | 1961–65 | 12–16 |
| Genoa | 1948 | ? | 1959 | 11 |
| Milan | 1945 | 1950 | 1953 | 8 |
| Naples | 1946 | *1958* | 1969? | 23 |
| Rome | 1954 | 1959, 1962 | 1965 | 11 |
| Turin | 1950 | 1958 | 1959 | 9 |
| Venice | 1955 | *1959* | 1961 | 6 |

Source: *Urbanistica* (March 1959, March 1963).
a. Underlined dates signify adoption by prefectoral commissioners.
b. Note that the delay between council adoption and national promulgation is more of a performance test for the national government than for the municipality submitting a master plan for approval. The Ministry of Public Works has often been slow in making its determinations, as it was in the case of the 1959 master plan adopted by the city of Rome.

less smoothly and where nationally approved plans were secured only in the 1960s. At the lowest level of performance are cities like Naples.

While Rome produced three officially approved plans between 1870 and the fall of Fascism—in 1883, and 1931—Naples managed to do so only once, in 1939. In 1944, studies for a new plan were begun in order to cope with the new problems created by the war, as well as those inherited from the past. The city adopted a plan in 1946 and sent it to the Ministry of Public Works for approval. Almost four years later the ministry returned the plan to the city for revision. The city council adopted a revised plan in 1951, but the right-wing (Lauro) administration that came into power after the elections of 1952 withdrew the plan because it "did not correspond to the new programs." In 1954 the ministry ordered Naples to adopt a plan. The city complied, but somewhat slowly; four years later, in 1958, the Monarchist administration produced a new master plan just before it was removed from office on grounds of corruption by the national government. The prefectoral commissioner appointed in 1958 to govern Naples adopted the plan on behalf of the city. Almost four years later the Ministry of Public Works rejected the plan and requested a new formulation. Late in 1962 a new commission presided over by Professor Luigi Piccinato, a leading actor in Roman city planning, was appointed, and produced a plan in 1964. Progressive resistance to this latest plan was holding up adoption as late as 1968.

Building in the city was still being regulated, after a fashion, in accordance with the zoning provisions of the 1939 master plan, but, in characteristic Neapolitan fashion, the colors on the official zoning map began to fade, leaving large areas formerly zoned as farmland now open for development. In 1966, the Ministry of Public Works sent two inspectors to Naples to examine the colors on the Naples zoning map and, after investigation, it acted to restore the orginal colors. The president of Naples province declared that the whole affair was really due "to the violent, incurable color-blindness that caused some functionaries in the planning department to perceive yellow as green. They had thus reclassified agricultural zones as development land, subject only to the general rules of the 1935 building code."[3]

## THE POWER OF PLANNERS

Professional planners have been a fairly cohesive and influential group in Rome since at least 1929 when the National Institute of Planners (INU) was founded. The connections between INU and government have been deliberately and formally close: since 1929, INU has in fact been officially chartered as an institute to give professional planning advice to government officials. City and national officials, administrators and politicians, have been regular members of the institute and active participants in its affairs. Influence has therefore flowed in both directions: INU proposals have become government policy and government has occasionally attempted to influence the stands taken by INU branches.[4]

INU members played an important role in shaping the 1931 master plan of Rome. Architect Marcello Piacentini, one of the founders of INU, was rapporteur for the commission that drafted the plan submitted for Mussolini's approval in 1930. The national secretary of INU, Professor Virgilio Testa, was also, between 1934 and 1943, secretary-general (that is, chief administrator) of the commune of Rome, immediately beneath the governor appointed by Mussolini. The zenith of INU influence upon the national government was reached in 1942 when Mussolini reluctantly gave his consent to a national Urban Planning Act (the Legge Urbanistica, No. 1150 of August 17, 1942), which translated many of the goals and techniques advocated by INU planners into national policy with the force of law.[5]

3. Cited in Salvatore Rhea, "Napoli perchè," Il Ponte, April 1968, p. 469. See also Giulio De Luca, "L'asse attrezzato e l'area metropolitana di Napoli," Nord e Sud, August 1964, pp. 65–78.
4. Il Messaggero, February 7, 1962.
5. The legislative (political) background to the 1942 Planning Act, including Mussolini's reluctance to approve it, is related by the then minister of public works, Giuseppe Gorla, in L'Italia nella seconda guerra mondiale (Milan, 1959). The book provides an interesting, if brief, case study of policymaking under Fascism. The sole policymaking actors were the various government ministries, not the "corporations" of the "corporate state." The consent of these ministries had to be achieved by a lengthy process of bargaining between proposing and opposing departments, mediated by the dictator. Seldom did the opposing departments act openly; they usually instigated the opposition of other departments. Gorla's problem as a minister proposing new and controversial legislation was to guess who were his real,rather than his apparent, opponents. Mussolini would not allow major policies to come before the Council of Ministers until general agreement among the departments was reached. Gorla won approval to draft a new bill in the spring of 1941. The bill, after laboriously clearing eleven departments and reaching the cabinet agenda twice, only to be removed by Mussolini just before the meeting began, finally received cabinet sanction in June 1942. King Victor Emmanuel III signed the bill, prior to its presentation to the Fascist "parliament," saying privately to Gorla, "I make an exception for Rome [with regard to the bill's principal stated objective: curbing urban growth]. It is a

But despite Fascist acceptance of many INU goals, an increasingly large segment of this organization became disenchanted as much with Fascist "imperial" planning and architecture as with Fascist social conservatism and political authoritarianism. For a period after the liberation (1944–46) antifascist members of INU were brought into the city administration to develop new planning policies for the city. But with the end in 1946 of the CLN (Resistance) administration, appointed by Allied Military Government officials, the antifascist planners left the city offices, and the city's planning reverted by inertia to the policies, personnel, and practices in vogue before the fall of Fascism. Since that time there has usually been a split between, on the one hand, the professional planners in INU, who work for government mostly as private consultants and are often deeply involved in the evolution of planning theory, and, on the other hand, the planners who work regularly for the City Planning Department, who have been less caught up in the postwar climate of reformism and revisionism and more absorbed in their day-by-day administrative responsibilities. Since the early postwar period, INU planners have tended to be critical of the competence, integrity, and outlook of the City Planning Department.

Characteristically, it was the planners of INU, rather than the Planning Department, who proposed in 1950 to scrap the master plan of 1931 in favor of a new scheme.[6] It was equally characteristic of the Planning Department to propose in 1951 the expressway through the heart of the historic district—a proposal that carried on the Fascist policy of modernizing rather than conserving the historic centers of Italian cities and towns.[7] The progressive planners in INU succeeded not only in blocking the proposed highway through the Baroque quarter but also in obtaining from the city a promise to prepare a new plan.

INU achieved "privileged access" in 1952 when, after the elections of that year, the lawyer Leone Cattani, a newly elected city councilman and a former national president of INU, was elected planning assessor in the new city giunta of Rome. The planning assessor in Rome, in addition to being a city councilman, the political head of the planning department, and a member of the mayor's giunta, is also a party leader and representative (in Cattani's case, the Liberal party). Cattani succeeded in securing giunta and council consent to establish the Special Office for the New Master Plan,[8] attached to, but not part of the plan-

good thing for Rome to become even larger, if only to make that Vatican City enclave over there seem smaller" (p. 325). The bill was attacked in Parliament and almost buried in committee on instigation from high party figures and ministers. A delegation from the Senate asked Gorla to withdraw the bill, but it finally was passed in July 1942 (p. 330–33).

6. Leonardo Benevolo, "Le discussioni e gli studi preparatori al Nuovo Piano Regolatore," pp. 205–10.

7. The story of the proposed demolition project involving Via Vittoria is related in Benevolo, ibid., pp. 210–15; by one of the leading participants, Antonio Cederna, in *I vandali in casa*, pp. 35–42; and by Italo Insolera in *Roma moderna*, pp. 203–04.

8. On the creation of the Special Office (Ufficio Speciale Nuovo Piano Regolatore or USNPR), see Mario Manieri-Elia, "L'attività dell'Ufficio Speciale per il Nuovo Piano Regolatore," in INU, *Roma: Città e piani*, pp. 272–76. Cattani described his stormy role in Roman planning in *Urbanistica Romana: Una battaglia liberale in Campidoglio* (n. p., 1954).

ning department. But in his zeal to curb illegal building activities he incurred the wrath of the interests close to the Christian Democratic party, then as now the dominant political party in Rome, and was forced to resign.

His successor, Enzo Storoni, was also a Liberal and a lawyer and, while not himself a member of INU, was personally close to leading members of the institute. Storoni requested INU to prepare reports on a new master plan for Rome and incorporated them in his own impressive *relazione* on the new plan to the city council on December 22, 1953. The council proceeded to endorse most of the principles dear to the professional planners of INU, such as conservation of the historic center, decentralization, and limitations on residential density, in its resolution of May 21, 1954, on the new master plan. The city council not only committed itself to the goals of the professional planners, it placed them in a strategic position within the master planning process. But despite their official standing and professional prestige, the planners found themselves hard pressed to convince other groups in Roman planning politics, particularly the laymen, politicians, and institutional spokesman on the Grand Commission and the city council, that their professional advice was valid.[9]

In June 1958, the city council voted to reject the CET plan and instead asked the giunta, with the aid of the regular city planning department, to bring in a new plan—one that was less controversial than the CET plan, even in its watered-down version. The plan adopted by the city council on June 24, 1959, represented an almost total defeat for the professional planning movement. Disregard for the values of the planning movement was also evident in the way the city government with the aid of some of the most renowned Italian architects, prepared for the 1960 Olympics by building facilities, and thus encouraging development, in the north, west, and south—rather than the east.[10]

The planning movement began to regain influence in city politics only after the riots of the summer of 1960, which reversed the trend toward a clerico-fascist regime in Italy and started the country in the other direction, toward the Center-Left coalition. With the Center-Left coalition that was formed nationally and locally in 1962 came a determination to break with previous policies of laissez-faire in order to correct the inequities and maladjustments then being created by rapid economic growth. Nationally, this attempt to harness the economic boom and mitigate some of its adverse side-effects took the form of

9. I have attempted to describe the predicament of professional planners of the CET in "Professionalism and Politics in Roman Planning," cited above, Chap. 1, n.8.

10. Pier Luigi Nervi, for example, was criticized by the progressive planners for ignoring the planning consequences of his individual designs for Olympic facilities, particularly the sports facilities and Corso Francia highway in the northern part of the city where planners wished to discourage further development. (See Cederna, *Mirabilia Urbis,* pp. 81–83). Leonardo Benevolo, in "Le facoltà di architettura e l'architettura della città," *Città e Società,* March-April 1968, pp. 15–34, criticized the seventy groups of architects, including some of the most famous in Italy who participated in the 1966 national design competition for an enlargement of the Parliament building in the heart of historic Rome, in complete disregard for the principles of intervention in historic centers elaborated by the planning movement.

proposed legislation to establish new forms of planning—economic and physical. A new national urban planning bill was prepared on the basis of a planning code formulated by INU in 1960. A national Five Year Economic Plan was also prepared. In Rome the forces of the Center-Left sought to undertake similar action at the local level. On December 18, 1962, the city council formally adopted a master plan supported, although not very enthusiastically, by the progressive planning movement.[11] But if adoption of the 1962 master plan represented something of a victory for the planners, slowness in implementing the plan represents a continuing defeat.

If the effectiveness of planning in Rome is gauged by the influence wielded by professional planners, one must conclude that the level of effectiveness has varied considerably over time; that planner influence has been at times practically nil, at other times considerable; that planner influence has been mostly at that level of general policy rather than concrete action; and that there has been a rather broad gap at times between formal planning policy in the city and the realities of planning administration.

It should also be said, however, that the planning movement has been successful in making planning issues the most salient issues in Roman politics for the past decade. Adoption and implementation of the new master plan has been at the top of every party coalition program since 1960. Since that time planning questions have been at the heart of Roman politics: the major object of interparty bargaining, intraparty factionalism, and electoral competition. Planning has been the major problem of Roman mayors since at least 1956. Planners have secured attention, if not action.

Rome does not seem to have been more fickle in its responsiveness to planners' demands than other Italian cities. One might think that the vicissitudes of planner influence in Rome were determined by the conservative cast of the city's politics, but planners seem to have fared no better in cities with leftist-oriented administrations. The experience of planners in Bologna may be instructive in this regard. The Communists have controlled the city government of Bologna since the Liberation. In 1956 the Christian Democrats waged a major electoral campaign to oust the Communists from office, asserting that they had become merely able administrators of the status quo, and charging that the master plan adopted in 1955 under Communist auspices was designed to preserve the existing social and economic nature of the city so as to also preserve Communist

11. The official INU report is very lukewarm about the 1962 master plan, calling it orthodox from a legal point of view, but outdated in terms of current concepts of city planning . . . .. Planning theory has for some time replaced the idea of a plan conceived of as a static legislative measure with that of the dynamic organization of technical and political intervention; as a corollary, theory now considers the planning of metropolitan areas and surrounding regions as an operation complementary to and inseparable from the planning of economic intervention.
The INU report is reproduced in *Urbanistica*, March 1964, pp. 68–75; the quotation can be found on p. 69.

voting strength. The Communists implicitly accepted these charges when, after 1959, a change in party leadership in the city gave a more dynamic and forward-looking image to city policymaking. In the 1960 elections the Bologna Communist party placed on its list a talented young architect-planner from Rome, Giuseppe Campos-Venuti. Despite the fact that he was completely unknown to them, the party's voters dutifully elected Campos-Venuti to the council and the party's council delegation dutifully elected him planning assessor for Bologna.[12] Campos-Venuti took charge of the Bologna intercommunal plan operation, involving some fourteen communes, and of the Law 167 low-cost housing program for the central city. At the same time a planning operation was launched in the form of capital programming. The emphasis in city policy was now to be economic development and change, rather than preservation of the status quo through zoning and laissez faire. The Bologna intercommunal plan was published in 1962 and a year later both an impressive Law 167 program and a five-year capital investment program appeared. With these plans the communists refuted charges that they had neglected physical and economic planning and had actually attempted to discourage economic development in order to retain power.

But before the intercommunal plan was actually presented to the Bologna city council, Campos-Venuti was ousted as planning assessor. The party dropped him from its lists in the 1966 elections. Campos-Venuti had privately criticized his party comrades for having favored land speculators in Bologna, not through corruption but through policies of fiscal conservatism which, in effect, left development initiative in private hands. He had also privately denounced the city's overindulgent policy in granting variances ("deroghe") to the master plan. Also, many officials in surrounding communes, though loyal Communists, were angered by what they saw as the Bologna Planning Department's tendency to impose its policies on them by means of the intercommunal plan and by means of party discipline. The imposition of new building restrictions, especially in surrounding communes, may also have threatened the traditional Communist policy of maintaining cordial relations with the Bologna business community.[13]

Thus, planners have experienced difficulties and failure even in Italian cities run by parties ostensibly favorable to planning. Italian planning journals tend to look outside Italy for examples of effective planning.

12. Actually, Campos-Venuti was the "first of the not-elected" on the party list and an old party functionary voluntarily resigned to allow him to take a seat on the council and become Planning Assessor in the giunta.

13. Mario Dezmann, "Mancini docet anche a Bologna," pp. 443–47; Giovanni Degli Esposti, Bologna PCI (Bologna, 1966), pp. 212–14; Robert H. Evans, Coexistence: Communism and its Practice in Bologna 1945–1965 (Notre Dame, 1967), Chap. 7; Campos-Venuti interview in L'Espresso, March 16, 1969; Resto del Carlino (Bologna), March 31, April 20, 1966; Indro Montanelli et al., Italia sotto inchiesta: "Corriere della Sera" 1963/65 (Florence, 1965), pp. 390–93. Further evidence on the conservatism of Communist policies in Bologna and other northern cities, see Fried, "Communism, Urban Budgets, and the Two Italies."

## BUDGETARY COMMITMENTS

It is not easy to test planning performance in Rome by examining actual budgetary allocations. The city budget does not make it very clear how money is allocated among purposes, or even among major functional units. The salaries of the higher planning officials, for example, are charged to the budget of the Personnel Department. In 1962, the city apparently spent 40.9 million lire (about $68,000) on higher administrative personnel, 60 million (about $100,000) for Special Office personnel, and 156 million (about $260,000) for special studies, the design of detailed plans, and so forth.[14] Total city expenditures that year were 95.5 billion lire (about 160 million dollars). Thus expenditures for planning represented a rather modest two-tenths of one percent of total city spending. With these funds the city was able to employ about thirty architects and engineers in the Planning Department and fifteen in the Special Office for the New Master Plan.

It cannot be said, however, that the city has been spending large amounts of money on other objects than planning or that it has ignored planning choices in its own budgetary determinations. The city has had relatively little money to spend in the postwar period on any object. It has received no grants from the national government for planning purposes. Since 1962 it has made some attempts to translate the master plan into its annual and long-range spending plans. Efforts to coordinate sectorial investments in accordance with master plan policies culminated in the city's first Five year Development Plan, adopted on July 26, 1967, by the city council. The Five Year Plan calculates the investment requirements in all sectors of city activity in accordance with master plan determinations. The major projects called for by the master plan are all included within the Five Year Plan. Unfortunately, the Five Year Plan—sometimes called the *"libro dei sogni"* or "book of dreams"—represents not so much how the city has decided to spend its own funds as a carefully worked out and not very successful plea for funds from the national government.

## THE STYLE OF PLANNING

A criticism of city planning efforts is that they tend to be middle class in orientation and to ignore the values and interests of low income groups.[15] This class bias seems to have been less true in Rome than in many American cities. Inhabitants of many of the borgate or illegal settlements around the city, generally people of low status and income, discovered that their settlements were zoned for farmland by the 1959 master plan and hundreds of them took

14. Comune di Roma, *Bilancio di previsione dell'entrata e della spesa per l'esercizio finanziario 1964* (Rome, 1964).
15. Herbert Gans, "City and Regional Planning," in *International Encyclopedia of the Social Sciences,* 12 (1968), 129–37.

advantage of the opportunity to present "observations" against the plan. If their settlements were zoned as farmland, their houses could be demolished and the city was not obligated to provide them with utilities and services. Thus, 1,217 of the observations against the 1959 plan came from the inhabitants of twenty illegally subdivided borgate who asked that their settlements be rezoned as Zone F, Urban Renewal, which would give them official recognition and a claim to city services and utilities. The rezoning campaign was successful: the master plan of 1962 made it official city policy to attempt to convert these "spontaneous" villages into more rationally organized communities.[16]

The interests of borgata inhabitants and those of other low income groups were also effectively articulated by the Communists and the Socialists. The Communists held meetings on the master plan in all the poorer sections of the city. Needless to say, the party attempted to shape, as well as to collect, ideas and reactions.

However, no party, interest group, or government agency in the city tried to discover general citizen or group preferences through opinion surveys. The first opinion surveys relevant to city planning were carried out only in 1966–67—after the plan was adopted and promulgated. Direct citizen participation in the planning process came *after* the plan was formulated, when the plan was put on display and observations were collected, examined, and in hundreds of cases accepted by the city.

The city council in 1954 was anxious to establish a democratic form of planning. The Grand Commission was created precisely for the purpose of representing all the interests with a stake in the planning process: all social groups, political parties, government departments, and public institutions. The planning machinery was rather proudly hailed as an innovation in Italian planning methods in the direction of greater democracy and participation. Professor Michele Valori, a sophisticated participant-observer, later wrote that "for the first time in its planning history, Rome had recognized the necessity of broad participation by public opinion . . . in the study and formulation of a modern, democratic plan."[17] Certainly, compared to the oligarchical way in which the 1931 master plan had been formulated, drafting of the new plan was highly democratic. The city council, periodically elected in fiercely competitive elections, remained in charge of the plan, able at any time to discharge either or both the Grand Commission and the CET and assume the burden of plan formulation itself. The planners were appointed by and responsible to democratically elected officials. Basic policy was set by the city council and the council had to approve the final product. In this sense the machinery of 1954 was incomparably more democratic than the machinery of 1931.

On the other hand, the Grand Commission itself was not really the organ for

16. Insolera, *Roma moderna*, pp. 270–71, n. 3.
17. Michele Valori, "I lavori per il Piano Regolatore di Roma: Quattro anni difficili," in *Roma: Città e piani*, p. 238.

democratic planning that some of its defenders believed it to be. Out of the ninety or so members, only twenty-two were elected by the people—the mayor, the six assessors, the fourteen city councilmen, and the president of Rome province. Except for the fifteen architects and engineers appointed by the city to the planning and building commissions, two representatives of the press, and a few other experts, all the rest were state and local bureaucrats. The Grand Commission represented less the community-at-large than the community of organizations. Two-thirds of the Grand Commission members had organizational rather than popular constituencies. The popularly elected members also had organizational constituencies, to be sure: the party apparatuses that had nominated them and, by steering the preference vote among party voters, had elected them. Six of the popularly elected officials were assessors—the political heads of city departments—perhaps more oriented to the enhancement of departmental interests than community-wide interests. Characteristically, there were no laymen, no leading citizens, no representatives of the "grassroots" on the Grand Commission—only institutional leaders and spokesmen. Long after the fall of Fascism and the advent of constitutional democracy, representation was still seen in corporatist rather than individualist terms.

Even so, the experiment in "democratic" planning was not, in the end, a success. The Grand Commission, representing (at least in theory) the major interests in the community, could come to no decision on the proposed new plan and after nearly four years of deliberation simply dissolved itself and passed the whole matter back to the city council. The city made no other attempt to create special representative organs for planning. After 1958 the plan was formulated by planning consultants and city officials, working and negotiating with interest groups, party leaders, and city councilmen. Formal discussion of planning proposals was confined to the city council and its committees. At the same time, however, there was considerable unofficial debate over planning issues in the Roman press and within the parties.

If the Grand Commission did not work well as a mechanism for democratic planning, it does not seem to have worked any better as a device for registering and adjusting the planning interests of the dozens of public institutions and government agencies represented on it. Most institutional representatives said little or nothing during the entire four years of commission deliberation. Commission discussions were dominated by those few agency representatives and councilmen with some degree of familiarity with planning questions. It is not clear whether agency representatives voted on the various questions *qua* agency representatives or simply as commission members. There is no evidence to suggest that giving the agencies representation in the planning process made them willing to express their preferences, reveal their intentions, or make any commitment to the resulting plan.

Parallel to and independent from the public planning process, there was an informal, private planning process in which individuals and agencies acted much as they wished and often in contrast to the policies emerging with such travail from the public planning process. Public agencies and private corporations preferred central to peripheral sites and acted accordingly. Private individuals, for their part, found it desirable to build illegal extra stories on the old buildings in the center and to build five-story apartment houses on suburban land not zoned for development; they found the lack of a building permit no hindrance to implementation of *their* plans. These private planning activities, undertaken without regard to the dictates of public plans, were the major form of citizen participation in the planning process in postwar Rome.

If the process by which the master plan of 1962 was formulated was quite comprehensive in the kinds of social and institutional perspectives it sought to incorporate and adjust, the plan that finally emerged was not based on very sophisticated research techniques or on interdisciplinary research and analysis. The 1962 plan, like its predecessors, is primarily the work of planners trained in design rather than in economic or social analysis. Little of the research and information upon which the plan is based has been published. The report accompanying the 1962 master plan consists of a forty-three-page explication of the zoning scheme.[18] The master plan itself consists of sixty-two zoning maps at a scale of 1:10,000 plus a brief set of technical implementation norms, divided into twenty-one articles. The lack of a major regional planning research institute in Rome, such as ILSES (Istituto Lombardo per gli Studi Economici e Sociali) in Milan or IRES (Istituto di Ricerche Economico-Sociali) in Turin, deprived the Roman planners of an imposing research base with which to justify their decisions.[19] The first use of more up-to-date planning techniques in the city came only with the 1963–64 traffic survey, modeled on similar surveys in the United States and Great Britain, which was the first in Italy and one of the first in Europe. The survey, it will be noted, was begun *after* adoption of the master plan.[20]

Many of the professional critics of the 1962 master plan consider it crude, arbitrary, and overly indulgent to private interests.[21] This is an unnecessarily harsh judgment. No professional critic has been able to show that better schemes were available to achieve the goals of imposing order on the city's development and, at the same time, saving its historic center. Any plan that an Italian city council might conceivably adopt is bound to be less coherent, rigorous, and Draconian than most planners would like. No amount of research or technical

18. See "Council Debates, 1962," pp. 463–506.

19. The 1962 master planners did have available the research produced by the 1959–60 intercommunal plan operation.

20. Comune di Roma, *Il traffico a Roma: La situazione attuale e le previsioni fino al 1985* (Rome, 1966).

21. See for example the INU observations on the plan, reproduced in *Urbanistica*, March 1964, pp. 68–81; Coppa, "La lunga strada," pp. 17–20; Vincenzo Cabianca, "Roma: verso un sistema generale del verde," *Urbanistica*, May 1966, pp. 6–17; and Insolera, *Roma moderna*, pp. 259–72.

sophistication can obviate the need for essentially arbitrary choices among competing interests. The plan adopted in 1962 consists of a refinement and elaboration of previous proposals. It is certainly adequate for the purposes of current capital programing and for the elaboration of new planning policies for the city. The defects of planning in Rome since 1962 lie not so much with the plan adopted in that year but with the failure to implement that plan and to continue the refinement process.

In several cases, as has been seen, plans were adopted by other cities much more speedily than in Rome. If, however, we look at planning style—the kind of plan adopted and the way it was formulated—somewhat different judgments may be called for. In two cities (Florence and Venice) where plans were adopted more speedily than in Rome, they were adopted by prefectoral commissioners rather than by democratically elected city councils. Florence and Venice were run by prefectoral commissioners between 1958 and 1961, after the city councils in those cities had been dissolved by the national government. When city councils in those cities were once again elected in 1961, they voted to change the commissioner-adopted plans.

In the cases of Milan and Bologna, plans were quickly adopted because they were not very innovative. Neither the Milan nor the Bologna plan was highly esteemed in professional planning circles. The Milan plan was criticized by conservationists for perpetuating the Fascist policy of massive demolitions in the older parts of the city. While planners admired certain features of the Milan plan, particularly its attempt to decentralize activity to a new "directive center," they thought this was inconsistent with the plan's equal emphasis on redevelopment of the existing center.[22] The plan formulated by the Communists in Bologna received the same low marks from the professional planning critics as the plan formulated by the Social Democrats in Milan. The Bologna general plan was criticized for being too passive, for ratifying existing oil-stain developmental tendencies in the city, rather than attempting to shape the form of development.[23] In neither Milan nor Bologna was there citizen participation in the planning process. In neither case was there any attempt at interdisciplinary planning: both the Milan and Bologna plans were formulated without reference to social or economic analysis.

For the development of more comprehensive perspectives in Italian planning, we must look not so much at the master planning operations carried out in

22. On Milan, see Cederna, *I vandali,* pp. 308–51, and "La politica urbanistica milanese," *Il Mulino,* May 1969, pp. 537–41. Prof. Luigi Piccinato, author of the master plans of many Italian cities, including Rome, Naples, and Padua, has written that "Milan is the most spectacular example in Italy, indeed in Europe, of the negation of planning and of the exaltation of non-planning." (*Roma Nuova, 1,* 69–70.)

23. On the early history of the master plan of Bologna, see Mario Dezmann, "Mancini Docet anche a Bologna," *Il Ponte,* April 1966, pp. 443–47, and Bruno Zevi, *L'Espresso,* September 15, 1957. The September 1969 issue of *Urbanistica* is dedicated to the recent planning problems and achievements of Bologna.

individual Italian cities but at the more recent *metropolitan area* planning
operations. This intercommunal planning has attempted to cope with the problems of conurbation by breaking away from the traditional legalistic and
design emphasis of master planning and turning to the perspectives of the region
and the techniques of economic analysis.[24] The emerging metropolitan plans,
such as those for Milan, Turin, and Bologna, are a good deal more sophisticated
and less parochial in their perspectives than the master plans prepared for the
central city in each area. Milan and Turin have been in the vanguard in creating
this new dimension in Italian planning. Milan proposed the formation of a
Milanese intercommunal plan as early as 1951 and it helped to establish a
regional economic research institute (ILSES) in 1960. Turin began working with
seventeen neighboring communes on the Turinese intercommunal plan in 1954
and helped to establish IRES, a regional economic research institute, in 1958.[25]

As in much Italian planning, the advances have been made at the level of
theory rather than practice.[26] Sophisticated designs have been worked out,
often using the latest analytical techniques, but the attempt to make planning
more comprehensive has also created new forms of conflict. There have been
major interdisciplinary conflicts between the economists and the city planners
in the formulation of the intercommunal plans, especially in Milan. The two-
way conflict between city planners and politicians has broadened out to become
a triangular struggle between economists, city planners, and politicians, making
adoption of any plan very difficult. The attempt to achieve territorial comprehensiveness has added still another dimension of conflict, as between the
central cities and surrounding communes. When and if ideological, political,
and professional conflicts can be settled and intercommunal plans can be
adopted, they still must be translated into the zoning and investment decisions
of dozens of independent communes. Implementation of the Milanese intercommunal plan, for example, calls for action by ninety-two separate local
authorities, many of them far from convinced of the worth of the whole operation.[27]

Conflicts of interest in the Bologna metropolitan planning district have been
no less intense than in Milan or Turin, but since all the communes of the district
are controlled by the Communist party, party discipline has been available to
ensure some measure of cooperation. Even so, party discipline has not always
been strong enough to overcome *municipalismo,* an "ism" with a longer and
stronger tradition in Italy than Communism.[28] Interestingly enough, no region-

24. *Urbanistica,* March and October 1967.
25. Carlo Beltrame, "Gli istituti regionali di ricerca socio-economica," *Esperienze Amministrative,* June 1964, pp. 66–109...
26. Stefano Ray, "Roma: vocazioni storiche e implicazioni metodologiche di un piano
regolatore," *Rivista di Sociologia,* January-April 1967, pp. 79–102.
27. Marco Romano, "L'esperienza del piano intercomunale milanese," *Urbanistica,* October
1967, pp. 32–44.
28. *L'Espresso,* March 16, 1969 (interview with G. Campos-Venuti).

al economic research institute on the model of the Milan and Turin has appeared in Bologna. The Rome intercommunal plan, unlike the Rome master plan, was based on considerable research but it has had no practical consequences; presented in 1960, it has never been adopted. Intercommunal planning, however, is less important for Rome, given the empty territory around the city, than it is for cities like Milan, Turin, Bologna, Genoa, and Florence, whose territories are approaching saturation. Roman *master planning* has been less comprehensive than the intercommunal planning in Bologna, Milan, Turin, but it does not suffer in comparison with the master planning in those cities.

THE ACHIEVEMENT OF PLANNING GOALS

It is still premature to judge the effectiveness of Roman planning by the criterion of goal achievement, for official approval of the 1962 master plan by the national government (the Ministry of Public Works) was secured only in 1966. Even then, approval was made conditional upon further revisions of the plan—revisions that were voted by the Rome city council in the General Variance of October 1967. And even after this the city seemed incapable of producing a complete, definitive, publishable version of the plan to guide public and private actors. Some provisions of the 1962 master plan went into effect, legally at least, even before the plan received government approval. Under Law 1902 of November 3, 1952, adoption of a master plan by an Italian city council automatically puts into effect so-called "safeguard norms" that permit the city to turn down building permits in conflict with the new plan, even though that plan has not yet become law. Legally, then, the zoning code of the 1962 master plan has been in effect since 1962.

The city thus did not need promulgation of the master plan in order to enforce the new zoning provisions, nor did it have to wait before carrying out those provisions of the plan calling for the spending of money rather than the exercise of police power. The city has been free, at least legally, to launch the major projects of the plan, using its existing powers of eminent domain. In addition, the city administration made certain pledges to the council in December 1962, committing the city to a series of specific actions on the plan within "120 days.[29] Table 10.3 shows that goal achievement, so far, has been modest.

Have other Italian cities been more successful than Rome in implementing their plans, in achieving the goals set forth in their plans? One way of answering this might be to look at the number of detailed plans of execution that each city has been able to issue since it adopted its plan. Under the Planning Act of 1942, detailed plans were to be the normal means of plan implementation. New districts of the city were to be designed by the city planning departments rather than by the planning offices of private subdividers. Table 10.4 shows how seldom this

29. See "Council Debates, 1962," pp. 531–34.

Table 10.3 The Record of Goal Achievement

| Master Plan Goals | Means | Achievement |
|---|---|---|
| 1. Save the historic center through decentralization. | a. Use-controls in the center; ban on street cutting and major alterations. | a. No public demolition, but considerable private alteration, some legal, some illegal. |
| | b. Establishment of new centers. | b. Study of the new centers began in 1966. |
| | c. Creation of eastern axis expressway system. | c. Study began in 1966. |
| | d. Selective expansion: ban on heavy expansion in north and west. | d. Development in north and west has been only moderate. |
| 2. Create public facilities and services in the borgate. | Detailed plans of investment for Zone F (borgate). | First detailed plans for some borgate adopted in 1968. |
| 3. Establish public control over new development and break up oil-stain pattern. | a. Restrict redevelopment in existing districts. | a. Partially effective. |
| | b. Reduce densities of development within 1931 master plan districts, as yet unbuilt. | b. Effective. |
| | c. Step up public housing program (Law 167). | c. Only moderate progress. |
| | d. Restrict new infrastructure to areas zoned for development. | d. Effective |
| | e. Tighten controls over private subdivisions. | e. Effective for legal subdivisions. New subdivision standards adopted in 1967. |
| | f. Strengthen regulatory capability of planning department. | f. Ineffective. |
| 4. Improve circulation within the city. | a. Ban downtown parking. | a. Partially effective. |
| | b. Build eastern axis. | b. Under study since 1966. |
| | c. Build subway system. | c. Ground broken in 1964; less than one mile built by 1970. |
| | d. Create corodinated traffic light system. | d. Installed but ineffective. |
| 5. Improve quality of new residential districts. | a. Tighten controls over private subdivisions. | a. First subdivisions under new master plan approved in 1967; apparently effective for legal subdivisions. Ineffective for illegal subdivisions. |
| | b. Build low-cost housing quarters under Law 167. | b. One out of 44 quarters built. |
| | c. Discourage illegal subdivisions. | c. Ineffective. |
| | d. Encourage expansion through syndicates ("*comparti*") rather than lot-by-lot. | d. None reported. |
| 6. Preserve agricultural, archeological, and scenic values of the Agro Romano. | a. Establish low density zoning. | a. Effective only for legal subdivisions. |

Table 10.3 (Continued)

| | |
|---|---|
| b. Curb illegal subdivisions. | b. Totally ineffective. |
| c. Prevent destruction of monuments and ruins. | c. Mostly ineffective. |
| 7. Increase the supply of public facilities in existing districts. | a. Borgate detailed plans. | a. Some borgate plans approved in 1968. |

| | | |
|---|---|---|
| 7. Increase the supply of public facilities in existing districts. | a. Borgate detailed plans. | a. Some borgate plans approved in 1968. |
| | b. Acquire sites for facilities in existing districts. | b. Little acquisition. |
| | c. Acquire and equip neighborhood parks. | c. Scheme formulated in 1966. Some purchases made and equipment bought. |
| | d. Rebuild sewers in old city; build sewers in newer sections. | d. Plan formulated in 1963. Some progress. |
| | e. Improve water supply and distribution. | e. Supply plan adopted in 1963. |
| | f. Build schools in new sections. | f. Triple sessions abolished in 1968. |

| *1962 City Administration Pledges to the Council* | *Fulfillment* |
|---|---|
| 1. Creation of a Permanent Planning Institute for regional planning research. | Budgeted in 1964; vetoed by national government. Rome province created a research institute in 1963. |
| 2. Reorganization of the Special Office for the Master Plan and the Planning Department. | Partial reorganization of the Planning Department in 1968. |
| 3. Conclusion of intercommunal plan. | No intercommunal planning since 1960. Some regional planning, however. |
| 4. City control over EUR. | EUR remains independent. |
| 5. Preference for Law 167 zones in east-south-east. | Spinaceto the only Law 167 project completed—in the west-south-west. |
| 6. Acquisition of the Appian Way Park. | Acquisition is to be financed by the national government, which has not yet acted. |

actually occurred in the major Italian cities with the exception of Milan. Most cities preferred to leave development initiative in the hands of private subdividers rather than incur the heavy costs of designing new districts themselves. Of course, if Roman experience with the implementation of the 1931 master plan through detailed plans is any guide, we cannot be sure that, even if detailed plans had been issued in other Italian cities, they would have been more faithful in master plan execution than were detailed plans in Rome.

Were other Italian cities better able than Rome to enforce their building and zoning regulations? Apparently not. Rapid economic growth and urbanization seem to have defeated public regulation of building throughout the peninsula. If northern cities were sometimes freer than Rome or southern cities from blatant official corruption, they were no more able to maintain the effectiveness of land-use controls. *"Abusi edilizi,"* or violations of the building and zoning codes, became just as common in the hinterlands of Milan and Turin as in the outskirts of Rome. Northern cities, including Communist Bologna, were as prone as cities further south to indulge in "spot zoning," to be overly generous in granting *deroghe* or variances to building and planning regulations. Had the cities of central and northern Italy been sterner than Rome in enforcing law and

Table 10.4. Comparative Numbers of Detailed Plans Approved as of 1963

|  | Number of detailed plans issued |
|---|---|
| Bologna | 2 |
| Florence | no information |
| Genoa | *"vari"* ("several") |
| Milan | 106 |
| Naples | 2 (1939 plan) |
| Palermo | no information |
| Rome | not yet promulgated |
| Turin | 1 or *"alcuni"* ("some") |
| Venice | 2 |

Source: *Urbanistica*, March 1963, pp. 84–115.

order in urban development, it would not have been so difficult, after all, to pass the urban planning reform legislation sponsored by successive ministers of public works since 1960. Parliament would not have been forced to pass a law in 1967 that required Ministry of Public Works approval for all subdivision permits and all *deroghe* in the eight thousand Italian communes.[30]

## THE QUALITY OF THE ENVIRONMENT

By some indicators, the quality of Rome as an urban environment is not so bleak as the lack of effective planning might suggest. The middle class amenities "measured" by Professor Burchard's scale (see above, p. 6)—the theaters, museums, squares, churches, and fountains—remain intact, if often in bad repair. No major changes have been made in the external aspects of the old city comparable to those perpetrated by Fascist modernization projects. Modern intrusions into the traditional Roman cityscape, like the FAO building or the Hilton Hotel, have not been common. The additional stories erected on hundreds of buildings in the historical sections have not altered the general appearance of these old neighborhoods. Sudden and massive invasion by the automobile has made the city less attractive and more difficult to enjoy; but the damage is not permanent and may eventually be reduced by measures to displace traffic into more suitable channels and districts. The dome of St. Peter's, some four hundred feet high, is still the tallest structure in the city. The historic sections and monuments of the city have thus survived the years of the "economic miracle" surprisingly intact, though not without the vigilance and relentless propaganda of the press and of preservationist groups like the *Italia Nostra* society. The major threat to historic Rome is now decrepitude, accelerated by the vibrations and pollutions of modern traffic.

But if the years of private progress have spared the legacy of public amenity inherited from the past, they have not been generous in endowing the city with

30. Michele Martuscelli, "La legge ponte: significato ed operatività," *Urbanistica*, October 1967, pp .5–13.

new forms of public service and convenience. The great postwar rise in private living standards has not been matched by a corresponding rise in community service standards.

The rise in private living standards has been spectacular, even in Rome. Despite rapid population growth and a slow rate of industrialization, Rome has participated in the national economic boom. Estimated per capita income in the city rose from $500 in 1951 to $1,120 in 1964.[31] Rising incomes have been reflected in the diffusion of telephones, automobiles, and household appliances. In 1930, Rome had 4.5 telephones per 100 persons; by 1951, this had risen to 15.7 telephones per 100 persons; fifteen years later, in 1966, it had reached 32.9 telephones per 100 persons—on a par with Paris, if not with Zurich, Stockholm, or Washington.[32] (See Table 10.5.)

The inundation of the city with automobiles was equally sudden and impressive. The accelerated pace of motorization can be seen in Table 10.6, showing the issuance dates for Rome province license plates, beginning with "ROMA 1" in 1927 to "ROMA B00000" (1.1 million) in 1967, though the cars with the earlier plates were no longer on the road. By 1967, there were 700,000 automobiles registered in Rome province, as compared to 40,000 in 1947, although

Table 10.5. Telephones per 100 Persons in Some Leading Cities, 1930–1966

|  | 1930 | 1966 |
|---|---|---|
| Rome | 4.5 | 32.9 |
| Paris | 12.5 | 33.3 |
| Zurich | 17.0 | 63.5 |
| Stockholm | 30.5 | 74.9 |
| Washington | 32.7 | 92.6 |

Source: Enrico Camaleone, "Roma: verso il milione di apparecchi telefonici," Capitolium, March 1967, pp. 128–29.

Table 10.6. Motor Vehicle Registration in Rome Province, 1927–1967

| License plate | Issuance | | Time lapse |
|---|---|---|---|
| Roma 1 | March | 1927 | |
| Roma 100,000 | March | 1947 | 360 months |
| Roma 200,000 | May | 1954 | 87 months |
| Roma 300,000 | October | 1957 | 41 months |
| Roma 400,000 | June | 1960 | 33 months |
| Roma 500,000 | January | 1962 | 19 months |
| Roma 600,000 | March | 1963 | 14 months |
| Roma 700,000 | January | 1964 | 10 months |
| Roma 800,000 | January | 1965 | 12 months |
| Roma 900,000 | January | 1966 | 12 months |
| Roma A00000 | November | 1966 | 10 months |
| Roma B00000 | August | 1967 | 9 months |

Source: Il Messaggero, August 24, 1967.

31. "Five Year Plan," p. 43.
32. Enrico Camaleone, "Roma: verso il milione di apparecchi telefonici," Capitolium, March 1967, pp. 128–29.

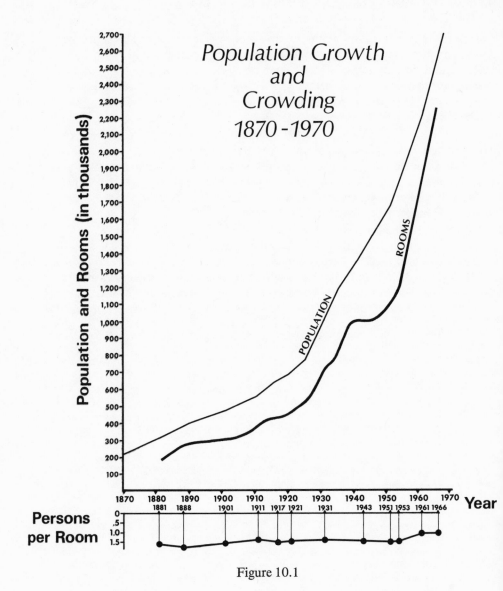

Figure 10.1

even in 1947 complaints about traffic had been loud and desperate. Between 1947 and 1957, the number of private motor vehicles in the province had risen from 32,000 to 157,000; ten years later the number of vehicles had again multiplied by five.[33]

There was also a major improvement in housing conditions. The citywide index of crowding, based on the number of persons per room, dropped from 1.4 in 1951 to 1.1 in 1961. In spite of heavy immigration and a slump in the building industry, the index remained at 1.1 even as late as 1966.[34] Since the index of crowding in Rome after 1870 had never dropped below 1.4 and on some occasions had climbed as high as 1.8, the drop to 1.1 persons per room was a major achievement. (See Figure 10.1.) This may be compared to the 1967 figures for the United States, as a whole, of 0.6 persons per room; Denmark, 0.7; England, 0.7; France, 1.0; and Italy, as a whole, 1.1.[35]

In 1951, 34 percent of all Roman dwelling units contained two or more persons per room; by 1966, only 12 percent were this overcrowded. When the housing survey of 1966 was taken, about one-third of the dwelling units were classified as "superior," that is, with under one person per room, and half were classified as "normal" because they housed between one and two persons per room; the remaining 15 percent of Roman dwelling units were classified by the Central Institute of Statistics as "inferior," because they contained two or more persons per room. Table 10.7 shows how the housing quality types related to the types of housing property within the city.

The improvement in Roman living standards was also registered in successive census data on the distribution of basic utilities, as shown in Table 10.8.

Table 10.7. Housing Types and Property Types, 1966

| | "Superior" | "Normal" | "Inferior" | | | | |
|---|---|---|---|---|---|---|---|
| Persons/room | 0–0.99 | 1–1.99 | 2–2.99 | 3–3.99 | 4 and over | Total |
| All types | 36.9% | 50.9% | 9.4% | 1.7% | 1.1% | 100% |
| Owner-occupied dwellings only | 48.4% | 46.2% | 4.1% | 0.7% | 0.5% | 100% |
| Rented dwellings (Public and private) | 31.5% | 53.8% | 11.8% | 1.9% | 1.0% | 100% |
| Public housing | 30.5% | 53.9% | 12.7% | 2.1% | 0.8% | 100% |

Source: Istat, *Indagine speciale sulle abitazioni al 1° gennaio 1966*, p. 92. The categories are defined on p. 16.

33. *Annuario Statistico Italiano, 1957*, pp. 66, 68; *1967*, pp. 190, 192; Antonio Pala, "La politica del traffico in un grande Comune: problemi, strumenti d'azione, prospettive," *L'Impresa Pubblica*, January 1966, pp. 11–18.

34. For 1951: "Popolazione e territorio," p. 332; for 1961: Istat, 10° Censimento, vol. 3, *Dati Sommari per Comune*, Fasc. 58, Provincia di Roma (Rome, 1966), p. 71; for 1966, calculated from Istat, "Indagine speciale," p. 47.

35. See the historical data on crowding in Roman housing in Comune di Roma, Ufficio Speciale Nuovo Piano Regolatore, *Relazione al Piano Regolatore Generale, Raccolta di Graffici allegati alla Relazione* (Rome, 1957); United Nations, *Compendium of Social Statistics: 1967* (New York, 1968), pp. 257–305.

Table 10.8. Improvement in Roman Housing, 1951–1961

*Percentage of regular occupied
dwellings equipped with the facility*

|  | 1951 | 1961 |
|---|---|---|
| Inside running water | 81.0 | 94.7 |
| Outside aqueduct water | 6.9 | 2.2 |
| Well water | 2.8 | 2.3 |
| Inside toilet | 82.7 | 97.7 |
| Outside toilet | 6.9 | 2.0 |
| Bath | 51.5 | 78.4 |
| Electric light | 90.6 | 99.6 |
| Industrial electric current |  | 59.2 |
| Piped gas | 66.8 | 80.8 |
| Bottled gas |  | 16.7 |
| Central heating | 32.8 | 48.5 |

*Sources: Roma: Popolazione e territorio,* p. 226, for 1951; *10° Censimento Generale della Populazione (15 ottobre 1961), vol. 3, Dati sommari per comune, Fasc. 58, Provincia di Roma* (Rome, 1966), pp. 70–71, for 1961.

Table 10.9. Distribution of Private Amenities, 1966–1967

| Services and appliances in apartments | Middle income district | | Lower income district | |
|---|---|---|---|---|
|  | yes | no | yes | no |
| Central heating | 33 | 17 | 24 | 26 |
| Telephone | 44 | 6 | 37 | 13 |
| TV | 43 | 7 | 42 | 8 |
| Washing machine | 35 | 15 | 20 | 30 |
| Floor polisher | 26 | 24 | 10 | 40 |
| Refrigerator | 43 | 7 | 35 | 15 |
| Attached garage | 3 | 47 | 3 | 47 |
| Garden | 18 | 32 | 2 | 48 |

*Source:* Franco Crespi and Franco Martinelli, "La dinamica delle relazioni sociali nel contesto urbano," *Rivista di Sociologia,* May-August 1968, p. 26.

Improvement went beyond the basic utilities. Sample surveys in a middle class and a lower middle class district in 1966–67 revealed the distribution of private amenities shown in Table 10.9.

The postwar period has also witnessed increased private home ownership. Almost all dwellings in Rome, it should be noted, are apartments in multi-family structures, with the exception of the often illegal one-family homes built out in the countryside or on the fringe. Home ownership in Rome is largely, then, apartment ownership. Despite the rising cost of apartments, owner-occupied apartments rose from 20.3 percent of all regular dwellings, with 19.2 percent of all rooms, in 1951, to 30.8 percent of dwellings and 41.3 percent of rooms in 1966. There was also a commensurate increase in the percentage of non-tenants in the total population from 20 to 31 percent.[36] Rents for many

36. For 1951; "Popolazione e territorio," pp. 332–33; for 1966, "Indagine speciale," pp. 38, 46.

Table 10.10 Apartment Rents in Rome, 1966

| Monthly rents in lire | All rentals | Public rentals | Private rentals | Rentals under 1947 rent controls | Rentals under 1963 rent controls | Rentals free of control |
|---|---|---|---|---|---|---|
| Up to 2,000 ($3.20) | 2,023 | 1,904 | 119 | — | 119 | — |
| 2,001–5,000 ($3.20–8.00) | 11,781 | 10,591 | 1,190 | 883 | 357 | — |
| 5,001–10,000 ($8.00–16.00) | 35,462 | 23,205 | 12,257 | 7,021 | 5,236 | — |
| 10,001–15,000 ($16.00–24.00) | 38,462 | 23,205 | 25,823 | 10,234 | 15,232 | 357 |
| 15,001–20,000 ($24.00–32.00) | 53,193 | 8,687 | 44,506 | 14,518 | 28,917 | 1,071 |
| 20,001–25,000 ($32.00–40.00) | 61,880 | 8,806 | 53,074 | 12,971 | 37,604 | 2,499 |
| over 25,000 (over $40.00) | 173,859 | 12,791 | 160,888 | 17,969 | 123,641 | 14,278 |
| Totals | 376,660 | 89,189 | 297,857 | 63,596 | 211,106 | 18,205 |

Source: Istat, Indagine speciale, pp. 130–52.

people, in any event, remained rather low: more than half the apartments in the city in 1966 rented for less than forty dollars a month, as can be seen in Table 10.10. Average rental in 1962 was about $35.00 per month; for rent-controlled apartments (17 percent of all rentals), about $25.00 a month; for uncontrolled apartments, about $40.00.[37] Roman families spent an average of only 13.3 percent of their income on housing in 1963–64.[38]

The improvement in living standards, measured objectively and in terms of objects possessed, was also reflected in other surveys that sought to determine the degree to which Romans were satisfied with their material surroundings and possessions. Surveys showed that Romans were generally satisfied with their living arrangements, even in the borgate. To be sure, one must interpret replies from borgata residents with care, since those who live in illegally built housing are not likely to complain about conditions in a way that might justify city action against them. The reader will notice in the 1962 borgata survey (Table 10.12) that the residents are generally satisfied with living in the borgata and satisfied with their home because they own it. Women in the borgata, however, are much less enchanted with living conditions than are the men.

Surveys in middle class and working class districts in 1966–67 revealed no general dissatisfaction with living conditions (see Table 10.11).

The housing indicators referred to up to this point all concern "regular" dwellings—dwellings considered suitable for human habitation. The statistics exclude the rather large number of "irregular" or improper dwellings that have

37. Il Messaggero, Septermber 6, 1964, reporting 1962 housing survey data.
38. Annuario Statistico Italiano 1967, p. 385. The estimates are for the entire area of central Italy.

Table 10.11. Satisfaction with Living Quarters, 1966–1967

| Satisfaction with own apartment | Middle class zone (Monte Sacro) | | Working class zone (Ardeatino) | |
|---|---|---|---|---|
| | Yes | No | Yes | No |
| Large enough | 25 | 25 | 28 | 22 |
| Well-furnished | 43 | 7 | 38 | 12 |
| Comfortable for family life | 36 | 14 | 37 | 13 |
| Suitable for having visitors | 35 | 15 | 30 | 20 |
| Suitable for dinner guests | 32 | 18 | 26 | 24 |
| Suitable for house guests | 14 | 36 | 9 | 41 |

Source: Crespi and Martinelli, "La dinamica," p. 27.

Table 10.12. Housing and Neighborhood Satisfaction in a Roman *Borgata*, 1962

1. Do you intend to remain in this *borgata*?

| | | |
|---|---|---|
| Yes | 273 | 78.0% |
| No | 10 | 2.8 |
| No reply | 67 | 19.0 |
| | 350 | 100.0 |

2. Are you satisfied with your present dwelling?

| | | |
|---|---|---|
| Yes | 246 | 70.0% |
| No | 21 | 6.0 |
| No reply | 83 | 23.0 |
| | 350 | 100.0 |

3. How would you feel about living in the city itself?

| | | |
|---|---|---|
| Would prefer the city | 17 | 18.9% |
| Could not stand the city | 38 | 42.2 |
| No preference | 4 | 4.5 |
| No reply | 31 | 34.4 |
| | 90 | 100.0 |

4. Why do you dislike the city?

| | | |
|---|---|---|
| Noise and traffic | 35 | 38.9% |
| Claustrophobia | 16 | 17.8 |
| Isolation | 1 | 1.1 |
| No reply | 38 | 42.2 |
| | 90 | 100.0 |

5. Are you satisfied to live in the *borgata*?

| | | |
|---|---|---|
| Yes | 80 | 88.9% |
| No | 10 | 11.1 |
| | 90 | 100.0 |

6. Degree of satisfaction with the home.

| | Men | | Women | | Total | |
|---|---|---|---|---|---|---|
| Very satisfied | 32 | 74.4% | 9 | 19.2% | 41 | 45.6% |
| A little satisfied | 3 | 7.0 | 12 | 25.5 | 15 | 16.7 |
| Dissatisfied | 4 | 9.3 | 8 | 17.0 | 12 | 13.3 |
| No indication | 4 | 9.3 | 18 | 38.3 | 22 | 24.4 |
| | 43 | 100.0 | 47 | 100.0 | 90 | 100.0 |

7. Reasons for satisfaction with the home.

| | Men | | Women | | Total | |
|---|---|---|---|---|---|---|
| Ownership | 31 | 72.1% | 23 | 48.9 | 54 | 60.0% |
| Other | 7 | 16.3 | 6 | 12.8 | 13 | 14.4 |
| No reply | 5 | 11.6 | 18 | 38.3 | 23 | 25.6 |
| | 43 | 100.0 | 47 | 100.0 | 90 | 100.0 |

Source: Franco Crespi, "Aspetti del rapporto tra strutture urbanistiche e relazioni sociali in una borgata alla periferia di Roma, "*Rivista di Sociologia,* May-August 1967, pp. 43–50.

housed a considerable, if never precisely determined, segment of the postwar Roman population. Since World War II and before, thousands of Romans have lived in shacks and caves, under bridges, and under the arches of old Roman aqueducts. The census takers in 1951 counted 27,961 dwellings of this sort, with 105,004 people living in them.[39] A special survey of "precarious lodgings" in 1957 identified 551 shanty settlements around the city, with 13,131 dwellings and 54,576 people.[40] The 1961 census reported the existence of 20,032 "improper" dwellings with 72,203 inhabitants.[41] Later in the sixties, on the eve of Rome's centennial anniversary as the national capital of Italy, another survey was made, in the hope that the anniversary might fittingly be celebrated by the elimination of the *baracche* (shacks) and the rehousing of the inhabitants in decent housing. The 1967 survey found 38,248 people, living in 8,984 dwellings, scattered in 522 different settlements. Most of the inhabitants—the *baraccati*— were found not in the historic center or in the open countryside, but on the fringe of recently built eastern districts, particularly along the ancient consular roads.[42]

In 1969 still another survey was made by the City Statistical Office, this time inquiring also into social characteristics of the *baraccati*. The survey found 29,318 people (7,532 families) living in *"alloggi precari"* ("precarious lodgings"). About two-thirds of these people (5,350 families) lived in structures they owned; about 15 percent were renting the structures they lived in; the rest were either enjoying free rent or living with the family that owned the structure. Of the 29,318 people, 9,218 were employed and 413 were out of work. Of this total labor force of 9,631, 34 percent were building workers, 21 percent worked in factories, 16 percent worked in commercial establishments, and 19 percent (mostly women) worked in the "services" sector, presumably as domestic help. As for housing types, they were distributed as follows:

| | |
|---|---:|
| Cantonments | 207 |
| Caves | 9 |
| Ruins | 131 |
| Shacks built of masonry | 6,200 |
| Other shacks | 875 |
| Other lodgings | 105 |
| Total lodgings | 7,527 |

39. "Popolazione e territorio," pp. 210–11.
40. *Notiziario Statistico Mensile,* October 1967.
41. 10° Censimento, vol. 3, *Dati sommari per commune,* Fasc, 58, Provincia di Roma, pp. 66–67.
42. *Notiziario Statistico Mensile,* October 1967. Note that irregular dwellings are built for the most part on private property which has been duly sold to the builders. Thus Rome, unlike the capital cities of many developing countries, does *not* have a major squatter problem— that is, masses of people occupying public and private land illegally and without permission. Property rights have been respected in Rome, but not public land use regulations. The major form of squatting in Rome has taken the form of sporadic occupation of unoccupied public housing by shantydwellers.

The structures were distributed among the parts of the city as follows:

| | |
|---|---:|
| Rioni | 131 |
| Quartieri urbani | 6,014 |
| Suburbi | 38 |
| Quartieri marini | 497 |
| Agro Romano | 847 |
| Total lodgings | 7,527 |

Most of the shanties were located in the quartieri urbani, particularly in the eastern sector. Two eastern quartieri, Tuscolano (1,138) and Collatino (1,038), had sizable concentrations.[43]

The degraded conditions under which these people have lived—on a par with the poorest inhabitants of southern Italy or of any country—must be kept in mind lest the statistics for regular dwellings in the city as a whole give a distortedly optimistic image of the Roman environment. There seems to have been some progress in reducing the numbers of people living in these squalid conditions since 1951, if official statistics can be relied upon. But such dwellings and their inhabitants have always been difficult and unrewarding to identify and count and their settlements have blended into the much vaster total of illegally built but often solid and substantial homes of the borgate.

Aggregate data for the city do not generally include the improper dwellings; nor do they reveal the considerable range of housing environments that are to be found among the city's various districts and social strata. Unfortunately, intracity data from the 1961 census have not yet been published so that distributive comparisons with 1951 are not possible. The 1951 census, however, delineated marked differences among the districts of the city in terms of housing quality. Table 10.13 brings out some of the differences in housing between the central districts (the rioni), the more recently built quartieri, the fringe districts (the suburbi), and the rural districts of the Agro Romano. It also shows the

Table 10.13. Housing Conditions in Various Roman Districts, 1951

| | Percentage of proper dwellings with: | | | | |
|---|---|---|---|---|---|
| | Running water | Inside toilet | Bath | Central heating | Persons per occupied room |
| Rioni | 88.1 | 86.5 | 44.2 | 27.1 | 1.32 |
| Quartieri | 86.6 | 87.3 | 63.1 | 41.7 | 1.34 |
| Suburbi | 57.3 | 67.1 | 15.8 | 5.4 | 2.09 |
| Agro | 37.6 | 50.1 | 17.5 | 6.7 | 1.76 |
| CITY | 81.0 | 82.7 | 51.5 | 32.8 | 1.40 |
| Parioli Q. | 79.1 | 80.1 | 73.1 | 68.1 | 0.86 |
| Pinciano Q. | 93.2 | 94.6 | 80.8 | 75.8 | 0.79 |
| Trastevere R. | 77.9 | 76.7 | 23.0 | 15.2 | 1.76 |
| Tiburtino Q. | 82.1 | 83.1 | 30.6 | 10.5 | 1.96 |

Source: Roma: Popolazione e Territorio, pp. 308–38.

43. Notiziario Statistico Mensile, February 1969.

Table 10. 14. Housing Types by Occupational Status of Breadwinner, 1961

*Percentage of occupants with:*

| Breadwinner's occupational status | Running water | Bathroom | Toilet | Central heating |
|---|---|---|---|---|
| Entrepreneur | 98.3 | 95.4 | 99.6 | 86.6 |
| Manager or salaried employee | 98.5 | 92.7 | 99.9 | 70.6 |
| Self-employed | 91.6 | 76.5 | 97.7 | 44.6 |
| Wage earner | 91.6 | 70.4 | 96.6 | 32.0 |
| Housewife-head of family | 96.8 | 73.1 | 98.1 | 39.6 |
| Pensioner | 97.4 | 74.4 | 99.1 | 40.1 |

*Percentage of occupants in:*

| | Noncrowded apartments (less than 1 person/room) | Moderately crowded apart- ments (1-2 persons/room) | Badly crowded apartments (more than 2 persons/room) |
|---|---|---|---|
| Entrepeneur | 73.9 | 24.0 | 1.4 |
| Manager or salaried employee | 58.4 | 38.4 | 3.7 |
| Self-employed | 39.6 | 49.9 | 11.8 |
| Wage earner | 24.6 | 56.5 | 19.2 |
| Housewife-head of family | 57.0 | 33.1 | 10.1 |
| Pensioner | 50.6 | 39.2 | 11.3 |

*Source:* Calculated from Istat, *10° Censimento, Vol. 8, Abitazioni* (Rome, 1967), pp. 532–33, 796–97.

differences between the wealthiest districts, such as Parioli and Pinciano quarters, and the low-income districts of the old center (such as Trastevere) and the eastern quarters (Tiburtino). Note that these statistics do not include improper dwellings.

Published returns from the 1961 census give an indication of the distribution of housing quality ("regular" housing, that is) among various social categories. Table 10.14 shows the differences between the homes of (1) entrepreneurs; (2) managers and salaried employees; (3) self-employed; (4) dependent workers; (5) farm helpers; (6) housewife-heads of family; and (7) pensioners. Not unexpectedly, these data show considerable differences among social strata in housing conditions. Upper income groups are much more apt to be apartment-owners and to enjoy various amenities.

If the percentage of people living in their own apartments rose from 20 to 31 percent between 1951 and 1961, that still left two-thirds of the Roman population as tenants, often subject to rapidly rising rents.[44] Apartments built before 1947 remained covered by rent controls, but those built after that date were not. Only in 1963 did the national government step in to freeze rents for apartments built since 1947. As of 1966, just prior to expiration of rent control, the situation was as shown in Table 10.15.

Rents were decontrolled in 1966, but the lack of low-cost housing and renewed inflation in housing prices provoked nationwide worker and student demon-

44. *Bollettino Statistico*, February 1967, pp. 70–75.

Table 10. 15. Apartment Tenancy, Ownership, and Rent Control, 1966

|  | *percentage of dwellings* |  | *percentage of rooms* |  |
|---|---|---|---|---|
| Owner-occupied | 36.8 |  | 41.3 |  |
| Rented | 57.5 |  | 54.1 |  |
| Rent controlled under 1947 act |  | 9.7 |  | 9.7 |
| Rent controlled under 1963 act |  | 32.3 |  | 29.7 |
| Uncontrolled rent |  | 3.5 |  | 3.0 |
| Public landlord |  | 12.0 |  | 11.7 |
|  |  | 57.5 |  | 54.1 |
| Other title | 6.5 |  | 4.6 |  |
| Total | 100.0 |  | 100.0 |  |

Source: Istat, *Indagine speciale*, p. 92.

Table 10. 16. Housing Conditions as of 1961
*(Percentages)*

| Conditions | Dwellings | Rooms | Families | Occupants |
|---|---|---|---|---|
| Non-crowded (1 person/room or less) | 49.4 | 56.4 | 47.4 | 37.1 |
| Moderately crowded (1-2) persons/room | 44.1 | 39.1 | 44.9 | 54.0 |
| Severely overcrowded (more than 2 persons/room) | 6.8 | 4.2 | 7.7 | 10.9 |
| Total | 100.0 | 100.0 | 100.0 | 100.0 |

Source: Istat, *10° Censimento, Vol. 8, Abitazioni* (Rome, 1967), pp. 532–33.

strations on behalf of better housing in the fall of 1969. Data published in 1967 referring back to the 1961 census, when compared to the data from the 1966 housing survey, showed that housing conditions were actually worsening in the city, as measured by the index of crowding. As Table 10.16 shows, if compared to the data in Table 10.7, the percent of dwellings in the severely overcrowded category (more than two persons per room) had risen from 6.8 percent of all dwellings in 1961 to 12.2 percent in 1966, despite the fact that the overall index of crowding for the city remained at 1.1 persons per room. Under pressure from the labor movement, the national government in 1969 reimposed rent controls and banned evictions in all the large Italian cities, including Rome.[45]

45. In 1965, in the midst of a severe crisis of overproduction in the housing industry, apartments were selling and renting for prices that Swedish and American, but not Roman, workers could afford to pay. Four-to-five-room apartments generally sold for between $20,000 and $50,000 or rented for between $100 and $350 a month. A Roman worker was lucky to earn $160 a month, while the average Roman white-collar employee was likely to be making about $250 a month. (*La Stampa*, February 21, 1965.) Rents in Rome rose from an index number (1938 = 100) of 1,191 in 1951 to 6,176 in 1962; during the same period the index of food prices rose from 6,172 to 7,767; clothing prices, from 7,187 to 6,951; utilities, from 3,171 to 3988; the total cost of living, from 4,794 to 7,144. The rise in rents seems simply to have brought housing costs into line with other costs, relative to prewar prices. Rents continued to rise in the 1960s, this time faster than all other items in the cost-of-living index. The cost of housing rose from an index of 100 in 1961 to 133.3 in 1966. (*Annuario Statistico Italiano 1967*, p. 364; *Annuario Statistico della Città di Roma 1964*, p. 254.) See also Diego Cuzzi and Enrico Fattinanzi, "Edilizia residenziale: prospettive 1970," *Tempi Moderni*, Winter 1968, pp. 75–82.

There are appreciable differences in housing conditions among districts and classes in Rome, but perhaps less than one might expect. In fact, one of the striking characteristics of postwar Roman development is not so much the inequalities among districts but the uniformities among them. One expects to find considerable variation in the services and environmental quality as between wealthier and poorer sections of the city, but instead one finds a lack of services and poor environmental quality in all districts, including the wealthiest. Many of the wealthier districts built during the postwar period have no more street space, green space, or recreational facilities than the low-income districts. The streets in upper-income districts are no cleaner than those in the less wealthy districts. There has been the same penchant toward maximum exploitation of property in both kinds of districts.

The real inequalities have been those between regularly built districts—whether rich or poor—and the *"bidonvilles,"* or shantytowns. The better districts usually have basic infrastructure ("primary urbanization"), such as streets, sewers, water, and electricity, while lacking community facilities ("secondary urbanization"), such as schools, markets, churches, parks, playgrounds, and social centers. The *borgate* and *bidonvilles* lack both kinds of infrastructure.

The seriousness of the city's failure to keep up with the demand for infrastructure is reflected, for example, in the need until 1968 to use *triple* sessions for Roman elementary and secondary schools. To cope with population growth and to eliminate triple sessions and the use of unsuitable places as classrooms, the city needed to build about 10,000 classrooms between 1956 and 1966; it was able to build 3,474 or 35 percent of the estimated need.[46]

The quantity and distribution of parks and playgrounds was even worse. The city had one of the lowest endowments in green space of any major city in the world—less than two square meters per person as compared to 1.5 in Milan, 7.4 in Paris, 11.0 in Moscow, 10.0 in the former County of London, and 20.0 in Cologne.[47] The population of the city had doubled since the 1930s but no new parks had been created. Rome, a city of 2.5 million people, had 19 swimming pools, 52 gymnasiums, 64 soccer fields, 143 tennis courts, and 18 basketabll courts. Relatively few of these facilities were open to the general public. Few Roman schools, it should be mentioned, have gymnasiums or playgrounds.[48]

The general advance in private living conditions was not matched by a commensurate advance in or even the maintenance of minimal levels of community service, whether in the field of education, recreation, water, sanitation, or public transportation. Rapid movement of population into and within the city, the scattered pattern of residential development, and rising consumption standards wrought havoc with the supply of public services, leaving some districts—the

46. "Piano Quinquennale," pp. 59–60.
47. Antonio Cederna, *Il Mondo,* October 12, 1963.
48. Carlo Bodo, "Le attrezzature sportive nel territorio del Comune di Roma," *Urbanistica,* May 1966, pp. 103–05.

declining districts of the historic center—with underutilized or worn-out facilities, and others—the newer districts of the periphery—with no facilities at all. Thus, a city famous for its aqueducts and fountains, a city that historically made no user charges for water, has found itself forced to ration water and to allow many of its residents to use illegal, often polluted, well water. In many cases, where water is brought to the newer districts it is not piped into the housing for lack of sewers.[49] While the older sections of the city can still rely upon the sewer net built by the ancient Romans (the *Cloaca Maxima,*) the newer sections empty wastes into local streams and open sewage ditches.[50]

Rising population, income, and consumption levels have also led to a drastic decline in sanitation in the city because of inadequate facilities for solid waste disposal.[51] Between 1956 and 1967 the sanitation department was faced with a 50 percent rise in the number of users and in the volume of waste—an increase that reflected rising consumption levels as well as population growth.[52] At the same time, the diffusion of automobiles made garbage collection and street cleaning increasingly inefficient and costly. Declining sanitary standards led the provincial medical officer, a national functionary, to denounce Rome in October 1967 as "the dirtiest city in Italy" and to warn of serious threats of epidemics due to defective sanitary conditions.[53]

Traffic congestion in Rome has become proverbial. To most Romans, it is the most serious problem in the city, followed only by the problem of city sanitation.[54] The rapid diffusion of private automobiles has not been matched by the creation of a modern circulation network. The historic center, still at the center of most city activities, remains the compulsory point of transit for cross-city traffic, even though it was built to accommodate the coach and cart traffic of the seventeenth and eighteenth centuries. There is less excuse for the poor circulation in the newer sections of the city, where districts have been added on by accretion with little thought for circulation requirements. Because of speculative pressure, streets in most of the newer districts have not been much wider and in some cases have even been narrower than streets in the historic center. The city has no limited access highways and until 1965 had no system of staggered

49. Mario Pediconi, "Il problema idrico nelle grandi città," *L'Impresa Pubblica,* September 1967, pp. 3–8.
50. Report of the Provincial Health Officer, *Il Messaggero,* November 10, 1967.
51. Carlo Rosato, "Il servizio di nettezza urbana in una grande città: problemi e soluzioni," *L'Impresa Pubblica,* November-December 1967, pp. 9–18.
52. Ibid., p. 9–10.
53. *Il Messaggero,* November 10, 1967.
54. The weekly *L'Espresso* sponsored an opinion survey in the city on the eve of the June 1971 elections. (Unfortunately, the results are not precisely or even clearly reported. Asked what was the worst problem facing the city, 39% of the people surveyed pointed to traffic congestion and 29% mentioned poor sanitation, while relatively few (how few is unspecified) mentioned crime, disorder, unemployment, lack of industry, or the lack of public facilities. (*L'Espresso,* June 13, 1971.) On Roman traffic, see Jack Long, "Europe's Traffic Jam," in Sylvia Fleis Fava, ed., *Urbanism in World Perspective* (New York: Crowell, 1968), pp. 496–502.

traffic lights. As late as 1962 there were only 72 traffic lights in the entire city.[55] Resistance to parking and traffic regulation is widespread and intense.

The growth of private motorization has severely damaged the system of public transportation, drawing away passengers, raising operating costs, and reducing operating speeds. Between 1950 and 1964, population rose by 35 percent while passenger loads on public transit rose only 3 percent.[56] Average speed on city buses fell to three miles per hour. The centrifugal growth of the city required a doubling of routes served, while traffic considerations forced the conversion to buses from more economical trolleys and trolley buses. In 1945, ATAC, one of the city transit companies, lost one lira or one-sixth of a cent for every passenger carried; by 1964, it was losing five cents a passenger. Two-thirds of the city government's operating deficit was caused by the deficits of the city transit companies. The city's only subway line, built to link Termini station with the World's Fair of 1942 at EUR, serves only some 24 of the city's 1500 square kilometers. Ground was broken for a new six-mile subway line in 1964; by 1970, only five stations and about 1.5 miles of line had been completed. Thus while Rome in 1967 had the same five autos per person as New York, it lacked the 210 miles of the New York City transit system. Whether the new subway system, if and when eventually built and completed, will be able to ease the traffic problem

Table 10. 17. Satisfaction with Neighborhood Quality in Rome, 1966

| Elements of Satisfaction | Zone A (middle class, Monte Sacro-Tufello) | | | Zone B (lower class, Ardeatino-Tor Marancio) | | |
|---|---|---|---|---|---|---|
| | Yes or partly yes | No | No reply | Yes or partly yes | No | No reply |
| Air purity | 44 | 6 | — | 48 | 2 | — |
| Quiet | 39 | 11 | — | 39 | 11 | — |
| Street cleanliness | 23 | 27 | — | 25 | 25 | — |
| Presence of green | 24 | 26 | — | 18 | 32 | — |
| Street connections | 42 | 7 | 1 | 45 | 4 | 1 |
| Public services | 43 | 7 | — | 42 | 8 | — |
| Parking space | 24 | 16 | 10 | 17 | 11 | 22 |
| Food stores | 49 | 1 | — | 41 | 8 | 1 |
| Clothing stores | 30 | 19 | 1 | 17 | 11 | 22 |
| Closeness of markets | 39 | 11 | 1 | 41 | 8 | 1 |
| Presence of movies | 29 | 14 | 7 | 28 | 14 | 8 |
| Closeness of schools | 35 | 9 | 6 | 45 | 2 | 3 |
| Closeness to relations | 26 | 18 | 6 | 30 | 17 | 3 |
| Closeness to friends | 28 | 10 | 12 | 22 | 16 | 12 |
| Play space for children | 17 | 25 | 8 | 12 | 35 | 3 |
| Youth recreation centers | 10 | 28 | 12 | 9 | 26 | 15 |

Source: Crespi and Martinelli, "La dinamica delle relazioni sociali nel contesto urbano," p. 27.

55. Pala, "La politica del traffico," p. 16.
56. Enrico Camaleone, "Trasporti collettivi e bilancio comunale: un contrasto insanabile," Capitolium, February 1966, pp. 104–18.

and increase the share of public transportation in total transportation (now only 45 percent as compared to 87 percent in Paris) remains to be seen.[57]

Surveys in various parts of the city reveal satisfaction with private living quarters and even, generally, with the local neighborhood; but there is also sharp dissatisfaction with the lack of clean streets, parks, and recreational facilities. (See Table 10.17.)

Interviews in a Roman borgata (Table 10.18) show much more basic unmet wants, such as drinking water, drainage, schools, pharmacies, street paving and lighting, and markets. Note that the borgata involved is not a shantytown: the houses, although built without city permits, are solidly built structures, many four-and-a-half stories in height.[58]

Table 10. 18. Perception of Neighborhood Quality in a Borgata, 1962

|  | Men | | Women | | Total | |
|---|---|---|---|---|---|---|
| Most-felt needs: | No. | % | No. | % | No. | % |
| Water and sewers | 25 | 58.1 | 15 | 31.9 | 40 | 44.5 |
| Stores and market | 1 | 2.3 | 11 | 23.4 | 12 | 13.4 |
| School | 12 | 27.9 | 16 | 34.0 | 28 | 31.1 |
| Streets | 4 | 9.3 | 6 | 12.8 | 10 | 11.1 |
| Pharmacy, doctor, midwife | 18 | 41.9 | 9 | 19.1 | 27 | 30.0 |
| Newspaper stand | 1 | 2.3 | 1 | 2.1 | 2 | 2.2 |
| Movie | 0 | — | 3 | 6.4 | 3 | 3.3 |
| Telephone | 1 | 2.3 | 2 | 4.3 | 3 | 3.3 |
| Streetlighting | 6 | 14.0 | — | — | 6 | 6.7 |
| Post office | 2 | 4.7 | — | — | 2 | 2.2 |
| No reply | 12 | 27.9 | 15 | 31.9 | 27 | 30.0 |
|  | 82 | 100.0 | 78 | 165.9 | 160 | 174.3 |

Source: Crespi, "Aspetti del rapporto tra strutture urbanistiche," p. 50.

In *The Politics of Despair,* Hadley Cantril reported the results from another survey in a Roman borgata taken in about 1953:

> When the inhabitants of the *borgata* were asked, "What illness most troubles you?" they did not list the ailments and diseases the authorities or experts thought they might, such as tuberculosis, bronchitis, rheumatism, syphilis. Instead, they gave overwhelming first place to the "itch." It is little wonder then that in the *borgata,* as in so much of Italy, the cry is for houses, running water, bathrooms, toilets, and the fundamental necessities of modern life.[59]

Twenty years later, the cry remains the same.

*Comparisons with Other Cities.* According to many if not all indicators of environmental decency and amenity, Rome is not very much better or worse than

57. Ibid. Slowness in building the subway can be blamed on the national government (Ministry of Transport) rather than the city government, which has no construction responsibilities. The pace of building has been so slow that some people have labeled the new subway *"il centrimetropolitano."*

58. Crespi, "Aspetti del rapporto," pp. 5–50.

59. *The Politics of Despair* (New York, 1962), p. 84.

other large Italian cities. The quality of postwar residential districts seems to have been uniformly bad in cities throughout Italy, whether northern or southern, Communist or Christian Democratic. The districts of no city are held up as examples of excellence, although some particular public housing quarters and some private developments (especially those built by SGI) are highly respected. The new Law 167 districts, if and when they are actually completed, will be the first large-scale districts built in Italy with reasonably low density and reasonably high facility standards.[60]

According to some housing quality indicators the Roman record is particularly bad. Table 10.19 shows the percentage of the actual population (1961) living in improper housing (shanties, caves, and so forth) in the leading Italian cities. Rome has the unfortunate distinction of possessing the largest relative and absolute number of shantydwellers among the major Italian cities. Of course, the shantydwellers in the North, around Milan, for example, are located mostly in the communes around the central city rather than in the central city itself. Bologna seems to have been the most successful among the rapidly growing metropolitan areas in providing decent housing for all of its new inhabitants.[61]

If we look at *regular* housing, Rome fares rather better. Table 10.20 shows

Table 10. 19. Numbers and Percentages of Total Population Living in
Irregular Housing, 1961

| City | Total population living in irregular housing | Percentage of total city population living in irregular housing |
|---|---|---|
| Turin | 3,857 | 0.38 |
| Genoa | 6,207 | 0.79 |
| Milan | 3,602 | 0.02 |
| Bologna | 1,621 | 0.36 |
| Venice | 3,840 | 1.10 |
| Florence | 2,600 | 0.60 |
| Rome | 72,203 | 3.30 |
| Naples | 21,514 | 1.82 |
| Palermo | 16,257 | 2.72 |

*Source:* Calculated from Istat, *10° Censimento,* vol. 8, *Abitazioni* (Rome, 1967).

60. A recent comparative study of the formulation and implementation of Law 167 housing programs in Bologna, Rome, Milan, Turin, and Genoa rates Bologna as by far the best and Milan and Genoa as by far the worst, with Rome and Turin somewhere in between. The Bologna operation is rated highest because it attempts more than any of the others to reshape the pattern of urban development. New low-cost housing districts have been located in semicentral areas of the city so as to break the normal pattern of Italian city development, which reserves the center for business, the semicentral neighborhoods for the middle-class residences, and peripheral areas for lower-class residences and industry. Most of the new development in Bologna has been steered into these new districts, where much low-cost housing has been built. Operations under Law 167 in other cities are given poor ratings because of the small scale of the programs, the choice of the usual remote areas for low-cost housing, and the slow pace of implementation. The Rome Law 167 program is given low marks on implementation but rather high marks for the scope of the program's intentions. See Valeria Erba, "Alcuni esempi di applicazione," pp. 46–53.

61. I. Montanelli et al., *Italia sotto inchiesta,* p. 383.

Table 10.20 Percentage of Regular Dwellings Equipped with Running Water and
Central Heating in Major Italian Cities, 1961

| City | percentage of regular dwellings with running water | percentage of regular dwellings with central heating |
|------|------|------|
| Turin | 93.9 | 70.4 |
| Genoa | 93.1 | 35.5 |
| Milan | 93.1 | 64.6 |
| Bologna | 97.3 | 50.0 |
| Venice | 91.6 | 31.1 |
| Florence | 91.9 | 29.6 |
| Rome | 94.7 | 48.5 |
| Naples | 90.5 | 6.3 |
| Palermo | 91.8 | 3.6 |

*Source:* Calculated from Istat, *10° Censimento,* vol. 8, *Abitazioni* (Rome, 1967).

Table 10. 21. Distribution of Dwellings by Degree of Crowding and Ownership
Type in Major Italian Cities, 1966

| City | Persons per room | | | | | |
|------|------|------|------|------|------|------|
| | Less than 1 person/ room | 1–2.99 persons/ room | 2–2.99 persons/ room | 3–3.99 persons/ room | 4 or more persons/ room | Total % |
| | *All dwellings* | | | | | |
| Rome | 36.9 | 50.9 | 9.4 | 1.7 | 1.1 | 100.0 |
| Milan | 35.0 | 49.4 | 12.6 | 2.0 | 1.0 | 100.0 |
| Naples | 31.9 | 43.5 | 13.4 | 5.8 | 5.4 | 100.0 |
| Turin | 25.3 | 60.2 | 11.2 | 2.3 | 1.0 | 100.0 |
| Genoa | 85.1 | 14.0 | 0.6 | 0.3 | 0.0 | 100.0 |
| Palermo | 35.4 | 35.5 | 14.1 | 2.7 | 2.3 | 100.0 |
| | *Owner-occupied dwellings* | | | | | |
| Rome | 48.4 | 46.2 | 4.2 | 0.7 | 0.5 | 100.0 |
| Milan | 51.4 | 41.9 | 5.9 | 0.4 | 0.4 | 100.0 |
| Naples | 58.2 | 34.7 | 5.2 | 1.2 | 0.7 | 100.0 |
| Turin | 48.1 | 43.7 | 6.8 | 1.4 | 0.0 | 100.0 |
| Genoa | 91.2 | 8.8 | 0.0 | 0.0 | 0.0 | 100.0 |
| Palermo | 55.4 | 38.8 | 4.8 | 0.5 | 0.5 | 100.0 |
| | *Rented dwellings* | | | | | |
| Rome | 31.5 | 53.8 | 11.8 | 1.9 | 1.0 | 100.0 |
| Milan | 31.4 | 51.4 | 14.0 | 2.2 | 1.0 | 100.0 |
| Naples | 22.7 | 46.6 | 16.3 | 7.2 | 7.2 | 100.0 |
| Turin | 21.3 | 63.2 | 12.1 | 2.2 | 1.2 | 100.0 |
| Genoa | 81.7 | 17.2 | 0.8 | 0.3 | 0.0 | 100.0 |
| Palermo | 24.2 | 51.4 | 18.5 | 3.4 | 2.5 | 100.0 |
| | *Publicly owned dwellings* | | | | | |
| Rome | 30.5 | 53.9 | 12.7 | 2.1 | 0.8 | 100.0 |
| Milan | 22.8 | 55.9 | 17.2 | 3.0 | 1.1 | 100.0 |
| Naples | 24.1 | 57.7 | 13.1 | 2.2 | 2.9 | 100.0 |
| Turin | 16.5 | 69.9 | 10.7 | 1.9 | 1.0 | 100.0 |
| Genoa | 66.2 | 28.6 | 3.9 | 1.3 | 0.0 | 100.0 |
| Palermo | 32.1 | 50.0 | 14.3 | 3.6 | 0.0 | 100.0 |

*Source:* Istat, *Indagine speciale sulle abitazioni al 20 gennaio 1966* (Rome, 1968), p. 108.

the percentage of regular housing equipped with running water and with central
heating in the major Italian cities. It will be noted that although it is located in a
much milder climatic zone, Rome had a greater percentage of centrally heated
dwellings than Florence, Venice, or Genoa.

Table 10.21 shows the distribution of dwellings in the various cities by type of crowding and type of ownership. According to this table, Rome has a larger proportion of its dwellings in the "superior" category (under one person per room) than any city except Genoa. A larger proportion of its dwellings are in the combined "superior" and "average" (one to two persons per room) categories than any city except Genoa. This seems to be true for owner-occupied dwellings as well as for rented dwellings, for publicly as well as privately owned dwellings.

Table 10.22 shows the distribution of dwellings among occupancy types in the leading cities as of January 1966. Note that Rome had the highest proportion of owner-occupied dwellings of any major Italian city—36 percent as compared to 21.8 percent for Milan. It also had the largest proportion of publicly owned dwellings—12 percent—of any city.

Rome, again, does not show up badly when its performance is appraised in terms of the age of the city building code (See Table 10.23). Rome has not yet

Table 10. 22. Distribution of Dwellings among Occupancy Types
in Leading Italian Cities, 1966
(Percentages)

|  | Owner-occupied | Rented from private owners | | | Publicly owned | Other title |
|---|---|---|---|---|---|---|
|  |  | Frozen[a] 1947 | Frozen[b] 1963 | Un-controlled |  |  |
| Rome | 36.0 | 9.7 | 32.3 | 3.5 | 12.0 | 6.5 |
| Milan | 21.8 | 19.3 | 37.4 | 4.3 | 11.0 | 6.2 |
| Naples | 23.5 | 23.7 | 35.8 | 3.2 | 7.5 | 6.3 |
| Turin | 16.4 | 5.0 | 48.1 | 10.0 | 6.1 | 4.4 |
| Genoa | 35.5 | 31.0 | 15.4 | 5.5 | 5.8 | 6.8 |
| Palermo | 28.1 | 13.3 | 41.1 | 5.8 | 3.8 | 7.9 |
| Mean | 27.1 | 14.3 | 38.3 | 5.1 | 9.0 | 6.2 |

Source: Istat, Indagine speciale sulle abitazioni al 20 gennaio 1966, (Rome, 1965), pp. 38–39.
a. Frozen, 1947: where the lease dates from before March 1, 1947, and the rental is fixed by Decree-haw of February 27, 1947, as amended, but where landlord and tenant have agreed to a different, usually higher, sum.
b. Frozen, 1963, and renegotiated: where leases date from March 1, 1947 and November 6, 1963, where rental is determined by Law 1444 of November 6, 1963, subject to private negotiation between landlord and tenant.

Table 10. 23. Comparative Age of the Building Code in Major
Italian Cities, as of 1963

| City | Approval date for building code |
|---|---|
| Turin | 1956 |
| Milan | 1921 |
| Venice | 1930 |
| Genoa | 1952 |
| Bologna | 1912 |
| Florence | 1943 |
| Rome | 1934 |
| Naples | 1935 |

Source: Urbanistica, March 1963, pp. 84–115.

Table 10.24. Square Meters per Person of Parks and Recreational Areas in Some
Leading Cities, 1962

| City | Square meters of parks and recreational areas per person |
|------|------|
| Naples | 0.58 |
| Milan | 1.00 |
| Rome | 1.50 |
| Turin | 1.90 |
| Paris | 7.00 |
| London | 11.00 |
| Copenhagen | 12.00 |
| Cologne | 20.00 |
| Amsterdam | 25.00 |
| Stockholm | 80.00 |
| Washington | 117.00 |

Source: Antonio Cederna, Mirabilia Urbis (Turin: Einaudi, 1965), p. 462.

Table 10.25. Sports Facilities in Leading Italian Cities*

| City | Gymnasiums | Soccer fields | Swimming pools | Playgrounds |
|------|-----------|--------------|----------------|-------------|
| Turin | 239 | 118 | 20 | 27 |
| Milan | 426 | 436 | 58 | 104 |
| Genoa | 83 | 48 | 10 | 14 |
| Venice | 99 | 66 | 4 | 35 |
| Bologna | 123 | 92 | 9 | 21 |
| Florence | 110 | 91 | 9 | 11 |
| Rome | 383 | 171 | 33 | 28 |
| Naples | 204 | 44 | 5 | 7 |
| Palermo | 41 | 31 | 1 | 1 |

Source: Istat, Statistica degli impianti sportivi al 1° gennaio 1961
(Rome, September 1964), pp. 52–55.
*Note that these include private facilities, many of which are closed to the public. Note also
that the figures apply to the entire province, not merely the provincial capital.

formulated a new code in conformity with the 1962 master plan and is thus still
working with the 1934 building code. But the last major revision of the Milan
building code was carried out in 1921 and of the Bologna building code in 1912.

The performance of other Italian cities in providing parks and recreational
facilities seems to have been no better than Rome's poor performance in this
regard. Milan had one square meter of parks and recreation areas per person as
compared to 1.5 square meters for Rome. Table 10.24 sets out the comparative
data for some Italian and foreign cities.

Rome, despite its population, has fewer sports and recreational facilities than
Milan but, as Table 10.25 suggests, no Italian city has done very much in this
area. As with parks, we do not know whether the facilities are few because
demand is light, or vice versa.

Environmental comparisons among major Italian cities can also be made in terms of public health indicators. Table 10.26 shows the incidence of typhoid fever per 10,000 residents in various Italian cities (provinces) and in various countries. In absolute terms, Rome province has more typhoid cases than the United States, indicating a serious malfunctioning in the city's environmental sanitation, even if not as serious as that in Naples or in Matera, another southern Italian town.[62]

It should also be said that Rome has relatively few crimes of violence, as compared to southern Italian cities and to U.S. cities. Rome remains a relative safe city despite the imposing social and demographic changes.[63] Table 10.27 shows a low absolute number of homicides per year in Rome, especially as compared to Naples. Table 10.28 shows the relatively few convictions for murder in Lazio region, as compared to the Naples region (Campania) and to Sicily. Table 10.29 shows the same dearth of violent crime among Roman youths, again measured in absolute terms, although it also shows a fairly high number of youthful crimes against property.

Table 10.26. Incidence of Typhoid and Paratyphoid Infection in Major Italian
Cities and Selected Countries, 1969

| City*<br>Country | Cases of typhoid<br>fever and paratyphoid<br>infection per 10,000<br>residents |
|---|---|
| Bologna | 0.44 |
| Florence | 0.65 |
| Milan | 1.6 |
| Rome | 1.7 |
| Naples | 5.7 |
| Matera | 18.5 |
| Norway | 0.03 |
| Denmark | 0.05 |
| Sweden | 0.12 |
| U.S.A. | 0.017 |
| England | 0.06 |
| Japan | 0.05 |
| France | 0.3 |
| Italy | 2.4 |

Source: Il Messaggero, September 18, 1960.
*The figures apply to the entire province, not merely to the provincial capital.

62. Il Messaggero, September 18, 1970.
63. There were about the same number of murders in Italy in 1965 as in the New York Metropolitan area in 1969. The U.S., with four times the population of Italy, in 1969 had 14,587 murders as compared to 1,130 for Italy in 1965. (1971 World Almanac, pp. 77–78; Annuario di Statistiche Giudiziarie 1965, Rome, 1968, p. 224). Crimes of violence are rare in Rome, compared to crimes against property. Nor, despite the constant confrontations in Rome between the police and political extremists, have there been many deaths caused by "political violence." L'Espresso (June 4, 1961) counted 64 deaths of civilians caused by encounters with the police in all of Italy since 1948, mostly during labor or peasant agitations, and none had occurred in Rome.

Table 10.27. Numbers of Voluntary Homicides in Various Regions of Italy, 1965

| Appellate court district | Voluntary homicides (1965) |
|---|---|
| Turin | 50 |
| Milan | 69 |
| Venice | 19 |
| Genoa | 42 |
| Bologna | 30 |
| Florence | 27 |
| Rome | 62 |
| Naples | 218 |
| Palermo | 91 |
| Total for Italy | 1,130 |

Source: Istat, *Annuario di Statistiche Giudiziare 1965* (Rome, 1968), pp. 219–24.

Table 10.28. Region of Residence of Those Found Guilty of Voluntary Homicide, 1965

| | |
|---|---|
| Piedmont (Turin) | 21 |
| Lombardy (Milan) | 19 |
| Veneto (Venice) | 7 |
| Liguria (Genoa) | 14 |
| Emilia-Romagna (Bologna) | 7 |
| Tuscany (Florence) | 7 |
| Lazio (Rome) | 7 |
| Campania (Naples) | 128 |
| Sicily (Palermo) | 99 |
| Total for Italy | 470 |

Source: Istat, *Annuario di Statistiche Giudiziarie 1965* (Rome, 1968), pp. 240–42.

Table 10.29. Juvenile Crimes against Persons and Property in Leading Italian Cities, 1965

| City where crime committed | Against persons | Against property |
|---|---|---|
| | 107 | 548 |
| Milan | 73 | 258 |
| Venice | 46 | 142 |
| Genoa | 102 | 181 |
| Bologna | 7 | 34 |
| Florence | 156 | 186 |
| Rome | 172 | 822 |
| Naples | 626 | 663 |
| Palermo | 86 | 340 |

Source: Istat, *Annuario di Statistiche Guidiziarie 1965* (Rome, 1968), p. 302.

### COMPARISONS AND EXPLANATIONS

By various standards Roman performance seems to lie about midway between that of the wealthier or more civic-minded cities of the Italian North and that of the poorer, less politically developed cities of the South.[64] This seems to be true

64. Average electoral turnout in the twenty-one largest cities in northern and central Italy in 1960–62 was 91.6%, while in the ten largest southern cities it was 86.0%. See Fried, "Communism, Urban Budgets, and the Two Italies".

Table 10.30. Fiscal Behavior in Rome as Compared to Northern and Southern Cities

| Fiscal variable | Average for 21 north-central cities | Rome | Average for 10 southern cities |
|---|---|---|---|
| Per capita city income tax, 1965 | 5,307 lire | 3,577 lire | 2,254 lire |
| Per capita city sales tax, 1965 | 10,751 lire | 8,483 lire | 7,327 lire |
| Per capita operating expenditures, 1961 | 25,010 lire | 32,130 lire | 24,890 lire |
| Per capita operating revenues, 1961 | 26,640 lire | 26,090 lire | 13,470 lire |
| Per capita city income tax as % of per capita provincial income | 1.02% | 0.63% | 0.74% |
| Collection costs as % of sales tax yields, 1966 | 17.2% | 13.2% | 28.5% |
| Years of operating deficit, 1951–61 | 5.4 years | 10 years | 9.1 years |
| Interest payments as % of operating revenues, 1964 | 19.9% | 38.6% | 49.7% |
| Salaries and interest payments as % of operating revenues, 1964 | 71.7% | 109.2% | 142.2% |
| Per capita interest payments, 1961 | 1,448 lire | 7,218 lire | 1,850 lire |

Source: R. Fried, "Communism, Urban Budgets, and the Two Italies: A Case Study in Comparative Urban Government," The Journal of Politics, 33 (1971), 1029.

not only for planning, but for other kinds of municipal outputs as well. The performance of Rome in the fiscal area has been compared in another study with that of the other thirty Italian cities with more than one hundred thousand people.[65] It was found that Rome in many ways behaved like a southern city in matters of municipal finance. Like southern cities, its taxes were low in relation to community wealth, while its expenditures far exceeded the revenues it was willing and able to collect. Like southern cities, it was forced in consequence to devote an increasingly large share of its operating revenues to interest payments on debts contracted to cover its operating deficit. And also like southern cities, its insolvency is chronic rather than recent. However, unlike southern cities, its tax collection costs have been low and the level of its per capita revenues and capital investments rather high (see Table 10:30).

In the previous chapters, planning performance in Rome has been related to a series of political, economic, and cultural variables. It is difficult to specify the relative importance of each of these variables in shaping the outcomes in Roman planning, but perhaps the findings of the comparative study of fiscal performance are applicable to planning also. The study of fiscal outputs suggests that "civic culture" (as indicated in Table 10.31 by "latitude" and "turnout"), socioeconomic development (income and industry), and city size are more strongly associated with performance differences—at least in the fiscal area—than such variables as national policy, the form of government, or even the nature of the local party system. Despite the polarization of Italian party politics, despite the fact that some cities are controlled by the Communists and others by the extreme Right, local party systems seem to have much less impact on municipal policies than region, economic development, and demography (see Table 10:31).

65. Ibid.

Table 10.31. Correlations between Sociopolitical Characteristics and Fiscal Outputs in the 31 Largest Italian Cities, 1961–1965*

| | Communist strength | Christian Democ. strength | Right-wing strength | Electoral turnout | Economic growth | Industry | Latitude | Per-capita income | Population size | Immigration growth | Rurality | Density | Literacy |
|---|---|---|---|---|---|---|---|---|---|---|---|---|---|
| Total operating revenues (1961) | | | | | | .307 | | .621 | .938 | .345 | −.399 | .424 | |
| Per capita operating revenues (1961) | | | −.506 | .609 | | .699 | .800 | .801 | .372 | .687 | −.373 | | .698 |
| Per capita city income tax | | | −.408 | .547 | | .718 | .648 | .489 | | .481 | | | .483 |
| Per capita city consumption tax receipts | | | −.513 | .630 | | .674 | .707 | .658 | | .617 | | | .520 |
| City income-tax pressure | | | | .378 | | .529 | .417 | | | | | | |
| Tax-collection costs | | | .550 | −.704 | | −.423 | −.702 | −.529 | | −.631 | | | −.618 |
| Total operating expenditures | | | .350 | | | | | .448 | .994 | | −.396 | .444 | |
| Per capita operating expenditures | | | | | | | | | .555 | | −.400 | .308 | |
| Operating expenditures / Operating revenues | | .314 | .403 | −.706 | | −.638 | −.816 | −.572 | | −.439 | | | −.612 |
| Per capita interest payments | −.389 | .317 | | −.376 | | | −.422 | | .430 | | | | |
| Interest payments / Operating revenues | −.398 | .381 | .323 | −.705 | | −.509 | −.768 | −.442 | | −.300 | | | −.556 |
| Per capita investment | | | | | | .421 | .338 | .336 | .374 | .349 | −.309 | .468 | .357 |
| Indirect taxes / Operating revenues | | | | | | | | | | | | | |
| Direct taxes / Operating revenues | | | −.318 | .345 | | .326 | | | | | | | |
| Incr. operating expenditures / Incr. operating revenues | | .352 | | −.493 | | −.553 | −.600 | | | −.401 | | | −.423 |
| Years of operating deficit | | | | | | .457 | −.543 | .374 | −.569 | −.760 | −.423 | | −.564 |

Source: Fried, "Communism, Urban Budgets, and the Two Italies," pp. 1032-24.
*Correlations with less than .05 significance have been omitted.

Assuming that the central tendencies identified in Table 10:31 apply to Rome, and to planning, the correlation coefficients in that table imply that Roman municipal behavior is largely to be explained by the fact that it is large in size, semi-southern, and non-industrial. While size and economic development seem plausible as constraints on performance, there may be some doubts as to the meaning of "southern-ness," or "latitude" as a constraint. "Latitude" is the most powerful single factor accounting (statistically) for differences in the fiscal and perhaps planning behavior of Italian cities. But while its impact is obvious, its exact nature is not obvious at all. "Latitude," in fact, cannot be reduced to any particular variable or combination of variables and its impact on performance remains, even when such factors as industrialization and economic development are held constant. Poor (and therefore atypical) northern cities tend to act like northern cities, while the wealthier, industrialized (and therefore atypical) southern cities tend to act like southern cities.

The comparative study of Italian municipal fiscal behavior suggests the existence of a dualistic or, more precisely, a polarized *governmental culture*, composed of distinctively northern and southern patterns of municipal behavior that cannot be entirely explained in terms of the usual political, social, and economic indicators. It is not clear whether this polarity derives from differences in political culture, differences in socioeconomic structure, or differences in culture generally. But even if the nature of "latitude" is not clear and even if it is obviously not a social force in itself, it does indicate by proxy some independent variables of considerable force in shaping the culture of Italian municipal government.[66] Thus Rome's middling performance would seem to derive from its position midway between northern and southern governmental cultures.

66. Ibid.

# 11

# STRATEGIES FOR
# IMPROVING
# PERFORMANCE

Of the constraints on planning effectiveness in Rome, which seem to be the most subject to change and manipulation? Which of the "independent variables" shaping performance offer the greatest leverage for improving performance in the planning field? Can planning effectiveness in Rome be improved more by changing the structures of Roman government, changing the pattern of the Roman economy, changing national urban policy, or changing community values and beliefs?

## CHANGING ROMAN GOVERNMENT

Several major reforms of governmental structure have been proposed to improve the city's planning performance. These include: creation of the Lazio regional government; creation of a metropolitan planning district *(comprensorio)*; reorganization and reform of the city planning departments; creation of the Permanent Planning Institute; and creation of district or borough councils.

The Lazio regional government, elected for the first time in June 1970, is empowered by the constitution to legislate in the field of urban planning, within the framework of the "general principles" laid down in an act of Parliament. Since Parliament has not yet passed the necessary "framework-law" *(legge-quadro)*, it is not quite clear what Lazio region (or any of the other regional governments) can do to change the general conditions—legislative and financial —under which Roman planning must be carried out. The first regional giunta, elected by the Lazio Assembly in September 1970, placed *"urbanistica"* or city planning at the head of its program, thus recognizing the importance of planning and acknowledging regional responsibilities in the matter.

The regions were created in the hope that they would break the immobilistic tendencies of the centralized, bureaucratic Italian state. Whether regional governments will be any more capable than the national government of stimulating more effective controls over urban and regional development remains to be seen. It should be said that much the same balance of political forces now exists in Lazio region as has existed for some time in the Parliament. Progress in reforming planning legislation at the national level has been paralyzed by bitter fights over the extent of property rights under the proposed new systems of planning. It is not likely that the forces of the Center-Left, paralyzed by the conflict between "collectivists" and "privatists," will be any more capable to resolving this conflict at the regional level than they have been at the national level.[1]

It is hoped that the region may be able to use its authority and good offices to reconcile emerging conflicts of interest within Lazio as a whole and between Rome and its immediate neighbors. The region may show greater interest than the national Ministry of Public Works in resuming the intercommunal plan operation around Rome. Planning, in fact, may be just the area in which Lazio region finds a reason for its existence.

Creation of metropolitan planning districts *(comprensori)* has been proposed in each of the several national urban planning bills but, since none of these bills has been passed, it is difficult to say what impact the proposed new planning districts would have.[2] Undoubtedly, some of Rome's problems could be eased by cooperative gestures on the part of neighboring communes, but there seems to be little reason for those communes to provide open spaces, recreational facilities, "planned development," or to make other land use commitments simply to serve the needs of Rome's population. The communes around Rome, like the communes around Milan, Turin, and Bologna, have all taken a narrow view of planning issues and have tended to welcome any and all building initiatives, regardless of the impact on adjacent communes or on their own long-term interests.

The intercommunal plan formulated in 1959–60 has languished since that time in the files of the Ministry of Public Works. None of the forty or so communes involved has taken the trouble to adopt the plan and incorporate its decisions in communal zoning ordinances, if any. Intercommunal planning ventures have suffered from the same ideological, economic, partisan, and personal conflicts that have marked master planning operations in the individual communes. In all Italian metropolitan areas there is strong suspicion of the metropolis and reluctance to surrender communal autonomy to collective metropolitan planning operations. The suspiciousness of the smaller communes is usually matched

1. For the program of the first regional giunta, see *Il Messaggero,* September 10, 1970. The first year of the Lazio region has not been encouraging; action by the regional government has been paralyzed by the same acute conflicts over policies and patronage that have plagued the Center-Left coalition at the national and local levels since the early 1960s.

2. On the problem of planning districts, see Paolo Ghera, *La problematica comprensoriale in Italia dal dopoguerra ad oggi* (Rome: Centro di Studi e Documentazione per la Pianificazione Territoriale, University of Rome, 1966).

by the disdain with which they are regarded by the officials of the metropolis. Intercommunal planning in Rome was long delayed, it is said, by the refusal of the mayor of Rome to sit down at the same table on a plane of seeming equality with the mayor of Monteporzio Catone. The communes around Milan revolted against the initial attempt by the city of Milan to decide by itself what the Milanese intercommunal plan was going to be and the operation was blocked until a more voluntaristic, egalitarian formula for collaboration could be found.[3] Central city–suburban diffidence has often been aggravated by partisan differences: the central city has usually been in moderate hands, while the suburban communes have often been dominated by the extreme Left. But even where both central city and suburbs are controlled by the same forces, as in Bologna, there is the same suburban resistance to planning leadership by the central city. Voluntary participation in a metropolitan planning district seems, somehow, less likely to produce the needed cooperative action in the metropolitan area than the intervention of a higher level authority, namely the region.

When the Rome master plan was adopted by the city council in December 1962, the giunta committed the Center-Left administration to a series of reforms, including the reorganization of the city's own planning offices and the creation of a new planning agency, the Permanent Planning Institute, with metropolitan area scope. In the years since passage of the plan there has been no major reform in planning administration, and the Permanent Planning Institute has not been created. Partisanship and factionalism have played a major role in this. The Christian Democrats, as the principal representatives of conservative planning interests and as the major government party, have publicly supported the notion of administrative reform but privately opposed it on grounds of party power. The DC has controlled the existing planning offices since 1960 and would view reform as a threat to its control over actual, day-to-day planning policy in the city. A Permanent Planning Institute, with its representatives of progressive planners (particularly Socialists) and of neighboring communes (leftists), would, if given charge of master plan implementation and revision, destroy the DC monopoly over plan administration. It would also place some measure of control over planning policy in Rome in the hands of communal officials from the surrounding areas. The Permanent Planning Institute was, in fact, to be part of metropolitan planning district, in which Rome might not have as much influence as it wished to have.[4]

Creation of the Permanent Planning Institute, given the uncertainties about the role it might play and about who would control it, becomes increasingly unlikely, as does any root-and-branch reform of the planning offices. Just possibly, improved performance by these offices—at least according to "pro-

3. Marco Romano, "L'esperienza del piano intercommunale milanese," pp. 16–25.
4. Piero Maria Lugli, "Prospettive di sviluppo di Roma nell'ambito della sua area metropolitana," *Studi Romani,* April-June 1968, pp. 177–90; Mario Fiorentino, "L'attività della Sezione Laziale nel biennio 1964–1965," *Urbanistica,* May 1966, pp. 149–64.

gressive" criteria—may come not from any dramatic structural change but rather from the gradual permeation of agency ideology with progressive values, or at least with the progressive values of some years ago. The mystique of the new master plan will undoubtedly become the conventional wisdom of the planning offices, as it becomes the *traditional* frame of reference for looking at the city's development.

There is a potential for more dramatic reform in efforts to convert the new district councils into active participants in the planning process. The Socialists have proposed that the twelve district councils appointed by the city council in 1969 take an active part in the repression of building illegalities and in the design of detailed plans of implementation.[5] This would constitute, in effect, a major reform of Roman planning administration, by setting up centers of power to rival and check the existing city planning offices. The Center-Left parties that dominate the city council also dominate the twelve district councils, since the latter are not elected by their districts but rather appointed by the city council. The districts may have as little influence on planning administration as their parent body, but it seems likely that at least some of them will try to justify their existence by mobilizing popular support for the kinds of environmental improvements defined in the master plan.[6]

CHANGING THE ROMAN ECONOMY

Economic variables have been of crucial importance in postwar Roman planning, weakening the public sector while at the same time creating an irresistibly strong private sector, based on heavy internal migration, strong demand for land and housing, overinvestment in real estate, and underinvestment in industry. The economic (and moral) inequities created by zoning decisions generated resistence to the whole idea of rezoning the city, which new master plan proposals required. Exorbitant land and housing prices made illegal building attractive and/or necessary, both in the suburbs and in the old center. Monopolistic control of development land and the steep rise in land prices lessened the amount of public housing and public facilities that could be built. Retarded industrialization, based in part on the enormous attractiveness of real estate speculation, impeded growth in the city's tax base, while the lack of significant real estate or income taxation made it difficult for government to discourage land speculation, raise revenues to pay the costs of urbanization, or use tax policy to bolster planning policy.

5. *Avanti!* June 17, 1970.
6. Some of the new district councils have, in fact, begun to assert a major role in the planning process. The tenth district council in December 1970 denounced hundreds of illegal builders to the investigating magistracy, while the eleventh district council rejected the proposal of the City Planning Department to approve the establishment of a new shopping center in the district. The eleventh district council called for more details before it would give approval. (*Il Messaggero,* December 11, 1970.)

Economic measures to relieve the city's plight and to make order in the development process economically feasible might include the following: regional development programs to reduce migratory pressure on the city; programs to industrialize the city itself so as to increase its tax base and its capacity to provide jobs for migrants; large-scale programs of public land acquisition designed to lower land prices and reduce or eliminate private land speculation; major low-cost housing programs to increase the housing supply and also to shape future development; and national programs to provide financial aid to the cities. Which of these strategies—regional development, industrialization, public land operations, public housing, or state aid—seems most likely to increase the city's control over development?

Successful development efforts in central and southern Italy through regional and national economic planning, particularly the investment planning of public enterprises, may help to reduce migratory pressure on the city and presumably lessen the demand for land, housing, and employment. But regional development programs, whether for Lazio region or for the entire *Mezzogiorno,* are not expected to eliminate, though they may reduce, the pressure of migrants on city resources. Even if they do, Rome will still have a high rate of *natural* increase, a rate much higher than the national average, because of previous immigration to the city of southern and rural families with high birth rates.[7]

Regional development programs may help or they may hinder implementation of the second proposed strategy of economic reform: industrialization. Most existing development programs are designed to stimulate industrial development everywhere around the city but not in the city itself. Only a few hundred acres of city land lie, by accident, within the jurisdiction of the *Cassa per il Mezzogiorno* or Fund for Southern Development. City officials have not been able to identify whether the city's true interest lies in industrializing the city's neighbors or in industrializing the city itself. Industrialists, for their part, have shunned the city in favor of communes further south, where they enjoy both proximity to Rome and the tax and credit incentives of the Fund for Southern Development. Because of its relatively high per capita income, Rome has been denied inclusion in either the Fund for Southern Development jurisdiction or the Program for Depressed Areas of Central and Northern Italy (Law No. 614, July 22, 1966). For this and other reasons, efforts to industrialize the city or to modernize its industry have not been very successful.[8]

7. "Five Year Plan," p. 42.

8. The regional economic development plan unanimously adopted by the Lazio regional economic planning committee on July 10, 1969, is a compromise between those anxious to promote development within the city and those pressing for development of the depressed towns of northern and eastern Lazio. See Mario D'Erme, "Vicende ed approvazione del piano regionale di sviluppo del Lazio," *Rassegna del Lazio,* November-December 1969, pp. 7–24. On industralization efforts, see the supplement *Roma produce* in *Capitolium,* March-April 1968, and *Urbanistica Romana,* No. 1, 1968, supplement to *Capitolium,* February 1968. The latter describes previous and current efforts to industrialize the city.

To be sure, industrialization, if it occurs, will bring with it not only new resources but also new problems, for industrial firms may have their own concepts of the public interest and the influence to make these concepts respected. The FIAT company, for example, decided in 1962 to locate a major repair installation for Rome on a site in the northern outskirts of the city that had been designated by the master planners as a green space because of its scenic qualities and its usefulness as a separation between development sectors in the west and east. FIAT's proposal, planners feared, would also increase traffic flowing through the historic center by way of Piazza del Popolo. Despite the protests of the planners, FIAT managed to secure a building permit from the city and went on to build its facility in the north.[9] Under the Planning Act of 1942, moreover, the Ministry of Industry and Commerce may disregard city master plans when it designates sites as industrial zones. Industrialization efforts, if successful, may actually increase the weight of the antiplanning coalition in the city.[10]

Italian planners, despairing of the prospects of regulating private enterprise, have come increasingly to favor public enterprise in the hope that public entrepreneurs will be more responsive to planning requirements than private entrepreneurs have been. The Marxist parties—the Socialists and Communists— have naturally favored this evolution. While seeking nationalization of land as an ultimate goal, the Marxists have supported schemes that call for immediate, large-scale public acquisition of development land at prices below current market value, and permanent public ownership. The centrist parties have been willing to go along with the idea of compensation at less than market value, but they have insisted on the resale of condemned land to private builders at a price that covers purchase price plus the costs of urbanization.

City governments, in the reformers' scenario, will define the particular areas around the city that should be developed, buy them up at prices somewhere between rural acreage and speculative development prices, urbanize them, and resell them at reasonable prices to private builders, cooperatives, and public housing agencies. By purchasing land at less than full market value, the city will be punishing speculators rather than rewarding them for antisocial behavior. When the city pays full market value for land, it transfers funds from taxpayers to the land speculators who have performed no service and have run no risk whatever. When the city pays full market value, moreover, it can buy relatively little land for low-cost housing, schools, or other public purposes.

Great hopes have been placed in the prospect of wholesale public acquisition

9. Luigi Piccinato, "Funzioni e limiti del piano regolatore," *Ulisse,* September 1963, p. 74.
10. The Ministry of Industry's authority to disregard city plans, which it apparently never used, was canceled in the 1967 bridge-law. See Ministero dei Lavori Pubblici, *Legge 6 agosto 1967,* pp. 88–89. Professor Forte has noted that "many businessmen and executives, personally, are real estate owners; and some companies count more on the rise in land values than on their productive energies to balance their books." (*La strategia,* p. 189.)

of development land. General expropriation in zones marked for expansion will, it is generally believed, take the planning process out of politics. The failures of Italian planning are attributed to the fact that planning decisions have not been neutral: they have created the fortunes of some property owners and destroyed the potential fortunes of others; the choice among property owners has not been based on objective factors but on political pressures or personal weaknesses. Municipalization of development land is designed to produce "indifference," that is, genuine neutrality, in the planning process. If everyone's land is taken and everyone is paid roughly the same rate of compensation, then no one will care how the land is used—whether for intensive development, low density residential development, or public facilities. Zoning decisions will create few inequities or controversies since expropriation will distribute the burdens and benefits of planning decisions so evenly as to remove any incentive for active, self-interested participation in the planning process. Furthermore, municipalization is expected to create absolute "indifference" among the *public* decision makers, who, freed from the pressures of private property owners, will be able to make decisions on the basis of objective analysis. They will have no ability to favor one set of owners over another; they will not be able to use planning authority for the purposes of extortion or discrimination.[11]

The idea of large-scale municipalization of development land at below market prices is as appealing as it is utopian. Abolition of the building land market assumes, first of all, that public authorities have the funds necessary for the operation; but Italian municipalities at present are barely able to pay the salaries of their employees and the interest payments on their loans. Nothing short of a revolution in local government finance will make the municipalization scheme feasible.

Second, the scheme assumes that Italian property owners will remain indifferent to proposals for wholesale semiconfiscatory land purchases, whereas events of recent years have demonstrated that nothing less than a revolution in attitudes toward private property would be required for such an innovation in national policy. Third, the scheme assumes that municipalization will have a similar revolutionary impact on the attitudes of public decision makers. Through municipalization, one of the leading Italian city planners has written, "plans will be removed from the arbitrary discretion of public and private decision makers and will be scientifically designed on the basis of mathematical methods for the identification of the optimal combination of factors that will minimize total costs at a given level of efficiency."[12]

Even if Italian communes acquired the necessary funds and even if Italian property owners somehow consented to the principle of compensation at less than market value, it may still be doubted that Italian public decisionmakers

11. Forte, *La strategia,* pp. 395–400; Corwin R. Mocine, "Urban Growth and a New Planning Law in Italy," *Land Economics, 41* (1965), 347–53; Sullo, *Lo scandalo,* passim.
12. Giuseppe Samonà, *L'urbanistica e l'avvenire della città* (Bari, 1967, p. 276.)

would be willing to surrender their hard-won control over development to cost-benefit analysts in their planning departments. It may also be likely that public enterpreneurs would be tempted to exploit their monopolistic powers for political purposes, or simply to fill empty municipal coffers.

Schemes for massive public intervention in the housing market have many of the same weaknesses. They assume a financial capability that does not exist on the part of the cities. Performance in the field of low-cost housing has been a national scandal.[13] Relatively little public investment has been made in low-cost housing in postwar Italy and even the monies appropriated have been spent with an infuriating slowness. Moreover, there has been little or no co-ordination among the several housing programs and no coordination at all between the housing programs and city planning.[14] Only in recent years, under Law 167, have some efforts been made to coordinate the activities of the housing agencies with each other and with the city planning departments. But despite agitation by student and labor groups, periodic invasions of unoccupied public housing, even demonstrations by shantydwellers in St. Peter's Square, the national government has stinted on appropriations for low-cost housing and relied instead on rent controls and bans on evictions to relieve the situation. Thus the Law 167 program in Rome, which many hoped would combine the resources and purposes of the housing and planning movements, has been stalled by lack of funds. As of late 1970, seven years after council adoption of the Law 167 program, not one of the new residential districts has been urbanized, built, and inhabited.

Another strategy for coping with the city's growth has involved the search for greater revenues in the form of increased state aid. During much of the postwar period, city officials focused their efforts and hopes on a special law for Rome that would not only provide greater revenues for the city, including regular state grants to the city as national capital, but at the same time increase the city's autonomy from the controls of the national government, make the city government more efficient by transferring authority from the council to the giunta, and create district councils.[15] In 1949, the first Rebecchini giunta succeeded in having a bipartite state-city commission established to study the question, but the notion of a special law for Rome set off a storm of protest from

13. Between 1951 and 1961 the Italian state contributed toward the building of 13% of Italian housing, as compared to government contributions of 69% in Holland, 56% in Denmark, 47% in France, 43% in Belgium, 36% in Sweden, and 27% in West Germany. (*Paese Sera*, May 17, 1966.)

14. M. Vittorini, *Pianificazione urbanistica*, passim; David Gazzani, "Il problema della casa oggi," *Rivista di Sociologia*, December 1969, pp. 189–200; Vittorio Chaia, "Vent'anni di edilizia sovvenzionate," *Casabella*, February 1968, pp. 20–25.

15. On the history of special laws for Rome, see L. Cattani et al., *Le leggi speciali per la città di Roma dal 1870 ad oggi* (Rome, 1956); Comune di Roma, *Una legge per la capitale* (Rome, 1956); A. Petrucci, *Un piano per Roma*, pp. 69–105; Atti Parlamentari, Legislatura II, Disegni di Legge e Relazioni, Documenti, Senato della Repubblica, No. 1296 and 1760-A (February 10, 1958).

all over the peninsula, especially in Milan. Anti-Romanism blocked action on the pledges and proposals of successive governments during the 1950s and early 1960s. Only in November 1964 did Parliament finally vote a special law, but it was far from the general law that the city had sought for all those years. The law merely authorized the city to borrow 25 million dollars from the state and foreign lenders, with a state guarantee, to be spent on specified public works (aqueducts, streets, sewers, schools) over a five-year period. By 1964 revenues were reduced to the point that, without the special law, the city could not pay for any capital improvements.

The special law was not, then, very successful in solving the city's basic revenue problems; it has provided emergency relief only. The rest of the country is not sympathetic to the idea of giving special treatment to the capital. Rome has long been seen as a perennial welfare client, undeserving, parasitic, taking life easy while other people have to work hard to produce the wealth that is then taxed to pay for Roman bread and circuses. Romans are thought to excel in the art of getting something for nothing; the Milanese believe, for example, that in Rome there are 20,000 free tickets available for every soccer game and 300 free tickets for every opera performance. There is, in effect, a variety of anti-Romanism to suit every taste. To anticlericals, Rome is papal; to hard-working businessmen, Rome is corrupt, backward, slothful, and bureaucratic; to fanatics and believers, Rome is skeptical and indifferent; to leftists, Rome is fascist, bourbonic, rhetorical; to northerners, Rome is southern; to aristocrats, Rome is plebeian.[16]

There are many cities and towns that feel just as qualified for state aid, even if none is the national capital. The Roman record for financial management and general management of civic affairs has not been considered exemplary. Ironically, the Radical campaign against the city in the fifties, which reinforced the identification of the city with corruption and *"malgoverno,"* is now preventing the city from securing sympathetic attention to its claims, even as a city that has reformed its ways. Most Italian legislation does not provide for grants-in-aid; the Italian state has simply not been very generous to provinces and communes, preferring to dispense services directly, and Rome's lack of success is typical of the other cities that have pressed for state aid. The state is usually willing to do no more than grant authority to a city to go further into debt.

## CHANGING ITALIAN NATIONAL POLICY

Rome's planning difficulties have derived in large degree from the city's own lack of internal cohesion, efficiency, and determination, but equally, if not more, from the mediocre support for planning provided by the Italian government. Despite the social and economic transformation of the country, created

16. See, for example, Filippo Sacchi, "Perchè gli italiani non amano Roma," *La Stampa,* June 10, 1956, and Arturo Carlo Jemolo, "Io defendo Roma," ibid., June 1, 1966.

by postwar industrialization and urbanization, the institutional framework for local government has remained what it was when Italy was basically rural and agrarian: there has been no major revision of the Provincial and Communal Acts of 1915 and 1934, of the Local Government Finance Act of 1931, or of the Urban Planning Act of 1942. Paradoxically, although Italy has long been a centralized, unitary state, the national government has never developed a coherent policy on how its vast powers of control should be used. The emphasis in Italian national urban policy has been predominantly negative: national controls have been used, though never very effectively or systematically, to prevent undesirable local activity rather than to encourage local initiative. Close central review of municipal decisionmaking has seldom prevented municipal corruption or raised the level of municipal performance. Municipal peccadillos have frequently, in fact, been tolerated as part of an implicit policy of reducing the drive for local autonomy. Financially, the policy of the national government has been to decentralize spending while centralizing revenues: to devolve program responsibilities on local governments while reserving to itself the major sources of revenue. Thus most of the financial costs created by postwar economic and urban development have been paid locally, while the increased public revenues generated by development have gone to the central government.[17]

Failure to reform the Provincial and Communal Acts forced Italian urban governments to cope with greatly increased operating responsibilities within a framework of government designed for a different epoch. The mass of procedural formalities that might have served some purpose in the remote past became an irrational hindrance in a period when more people needed more services delivered more rapidly than ever before. The numerous controls inherited from the past were effective not in checking municipal corruption or lethargy but in stifling municipal initiative. The spirit of the old legislation was expressed in a 1961 circular of the Ministry of the Interior which forbade provinces or municipalities from engaging in development planning; most prefects wisely refrained from enforcing the circular.[18] Failure to reform the Local Finance Act of 1931 meant that even the wealthiest and most circumspect communes found themselves forced to borrow funds in order to cover their mounting operating expenses.

The major legislative acts that were passed in order to provide some relief for the cities, such as the 1963 Act to Tax Capital Gains in Building Lots and its companion Act on Low Cost Housing (Law 167), have been enormous disappointments. The tax on building lots, which conservatives had already gutted in Parliament, was further crippled by adverse court decisions. The tax act was designed to provide the cities with funds for investment in Law 167 low-cost housing programs. But yields from the tax on building lots have been so small,

17. Antonio Gori, "Condizioni e prospettive della finanza locale," *Esperienze Amministrative,* December 1964, pp. 41–54.
18. C. Beltrame, "Gli istituti regionali," pp. 69–70

especially given the tendency to litigate almost every single assessment, that there have been no funds available for low-cost housing. The national government has not stepped in to provide alternative sources of funding.[19] Despite the shift to the Center-Left in the early sixties, the Italian government remained wedded to its traditional policy of emphasizing controls over local government, rather than stimulation and assistance, The national government has continued to seek implementation of its goals for Italian cities by means of regulations and moral exhortation rather than by means of spending programs. It has been slow to respond to the Italian urban crisis, and when it has finally acted the actions have not been very effective. The record of national performance in the urban field does not provide encouragement for those who hope to find in national policy the leverage for improving conditions in Rome.

CHANGING ROMAN POLITICS

Two political reforms, both controversial, might help planning in Rome by changing the balance of power in city politics. One would involve restoring the electoral law of 1952; in that year, the party or coalition that received a relative majority of the total vote was given two-thirds of the seats on the city council. Since the Center-Left coalition would presumably win a plurality in Rome, under the 1952 election law (actually Law 84 of February 24, 1951), it would receive the "majority premium" and thus enjoy for the first time a strong and substantial majority for plan implementation and policymaking in general.[20] Under the present electoral law, which dates from 1956, there is a rather exact correspondence between shares of the vote and shares of council seats; exact proportionality has given the Center-Left coalition a bare and weak majority with which to carry out its programs. But the electoral reform idea has certain drawbacks. First, the 1951–52 electoral law gave the Christian Democrats a near majority of thirty-nine out of eighty seats on the council though they received only 31.1 percent of the vote.[21] With thirty-nine seats the Christian Democrats would again be able to govern almost by themselves, to the great disadvantage of their quondam coalition partners. Thus the allies of the DC party are not likely to support reversion to the 1951–52 law, for, though it would greatly strengthen the Center-Left as a whole, it would reduce the weight within that coalition of the lesser parties. An even more serious drawback to this kind of political engineering is that it would be considered fraudulent and illegitimate by much of the Italian public.[22] In 1952 the opposition parties successfully

19. Bruno Zevi, *L'Espresso*, March 1, 1970.
20. On the electoral laws of 1952 and since, see Ministero dell'Interno, *Compendio dei risultati delle elezioni comunali e provinciali dal 1946 al 1960* (Rome, 1961), pp. 3–14.
21. Ibid., p. 169.
22. Cf. Giovanni Sartori, "Political Development and Political Engineering," *Public Policy 1968* (Cambridge, Mass., 1968).

mobilized Italian public opinion against a bill that would have similarly abolished straight proportionality at the national level. The proposed bill was successfully defined as the *"legge-truffa,"* or "swindle law," and the same label would undoubtedly be attached to a similar electoral law for Italian cities if it were again proposed. To change the electoral law would require parliamentary action. Parliament is unlikely to pass a law that might widely be regarded as an attempt by the "losers" to change the rules of the game.

Far more likely, though just as controversial, is the second political reform, involving entry of the Communists into the governing coalition. Frustrations over failure to implement the master plan have led the Socialist leadership in Rome to call for an "opening" to the Communists, as the only way for the city to move ahead on its master plan.[23] Communist participation might vary from common voting in the city council to the actual appointment of Communists to the city giunta—for the first time since 1946.

Since 1962 the Communists have claimed that no progressive planning policy for Rome could be carried out without their active support. They contend that the Socialists, by themselves, lack sufficient force to counteract the conservative pressures on their Christian Democratic allies. Certainly a tripartite coalition of Christian Democrats, Socialists, and Communists would be a good deal further to the left than the existing Christian Democratic–Socialist alliance. But the preconditions for such a tripartite coalition do not seem to exist at present nor are they likely to occur in the near future, at least in Rome.

Christian Democrats in other Italian cities and at the national level are more apt to accept Communist collaboration than are Christian Democrats in Rome.[24] The Socialists may well conclude that their period of collaboration with the Christian Democrats in the Center-Left has meant symbolic victories, such as the master plan of 1962, and some government patronage, but little else. If they decide to insist upon bringing the Communists in to share the responsibilities of power, the Christian Democrats will probably decide, as they did in 1946 and again in 1961, that no coalition is better than a bad coalition.

23. *Avanti!* June 17, 1970. As their precondition for returning to the giunta with the Christian Democrats after the elections of June 1971, the Socialists insisted on a major revision of the master plan that would scale down new development in Rome in favor of development in other parts of Lazio region. The Socialists also demanded a "more democratic and collegial management of master plan administration." Satisfied on neither score, the Socialists refused to reconstitute the Christian Democrat–Socialist (Center-Left) giunta. They did, however, agree to vote with the Christian Democrats on the city council in what amounted to a watered-down version of the Center-Left coalition. (*Il Messaggero,* October 21, 1971.)

24. In its opinion survey in Rome on the eve of the June 1971 elections, the weekly *L'Espresso* asked prospective voters whether, if forced to make the choice, they would prefer to have the Communists brought into the governing coalition, or the neofascists. Fifty-four percent of the sample chose government with neofascist support over government with Communist support; 17% rejected both alternatives; and 30% refused to answer the question. Forty-six percent of the sample opposed incorporation of the Communists into the governing majority in the city, while the same percentage indicated approval of occasional or constant reliance on Communist votes for the passage of measures on the city council. (*L'Espresso,* June 13, 1971.)

Should the Center-Left break down, as it has threatened to do several times since 1962, a prefectoral commissioner for Rome is quite likely and perhaps for a long term.

What coalition will emerge in Rome after the prefectoral commissioner is appointed would undoubtedly depend on the coalition formula determined at the national level. If the national DC decides to turn further to the left and to accept the Communists as active or passive coalition partners, the Rome DC will eventually have to follow the national party line and form the same coalition in Rome. Short of such an eventuality, the prospects for incorporating the Communists into the governing majority at the local level in Rome seem remote.

Even if the Communists were to become part of the governing majority, there is no guarantee that this would affect planning policy for the city in a positive direction. As seen in Bologna, Communists in power can be able managers of the status quo. In Rome, on planning matters, however, their record has been one of responsible, constructive opposition. The Communists have been perhaps the most effective party in shaping and criticizing planning policy, although they have had less impact on the administrative level. They have taken pains at all times since the war to have on their delegation extremely competent spokesmen, both professional planners and politicians experienced in planning matters. Although the Christian Democrats have held power they have not had first-class spokesmen in the planning field, at least in council debates.[25]

Among the determinants of planning performance, the party system is perhaps the one least susceptible to analysis based on linear models and relationships, the one most requiring a complex field theory for adequate understanding. It is difficult to state with any degree of certainty what the effects of a given movement in coalition politics will mean for city policy, so many are the possible countermovements that can intervene between changes in coalition politics and policy outcomes. The complexities of Roman coalition politics are compounded by other aspects of the party system: factionalism, centralized control, bureaucratization, and ideology. A movement at the interparty level may set off a chain reaction of factional conflicts, national party interventions, interest group defections, and cross-party ideological coalitions that make the ultimate consequences for policy very difficult to predict. Thus, for example, if the Socialists move to bring the Communists into the governing coalition, the Christian Democrats may respond by making concessions in planning policy— concessions designed to forestall incorporation of the Communists into the majority. The Byzantine calculations and strategies that make the party system "work" defy the rational imagination.

Is there any prospect or possibility of strengthening the proplanning groups and weakening the antiplanning forces? Certainly a shift to the left in the party system would give the proplanning forces considerably greater and more effec-

25. The leading spokesman for the DC on planning matters during much of the postwar period was Councilman Greggi, whose qualifications have been described above, chap. 8, n. 10

tive access than they have had, just as did the shift to the left involved in the formation of the Center-Left in 1962, both nationally and locally. But despite the fact that a coalition sympathetic to the planning movement has been in power, this has been a period of extraordinary frustration for the planners. The Center-Left, nationally and in Rome, has been unable to keep its pledges of reform in the urban planning field. Nationally, the parties of the Center-Left have found it impossible to agree on the terms of a new general urban planning act; and locally, the Center-Left parties cannot agree on how and when the master plan of 1962 should be implemented. Center-Left promises made in 1962—to create new planning institutions, reform existing plan administration, and commence the major projects of the master plan—have not been kept.

The situation since 1962 has been something of a stalemate rather than, as previously, a one-sided game in favor of the antiplanning interests. Since 1962 the proplanning forces have been able to win at least symbolic or verbal battles at the local and national level, but little more. National and local governments, trapped in the crossfire of intransigent, "maximalist" *fazioni,* have done perhaps all they could do—namely, nothing.

The group pattern has not, however, remained static. On both sides there has emerged, locally and nationally, a growing sector of accommodation, working toward *combinazione.* Conservative forces, especially the larger, more responsible business firms, have come to discern some possible benefits in more orderly urban development patterns and to see planning reform as inevitable and in some respects desirable. Progressives, on the other hand, are perhaps more willing to compromise than before and to acknowledge the legitimacy of some private development interests. Thus conservative journals in Rome can now be found supporting the idea of building the parallel Rome in the east, while Communists, though not the Maoist Proletarian Socialists, are willing to give city approval to a series of private subdivision conventions in the west.[26] There is still a serious dispute, however, about property arrangements in the new eastern directive centers. The Left prefers maximum extension of public ownership, while private builders refuse to build unless they are given the traditional complete title. The progressives have been strengthened to some extent by recent protest demonstrations by Italian labor unions and students on behalf of public housing. They would be further strengthened if the coalition between the building industry and the land speculators could be broken. They will probably benefit from the looser ties between the church and the largest Italian building and real estate corporation, SGI. They would be immensely strengthened if the national government and the city could work out arragements for financing and commencing the vast projects in the east. From such projects the building industry can expect enormous contracts; the institutional interest groups can expect suitable office space; and lower income groups can expect more jobs as

26. *Il Messaggero,* June 7, 1967, and *Giornale d'Italia,* November 10, 1969.

well as the general rehabilitation of the eastern sections of the city. But, in
Lewis Carroll terms, this is tantamount to saying that if planning can become
effective the planning groups will become more powerful, rather than vice versa.

CHANGING COMMUNITY VALUES

We come now to the last variable affecting planning performance in Rome:
the values and beliefs of its citizens. Many of these values and beliefs, as already
noted, run contrary to what seems to be necessary for good planning. Can they
be changed? Can the environmental standards and expectations of the city's
social groups be raised? Can this be done with due regard for the possibilities of
satisfying those higher standards of performance? Can Romans be transformed
into good citizens, oriented to the achievement of collective goods? Can Romans
be made into law-abiding citizens, predisposed to obey the terms of the building
and zoning codes, patient enough to wait for the issuance of a permit before
subdividing and building, and conscientious enough to abide by the terms of
subdivision and building permits? Can Romans be made to refuse to buy apartments in neighborhoods without light, open space, green, or even paved streets
and sewers? Can they be made to applaud the demolition of illegally built
structures and to condemn, rather than admire, the producers of unauthorized
building lots and buildings? Can Romans be persuaded to have less concern with
private property rights and more concern for the quality of their civic environment?

A cynic might answer these questions with another: if Romans are to be
transformed through a process of civic education or reeducation, who is to
serve as their teacher? Some cynicism is undoubtedly called for. In too many
cases, the preservationists and planners who moralize on the shortcomings of
Roman politics and planning have behaved rather differently in their own
activities *qua* architects and builders. Thus, for example, in 1965 it was discovered that some of the planners and architects most active and vehement in
defending the Appian Way district from private development had themselves
built villas there, in company with movie stars, princesses, and other members
of the Roman establishment.[27]

But in this case as in others the cynic is able to explain only part of the past
thus he is able to predict only part of the future. For the propaganda of planning
pressure groups, of Roman parties, of the press, and even of the Rome city
government has gradually created a powerful, if not dominant, constituency
for planning in the city. Truthfully, not much is known about Roman values that
are relevant to planning and exactly how they have affected planning performance. The way the city's neighborhoods have developed may have been roughly
in accordance with popular preferences, it may have been a matter of indifference to many people, or it may have made people angry about something they

27. *Avvenire d'Italia* (Rome), December 11, 1965.

felt unable or unwilling to do much about. The evidence suggests that most Romans place primary emphasis on their individual apartments, with only general, mostly social, requirements for neighborhood quality. There is no evidence to suggest that, once standards for apartment quality and neighborhood social quality have been met, Romans are indifferent to the lack of paved streets, schools, parks, playgrounds, sewers, or markets; the seeming indifference to the physical quality of the environment may simply reflect a reasonable ordering of priorities that sets apartment quality and neighborhood social quality above the quality of neighborhood physical facilities. If this is true, it is not so much the demand for services that needs changing, but the supply.

The pattern of postwar development in Rome suggests that an implicit community decision was made that economic growth and full employment were worth their costs in municipal indebtedness, poor facilities, and congestion. Certainly the type of socioeconomic development that came to Rome and Italy in the late fifties and early sixties was totally new. Institutional structures, legislative frameworks, and accumulated social knowledge could not possibly have dealt wisely with something as powerful and novel as a sudden, sharp rise in personal mobility and prosperity. Community opinion in Rome, and throughout Italy, was so strongly oriented toward rapid growth in private welfare that any attempt to shape the pattern of private consumption or to divert income into the public sector would have been intolerable.

The kind of physical improvement of the community desired by city planners may be more attainable at the stage of economic development when immediate personal consumption needs and drives have been met and city authorities are no longer haunted, as they were in Rome after the war, by the specter of chronic mass unemployment. Rising levels of economic development may eventually permit the satisfaction of lower priority desires, such as neighborhood and city amenity. But approaching affluence does not guarantee any change in attitudes toward government: affluent Romans may be just as suspicious of government and of community action as their poorer if nobler progenitors. And so the emerging mass constituency for planning in Rome may never become either a source of power to enforce the norms of the new master plan or a willing source of revenues to pay for the facilities it requires.

The new structures of Roman government—the Lazio regional government and, within the city, the twelve district councils—perhaps will be more effective than the Italian state or the city government of Rome have been in making good Roman citizens. Roman government and planning may, indeed, be revolutionized from above and from below: from above by the new Lazio region, with its potential for new policy, and from below by the new district councils, with their potential for citizen participation. Supported from above with regional financial and political support, and spurred from below by district expectations and demands, the city may find the impetus it needs to realize the ambitious goals set forth in its new master plan. And even partial achievement of these goals should allow a Roman to say once again with pride: *Civis Romanus sum*.

# APPENDIX:

# CHRONOLOGY OF

# PLAN FORMULATION

STAGE ONE: SECURING OFFICIAL COMMITMENT TO PRODUCE A NEW PLAN
(1950–54)

November 10, 1946   The first city council elections since 1920 are held, with the following results:

| | | |
|---|---|---|
| Popular Bloc (Socialists and Communists) | 36.9% | 30 seats |
| Republicans (anticlericals) | 7.8 | 6 |
| Christian Democrats (DC) | 20.3 | 17 |
| Liberals (conservatives) | 5.0 | 4 |
| *Qualunquisti* (right-wing protest) | 20.7 | 17 |
| Monarchists | 7.0 | 5 |
| Local | 1.6 | 1 |
| | | 80 |

The Christian Democrats in the center refuse to ally themselves with either the Left (Communists and Socialists) or the Right (Liberals, *Qualunquisti,* Monarchists). For lack of a majority coalition, the city council is dissolved and the city government is placed in the hands of a prefectoral commissioner appointed by the national government.

October 12, 1947   Elections are held again, almost one year later, with the following results:

| | | |
|---|---|---|
| Communists-Socialists | 33.5% | 28 seats |
| Social Democrats (split-off from Socialists) | 3.9 | 3 |

| | | |
|---|---|---|
| Republicans | 5.9 | 5 |
| Christian Democrats | 32.8 | 27 |
| Liberals | 1.9 | 1 |
| *Qualunquisti* | 10.2 | 8 |
| Monarchists | 5.3 | 4 |
| Neofascists (MSI) | 4.0 | 3 |
| Dissident Monarchists | 1.6 | 1 |
| | | 80 |

November 5, 1947   The city council elects a Christian Democrat, Salvatore Rebecchini, to be first postwar mayor of Rome. Voting in favor: 27 Christian Democrats, 3 Social Democrats, 1 Liberal, 8 *Qualunquisti,* 3 Neofascists. Voting against: 28 Communists-Socialists, 5 Republicans, 4 Monarchists, 2 Independents. The *giunta* (city cabinet) consists of 12 Christian Democrats, 5 *Qualunquisti,* 1 Liberal.

July 18, 1950   The Rome branch of INU *(Istituto Nazionale di Urbanistica* or National Planners Institute) proposes the preparation of a new master plan to replace the existing master plan of 1931, due to expire in 1952. It receives no answer to its proposal from Mayor Rebecchini.

1950–51   Most Roman newspapers, including the influential rightwing daily, *Il Tempo,* join in the campaign for a new plan.

October 12, 1951   The giunta reports on the general criteria for a new plan: preservation of the historic center; decentralization of traffic generators to new city centers without "sterilizing" the existing center; promotion of residential expansion toward the southwest and the southeast; utilization of EUR (the half-built site of the "World's Fair of 1942") as the major new city center; and an end to street-cutting in the historic center in order to ease traffic. The city council approves these criteria but takes no further action.

November 1951   The giunta, violating its own report, proposes to build a rapid highway through the historic center; the project, involving extensive demolitions in the old center, is approved by the city council.

May 25, 1952   Elections are held under a new electoral law, which gives two-thirds of the council seats to the coalition winning a simple plurality.
    1. Left coalition
       (Communists-Socialists) 34.3%   16 seats

|  | 2. Center coalition | 41.8% |  | 53 seats |
|---|---|---|---|---|
|  | Social Democrats |  | 3.3 | 4 |
|  | Republicans |  | 2.2 | 3 |
|  | Christian Democrats |  | 31.1 | 39 |
|  | Liberals |  | 4.3 | 6 |
|  | Independent |  | 0.9 | 1 |
|  | 3. Monarchists | 5.9 | 3 |  |
|  | 4. Neofascists | 15.6 | 8 |  |

Mayor Rebecchini, again heading the Center coalition, is reelected to office. With a giunta of Christian Democrats, Liberals, Republicans, and Social Democrats, a Liberal (Cattani) is appointed Planning Assessor.

April 20, 1952     Parliament passes Law No. 504, extending the validity of those master plans due to expire in September 1952 to December 31, 1955. Rome now has three years in which to adopt a new plan.

August  3, 1952     The Ministry of Public Works refuses to approve the proposed highway through the historic center, following protests by the Roman press and eminent members of the Italian intelligentsia.

February 22, 1953     The Ministry of Public Works installs a committee to prepare a regional plan for Lazio, the region around Rome. (The regional plan is finally produced in 1967.)

March 20, 1953     Planning Assessor Cattani secures the establishment of the Special Office for the New Master Plan (Ufficio Speciale Nuovo Piano Regolatore) attached to, but not part of the Planning Department. The Special Office (USNPR) is to conduct research for the new plan.

December 22, 1953     Following Cattani's resignation from the giunta, a new Planning Assessor, Enzo Storoni (Liberal) reports in depth on the administration of the existing plan of 1931 and on the problems of preparing a new plan.

December 22, 1953–     The city council debates the criteria for the new plan.
May 21, 1954

May 21, 1954     The city council *unanimously* adopts a resolution on the new master plan, based on (1) conservation of the historic center and its "vitality"; (2) "gradual" decentralization of "certain" activities; (3) a maximum density of 750 inhabitants per hectare (1,875 per acre) in the new residential districts; (4) promotion of industrial development; (5) provision of "adequate" green zones in and around the city; (6) prosecution of illegal subdividers and regularization of existing illegal subdivisions; (7) elimination of tax exempt status for unauthorized residential construction; (8) continued expansion of the city through conventions with private subdividers and possibly through city land condemnation; (9) promotion in Parliament of a tax on capital gains in land.

July 28–30, 1954   The city council elects a Grand Commission (consisting of the mayor, 6 assessors, 14 councilmen, 9 city functionaries, 38 representatives of ministries and public bodies, the six nonbureaucratic members of the City Planning Commission, and the 9 nonbureaucratic members of the City Building Commission) to prepare the new plan in accordance with city council directives. The actual drafting is to be carried out by a Committee for Technical Elaboration (CET), consisting of 8 professional city planners, the city engineer, and the technical director of the Special Office (USNPR). Of the 14 city councilmen on the Grand Commission, 6 represent the minority parties (Communists, Socialists, neofascists, Monarchists), 8 the majority coalition (DC, Liberals, Social Democrats). Of the 8 members of the CET, one is closely identified with the Left, another with the Neofascists.

STAGE TWO: FORMULATING THE NEW PLAN (1954–57)

January 27, 1955   The CET, composed of professional planners, makes its first reports to the Grand Commission. The majority report stresses the need for absolute conservation of the historic center and calls for heavy eastern expansion; decentralization of employment to new "directive centers" in the east; construction of an "eastern axis" or freeway to serve as the "linear center" of the new city. The minority (of one) report calls for residential expansion in the north, the west, the southwest, and the southeast.

Summer 1955        Four resolutions are presented to the Grand Commission. A right-wing resolution calls for expansion to the southwest and northwest, avoiding expansion to the east. Two "centrist" resolutions called for a combination of eastern expansion, favored by the CET, with southwestern expansion toward the sea. The Left presents a resolution banning expansion in the west, drastically curtailing it in the north and southwest, and favoring it only in the east.

November 17, 1955    The Grand Commission, by a vote of 55 to 0, adopts a compromise resolution favoring expansion in the east *and* southwest, with emphasis on the latter; "moderate" expansion is to be allowed in the north. Expansion of the city is to take place in accordance with the following formula:

40% south (between Via Ostiense and Via Ardeatina)
30% east (between Via Appia and Via Tiburtina)
15% north (between Via Tiburtina and Via Trionfale)
15% west (between Via Portuense and Via Trionfale)

A major expressway (the "eastern axis") is to be built in the east, but, the major new administrative center of the city is to be in the west at EUR, planned and half-built by the Fascist regime.

December 11, 1955–    An anticlerical weekly, *L'Espresso,* organ of the new
January 22, 1956    Radical party, begins a campaign against the undue influence of private interests, particularly those close to Vatican circles, in Roman planning administration. Cristicism is focused on efforts by SGI, the Vatican-owned real estate company, to secure a variance for the construction of a Hilton hotel on Monte Mario, over the protest of the Rome branch of the National Planners Institute.

April 6, 1956    The city council refuses to approve Mayor Rebecchini's sudden request for the Hilton variance.

April 10, 1956    The Christian Democrats drop Rebecchini as their candidate for mayor in favor of Senator Umberto Tupini.

May 27, 1956    Elections are held under a new electoral law, this time providing for straight proportional representation. The Center coalition drops from a majority of 53 to a minority of 34, although its combined share of the vote rises from 41.9% to 42.5%. The Christian Democratic delegation on the council drops from 39 to 27. Extreme Right and extreme Left, together, now have 45 out of the 80 council seats.

| | | | |
|---|---|---|---|
| Communists | 24.2% | 20 seats | (+12 seats) |
| Socialists | 10.6% | 9 seats | (+ 5 seats) |
| Radicals | 1.2% | 1 seat | (new party) |
| Social Democrats | 4.5% | 3 seats | (− 1 seat) |
| Republicans | 1.6% | 1 seat | (− 2 seats) |
| Christian Democrats | 32.1% | 27 seats | (−12 seats) |
| Monarchists | 9.3% | 6 seats | (+ 3 seats) |
| Neofascists | 12.1% | 10 seats | (+ 2 seats) |

July  7, 1956 — Senator Tupini is elected second postwar mayor of Rome with votes from the Center parties plus the neofascists. The Christian Democrats, facing the choice between alliance with the Socialists (now detached from the Communists) or with the neofascists, choose the neofascists.

November  8, 1956 — The CET presents to the Grand Commission its general proposals for zoning, traffic control, and regional planning. It is repeatedly accused by Grand Commission members of attempting to usurp the Commission's policy making authority.

December 13, 1956 — The CET receives unexpected right-wing support from architect Alberto Calza-Bini, one of the founders in 1929 of the National Institute of Planners and leading planning consultant to the Fascist government. A Subcommittee of 42 is appointed by the Grand Commission to determine whether, as Calza-Bini affirms, the CET in its proposals has been faithful to resolutions of the city council and the Grand Commission.

February 20, 1957 — The Subcommittee of 42 reports favorably on the CET proposals to the Grand Commission.

June 15, 1957 — After further debate in the Subcommittee of 42, the Grand Commission approves the work of the CET and authorizes it to prepare a final draft.

STAGE THREE: KILLING THE NEW PLAN AND PREPARING A SECOND (1957–59)

December  2, 1957 — The CET presents its final draft. A motion against the CET plan is presented by Lt. Col. Amici, representing the Ministry of Defense (Civil Aviation) and director of construction at Fiumicino International Airport. The Amici motion is signed by conservative planners and right-wing councilmen, but also by the leaders of the Christian Democrats and the representatives of the Ministry of Public Works on the Grand Commission.

December 10, 1957  The city council approves a variance permitting the subdivision of Villa Chigi, a private estate owned by Prince Sigismundo Chigi, who is Keeper of the Conclave, the highest lay dignitary in the church, and future (1962) councilmanic candidate of the neofascist party.

January  9, 1958  Sen. Tupini, a distinguished antifascist, resigns in order to retain his seat in the Senate. Urbano Cioccetti is elected mayor of Rome with the votes of the Christian Democrats, Liberals, Social Democrats, Monarchists, and neofascists. After hesitating and resisting, the Social Democrats withdraw from the governing coalition. For the first time in postwar Rome, the Center and extreme Right are joined in government, while the left-of-center forces are joined with the Communists in opposition.

February 1958  The Union of Catholic Technicians denounces the movement to kill the CET plan.

February 16, 1958  The Rome Committee of the DC (Christian Democrats) announces acceptance of the CET plan, with reservations.

March 1958  The Union of Roman Merchants denounces the decentralization proposals of the CET plan as a threat to downtown business interests.

March 1958  The *Unione Provinciale Agricoltori* or Farmowners Union denounces the intent of the CET plan to restrict development in the northern and western suburbs and in the Agro Romano, the countryside around the city.

March 10, 1958  Mayor Cioccetti appoints a committee of nine experts, mostly state bureaucrats, to examine the congruence between the CET plan and city council and Grand Commission policy directives.

April 30, 1958  The committee of nine experts reports against CET plan; all parties on the Grand Commission agree to dissolve both the Grand Commission and the CET and to turn the whole matter over to the city council, without any recommendations.

June  7–26, 1958  The city council debates CET plan.

June 18, 1958            The Christian Democrats move to reject the CET plan and
                         to delegate authority to the giunta to draft a second plan.
                         The leading newspaper in Rome, the conservative *Il
                         Messaggero,* comes out in favor of the CET plan.

June 26, 1958            The city council votes, 39–27, to reject the CET plan;
                         it delegates authority to the giunta to draft a new plan,
                         even though the deadline for city adoption of a new plan
                         has been set by the Ministry of Public Works for August
                         31, 1958. Voting against the CET plan: the Christian
                         Democrats, Liberals, Monarchists, and neofascists.

June 27, 1958            Debate on the variance for the Hilton hotel on Monte
                         Mario begins; approval is voted on September 24, 1958.

November 15, 1958        The Ministry of Public Works, which has allowed the
                         city to pass the deadline for action on the master plan
                         without penalty, now authorizes the city to cooperate
                         with 40 neighboring communes in the formation of an
                         intercommunal plan.

February 26, 1959        The giunta presents a second plan to the council. The
                         plan differs from the CET plan in several respects: (1)
                         instead of asymmetrical, selective expansion to the south-
                         east and southwest, the giunta plan contains no expansion
                         directives at all, except for the southwest; (2) the new
                         "directive centers" in the east—Pietralata and Centocelle
                         —are eliminated in favor of EUR; (3) the eastern axis is
                         demoted to the status of an urban segment of the *Auto-
                         strada del Sole* and is offset by a similar expressway in
                         the west; (4) subway lines are to run through the historic
                         center, rather than around it; (5) more areas in the Agro
                         Romano are zoned for development and more intensive
                         development; (6) within the perimeter of the 1931 master
                         plan, there is to be much greater development in the north-
                         ern and western suburbs and, generally, saturation of the
                         unbuilt areas.

February 26–             The city council debates the giunta plan. Over the pro-
June 24, 1959            tests of the Communists, the Socialists propose a series of
                         amendments and declare their willingness to vote for the
                         plan if their amendments are accepted. The giunta plan
                         is attacked by the Union of Catholic Technicians, the
                         National Institute of Urbanists, the *Italia Nostra* con-
                         servation society, *Il Messaggero,* and all political forces
                         left of center.

May 29, 1959        Mayor Cioccetti declares that, for the first time, the city will not celebrate June 4th, Liberation Day, anniversary of the Allied occupation of the city on June 4, 1944.

June 23, 1959        The city council votes down a motion to remove Mayor Cioccetti from office because of his failure to celebrate Liberation Day. The mayor's action is supported by the Christian Democrats, Liberals, Monarchists, and neofascists.

June 24, 1959        The same Center-Right coalition (Christian Democrats, Liberals, Monarchists, and neofascists) adopts the giunta plan as the new Master Plan of Rome. The Christian Democrat majority leader on the council declares that "the mobilization of all the atheistic and anti-Catholic forces against the Plan just adopted is an indirect confirmation that it corresponds to the true interests of Rome."

STAGE FOUR : SECURING APPROVAL OF THE SECOND (1959) PLAN

September 26–
October 25, 1959      The new plan is put on public display; written "observations" on the plan are collected from the public.

October 1–
December 30, 1959      An ad hoc commission of bureaucrats examines the 2,669 written "observations" and formulates recommendations ("counter-deductions") as to whether the plan should be changed to meet the various objections.

January 27, 1960      The plan, observations, and counter-deductions are forwarded to the Ministry of Public Works for approval.

July 1960         An attempt to reproduce on the national level the same Center-Right (Catholic-neofascist) alliance that is governing Rome leads to riots and bloodshed in several Italian cities; the attempt fails and the pendulum nationally begins to swing to the left. Patrons of the Catholic-neofascist alliance in the church, Catholic Action, and the DC party are defeated. Preparations begin for an eventual national alliance between the Catholics and the Socialists (the Center-Left). Control of the Ministry of Public Works passes from a supporter of the Center-Right (Togni) to a more moderate Christian Democrat (Zaccagnini).

July 26, 1960       An unofficial draft of the intercommunal plan is presented to the public by Planning Assessor D'Andrea

(Liberal). Though involving much the same kinds of decisions as the Rome master plan, the intercommunal plan is produced without controversy. It is never legally adopted by any of the forty-one sponsoring communes. It tends to confirm the validity of the expansion directives proposed by the CET plan.

August 1960    The XVII Olympics are held in Rome. Progressive planners condemn the location of new facilities in the north and at EUR (in the southwest), as well as the route of the connecting highway, Via Olimpica. The latter cuts in half a proposed public park in Villa Doria Pamphili, and its construction in the western part of the city seems designed to enhance the value of properties held in that part of the city by numerous religious orders

November 6, 1960    Elections are held, leaving the composition of the council virtually unchanged.

| Communists | 23.1% | 19 seats (−1 seat) |
|---|---|---|
| Socialists | 13.2% | 11 seats (+2 seats) |
| Social Democrats | 4.7% | 3 seats (no change) |
| Republicans | 1.5% | 1 seat (no change) |
| Christian Democrats | 33.9% | 28 seats (+1 seat) |
| Monarchists | 4.0% | 3 seats (−3 seats) |
| Neofascists | 15.2% | 12 seats (+2 seats) |

During the campaign, no party is willing to defend the 1959 master plan. Mayor Cioccetti, renominated as Christian Democratic leader, declares that the DC is willing to discuss revision of the plan; he also makes strong declarations of antifascism. National DC party secretary Aldo Moro precludes the formation of Catholic-neofascist alliances in any important city.

May 5, 1961    Parliament passes Law No. 325 authorizing an investigation into scandals surrounding the construction of Fiumicino International Airport, opened in January 1961. The scandals involve major leaders of the conservative planning coalition.

July 10, 1961    The city council of Rome is dissolved and the city placed under a prefectoral commissioner, Prefect Francesco Diana. The church is not willing yet to allow the DC in Rome to ally itself with the Socialists to form a Center-Left alliance, such as has been formed in Milan and Genoa. Since Catholic-neofascist alliances have been banned, the only alternative is government by a prefectoral commissioner.

July 12, 1961    A high functionary of the Ministry of Public Works is appointed subcommissioner for planning in the Rome city government, under Prefectoral Commissioner Diana. The national government can now act in the name of the city in planning matters.

July 27–
November 23, 1961    The Superior Council of Public Works in the Ministry of Public Works debates the 1959 master plan, in private.

November 13, 1961    The Rome Christian Democrats vote to accept major revisions in the master plan, including lessened development in the west and in the Agro Romano, and top priority for the eastern axis as the "linear center" of the new city.

November 23, 1961    The Superior Council of Public Works issues an ambiguous ruling on the 1959 master plan, approving it but requiring changes. The summary of its decisions in the form of a press release seems favorable to progressive demands; the full text of the decision, revealed in January 1962, favors conservative demands, such as western development, higher densities in the Agro Romano, subway lines through the historic center, etc. The decision leaves the way open for modest revision, favoring the conservatives, or radical revision, favoring the progressives.

STAGE FIVE: KILLING PLAN NUMBER TWO AND SECURING ADOPTION OF
PLAN NUMBER THREE

February 22, 1962    The first national cabinet based on Catholic-Socialist (Center-Left) cooperation takes office. One of the terms of the national interparty agreements involves a pledge to secure a new master plan for Rome satisfactory to the progressives. A planning progressive, Fiorentino Sullo (DC), is appointed minister of public works.
The Center-Left cabinet announces that elections will be held in Rome and other major cities. The 1959 plan is thus to be revised in the heat of an election campaign.

March 12, 1962    Minister of Public Works Sullo announces an agreement with Prefectoral Commissioner Diana to have a new plan produced and adopted by the city by June 24, when existing zoning and building regulations in the city are due to expire. Five experts, representing the political forces in the Center-Left coalition, are appointed to help prepare the new plan. The new planning operation is violently attacked not only by the conservatives, but by the Communists, now, with the formation of the Center-Left, isolated on the Left.

June 9, 1962     The new plan, signed by the five experts and by representatives of the Ministry of Public Works, is presented for adoption in the name of the city by Prefectoral Commissioner Diana. Diana, amidst universal astonishment and on the eve of city elections, refuses to sign the new plan.

June 10, 1962     Elections are held. City council seats are distributed as follows:

| | | |
|---|---|---|
| Communists | 19 | (no change) |
| Socialists | 10 | (−1 seat) |
| Republicans | 1 | (no change) |
| Social Democrats | 5 | (+2 seats) |
| Christian Democrats | 24 | (−4 seats) |
| Liberals | 6 | (+3 seats) |
| Monarchists | 2 | (−1 seat) |
| Neofascists | 13 | (+1 seat) |

June 19, 1962     The situation in Rome is rescued, after Diana's refusal to sign the new plan, when the Italian Council of Ministers, on the recommendation of Minister of Public Works Sullo, promulgates an emergency decree putting the norms of the June master plan into effect for six months, subject to revision and approval by the newly elected Rome city council. The same cabinet meeting nationalizes the Italian electricity industry.

July 17, 1962     A professional economic planner on the DC party ticket, prof. Glauco Della Porta (DC) is elected mayor of Rome, heading a giunta of Christian Democrats and Socialists. The political secretary of the Rome DC, Amerigo Petrucci, is appointed planning assessor.

July 17, 1962     Over the protests of the General Confederation of Agriculture, the Rome Building Contractors Association, and the Association of Roman Property Owners, the

National Chamber of Deputies approves the conversion into law of the cabinet decree of June 19, 1962. The Senate follows with its approval on July 26.

July 2-July 17, 1962    The June plan is put on public display.

August 7-               An ad hoc committee of the city council revises the June
November 14, 1962       plan under the leadership of the party leaders of the Center-Left and Planning Assessor Petrucci.

November 19-            The city council debates the new plan, as revised in
December 18, 1962       committee.

December 18, 1962       The new master plan is adopted by the Rome city council by a vote of 41 to 32. Voting in favor: Christian Democrats, Republicans, Social Democrats, Socialists, and one Monarchist. Voting against: Liberals, neofascists, Communists, and one Monarchist. The adopted plan contains most of the provisions demanded by the progressives, including eastern expansion, reduced densities in the Agro Romano, a tangential rather than circumferential circulation scheme, directive centers in the east, major emphasis on the eastern axis, enhanced protective norms for the historic center, increased provision for public parks, and precise standards for the distribution of public facilities among the existing and new districts.

STAGE SIX: SECURING NATIONAL APPROVAL OF PLAN NUMBER THREE
(1962–66)

February 12-            The 1962 master plan is put on public display; 4,635
March 13, 1963          written observations are collected.

March 13, 1963-         An ad hoc city council committee examines and formu-
February 24, 1965       lates counter-deductions to the 4,635 observations.

April 13, 1963          The Christian Democratic party publicly disowns a new national urban planning bill sponsored by its own Minister of Public Works, Fiorentino Sullo, on the eve of national parliamentary elections.

February 26, 1964       The city council approves a large scheme of land acquisition and urbanization for low-cost housing under Law 167 of April 18, 1962. The city is to acquire some 12,500 acres of land for the housing of 700,000 people during the period 1964–74. Land is to be purchased at 1962 prices, rather than current market value, mostly in areas zoned for expansion or redevelopment by the 1962 master plan.

March 1964            Following the national and local secession of the left wing of the Socialist party (PSI) to form a new pro-Communist, pro-Chinese party (the PSIUP), the Center-Left majority on the city council loses one council vote to the opposition. The loss is offset by the acceptance into the Christian Democratic council group of Dr. Pompei, former neo-fascist party secretary in Rome. Mayor Della Porta is replaced by Planning Assessor Petrucci as mayor.

March 12, 1964        Ground is broken on the first line of the new subway system, approved by Parliament in 1959. The first line is to be completed by 1967. (As of early 1970, less than half of the line was completed.)

November 25, 1964     Parliament votes a special law for Rome, allowing the city to borrow million $25 over a five-year period for specified kinds of capital improvement.

February 24, 1965     The city transmits the 1962 master plan, the 4,635 observations, and the city's counter-deductions to the Ministry of Public Works for approval.

April 9, 1965         The Constitutional Court declares sections of Law 167 unconstitutional, particularly its compensation provisions. These provisions, which would allow the city to pay 1962 prices for land purchased as late as 1974, are held to violate constitutional guarantees of just compensation.

June 4, 1965          The city council adopts, 52–16, the first zone plan under Law 167, involving 47 acres of land for about 26,000 people at Spinaceto. The land is already owned by the city; litigation paralyzes efforts to carry out Law 167 through the compulsory purchase of private land. Voting in favor: the Center-Left, the Communists, and Left-Socialists.

July 21, 1965         Parliament passes Law 904 to modify the compensation provisions of Law 167 so as to base compensation on the percentage of current market value fixed by the 1885 Law on the Reclamation of Naples.

September 20, 1965    The Ministry of Public Works approves the technical features of the Rome master plan and transmits it to the Council of State for examination of the plan's legal aspects.

October 20, 1965       The Council of State in its advisory capacity approves the legality of the plan, with some exceptions.

December 16, 1965      The President of the Italian Republic signs the decree promulgating the new master plan. Difficulties with the Court of Accounts *(Corte dei Conti)* hold up actual promulgation in the *Gazzetta Ufficiale* until February 11, 1966.

STAGE SEVEN: THE IMPLEMENTATION PHASE OPENS (1966–    )

February 11, 1966      The decree promulgating the master plan as law is published in the official gazette, revealing the amendments made and required by the national government.

March 31, 1966         The city council votes to divide the city into twelve districts for the purpose of decentralizing city government. Each district is to have a council, elected by the city council itself, with the same party composition as in the city council; in addition, each district is to have a deputy mayor and field offices of the city departments.

June 12, 1966          Elections are held in the city, with the following results:

| | | | |
|---|---|---|---|
| Extreme Left { | Communists | 21 seats | +two seats |
| | Left Socialists | 1 seat | (did not exist in 1962) |
| Center-Left { | Socialists | 6 seats | −four seats |
| | Social Democrats | 8 seats | +three seats |
| | Republicans | 1 seat | no change |
| | Christian Democrats | 25 seats | +one seat |
| Right { | Liberals | 9 seats | +three seats |
| | Monarchists | 1 seat | −one seat |
| | Neofascists | 7 seats | −six seats |

The Center-Left coalition enters and emerges from the elections with forty out of eighty seats, i.e., without an absolute majority. Mayor Petrucci is confirmed in office, again heading a Center-Left giunta.

July 26, 1967          The council adopts the city's first Five Year Development Plan—an inventory of needed capital improvements.

August 6, 1967         Parliament adopts Law No. 765, the *Legge-Ponte* or "Bridge-Law," as an interim reform of the 1942 Planning Act. The Ministry of Public Works in Rome must now approve all subdivision applications throughout the country. Fines are increased for violating planning and building laws and regulations. Tax credits are abolished for illegally built structures. Local governments lose most of their much-abused authority to grant exceptions *("deroghe")* to building and zoning requirements. The procedure for master plan approval is streamlined. Minimum national standards are established for building volume, height, and setback.

October 17, 1967    The city council approves (38–18) a general variance to the 1962 master plan, incorporating the changes demanded by the Ministry of Public Works and the changes required by city acceptance of some 700 of the 4,365 observations. Voting for: the Center-Left plus the Right (Liberals, neofascists).

December 21, 1967    Mayor Petrucci resigns in order to run for the Chamber of Deputies and is replaced by Planning Assessor Rinaldo Santini (DC). Implementation of the master plan is the first item in the new mayor's program.

May 29, 1968    The Constitutional Court strikes down sections of the 1942 Planning Act as an unconstitutional abridgment of property rights. Local governments must compensate owners for property marked for eventual public acquisition when master plans are formulated, rather than when the land is actually taken, if ever.

November 19, 1968    Law No. 1187 modifies the Planning Act of 1942 by limiting the validity of certain zoning decisions to five years. If within that period the city has not acted to compensate affected property owners, zoning provisions banning development entirely or designating land for public acquisition lose their validity.

November 25, 1968    The city council unanimously approves the appointment of a special commission to work out a general plan for the conservation of the historic center.

March 18, 1969    Mayor Santini and his giunta resign. The Center-Left coalition breaks down over failure to implement the master plan, version 3, and conflicts over the methods of implementation.

July 4, 1969    The Socialist party, locally and nationally, after a brief period of unification with the Social Democrats (1966–69)

splits again into separate Socialist and Social Democratic
Democratic parties.

July 30, 1969          After 120 days of "crisis," the Center-Left coalition is
                       reconstituted under a new mayor, Clelio Darida (DC).
                       The giunta is composed of ten Christian Democrats, four
                       Social Democrats, and four Socialists. The tiny Republi-
                       can party withdraws from the Center-Left, refusing to
                       accept the compromises negotiated with regard to imple-
                       mentation of the master plan. The new coalition is pledged
                       to the creation of the billion-dollar "linear center" in the
                       east to be built in collaboration with private enterprise
                       and agencies of the national government.

November 1969          The Center-Left coalition verges on collapse over the
                       question of the new linear center and the respective roles
                       to be played by the city, private enterprise, and the na-
                       tional government. The Socialists, seeking to minimize
                       private and national control over the operation, call for
                       the inclusion of the Communists in the governing major-
                       ity.

September 20, 1970     Rome celebrates its 100th year as the capital of Italy.

# SELECTED
# BIBLIOGRAPHY

The following bibliography contains only those items found useful in writing this book. More extensive references, particularly for the history of city planning in Rome, may be found in *Topografia e urbanistica di Roma* by Ferdinando Castagnoli, Carlo Cecchelli, Gustavo Giovannoni, and Mario Zocca, volume 22 in the history of Rome sponsored by the Istituto di Studi Romani. (Bologna: Cappelli, 1958). References on the history of city planning in Rome up to 1958 may also be found in the equally indispensable *Roma: Città e piani* published by the Istituto Nazionale di Urbanistica (Turin: Istituto Nazionale di Urbanistica, n.d.) Complete bibliographical references for all aspects of postwar Roman life may be found in the annual volumes of the *Bibliografia romana,* edited by "Ceccarius" (Giuseppe Ceccharelli) and published by the Istituto di Studi Romani.

PUBLIC DOCUMENTS

*A. National Government*

Atti Parlamentari, II Legislatura, Senato, Disegni. Docs. No. 1296 and 1760-A February 10, 1958 (Special Law for Rome).
Atti Parlamentari, III Legislatura, Camera dei Deputati. Doc. No. XI, 2, Commissione Parlamentare d'Inchiesta sulla Costruzione dell'aeroporto di Fiumicino. *Relazione.* Rome, December 23, 1961.
Atti Parlamentari, III Legislatura, Camera dei Deputati. Doc. Dis. di legge No. 3881, No. 3881-A. Conversione in legge del decreto-legge 19 giugno 1962, n. 473, concernente misure speciali di salvaguardia per il piano regolatore di Roma (Seduta del 19 giugno 1962). Discussioni, Seduta del 14 luglio 1962. Senato della Repubblica, Disegno di Legge no. 2108; Relazione della 7a Commissione Permanente, No. 2108-A.
Camera dei Deputati. *Esame dello stato della finanza locale in Italia.* 2 vols. Rome, 1967.
_____. *Atti della Commissione Parlamentare di Inchiesta sulla Miseria in Italia e sui Mezzi per Combatterla,* Vol. 6, *La Miseria nelle Grandi Città.* Rome, 1953.
_____. Commissione Parlamentare d'Inchiesta sulla Disoccupazione. *La Disoccupazione in Italia.* Vol. 3, Tome 3. Monografie Regionali: Lazio, Campania, Abruzzi e Molise. Rome, 1953.
_____, Segretariato Generale. *Ricerca sull'urbanistica.* Part 1. Rome, 1965.
Comitato Regionale per la Programmazione Economica del Lazio. *Schema generale del piano di studi e ricerche.* Rome, 1966.
Consiglio di Stato. "Parere del Consiglio di Stato sul Piano Regolatore Generale di Rome (20–10–1965)." *Urbanistica,* May 1966, pp. 131–34.

Istituto Centrale di Statistica (Istat). IX Censimento Generale della Popolazione, III Censimento Generale dell'Industria e del Commercio. *Caratteristiche demografiche ed economiche dei grandi comuni. Vol.* 1. Rome, 1959.

_____. *Annuario di Statistiche Giudiziarie 1965.* Rome, 1968.

_____. *Annuario Statistico dell'Attività Edilizia e delle Opere Pubbliche.* Rome, 1950–1966.

_____. *Annuario Statistico Italiano.*

_____. *Bilanci delle amministrazioni regionali, provinciali, e comunali: conti consuntivi anni 1953 e 1954.* Rome, 1956.

_____. *Indagine speciale sulle abitazioni al 20 gennaio 1966.* Note e relazioni No. 35, March 1968.

Ministero dei Lavori Pubblici. *Legge 6 Agosto 1967, N. 765.* Rome, 1968.

_____. "Riassunto del parere espresso dal Consiglio Superiore dei Lavori Pubblici nella adunanza in assemblea generale in data 23 november 1961, in merito al progetto di piano regolatore generale di Roma adottato il 24 giugno 1959."

Ministero dei Lavori Pubblici, Consiglio Superiore dei Lavori Pubblici. "Parere espresso dal Consiglio Superiore dei Lavori Pubblici nella adunanza in assemblea generale in data 23 novembre 1961, in merito al progetto di piano regolatore generale di Roma adottato il 24 giugno 1959." *Informazioni Urbanistiche,* September-December 1961, pp. 3–68.

Ministero delle Finanze. *Imposte comunali sui consumi, 1957-1958.* Rome, 1960.

_____. *Imposte comunali sui consumi, 1966.* Rome, 1968.

Ministero dell'Interno. *Compendio dei risultati delle elezioni comunali e provinciali dal 1946 al 1960.* Rome, 1961.

Presidenza della Repubblica. "Decreto 16 dicembre 1965 di approvazione del Piano Regolatore Generale del Comune di Roma adottato dal Consiglio Comunale il 18 dicembre 1962." *Urbanistica,* May 1966, pp. 135–45,.

Tribunale di Roma, Sezione IV. "Sentenza del 29 mese di dicembre 1956." Typescript.

*B. City Government*

Comune di Roma. *Bilancio di Previsione dell'entrata e della spesa per l'esercizio finanziario 1964.* Rome, 1964.

_____. *La Commune de Rome: Notes sur l'organisation administrative communale.* Rome, 1963.

_____. *Controdeduzioni alle osservazioni sul Nuovo Piano Regolatore Generale: Deliberazione della Giunta Municipale n. 187 del 20 gennaio 1960.* Rome, 1960.

_____. *Controdeduzioni alle osservazioni sul nuovo Piano Regolatore Generale di Roma adottato dal Consiglio Comunale in data 18 dicembre 1962: deliberazione della Giunta Municipale N. 984 del 24–2–1965.* Rome, 1965.

_____. "Il Decentramento amministrativo del Comune di Roma," *Capitolium,* June 1966 (Documentazione del Comune di Roma, 1966, No. 1).

_____. *Decisioni del Consiglio Comunale in ordine all'urbanistica cittadina e al nuovo piano regolatore.* Rome, 1955.

_____. *Il traffico a Roma: La situazione attuale e le previsioni fino al 1985.* Rome, 1966.

_____. *Piano delle zone da destinare alla construzione di alloggi a carattere economico e popolare in esecuzione della Legge 18 aprile 1962, No. 167.* Rome, 1964.

_____. *Piano Regolatore Generale della Città di Roma: Estratto dal Verbale delle deliberazioni del Consiglio Comunale.* Rome, 1959.

_____. *Piano Regolatore Generale della Città di Roma: Estratto dal Verbale delle deliberazioni del Consiglio Comunale.* Rome, 1963.

_____. "Riordinamento degli Uffici del Piano Regolatore, dell'urbanistica e dell'-

Edilizia Privata: Relazione dell'Assessore all'Urbanistica Dott. Amerigo Petrucci."
(n.d.)
_____. *Roma Oggi.*
_____. *Una legge per la capitale.* Rome, 1957.
_____. "Un programma quinquennale per Roma." *Capitolium,* May-June 1967.
_____. "Variante Generale del 17 ottobre 1967." *Capitolium,* January 1968.
_____, Gabinetto del Sindaco, Ufficio Stampa. "Sintesi del discorso pronunciato dal
sindaco in Campidoglio per l'insediamento della commissione di studio per il nuovo
piano regolatore e del comitato di elaborazione tecnica." Mimeographed. Oct. 11,
1954.
_____, Ufficio di Statistica e Censimento. *Roma: Popolazione e territorio dal 1860 al
1960.* Rome, 1960.
_____. *Annuario Statistico della Città di Roma 1964.* Rome, 1968.
_____. *Bollettino Statistico Mensile.*
_____. *Notiziario Statistico Mensile.*
_____, Ufficio Speciale Nuovo Piano Regolatore. *Attuazione della legge 18 aprile n.
167 per il piano delle zone da destinare all'edilizia economica e popolare: Norme
Techniche Generale.* Rome, 1963.
_____. "Comitato per l'esame dello schema di massima del Nuovo Piano Regolatore."
Mimeographed. Rome, 1957.
_____. "Commissione Speciale per l'Esame del Piano Regolatore Generale." Mi-
meographed. Rome, 1962.
_____. "Esame della situazione urbanistica di Roma come premessa allo studio del
nuovo piano regolatore." Mimeographed. January 27, 1955.
_____. "Piano Regolatore Intercomunale." 7 vols. Rome, 1960.
_____. *Progetto di Nuovo Piano Regolatore Generale di Roma in data 9 giugno 1962:
Relazione e Norme Techniche.* Rome, 1962.
_____. *Raccolta di graffici.* Rome, 1958.
_____. *Relazione al Piano Regolatore Generale.* Rome, 1957.

BOOKS

Abrams, Charles. *Man's Struggle for Shelter in an Urbanizing World.* Cambridge:
M.I.T. Press, 1966.
Almagià, Roberto. *Lazio.* Turin: Unione Tipografica Editoriale Torinese, 1966.
Almond, Gabriel and Sindney Verba. *The Civic Culture.* Princeton: Princeton Univer-
sity Press, 1963.
Almond, Gabriel, and G. Bingham Powell, Jr. *Comparative Politics: A Developmental
Approach.* Boston: Little Brown, 1966.
Altschuler, Alan. *The City Planning Process: A Political Analysis.* Ithaca: Cornell
University Press, 1965.
*Annuario Politico Italiano, 1963.* Milan: Comunità, 1964.
Aquarone, Alberto. *Grandi città e aree metropolitane in Italia: Problemi amministrativi
e prospettive di riforma.* Bologna: Zanichelli, 1961.
_____, *L'organizzazione dello Stato totalitario.* Turin: Einaudi, 1965.
Associazione Nazionale dei Comuni Italiani. *La finanza locale oggi.* Rome: ANCI,
1966.
Aymonimo, Carlo et al. *La città territorio: un esperimento didattico sul Centro dire-
zionale di Centocelle in Roma.* Bari: Leonardo da Vinci, 1964.
Banfield, Edward. *Big City Politics.* New York: Random House, 1965.
Barbacci, Alfredo. *Il guasto della città.* Florence: Le Monnier, 1962.

Benevolo, Leonardo. *L'architettura delle città nell'Italia contemporanea*. Bari: Laterza, 1968.

Berlinguer, Giovanni, and Piero Della Seta. *Le borgate romane*. Rome: Editori Riuniti, 1960.

Braga, Giorgio. *Il comunismo fra gli italiani*. Milan: Edizioni di Comunità, 1956.

Brown, William H., Jr., and Charles E. Gilbert. *Planning Municipal Investment: A Case Study of Philadelphia*. Philadelphia: University of Pennsylvania Press, 1961.

Burgalassi, S. *Il comportamento religioso degli italiani*. Florence: Vallecchi, 1968.

Campos Venuti, Giuseppe. *Amministrare l'urbanistica*. Turin: Einaudi, 1967.

Cantril, Hadley. *The Politics of Despair*. New York: Collier, 1962.

Caracciolo, Alberto. *Roma capitale: dal risorgimento alla crisi dello stato liberale*. Rome: Rinascita, 1956.

Castagnoli, Ferdinando et al. *Topografia e urbanistica di Roma*. Bologna: Cappelli, 1958.

Cattani, Leone et al. *Le leggi speciali per la città di Roma dal 1870 ad oggi*. Rome: Centro di Studi su Roma Moderna, 1954.

_____. *Urbanistica romana: una battaglia liberale in Campidoglio*. Rome, 1954.

Cederna, Antonio. *I vandali in casa*. Bari: Laterza, 1956.

_____. *Mirabilia Urbis: Cronache romane 1957–1965*. Turin: Einaudi, 1965.

Cioccetti, Urbano. *Amministrando Roma: discorsi di tre anni (1958–1960)*. Rome: Comitato Romano della Democrazia Cristiana, 1960.

Cobb, Charles K., Jr., and Francesco Forte. *Taxation in Italy*. World Tax Series, Harvard Law School, International Program in Taxation. Chicago: Commerce Clearing House, 1964.

Compagna, Francesco. *La politica della città*. Bari: Laterza, 1967.

Conigliaro, Angelo, ed. *I pardoni della città*. Bari: Laterza, 1957.

DeCarlo, Giancarlo. *La pianificazione territoriale urbanistica nell'area torinese*. Padua: Marsilio, 1964.

DeGasperi, Maria Romana Catti. *DeGasperi uomo solo*. Milan: Mondadori, 1964.

Degli Esposti, Giovanni. *Bologna PCI*. Bologna: Il Mulino, 1966.

Della Seta, Piero, Carlo Melograni, and Aldo Natoli. *Il piano regolatore di Roma*. Rome: Editori Riuniti, 1963.

Evans, Robert H. *Coexistence: Communism and Its Practice in Bologna 1945–1965*. Notre Dame: University of Notre Dame Press, 1967.

Falconi, Carlo. *Il pentagono vaticano*. Bari: Laterza, 1956.

Forte, Francesco. *La strategia delle riforme*. Milan: Etas Kompass, 1968.

_____. *Saggi sull'economia urbanistica*. Naples: Morano, 1964.

Fried, Robert. *The Italian Prefects*. New Haven: Yale University Press, 1963.

Fried, Robert, and Francine F. Rabinovitz. *Comparative Urban Politics*. Englewood Cliffs: Prentice-Hall, in press.

Frieden, Bernard J., and Robert Morris, eds. *Urban Planning and Social Policy*. New York: Basic Books, 1968.

Gay, F., and P. Wagret. *L'économie de l'Italie*. Paris: Presses Universitaires de France, 1964.

Ghera, Paolo. *La problematica comprensoriale in Italia dal dopoguerra ad oggi*. Rome: Centro di Studi per la Pianificazione Territoriale, University of Rome, 1966.

Ghio, Mario, and Vittoria Calzolari. *Verde per la città*. Rome: De Luca, 1961.

Ginsburg, Norton. *Altas of Economic Development*. Chicago: University of Chicago Press, 1964.

Giovenco, Luigi. *L'ordinamento comunale*. Milan: Giuffrè, 1962.

Gorla, Giuseppe. *L'Italia nella seconda guerra mondiale*. Milan: Baldini and Castoldi, 1959.

Grilli, Giovanni. *La finanza vaticana in Italia*. Rome: Editori Riuniti, 1961.

Gunther, John. *Twelve Cities*. New York: Harper and Row, 1969.

Hanson, Bertil Lennart. "Stockholm Municipal Politics." Mimeographed. Cambridge: Joint Center for Urban Studies of the Massachusetts Institute of Technology and Harvard University, 1960

Homo, Léon. *Rome Impériale et l'urbanisme dans l'antiquité*. Paris: Albin Michel, 1951.

Insolera, Italo. *Roma moderna: un secolo di storia urbanistica*. Turin: Einaudi, 1962.

Istituto Nazionale di Architettura. *III Convegno sui problemi dello sviluppo di Roma: Atti*. Rome: IN/arch, 1965.

Istituto Nazionale di Urbanistica (INU). *La pianificazione intercomunale*. Turin: INU, 1957.

_____. *La pianificazione reoginale*. Turin: INU, 1953.

_____. *Roma: Città e piani*. Turin, INU, n.d.

Kogan, Norman. *A Political History of Postwar Italy*. New York: Praeger, 1966.

LaPalombara, Joseph. *Interest Groups and Italian Politics*. Princeton: Princeton University Press, 1964.

Latini, Antonio. *La città dinamica e progressiva*. Florence: Olschki, 1964.

Lijphart, Arend. *The Politics of Accommodation: Pluralism and Democracy in the Netherlands*. Berkeley: University of California Prass, 1968.

LoBello, Nino. *The Vatican Empire*. New York: Trident Press, 1968.

Lugli, Piero Maria. *Storia e cultura della città italiana*. Bari: Laterza, 1967.

Luzzatto Fegis, Pierpaolo. *Il volto sconosciuto dell'Italia: seconda serie 1956–1965*. Milan: Giuffrè, 1966.

Montanelli, Indro et al. *Italia sotto inchiesta: 'Corriere della Sera' 1963/65*. Florence: Sansoni, 1965.

Morini, Mario. *Atlante di storia dell'urbanistica*. Milan: Hoepli, 1963.

Natoli, Aldo et al. *Introduzione a Roma contemporanea*. Rome: Centro di Studi su Roma Moderna, 1954.

Negro, Silvio. *Seconda Roma: 1850–1870*. Venice: Neri Pozza, 1966.

Pacelli, Mario. *La pianificazione urbanistica nella costituzione*. Milan: Giuffrè, 1966.

Pantaleone, Michele. *Antimafia: occasioni mancate*. Turin: Einaudi, 1969.

Petrucci, Amerigo. *Un piano per Roma*. Rome: Editoriale Romana, 1966.

Piccinato, Luigi, ed. *Problemi urbanistici di Roma*. Milan: Sperling and Kupfer, 1960.

Pozzani, Silvio, ed. *Roma nuova: la capitale nella vita economica italiana*. 2 vols. Milan: Banca Popolare di Milano-Nuovo Mercurio, 1964.

Rabinovitz, Francine F. *City Politics and Planning*. New York: Atherton, 1969.

Ranney, David C. *Planning and Politics in the Metropolis*. Columbus: Merrill, 1969.

Samonà, Giuseppe. *L'urbanistica e l'avvenire della città*. Bari: Laterza, 1967.

Settembrini, Domenico. *La Chiesa nella politica italiana, 1944–1963*. Pisa: Nistri-Lischi, 1964.

Società di Architettura e Urbanistica. *Il piano regolatore di Roma, ottobre 1961-dicembre 1962*. Rome: SAU, 1963.

Società Generale Immobiliare. *Alcune caratteristiche dei quartieri di Roma*. Quaderni della Società Immobiliare, 1960.

Sullo, Fiorentino. *Lo scandalo urbanistico: storia di un progetto di legge*. Florence: Vallecchi, 1964.

Tafuri, Manfredo. *Ludovico Quaroni e lo sviluppo dell'architettura moderna in Italia*. Milan: Comunità, 1964.

Tagliacarne, Guglielmo, ed. *260 aree economiche in Italia.* Milan: Giuffrè, 1966.
Testa, Virgilio. *Disciplina urbanistica.* Milan: Giuffrè, 1961.
Unione degli Industriali del Lazio. *L'industria di Roma a del Lazio: Problemi e prospettive 1967–68.* Rome: UIL, 1968,.
Unione Italiana delle Camere di Commercio, Industria e Agricoltura. *Lineamenti economici e prospettive di sviluppo delle province italiane.* Milan: Giuffrè, 1964.
Villani, Andrea. *Le strutture amministrative locali.* 2 vols. Milan: Franco Angeli, 1968.
Vittorini, Marcello. *Pianificazione urbanistica e politica edilizia.* N.p., n.d.
Walsh, Annmarie Hauck. *The Urban Challenge to Government.* New York: Praeger, 1969.
Whyte, William F. *The Last Landscape.* New York: Doubleday, 1969,.

ARTICLES

ACER-Unione Costruttori Romani. *Notiziario dei Costruttori Romani.* November 1966, whole issue.
Archibugi, Franco. "The Growth of Cities in Italy," *Review of the Economic Conditions in Italy* (Banco di Roma), January 1965, pp. 42–58.
Astengo, Giovanni. "Le nostre tigri di carta," *Il Ponte,* December 1968, pp. 1493–1510.
_____. "Relazione generale introduttiva: venti anni di battaglie urbanistiche." *Urbanistica,* September 1969, pp. 45–52.
Aymonimo, Carlo. "Il sistema dei centri direzionali nella capitale." *Casabella,* June 1962, pp. 21–26.
_____. "La condizione edilizia a Roma." *Casabella,* September 1963, pp. 4–25.
Beltrame, Carlo. "Gli istituti regionali di ricerca socio-economica." *Esperienze Amministrative,* June 1964, pp. 66–109.
Benevolo, Leonardo. "Il rifiuto del Piano del CET ed il Nuovo Piano della Giunta," *Urbanistica,* October 1959, pp. 169–84.
_____. "Il piano regolatore di Roma." *Italia Nostra,* January-February 1958, pp. 1–4.
_____. "Le facoltà di architetturà e l'architettura della città." *Città e Società,* March-April 1968, pp. 15–34.
_____. "Osservazioni sui lavori per il piano regolatore di Roma." *Casabella,* May 1958, pp. 4–15.
Bodo, Carlo. "Le attrezzature sportive nel territorio del Comune di Roma." *Urbanistica,* May 1966, pp. 103–05.
Bonamico, Sergio et al. "Studio metodologico propedeutico ad un restauro conservativo nel Centro Storico." *Capitolium,* September-October 1966, pp. 5–38.
Bonelli, Renato. "Principi, metodi e strumenti della tutela." Paper presented to the 1966 national congress of the Italia Nostra Society.
Bosi, Mario. "Il problema finanziario odierno di Roma." *Studi Romani,* October-December 1968, pp. 458–82.
Burchard, John, "The Culture of Urban America." In *Environment and Change: The Next Fifty Years,* edited by William R. Ewald, Jr., pp. 189–213. Bloomington: Indiana University Press, 1968.
Cabianca, Vincenzo. "Roma: verso un sistema generale del verde." *Urbanistica,* May 1966, pp. 6–17.
Cagianelli, Gianni. "L'assistenza." *Capitolium,* April-May 1969, pp. 85–86.
Calzolari Ghio, Vittoria. "Roma, luglio 1966: nuovo piano regolatore, nuova amministrazione, nuovo verde?" *Italia Nostra,* May-June 1966, pp. 32–42.
Camaleone, Enrico. "Preparare la città-regione." *Capitolium,* July-August 1967, pp. 276–87.

_____. "Roma: verso il milione di apparecchi telefonici." *Capitolium*, March 1967, pp. 126–32.

_____. "Trasporti collettivi e bilancio comunale: un contrasto insanabile." *Capitolium*, February 1966, pp. 104–18.

Campolongo, Alberto. "Sul divario del Mezzogiorno." *Studi economici*, January-April 1968, pp. 1–6.

Campos-Venuti, Giuseppe. "Il piano intercomunale del comprensorio romano." *Urbanistica*, July 1960, pp. 92–93.

Capurso, Gian Luigi. "Cronache amministrative: Palermo." *Nord e Sud*, July 1964, pp. 52–56.

Caracciolo, Alberto. "Continuità della struttura economica di Roma." *Nuova Rivista Storica*, January-June 1954, pp. 182–206, July-September 1954, pp. 326–47.

Cassio, G. P. "Vicende di un'imposta sulle aree fabbricabili." *Città e Società*, July-August 1966, pp. 77–84.

Cederna, Antonio. "Il verde a Roma: cronaca di una rovina." *Casabella*, April 9164, pp. 29–36.

Chiarelli, Giuseppe. "Rome." In *Great Cities of the World*, edited by William A. Robson, pp. 514–46. 2nd. ed. London: George Allen and Unwin, 1957.

Civico, Vincenzo. "Urbanistica Romana." *Studi Romani*, 1954 to present.

Coppa, Mario. "La lunga strada per il piano di Roma." *Urbanistica*, March 1964, pp. 13–20.

Coquery, Michel. "Aspects démographiques et problèmes de croissance d'une ville 'millionaire': le cas de Naples." *Annales de Géographie 72* (1963), 572–604.

Cortesi, Aurelio. "La speculazione eterna." *Casabella*, September 1963, pp. 29–33.

Coulter, Philip B. "Comparative Community Politics and Public Policy." *Polity*, 3 (Fall 1970), 22–43.

Crescenzi, Carlo. "Il piano di zone di Spinaceto e l'attuazione della 167." *Urbanistica*, December 1965, pp. 85–87.

Crespi, Franco. "Aspetti del rapporto tra strutture urbanistiche e relazioni sociali in una borgata alla periferia di Roma." *Rivista di Sociologia*, May-August 1967, pp. 5–50.

Crespi, Franco and Franco Martinelli. "La dinamica delle relazioni sociali nel contesto urbano." *Rivista di Sociologia*, May 1968, pp. 5–62.

Cuzzi, Diego, and Enrico Fattinanzi. "Edilizia residenziale: prospettive 1970." *Tempi moderni*, Winter 1968, pp. 75–82,.

D'Andrea, Ugo. "Una legge valida per i paesi d'oltre cortina." *Ulisse*, September 1963, pp. 81–87.

Del Bosco, Manlio. "La Chiesa ed il partito." *Il Mondo*, October 20, 1965.

DeLuca, Emilio Vega. "Politica territoriale e crisi dell'amministrazione dei lavori pubblici." *Città e Società*, January-March 1968, pp. 31–36.

DeMartino, Umberto. "Cento anni di dibattiti sul problema dei centri storici." *Rassegna dell'Istituto di Architettura e Urbanistica*. Facoltà di Ingegneria, University of Rome, April 1966, pp. 75–116.

D'Erme, Mario. "Il disegno di Roma nel nuovo Piano Regolatore." *Capitolium*, October 1965, pp. 456–59.

_____. "L'elaborazione del piano regolatore di Roma." *Battaglie Politiche*, December 1, 1957, pp. 6–8.

_____. "L'ombra di Villa Chigi sulla vita della città." *Rinnovamento*, January 1958.

D'Erme, Mario et al. "Quadro di riferimento per la pianificazione territoriale del Lazio." *Rassegna del Lazio*, July-September 1964, pp. 1–24.

Dezmann, Mario. "Mancini docet anche a Bologna." *Il Ponte*, April 1966, pp. 443–47.

Diana, Francesco. "Motivi del Rifiuto del commissario Diana." *Informazioni Urbanistiche,* April-August 1962, pp. 17–19.

Dogan, Mattei. "La stratificazione sociale dei suffragi." In *Elezioni e comportamento politico in Italia* edited by Joseph LaPalombara and Alberto Spreafico, pp. 407–74. Milan: Comunità , 1963.

Erba, Valeria. "Alcuni esempi di applicazione e attuazione della legge 167." *Città e Società,* July-August 1970, pp. 46–53.

Eulau, Heinz and Robert Eyestone. "Policy Maps of City Councils and Policy Outcomes: A Developmental Analysis." *American Political Science Review, 62* (March 1968), pp. 124–43.

Fasola-Bologna, Alfredo. "Il ruolo del sacerdote nelle aspettative della popolazione di una parocchia romana." *Rivista di Sociologia,* January-April 1968, pp. 69–88.

Fiorentino, Mario. "L'attività della Sezione Laziale nel biennio 1964–1965." *Urbanistica,* May 1966, pp. 149–64.

Fried, Robert. "Administrative Pluralism and Italian Regional Planning." *Public Administration* (London), *47* (Winter 1968) 375–91.

_____. "Communism, Urban Budgets, and the Two Italies: A Case Study in Comparative Urban Government." *Journal of Politics, 33* (1971), 1008–51.

_____. "Politics, Economics, and Federalism: Aspects of Urban Government in *Mittel-Europa."* In Terry N. Clark, ed., *Comparative Community Politics.* New York: Wiley, in press.

_____. "Professionalism and Politics in Roman Planning." *Journal of the American Institute of Planners, 35* (1969), 150–59.

_____. "Urbanization and Italian Politics." *Journal of Politics, 29* (1967), 505–34.

Gans, Herbert. "City and Regional Planning." In *International Encyclopedia of the Social Sciences, 12,* (1968), 129–37.

Garano, Stefano. "I problemi della ristrutturazione della periferia di Roma." *Città e Società,* May-June 1970, pp. 89–100.

Gatti, Alberto. "Il 'Piano Quadro' strumento e metodo di attuazione del Piano Regolatore Generale." *Capitolium,* January 1966.

Gazzani, David. "Il problema della casa oggi." *Rivista di Sociologia,* December 1969, pp. 189–220.

Girelli, Marcello. "Il piano per l'attuazione della legge 167 a Roma." *Urbanistica,* March 1964, pp. 85–87.

Giura Longo, Tommaso. "I servizi pubblici allo sviluppo della città moderna." *Ulisse,* September 1963, pp. 124–31.

Glisenti, Giuseppe. "Esame analitico dei risultati elettorali romani." *Cronache Sociali,* October 31, 1947, pp. 4–7.

Gori, Antonio. "Condizioni e prospettive della finanza locale." *Esperienze Amministrative,* December 1964, pp. 41–54.

Hoyt, Homer. "Importance of Manufacturing in Basic Employment." *Land Economics, 45* (August 1969), 344–49.

Insolera, Italo. "La capitale in espansione." *Urbanistica,* October 1959, pp. 6–90.

_____. "L'istituto del Regolamento Edilizio nell'ultimo secolo di urbanistica romana." *Urbanistica,* October 1959, pp. 197–208.

_____. "Storia del primo Piano Regolatore di Roma: 1870–1874." *Urbanistica,* June 1959, pp. 74–90.

Insolera, Italo and Mario Manieri-Elia. "Tre anni di cronaca romana." *Urbanistica,* March 1964, pp. 41–84.

_____. "Vicende del parco Appio." *Casabella,* April 1964, pp. 37–41.

LaPalombara, Joseph. "Italy: Fragmentation, Isolation, Alienation." In *Political Culture and Political Development,* edited by Lucian W. Pye and Sidney Verba, pp. 282–329. Princeton: Princeton University Press, 1965.

Lenzi, Luigi. "The New Rome." *The Town Planning Review,* May 1931, pp. 145–62.

Lilli, Virgilio. "Caos sui tetti di Roma." *Corriere della Sera,* November 19, 1966.

Liverani, Pier Giorgio. "Un inferno chiamato baracca." *Capitolium,* January 1970, pp. 7–15.

Lombardini, Siro. "La normalizzazione dei mercati delle aree e degli alloggi attraverso la nuova legge urbanistica." *Urbanistica,* March 1963, pp. 7–12.

Lugli, Piero Maria. "Prospettive di sviluppo di Roma nell'ambito della sua area metropolitana." *Studi Romani,* April-June 1968, pp. 178–90.

Luzzi, Paolo. "La '167' del Comune di Roma." *Città e Società,* January-February 1967, pp. 63–71.

Luzzi, Paolo, and Camilla Nucci. "Il sistema direzionale a Roma: un dibattito ancora aperto." *Città e Società,* March-April 1969, pp. 74–92.

McElrath, Dennis C. "The Social Areas of Rome: A Comparative Analysis." *American Sociological Review, 27* (June 1962), 376–91.

Manieri-Elia, Mario. "L'attività dell'Ufficio Speciale per il Nuovo Piano Regolatore." *Urbanistica,* October 1959, pp. 164–68.

———. "Roma: Olimpiadi e miliardi." *Urbanistica,* December 1960, pp. 106–19.

Martinelli, Franco. "Contributo allo studio della morfologia sociale della città di Roma." *Rivista di Sociologia,* January-April 1968, pp. 89–122.

Martuscelli, Michele. "La legge ponte: significato ed operatività." *Urbanistica,* October 1967, pp. 5–13.

Melograni, Carlo. "Dalla casa popolare all'unità d'abitazione." *Ulisse,* September 1963, pp. 113–23.

Mocine, Corwin R. "New Business Centers for Italian Cities." *Journal of the American Institute of Planners, 31* (August 1965), 210–21.

———. "The New Plan for Rome." *Journal of the American Institute of Planners, 35* (November 1969), 376–82.

———. "Urban Growth and a New Planning Law in Italy." *Land Economics, 41* (November 1965), 347–53.

Monaco, Vincenzo. "Relazione di minoranza del C.E.T. (Monaco)." *Urbanistica,* March 1960, pp. 115–18.

Mura, Giancarlo. "Correnti e Gruppi nella storia della D.C. romana." *Battaglie Politiche,* April 6, 1956, pp. 7–11.

Murphy, F. X. "Rome." *New Catholic Encyclopedia.* New York: McGraw-Hill, 1967.

Nicolosi, Giuseppe. "Posizioni ed esperienze sulla questione dei centri storici." *Rassegna dell'Istituto di Architettura e Urbanistica.* Facoltà di Ingegneria, University of Rome, April 1966, pp. 19–48.

Nucci, Camilla. "Attuazione del P.R.G. di Roma." *Città e Società,* September-October 1967, pp. 92–93.

———. "Considerazioni sulla pianificazione del territorio del Lazio." *Città e Società,* November-December 1966, pp. 51–65.

———. "Un difficile piano regolatore per Roma." *Città e Società,* May-June 1966, pp. 50–57.

Nucci, Camilla and Luzzi, Paolo. "Il sistema direzionale di Roma: un dibattito ancora aperto." *Città e Società,* March-April 1969, pp. 74–92.

Pala, Antonio. "I problemi del traffico di una grande città." *L'Impresa Pubblica,* May 1967, pp. 24–32.

Passigli, Stefano. "Italy." *The Journal of Politics, 25* (November 1963), 718–36.
Pediconi, Mario. "Il problema idrico nelle grandi città." *L'Impresa Pubblica,* September 1967, pp. 3–8.
Petrucci, Amerigo. "Problemi della Roma d'oggi." *Studi Romani,* January-March 1965, pp. 44–73.
_____. "The New General Town Plan of Rome." *Review of the Economic Conditions in Italy* (Banco di Roma *17*), (May 1963), 159–62.
Piccinato, Luigi. "Ancora Roma." *Urbanistica,* March 1964, p. 11.
_____. "Funzioni e limiti del piano regolatore." *Ulisse,* September 1963, pp. 70–76.
_____. "Il momento urbanistico alla prima Mostra Nazionale dei Piani Regolatori." *Architetture e Arti Decorative,* January 1930, pp. 199–235.
_____. "Il piano regolatore e le zone di nuova industrializzazione." In *Roma nuova,* edited by Silvio Pozzani, *1,* 65–103. Milan: Nuovo Mercurio, 1964.
_____. "L'esperienza del Piano di Roma." *Urbanistica,* October 1959, pp. 189–94.
_____. "Urbanistica." *Enciclopedia Italiana, 34* (1933), 768–71.
Predieri, Alberto. "Il pseudoesperto come politico di 'serie C.'" *Il Mulino,* May 1968, p. 406–08.
Quaroni, Ludovico. "I problemi del Piano Regolatore di Roma." *Urbanistica,* Nos. 15–16 (1955), pp. 96–99.
_____. "Una città eterna—quattro lezioni da 27 secoli." *Urbanistica,* June 1959, pp. 5–72.
Radice, Piero. "Fiumicino e dintorni." *Il Ponte,* January 1962, pp. 23–28.
Ravaglioli, Armando. "A Roma s'invecchia." *Capitolium,* January 1967, pp. 2–3.
Ray, Stefano. "Roma: vocazioni storiche e implicazioni metodologiche di un piano regolatore." *Rivista di Sociologia,* January-April 1967, pp. 79–102.
Rebecchini, Salvatore. "Passato e avvenire del centro storico di Roma." *Studi Romani,* April-June 1965, pp. 200–19.
Reed, Henry Hope. "Rome: The Third Sack." *The Architectural Review, 107* (February 1950), 91–110.
Rhea, Salvatore. "Napoli perchà." *Il Ponte,* April 1968, pp. 457–86.
Rodella, Domenico. "La legge ponte urbanistica e la conservazione ambientale." *Città e Società,* October-December 1967, pp. 14–21.
"Roma." *Enciclopedia Italiana, 29,* 589–928. Rome, 1936.
Romano, Marco. "L'esperienza del piano intercomunale milanese." *Urbanistica,* October 1967, pp. 16–64.
Rosato, Carlo. "Il servizio di nettezza urbana di una grande città: problemi e soluzioni." *L'Impresa Pubblica,* November-December 1967, pp. 9–18.
Salzano, Edoardo. "Sull'asse attrezzatto e i centri direzionali di Roma." *Città e Società,* July-August 1969, pp. 102–08.
Samperi, Piero. "Le caratteristiche urbanistiche del piano di zona." *Urbanistica,* March 1964, pp. 88–92.
Sartori, Giovanni. "European Political Parties: The Case of Polarized Pluralism." In *Political Parties and Political Development,* edited by Joseph LaPalombara and Myron Weiner, pp. 137–76. Princeton: Princeton University Press, 1966.
_____. "Political Development and Political Engineering." *Public Policy 1968.* Cambridge: Harvard University Press, 1968, pp. 261–98.
Savini, Carlo. "Fenomenologia delle migrazioni e indagini sociologiche in un'inchiesta dell'E.C.A. di Roma." *Rassegna del Lazio,* July-September 1963, pp. 85–90.
Sermonti, Enrico. "Contributo della conoscenza dell'agricoltura nella scelta della localizzazione delle aree a bosco e a parco in Agro Romano." *Urbanistica,* May 1966, pp. 117–21.

Seronde, Anne-Marie. "Le rôle de l'industrie dans la vie de l'agglomération romaine." *Bulletin de l'Association de Géographes Français*, June-July 1958, pp. 46–60.

Sharkansky, Ira. "Government Expenditures and Public Services in the American States." *American Political Science Review, 61* (1967), 1066–77.

Signorello, Nicola. "La migrazione a Roma." *Studi Romani*, July-September 1965, pp. 328–45.

Sullo, Fiorentino. "L'urbanistica nell'opinione pubblica." *Ulisse*, September 1963, pp. 77–80.

Tafuri, Manfredo. "Studi e ipotesi di lavoro per il sistema direzionale di Roma." *Casabella*, June 1962, pp. 27–35.

Tagliacarne, Guglielmo. "I conti provinciali." *Moneta e Credito*, September 1966, pp. 265–351.

Testa, Virgilio. "L'E.U.R.: centro direzionale e quartiere moderno alla periferia di Roma." *Studi Romani*, January-March 1970, pp. 39–50.

Ugazzi, Mario. "Una chimera, per i romani, l'orario continuato?" *Capitolium*, January 1967, pp. 5–9.

Valori, Michele. "Fare del proprio peggio." *Urbanistica*, October 1959, pp. 185–88.

_____. "I lavori per il Piano Regolatore di Roma: Quattro anni difficili." *Urbanistica*, October 1959, pp. 127–63.

_____. "Programmazione economica regionale e piani territoriali di coordinamento." *Città e Società*, March-April 1968, pp. 59–65.

Volpi, Franco. "La crisi degli enti locali nell'economia dei consumi di massa." *Studi Economici*, September-December 1968, pp. 373–97.

Wendt, Paul. "Post World War II Housing Policies in Italy." *Land Economics, 38* (May 1962), 113–33.

Zampetti, Enrico. "Le elezioni comunali a Roma da 1870 ad oggi." *Concretezza*, June 1, 1966, pp. 25–34.

# INDEX

Most references to Rome will be found under the appropriate topical heading. Acronyms for public agencies or programs are spelled out in the abbreviations list, pp. xvi and xvii. Page numbers in italics refer to tables and figures.